Praise for *Smoke and Ashes*

"Ghosh's elegant history of the plant's influence is both a tribute to what he calls 'the historical agency of botanical matter' and a reckoning with the imperial past." —*The Economist*

"Propulsive and revelatory . . . A skilled storyteller, [Ghosh] triumphs in laying out the shame of the British empire's opium trade for all to see." —Anjana Ahuja, *Financial Times*

"Expansive and thoughtful . . . *Smoke and Ashes* is a lovely blend of historical writing, travelogue and personal reflection." —Peter Frankopan, *The Spectator*

"Ghosh has produced, with *Smoke and Ashes*, a remarkable work of scholarship. His writing is as lush and dramatically effective as it is scrupulously researched, offering readers an image of emergent and contemporary modernity utterly estranged from Enlightenment ideals of progress, equality, and fraternity." —Noah Sparkes, *Los Angeles Review of Books*

"A scintillating and kaleidoscopic vision of opium's role in the past several centuries of global history . . . Exquisitely written and packed with astonishing insight, this is a must-read." —*Publishers Weekly* (starred review)

"Ghosh's literary prowess supercharges this eye-opening excavation of the full extent of the opium-industrial complex." —Donna Seaman, *Booklist* (starred review)

AMITAV GHOSH

SMOKE AND ASHES

Amitav Ghosh is the author of the bestselling Ibis Trilogy, composed of *Sea of Poppies* (shortlisted for the Man Booker Prize), *River of Smoke*, and *Flood of Fire*. His other novels include *The Circle of Reason*, which won the Prix Médicis étranger, and *The Glass Palace*. He is the author of many works of nonfiction, including *The Great Derangement: Climate Change and the Unthinkable* and *The Nutmeg's Curse: Parables for a Planet in Crisis*. He has received two lifetime achievement awards and five honorary doctorates. In 2018, Ghosh became the first English-language writer to win the Jnanpith Award, India's highest literary honor. He lives in Brooklyn, New York.

ALSO BY AMITAV GHOSH

Fiction

Jungle Nama

Gun Island

Flood of Fire

River of Smoke

Sea of Poppies

The Hungry Tide

The Glass Palace

The Calcutta Chromosome

The Shadow Lines

The Circle of Reason

Nonfiction

The Living Mountain: A Fable for Our Times

Uncanny and Improbable Events

The Nutmeg's Curse: Parables for a Planet in Crisis

The Great Derangement: Climate Change and the Unthinkable

Incendiary Circumstances: A Chronicle of the Turmoil of Our Times

Dancing in Cambodia and at Large in Burma

In an Antique Land

SMOKE
and
ASHES

SMOKE

and

ASHES

Opium's Hidden Histories

AMITAV
GHOSH

Picador / Farrar, Straus and Giroux
New York

Picador
120 Broadway, New York 10271

Illustration credits can be found on pages 395–398.

The Library of Congress has catalogued the Farrar, Straus
and Giroux hardcover edition as follows:
Names: Ghosh, Amitav, 1956– author.
Title: Smoke and ashes : opium's hidden histories / Amitav Ghosh.
Description: First American edition. | New York : Farrar, Straus and
Giroux, 2024. | Includes bibliographical references.
Identifiers: LCCN 2023039020 | ISBN 9780374602925 (hardcover)
Subjects: LCSH: Opium trade—History. | China—Commerce—History. |
India—Commerce—History. | Great Britain—Commerce—History. |
Ghosh, Amitav, 1956– —Travel | Ghosh, Amitav, 1956– —Family
Classification: LCC HD9675.O652 G467 2024 | DDC 338.4/7362293—
dc23/eng/20231003
LC record available at https://lccn.loc.gov/2023039020

Paperback ISBN: 978-1-250-37187-4

For Rahul Srivastava and Aradhana Seth

in celebration of neighbourliness

Contents

One	Here Be Dragons	3
Two	Seeds	14
Three	'An Actor in Its Own Right'	24
Four	Frenemies	36
Five	The Opium Department	50
Six	Big Brother	64
Seven	Visions	80
Eight	Family Story	91
Nine	Malwa	100
Ten	East and West	119
Eleven	Diasporas	138
Twelve	Boston Brahmins	161
Thirteen	American Stories	180
Fourteen	Guangzhou	218
Fifteen	The Sea-Calming Tower	243
Sixteen	Pillar of Empire	258
Seventeen	Parallels	280
Eighteen	Portents	305
	Notes	321
	Acknowledgements	393

SMOKE

and

ASHES

ONE

Here Be Dragons

A fact that confounds me now, when I think back on it, is that for most of my life China was for me a vast, uniform blankness. The huge space that hovered above India on maps might just as well have been marked: 'Here be dragons'.

As it happens, I was born in West Bengal, an Indian state that almost touches China, and grew up in a city, Calcutta (now Kolkata), that has a small but significant Chinese community. Yet, I had no interest whatsoever in Chinese history, geography or culture. Nor, despite the fact that I have always loved to travel, did it ever occur to me to visit, say, Yunnan, even though the capital of the province, Kunming, is not much farther from Calcutta than New Delhi, as the crow flies. Somehow Kunming seemed to belong to another world, one that was cut off from mine not just by a towering range of mountains but also by a Himalaya of the mind.

It was not till 2004, when I started writing my novel *Sea of Poppies*, that I thought of visiting China for the first time. The novel's central characters are a couple called Deeti and Kalua who set off on a journey to Mauritius, in 1838, as indentured workers. This being the basic arc of the narrative, I knew that the research for the book would take me to Mauritius—and so it did—but it also led me in another, completely unexpected direction. As I got deeper into the research, I realized that the story's background was formed not just by India and Mauritius but also by the stretch of water that separates (and also joins) the two countries: the Indian Ocean.

To write about the sea is not like writing about land. The horizons are larger and the settings lack the fixity that enables novelists to convey 'a sense of place'. If a ship happens to be the principal location, as the schooner *Ibis* is in *Sea of Poppies*, then you become very aware of currents, and winds, and flows of traffic. And the more I explored the background, the clearer it became that the flow of seaborne traffic in the period I was writing about, the first half of the nineteenth century, was not primarily between India and the West, as I had imagined, but between India and China—or, rather, one particular place in China, a city called 'Canton'.

I had come across this name often in the past without being quite sure of exactly where the city was. Now, as I began to steep myself in nineteenth-century nautical writing, I became increasingly curious: what was so special about Canton that the very thought of setting sail for it could induce raptures in nineteenth-century sailors and travellers?

Had I been at all informed about China and Chinese history, I would have known that 'Canton' was a word Europeans once used, rather loosely, to refer to the province of Guangdong in general, and to the city of Guangzhou in particular.[1] But at that time my knowledge of China and its geography was so sketchy that I had only a dim idea of where Guangzhou was.

Thinking back, it seems to me that my blankness in relation to China was not the result of a lack of curiosity, or opportunity, or anything circumstantial. I am convinced that it was the product of an inner barrier that has been implanted in the minds of not just Indians but also Americans, Europeans and many other people across the world, through certain patterns of global history. And as the years go by and China's shadow lengthens upon the world, these barriers are clearly hardening, especially in India and the United States.

There is, I think, something important to be learnt by taking a closer look at this condition—not only because of its bearing on China, but also because of what it tells us about the ways in which the world is perceived and understood.

On the Indian side, the memory that dominates, indeed overwhelms, all others in relation to China is that of the Sino-Indian war of 1962, in which India suffered a resounding defeat.[2]

I was six years old then but my memories of that time are still vivid. I remember my mother tearfully picking out gold bangles to contribute to the war effort; I remember my father collecting blankets and woollens to send to the front; I remember my parents and their friends arguing endlessly about the causes of the war and who was to blame for the debacle.

There is still no consensus on these issues. A 2021 study by the former head of the Historical Division of India's Ministry of External Affairs, Avtar Singh Bhasin, suggests that misunderstandings and blunders on the part of the country's then Prime Minister, Jawaharlal Nehru, played a significant role in precipitating the war. 'It was Nehru taking liberty with the western border that had invited trouble,' writes Bhasin. 'India became a victim of its wrong presumptions.'[3] Nehru was in many ways an admirable man and a visionary statesman, yet he seems to have been peculiarly inept in his handling of this crisis.

The whole truth will probably never be known anyway because some of the most important historical materials have yet to see the light of day. What is certain, however, is that the 1962 war was to some extent a consequence of the cultural and political shadows cast by the Himalaya—misreadings, misjudgements and faulty understandings played no small part in triggering the conflict.[4]

The issues that catalysed the 1962 war are by no means settled. The conflict has continued over decades and is still ongoing, with clashes between Chinese and Indian troops occurring regularly along the border. Nor is there an end in sight to these clashes: China is today an increasingly assertive and bellicose neighbour and India has no option but to stand its ground as best it can.[5]

There can be no doubt that this ongoing confrontation has added many layers of fear, resentment and hostility to Indian attitudes towards China. The extreme rancour against China that is now increasingly evident in the United States has existed in India for most of my life.

But extreme tensions exist also between India and Pakistan: they have fought several wars, and in both countries there are large numbers of people who are bitterly hostile towards each other. Yet, there is no lack of interest and curiosity on either side of the border. Quite the contrary: India and Pakistan have an obsessive interest in each other's politics, culture, history, current events, sport and so on.

This is by no means an unusual circumstance: conflict often tends to cause a deepening of cultural and imaginative engagements. In the United States, for example, there was a surge of enrolments in Arabic language classes after the 2001 attacks on the World Trade Center. The flow of books, articles and films on Iraq and Afghanistan has increased steadily ever since.

Nothing like that happened in India after 1962. Instead of a spike in interest, there was a spasmodic recoiling, accompanied by an upsurge of shame, suspicion and fear. After the war, which lasted only a few weeks, India's small, scattered communities of Chinese-origin migrants became scapegoats for the disaster.

The roots of India's Chinese communities go back to the late eighteenth century, when the first Hakka migrants settled near Calcutta.[6] Over time the community thrived; it ran several schools, temples and newspapers, and many of its members became successful professionals and entrepreneurs.[7] Many Chinese Indians never visited China and had no connections with that country; a substantial number were anti-Communists. But still, the 1962 war was no sooner over than the Indian government passed a law allowing for the 'apprehension and detention in custody of any person [suspected] of being of hostile origin'.

Thousands of ethnic Chinese were forced to leave India; many became stateless refugees. Thousands more were interned within India, remaining in internment camps for years, without trial. When they were released, most returned to find that their homes and businesses had been seized or sold off. For years afterwards they had to report monthly to police stations. The atmosphere of suspicion extended even to the few Indian scholars who studied China.

In the years after the war, Calcutta's ethnic-Chinese population halved in number, falling from 20,000 to 10,000. Many of those who remained were forced to relocate from the old Chinatown, in the city centre, to Tangra, a swampy marshland on the urban periphery. It is a testament of the community's resilience and enterprise that this neighbourhood has become a vibrant new Chinatown, dotted with factories, workshops, temples and restaurants.

The scapegoating of the Chinese Indian community after 1962 is, without a doubt, a very ugly chapter in the history of independent India. But India too has paid a price for it, Calcutta most of all. The 1960s and 1970s were exactly the time when diasporic Chinese communities were bringing about an economic transformation in many parts of Southeast Asia by funnelling in foreign capital, and by creating new businesses and industries. Had the Sino-Indian community not been devastated by the 1962 war it might have helped revitalize Calcutta too.

I was forcibly reminded of this in 2010 when my wife and I spent a few days in Coloane, at the southernmost tip of the Macau peninsula. Our tranquil, sun-bathed hotel stood above a sandy beach, commanding a spectacular view of the sea; its kitchens produced some of the finest Macanese fare in that famously epicurean city. One morning I discovered, to my surprise, that the hotel's proprietor, a woman in her mid-fifties, had grown up in Calcutta: she spoke fluent English, Bengali and Cantonese (but not Mandarin). Her family had owned restaurants in Calcutta, she told me, and they had always wanted to run a hotel as well. But after 1962 they had been compelled to leave. It had taken many years of struggle before they finally managed to realize their dream—except that their hotel was in Macau, not Calcutta.

What part, then, did the 1962 war play in shaping my view of China? That it played some part, I do not doubt—but the most notable thing about my perspective on China, really, was that it scarcely existed. And this was, I think, the result of a certain way of perceiving not just China but also the world in general: it is an outlook in which the West looms so large that it obscures everything else.

The presence of the West is inescapable across the Indian subcontinent, no matter whether it concerns language, clothing, sport, material objects or art. In fact it has long been a default assumption, among Indians as well as many Westerners, that the transformation of social, cultural and material life that occurred in the region over the period of colonization was largely due to a process called 'Westernization'.[8] Underlying this, in turn, is the assumption that modernity was an exclusively Western creation that was transmitted to India, and the rest of the world, through contact, like 'a virus that spreads from one place to another'.[9]

Another part of the world that has had a long and visible presence in the Indian subcontinent is the Middle East. Across the region, Middle Eastern influences are apparent everywhere—in art, architecture, food, clothing and language. The vocabularies of the major subcontinental languages all draw massively on Persian and Arabic. Even as a teenager I was aware that I used dozens of words of Arabic and Persian origin while speaking Bengali, Hindi or English. But I would not have been able to name a single word of Chinese origin in any of those languages; indeed, the very idea that I might be using words of Chinese derivation in my everyday life would have seemed bizarre. The same was true also of everyday objects and practices: it would not have occurred to me that anything in my material or cultural world might point in the direction of China rather than to the Middle East or Europe.

It was not until I visited China for the first time, in September 2005, that I discovered how profoundly mistaken I was.

That first visit to China was revelatory in many ways even though I spent only a few weeks in the country, almost all of them in Guangzhou. But my epiphany did not occur while I was in China; it happened after I returned to India.

One day, soon after my trip to Guangzhou, I was sitting in my family home in Calcutta drinking a cup of tea in my study. This ritual was as much a part of my everyday routine as getting out of bed; I've sat at that same desk, in the same chair, with a tea tray in front of me, thousands of times.

But that day was somehow different. When I looked into my cup of tea—or 'cha' as it is called in Bengali—I suddenly remembered a word that I had recently used in Guangzhou: 'chah'. I looked at the cup again and saw that it was made of porcelain—'China' in English, or 'Chinémati' (Chinese clay) in Bangla. It struck me then that this too was something that had entered my orbit through Guangzhou, which for centuries had exported vast quantities of 'China-ware' to the world.[10]

Sitting on the tea tray, along with the cup and saucer, was a bowl of white sugar: this is arguably, of all flavourings, the most beloved of the Indian tongue. And what is it called? In Bengal, as in much of India, it goes by the name 'cheeni'—which is but a common word for 'Chinese'.[11] I had been using this word all my life, yet it had never occurred to me to wonder about its origins. And then there was the tea tray, a cheap lacquerware object, of a kind that is very commonly seen in India. This too was so much of a piece with my surroundings that it had never stood out or raised any questions. But on that day it conjured up visual memories of the collections of lacquerware I had recently seen in Guangzhou: it struck me then that the tray too might have Chinese antecedents.

I looked around that room and suddenly I could see China everywhere: in a jar of peanuts (which are known in Bengali as 'Chinese nuts' or 'chinébadam'); in chrysanthemums in a vase; in goldfish in a bowl; in envelopes and incense sticks. It was as though an invisible hand had appeared in the room and were pointing out a whole range of objects that, in their very familiarity, had sunk so deep into my consciousness as to evade notice. These things—tea, sugar, porcelain—had never meant anything to me in themselves: they were just things, inanimate, silent and devoid of communicative ability.

A few weeks later, on returning to Brooklyn, where I live, I had the same experience in my study there. Apart from a similar ensemble of things related to tea there was an old rug, a paperweight and, of course, a plethora of 'Made in China' gadgets and devices. Everywhere I looked there was something, old or new, that harked back to China.

What dawned on me then was that certain objects are themselves the material, silent equivalent of words spoken by invisible, spectral forces and agencies that often form our lives without our being aware of it. In a strange reversal, the inanimate articles around me suddenly became my teachers, showing me that my physical existence spoke of a past that was completely different from the histories I had read about in books and documents. In my mental universe China almost didn't exist; in my material world China was everywhere.

In the years that followed, *Sea of Poppies* grew into a sprawling trilogy of novels, named after the schooner *Ibis*. Many chapters in the last two volumes of the Ibis Trilogy (*River of Smoke* and *Flood of Fire*) are set in and around Guangzhou and the Pearl River Delta. As I immersed myself in the research for the books, I realized that what was true of me was true also of much of the planet: China looms large within our material and cultural lives, yet its presence often passes unnoticed.

Why is this so?

In wrestling with this question, I eventually came to accept that China's historical presence in my world was easy to overlook because it was for the most part non-verbal: it was not usually attached to the kinds of discursive concepts, like 'development' and 'progress', that have played such a large part in the writing of modern history.

Or, put differently, while the West's influence on my world was exerted through a near-obsessive elaboration of words and concepts, China's influence was more subtle, almost invisible, wielded through the diffusion of practices, and through objects, like those that were arrayed on my desks in Calcutta and Brooklyn. Because objects are mute, and do not of themselves supply an explanation for their presence, it requires a conceptual shift to become aware of what it is that they do, in fact, communicate. This shift is especially taxing for those of us who, through training and education, have become accustomed to thinking about the world in ways that depend, almost exclusively, on language. And since language, of the human kind, is by definition an attribute of the species *Homo sapiens*, this means that all things non-human are, in principle, mute, in the sense that they cannot speak.

Of course, the objects that sparked my epiphany were not 'speaking' in any sense. Yet, they were communicating something to me silently, something that pointed to historical and cultural connections that were quite different from those suggested by abstract concepts like 'Westernization', 'modernity', 'colonialism' and so on. But in this too there was a problem, for the things that were assembled in front of me were not all definable as objects: the teacup, the tray and the sugar bowl certainly were objects, but what of the tea itself? The pale brown liquid in my teacup was something far more complicated than an object: tea exists also as dried leaves, as a living plant and as a species that covers a significant part of the Earth's surface. 'Tea', then, is a vast complex of plant matter that is found in multiple forms; without that network of forms, the objects in front of me that day—the cup, the tray, the sugar bowl—would have no coherence. To think of those things on the analogy of words, then, would imply that there was a grammar or syntax that tied them together: and what could that grammar be other than 'tea' itself, a thing that is not a single object but a living entity, continuously evolving and finding new modes of articulation? This, in turn, would mean that the thing I had always so easily and unproblematically identified as 'tea' had a certain kind of vitality, a life that manifested itself in innumerable ways, seen and unseen.

To think of botanical matter in this way is to acknowledge that when humans interact with certain plants the relationship is not unidirectional; people too are changed by that association. This gives us an inkling of why some cultures regard certain plants as spirits or deities, whose interactions with human beings are mysterious, sometimes benign and sometimes vengeful. In the words of the Potawatomi botanist Robin Wall Kimmerer:

In the indigenous view, humans are viewed as somewhat lesser beings in the democracy of species. We are referred to as the younger brother of Creation, so like younger brothers we must learn from our elders. Plants were here first and have had a long time to figure things out. They live both above and below ground and hold the earth in place.[12]

To look at China's relationship with India through this lens is disorienting, but also, in some ways, enlightening. For this relationship is one in which botanical materials have played an inordinately large part, with certain plants entering into it so forcefully as to create patterns that have invisibly shaped culture and history, not just within Asia but also in Britain and America. So powerful, indeed, is the imprint of botanical matter on China's relationship with the world that it demands exactly the kind of species-level humility that Kimmerer calls for, where it is acknowledged that there are beings and entities on this planet that have the power to amplify human intentions and intervene in relations between people.

This is not, by any means, to diminish the importance of the historical agency of humans. Far from it. It is to emphasize, rather, that humans have used many kinds of non-human entities in their relations with each other. Paradoxically, it is only by thinking of history without according primacy to humans, and by acknowledging the historical agency of botanical matter, that we can recognize the true nature of human intentions with regard to plants like tea. Conversely, it is the denial of the agency of certain non-human forces that often serves to occlude the intentions of humans who have used plants and other non-human entities to wage war upon their rivals and enemies.

TWO
Seeds

The seed from which this story begins is that of the tea bush (*Camellia sinensis*), which produces most of the world's tea. The oldest tea leaves go back 2,150 years and were found in the tomb of China's Jia Ding Emperor. Beginning as an elite practice, tea drinking advanced quickly through China and became widespread by the early middle ages.[1]

Chinese tea is said to have been introduced to England by the wife of King Charles II, Catherine of Braganza.[2] The bride's native country, Portugal, was the first European nation to enter the Indian Ocean; its network of bases and colonies included Macao, in southern China, which was leased to the Portuguese in 1557 by the ruling Ming dynasty. By 1662, when Catherine of Braganza's marriage was celebrated, the Ming were in the last stages of their overthrow by the Qing dynasty, but the status of Macao remained unchanged. This meant that at the time of the wedding, Portugal had been consuming Chinese products for over a century, so the practice of tea drinking was already well-established among the country's upper classes. In her dowry, Catherine brought with her two things that would prove to be of world-historical importance: a casket of tea and a set of six small islands that would later become Bombay (now Mumbai).

Tea drinking caught on quickly in England, and by the early eighteenth century, even before Britain established its empire in India, Chinese tea was already an important article of trade for the British economy.[3] In the decades that followed, the value of Chinese tea for the British increased even faster. Throughout the eighteenth century, even as the British were conquering immense swaths of territory in North America and the Indian subcontinent, Chinese tea remained the British East India Company's prime source of revenue, much of which was used to finance British colonial expansion: 'During the eighteenth century,' writes the historian Erika Rappaport, 'tea paid for war, but war also paid for tea.'[4] By the late eighteenth century, tea 'had become so much the national drink that the Company was required by Act of Parliament to keep a year's supply always in stock'.[5]

The degree to which the fortunes of the British Empire were enmeshed with tea seems astounding in this post-industrial age. Is it really possible that the country that pioneered the Industrial Revolution was financially dependent, through the very period when it was industrializing, on a plant reared by humble peasants in the Far East? But so it was. 'As the British Empire entered into battles in Europe and North America,' writes the historian Andrew Liu, 'the state increasingly relied upon raising tea duties to pay for war.'[6]

The importation of tea was for centuries a monopoly of the East India Company, and the customs duty on it was for a long time one of Britain's most important sources of revenue. The duty ranged from 75 per cent to 125 per cent of the estimated value, which meant that the customs duty on tea fetched higher revenues for Britain than it did for China, which charged an export duty of only 10 per cent.[7]

Largely because of tea, China was consistently among the top four countries from which Britain bought its imports. The value of the goods that Britain received from China vastly exceeded what it got from most of its colonies: 'In 1857, for example, the computed real value of imports into the United Kingdom from China was 1.8 times that from British North America, twice that from Australia, 2.2 times that from the British West Indies, 6.4 times that from British possessions in South Africa, and 72.2 times that from New Zealand.'[8]

Through much of the eighteenth and nineteenth centuries, the tax on tea accounted for nearly a tenth of Britain's revenues.[9] It earned the British government as much as all land, property and income taxes put together: so vast was this sum of money that it could pay for the salaries of all government servants; for all public works and buildings; for all expenses related to law, justice, education, art and science; and for Her Majesty's colonial, consular and foreign establishments—*combined*.[10] Nor were these the only benefits that tea conferred upon Britain's economy. A large part of the British merchant marine was engaged in transporting tea, not only from China to Britain but also from Britain to its colonies.[11] In short, through much of the Industrial Revolution, the finances of the British government were heavily dependent on tea, the vast bulk of which came from China.

The problem was that Britain had nothing much to sell to China in return; the Chinese had little interest in, and no need for, most Western goods.[12] China's Qianlong Emperor made this quite clear in a letter sent to George III in 1793: 'We have never valued ingenious articles, nor do we have the slightest need of your country's manufactures.'[13]

China's lack of interest in foreign goods was irksome to the British for many reasons, not all of them financial (one scholar has made the intriguing suggestion that Chinese self-sufficiency was a source of anxiety to the British because they discerned in it the possibility of a rival 'master race').[14] A more immediate concern for Westerners, however, was that Chinese goods generally had to be paid for with silver. Because of the imbalance in trade, there was a huge outflow of bullion from the West to China. Despite the enormous imbalance between exports and imports, the trade was still profitable because Chinese goods bought with silver could be sold in Europe for two or three times what they had cost.

Transfers of bullion on that scale were possible only because the world's supply of precious metals had been hugely increased by the mines of the Americas.[15] The European conquest of the Americas thus made the financing of the China trade possible by providing Europeans with massive stocks of bullion, mined by vast numbers of enslaved indigenous and African workers. But over time these supplies dwindled, and by the mid-eighteenth century it had become increasingly difficult for the East India Company to procure the quantities of silver that were needed to sustain its trade with China: finding a means of offsetting the drain of bullion now became a matter of increasing urgency, even desperation.[16]

One simple solution to the problem would have been to start growing tea in India. This was indeed a dream that the Company had pursued since the late 1700s, dispatching skilled botanists and plant hunters to China in the hope of stealing the plants and the know-how associated with the cultivation of tea.[17] But that goal proved elusive. The Chinese were well aware of the value of the plant, and taking seeds or seedlings of the tea bush out of the country was strictly forbidden. Nor could foreigners roam around China, grabbing whichever plants they wanted—there were many restrictions on their movements there. To the British, and other Europeans, this was a source of intense frustration, for they were accustomed to seizing plants at will wherever they went. But with tea their efforts at stealing the technology were constantly thwarted through the eighteenth century, even as their balance of payments problem was worsening.

This left the East India Company with only one means of addressing its balance of trade problem with China: increasing the flow of exports from its Indian colonies. Cotton from India was one product for which there was already a considerable market in China. Another commodity in which there was a small but brisk trade was opium, harvested from a variety of poppy, *Papaver somniferum*. It was this plant that would become the solution for the problem posed by *Camellia sinensis*.

So it happened that a plant that was already playing an important role in history opened the door for the proliferation of another, even more mysterious and powerful plant.

India's chai, which is thought of by many today as primordially desi, was a latecomer to this centuries-old story. This is humbling to think of, even at a personal level.

For me, as for many Indians, tea is now essential, indispensable, a constitutional necessity: I literally cannot function without it. This was true also of my mother and almost everyone I knew when I was growing up. Tea was not only integral to our well-being but also seen as an important element of the Indian identity. This identification has come to be embraced by the world at large so that every Indian is thought to be a swiller of tea. In short, today, chai is to Indians what apple pie is to Americans.

Yet, the reality is that chai drinking in India has a rather short history, rooted not in the soil of the subcontinent but, rather, in Britain's relationship with China. Indians were introduced to tea drinking almost as an afterthought, and that too at the cost of much effort.

Before the twentieth century most Indians tended to regard tea with dislike, even suspicion. It took several ingenious advertising campaigns, launched by branches of the tea industry, to change people's minds. However, it was not till the 1940s that tea gained popularity in the subcontinent, and even that was the result of what is probably the most brilliant advertising campaign in the history of modern India, involving some of the foremost artists and designers of the period, including Satyajit Ray, the great film director, and Annada Munshi, a pioneer of commercial design in India (see insert image 1).[18]

Indeed, the true mystery in the story of Indian tea is why the subcontinent was so slow to adopt the brew. Tea was traded in Surat as early as the seventeenth century and the beverage is known to have been consumed locally.[19] Yet, the taste for tea does not seem to have spread beyond the city, which is puzzling because the Indian subcontinent is surrounded by tea-drinking cultures. Tibet had adopted tea as far back as the seventh century, and from there the beverage had filtered through to adjacent regions, like northern Nepal, Sikkim, Bhutan, Ladakh and Kashmir. Moreover, the tea plant was actually native to parts of north-eastern India, and a concoction made from its leaves was popular among some indigenous communities.[20]

But the fact that a variety of *Camellia sinensis* grew naturally in north-eastern India did not come to the notice of British officials until the 1820s.[21] When the find was confirmed a decade later, there was much rejoicing in the East India Company: the old dream of using India to reduce Britain's financial dependence on Chinese tea was at last within reach![22]

Despite fierce resistance from indigenous communities, India's first tea plantations were established in Assam within a few years, but strangely, considering that *Camellia sinensis* was native to the region, the estates were not planted with local seeds.[23] British planters didn't have much faith in the native variety so they used seeds and stock that had been smuggled over from China.[24] Nor did they trust Indian workers who, in the view prevalent among the British, 'want the skill and enterprise of the Chinese'.[25] So, along with the plants, Chinese tea growers were also brought in, to provide instruction in the cultivation and processing of tea.[26]

The appropriation of Chinese know-how became much easier after the British inflicted a crushing defeat on the Qing state in the First Opium War (1839–42). The war ensured much greater freedom for Europeans in China: no longer was it difficult to circumvent the restrictions that had previously hindered them in stealing technology and trained workers. (This instance of knowledge-theft by the West is, of course, now conveniently forgotten.)

It will be clear from this that the colonial tea industry in India was, from the start, thoroughly dependent on Chinese expertise, labour and, in the words of a British Governor General, 'Chinese agency'.[27] And so it happened that small Chinese communities took root in rural Assam: they too would be forcibly uprooted during the war of 1962 (a story that has been told beautifully by the Assamese writer Rita Choudhury in her novel *Chinatown Days* [*Makam*]).[28]

The one thing the British did not borrow from China was the pattern of tenancy under which tea was mainly produced there, with farmers working on small holdings with family labour.[29] In India tea was cultivated by a semi-free labour force of indentured workers, toiling on vast plantations that were mainly owned by white planters.[30]

After a slow beginning the Indian tea industry made rapid strides until the subcontinent's exports came to eclipse those of China. 'By the turn of the [nineteenth] century, Indian tea exports had surpassed those of their Chinese rivals, and the industry had become the leader in world production.'[31] This huge surge in productivity came about not because of the efficiency of British-style capitalism, as is often claimed, but because the colonial state enforced a highly racialized mode of production in which plantation owners were given tax concessions, free land and an indentured labour force that worked in thoroughly coercive conditions.[32] The same colonial state that waged war on China in the name of capitalism and Free Trade had no compunctions about enforcing a system of unfree labour within its own borders.[33] This appalling legacy haunts the Indian tea industry to this day, with many plantations still being structured around hierarchies of caste and ethnicity (although it should be noted that a number of producers, large and small, have broken with colonial productive practices, and adopted methods that are more socially and environmentally benign).[34]

Nor was India the only colony where tea was grown in this fashion: the same system was implemented in British-ruled Ceylon (Sri Lanka), Kenya and Malaya, with similar results in terms of productivity. Crucial to the ascendancy of the teas of the British Empire was the promotion of the idea that Chinese teas were dirty and unhygienic while colonial teas were somehow 'modern' and 'pure'.[35] In time tea came to be so much identified with India and other British colonies that it began to be asked: 'Is there tea in China too?'[36]

In effect, a pillar of the Chinese export economy was demolished through a process of technological theft initiated by the British Empire. That this was warfare by other means was explicitly recognized on both sides. As Andrew Liu points out in his excellent comparative study of the Chinese and Indian tea industries: 'British officials in India championed tea cultivation in the northeast Brahmaputra Valley by using the same rhetoric of the Opium War hawks, claiming that Indian tea would "destroy" and "annihilate the Chinese monopoly".'[37] On the Chinese side too, the assault on the country's most important export industry was recognized as 'commercial warfare'.[38] This indeed is why Liu's book is titled *Tea War*.

In other words, tea came to India as a corollary of a sustained contest—economic, social and military—between the West and China. This struggle has unfolded over centuries and is far from over; it has shaped the modern world in many ways, and will continue to do so in the years to come. Yet, this structural, long-term conflict has only rarely intensified into actual wars, fought by soldiers. At other times the conflict has been mediated through non-human entities, specifically tea and opium. This is analogous to the devastation that Europeans had earlier unleashed on the Native peoples of the Americas and Australia, much of which was inflicted through non-human forces like diseases, pathogens, processes of terraforming and the introduction of non-native fauna and flora. These were structural, biopolitical struggles where outbreaks of war were the exception rather than the rule; instead, the deadly effects of processes like terraforming and the spread of pathogens made themselves felt over decades and centuries.

The conquest and colonization of the Americas had given Europeans a deep familiarity with this form of conflict. The English, in particular, had not only grown very skilled at it, but also succeeded in persuading themselves that their methods were less violent than those of the Spanish Empire because they relied more on structural rather than physical aggression in eliminating Native populations. This astonishing feat of doublethink was made possible by the fact that Europeans had come to conceive of 'Nature' as a domain that was completely separate from the human. Hence, they absolved themselves of all responsibility for the spread of disease, for example, by claiming that it was a 'natural' process over which they had no control, even though they often actively fomented the dispersion of pathogens by refusing to initiate measures that might have halted epidemics or environmental changes. Destruction through inaction thus became one of the essential features of biopolitical conflict.[39]

However, such contests did not preclude the appropriation of ideas and technologies. European settlers in the Americas admired many aspects of Native American culture, and, as David Graeber and David Wengrow have shown in their pathbreaking book *The Dawn of Everything*, they even adopted Native American critiques of

Western civilization, including ideas like 'freedom' and 'equality': the concealment of their sources made those ideas appear to be of purely Western derivation.[40] Similarly, many Europeans held Chinese civilization in the highest regard even as they were exploiting its every weakness.

European colonizers would also typically enter into a broad range of alliances with non-Europeans, some of whom would profit from offering them their support. This too is an important aspect of the biopolitical conflicts that unfolded in nineteenth-century Asia through the mediation of plant species. The British had many allies in China, who benefited greatly from their mutual dealings. But their most important allies were from the Indian subcontinent, and they included Parsi and Marwari merchants, mercenary soldiers ('sepoys') and sailors ('lascars'), as well as vast numbers of workers in various bureaucracies and ancillary industries. It was through these extended networks and connections that the struggle between Britain and China, profoundly yet invisibly, transformed the economic and material life of the Indian subcontinent.

THREE

'An Actor in Its Own Right'

The opium poppy, *Papaver somniferum*, is believed to have originated in central or eastern Europe, possibly the Balkans, or around the coast of the Black Sea.[1] The flower appears to have forged, very early on, a special relationship with human beings: indeed, it is possible that the plant developed its chemical structure precisely to ensure that humans would propagate it.[2] This may be why there are no truly wild varieties of the opium poppy; they are all cultivars that evolved in collaboration with human beings, to enhance their medical and psychoactive properties.[3]

Opium has been found at a 6,000-year-old archaeological site in Switzerland, and in an Egyptian tomb that dates back to the second millennium before the Common Era.[4] The substance was well known in the Greek and Roman worlds, and is mentioned by Homer, Virgil, Livy, Pliny and Ovid.[5] There are possibly references to it also in the Bible.[6] In the eleventh century, Avicenna described opium as the 'most powerful of stupefacients', a substance that possessed extraordinary properties both as a painkiller and as a poison.[7]

However, awareness of the powers of the poppy almost certainly preceded these references by several centuries. Long before the beginnings of recorded history, many groups of people seem to have discovered, independently of each other, that the opium poppy produces a uniquely powerful medicinal substance that can be used to treat coughs, stomach disorders and many other ailments.[8] It takes only a glance at the list of chemicals in several commonly used medications to see that opium remains pharmacologically indispensable to this day. Simply put, opium is perhaps the oldest and most powerful medicine known to man. As Thomas Sydenham, a seventeenth-century English apothecary, noted: 'Among the remedies which it has pleased Almighty God to give to man to relieve his suffering, none is so universal or efficacious as opium.'[9]

Today pretty much everyone who uses modern medicines has been exposed to opium. Back when I was doing readings from *Sea of Poppies*, I would often be asked whether I had ever used opium. I would explain that I had never used opioids recreationally (indeed, in the course of writing the novel I had developed so much respect for the opium poppy that I could not bring myself to take opioid painkillers even when I was recuperating from a surgical procedure). Yet, whether unconsciously or not, I have still ingested a fair amount of opium over the years through medications like Imodium, Corex and other codeine-based cough medicines. Opium has so many medicinal applications that it remains indispensable for the modern drug industry, just as it was for medieval apothecaries.

Indispensable as opium is as a medication, it is even more valuable as an anaesthetic: its extraordinary ability to assuage pain has been known since antiquity, and it has long been used in surgical and dental procedures. Even today many, if not most, anaesthetics are derived from opioids. It is not uncommon for opioid-based anaesthetics to induce an unexpected sense of elation, which is why the otherwise ghastly experience of a colonoscopy can end with a strange feeling of euphoria. I remember, as a teenager, waking from a minor surgical procedure and experiencing a sense of rapture so extreme that I wanted to jump off the bed and fling my arms around the nurse. That feeling was so peculiar that I have never forgotten it. It took me decades to figure out that I had been given an opioid-based anaesthetic—because the role of opium in modern life has come to be so thoroughly repressed that it is quite common for people to say: 'Oh well, it might have been great to live in the middle ages, but what if you had to have a tooth pulled or a limb amputated?' The answer, of course, is that then, as now, you would have been given a strong dose of some opioid.

As an anaesthetic opium is so important that during the World Wars it was treated as a vital strategic resource. This being the case even in modern times, it can well be imagined how valuable opium was in earlier eras when medicinal substances were far fewer in number. It is hardly surprising then that a trade in medicinal opium should have come into being very early across Europe, Asia and Africa.

That opium can induce changes in consciousness has, of course, also been known since antiquity. But this does not seem to always have been a major factor in the circulation of the drug. In this, opium is completely different from wine, toddy, marijuana, coca, kava, peyote, ayahuasca, mescalin, psilocybin mushrooms, pituri and most other mind-altering substances known to humans—and, as is well known, there has, historically, never been any human society that did *not* use some mind-altering substance, or develop techniques like meditation, fasting or ordeals, to enter into altered states of consciousness.[10] As David Courtwright has pointed out, the urge to alter their normal consciousness is so powerful in humans that '[c]hildren at play will whirl themselves into a vertiginous stupor'.[11] Indeed, it is difficult to imagine what it would be like to live always at a single, unvarying pitch of sobriety: such a state would probably be indistinguishable from clinical depression.

Various other animals are also known to seek out mind-altering plants, so it is quite possible that humans learnt about psychoactive substances from other species, perhaps even before the emergence of *Homo sapiens*.[12] Since many plants with psychoactive properties grew wild in forests and grasslands, they were easily collected by foragers, nomads, forest dwellers or indeed anyone who had any familiarity with plants. Some of these plants are so vigorous and hardy that they are virtually impossible to eradicate: *Cannabis sativa*, for instance, is among the world's fastest-growing plants. While travelling around southern China in 2012 I remember seeing cannabis growing luxuriantly, not just in forests but also around towns and villages.

Because of their widespread availability within their own traditional habitats, palm wine, toddy, cannabis, coca, betel nut, kava, peyote, tobacco, pituri, psilocybin mushrooms, ayahuasca, mescalin and the like might be described as 'grassroots psychoactives'.[13] One distinctive feature of these substances is that they were used *primarily* for their ability to alter states of mind (rather than their medicinal qualities, as was the case with opium). The fact that the properties of these substances were well known within their native regions meant that the local populace was able to develop certain protocols and rituals for their use, so as to limit the scope for abuse. These traditional societal usages were typically developed over very long durations of time, certainly centuries if not millennia.

Opium differs from grassroots psychoactives in many respects, not the least of them being the time span over which it became a substance that large numbers of people began to use for the specific purpose of altering their consciousness. This happened only a few hundred years ago, which is significant because it suggests that opium developed its distinctive user profiles relatively recently in comparison with grassroots psychoactives. The time frame within which opioid use develops in a society is, in fact, critical to how its wider societal effects play out.

Spatially too there are important distinctions in the ways in which mind-altering substances circulated. The use of grassroots psychoactives tended to be localized, being specific to certain cultures and regions. The chewing of coca leaves, for instance, was limited to certain societies in South America and has remained so to this day. The practice did not spread beyond the continent even when substances derived from coca leaves, such as cocaine, became commodified as recreational drugs. In the late nineteenth century the Dutch cultivated coca on a large scale in Java, but the practice of chewing the leaves was never adopted by the farmers who grew the plant, even though other psychoactives, like opium, were widely used on the island at that time.[14] Unlike coca, cannabis was an 'Old World' plant that had a wide geographic range across continents, and was, moreover, exceptionally hardy and vigorous. Yet, cannabis was not used as a psychoactive everywhere that it grew: in many places, such as Italy, it was cultivated for its fibre (hemp).[15] Back then the European preference was for wine and spirits. In the Indian subcontinent, on the other hand, the mood-altering properties of cannabis were embraced so early and so eagerly that 'India has been called the world's first cannabis-oriented culture'.[16]

Another respect in which grassroots psychoactives differ from opioids is that they generally require very little processing; most of them can be chewed or smoked, or otherwise consumed almost as soon as they are harvested; some can be used after being dried, and others straight off the plant, like palm toddy. The sap of poppy bulbs, on the other hand, requires a significant amount of processing for it to be transformed into opium. Even as recently as the eighteenth and nineteenth centuries it would take almost an entire year for poppy sap to be converted into usable opium; it cannot be used fresh off the plant, like marijuana, qat or coca leaves. This is probably why the pre-modern trade in opium was largely medicinal: the processing that the raw gum required may have imposed a natural limit on the quantities of the drug that could be in circulation.

The fact that opium had to be processed meant also that it was expensive, so it is no coincidence that early adopters were often cultural elites and literati.[17] This has remained a constant feature of opioid use, from medieval courts to the present day.[18] In the contemporary West too, musicians, artists and writers were often the pioneers in opioid-use because 'there was a certain glamour in it'.[19] The early embrace of opium by elites is another factor that sets the substance apart from grassroots psychoactives. Toddy, marijuana and mahua, for example, were looked down upon by elites because they grew in the 'wild' and were consumed by poor peasants and foragers.[20] Their own preferences, by contrast, tended to be for highly refined consciousness-altering substances like wine, spirits and, especially, aphrodisiacs (which opium was mistakenly thought to be). It is not surprising then that opium, which also required refining, held a special appeal for connoisseurs and literati, ranging from writers like Thomas De Quincey in England, Jean Cocteau in France and William S. Burroughs in the United States to Zhang Changjia in China.[21] This appeal did not wane over time; if anything it grew stronger. According to Beth Macy: 'The term "hipster", in fact, drew from the Chinese opium smoker of the 1800s, who'd spent much of his time smoking while reclining on one hip. The hipster counter-culture took inspiration from heroin-addicted jazz greats like Charlie Parker and John Coltrane.'[22]

The plant whose profile most closely resembles that of the opium poppy is the coca bush (*Erythroxylum coca*), the leaves of which can also be processed into the addictive drug cocaine. But for most of its long history coca was a grassroots psychoactive, used by indigenous populations in South America, where large numbers of people continue to use it in that fashion to this day. However, chewers of coca were not responsible for transforming the leaves of the bush into cocaine. It was a German chemist who isolated the cocaine alkaloid in 1855, though the drug did not become a trade commodity until later in the nineteenth century, some 300 years after opium. So, in effect, cocaine followed in the footsteps of opium, which had long since established certain patterns which, as the historian Alfred McCoy observes, 'have been repeated, years or even decades later, in the Andes coca zone'.[23]

Opium, therefore, is quite distinctive in its social history. The lumping together of opioids with other psychoactives, as a 'drug', is not just misleading; it has also led to profoundly mistaken public health approaches, depriving people of some substances, like cannabis and peyote, that are now known to have many beneficial properties. Indeed, the only effective means of combating the continuing spread of opioids may lie in forging alliances with other plants—that is by making grassroots psychoactives like cannabis and peyote more easily available.

Of course, opium also has innumerable beneficial uses, perhaps more so than any other psychoactive. It is precisely because of its extraordinary properties that opium also possesses the ability to generate a continually ascending series of more addictive forms, from the ma'jûn of the Middle Ages to chandu, morphine, heroin and oxycodone. Opium's ability to spin off new and more potent versions of itself—even synthetic analogues like fentanyl—is one of the many tricks that the genie has often used to break out of its bottle. Once it escapes, it has a way of quickly transcending class and spreading from elites to those at the other end of the social ladder. This pattern too has repeated itself many times over throughout history.[24]

These properties have endowed opium with a distinctive ability to interact with human societies in ways that can shape history. '[I]t is perhaps appropriate,' writes William B. McAllister, a US diplomat and historian, 'to interpret opium as an actor in its own right. Rather than simply an inert substance, opium might be seen over the last three or four centuries as a sort of independent biological imperial agent. In recent decades [opium's] worldwide ubiquity only confirms its power; opium appears to have bested all its human contenders.'[25]

It is because opium is a historical force in its own right that it must be approached with due attention to the ways in which it has interacted with humans over time. If these interactions are difficult to conceptualize it is largely because they are very strongly inflected by class and power differentials. But those difficulties are further compounded by the fact that the necessary vocabulary does not yet exist for thinking about history in a way that allows for the agency of non-human entities.

Through most of human history, opium circulated in very small quantities and was used primarily as a medicine. Anatolia was probably the region in which farmers first began to cultivate poppies as an important commercial crop, and the practice is thought to have spread outwards from there. The armies of Alexander the Great are believed to have carried opium into Iran, hence the derivation of the Persian and Arabic words for opium, 'afyun', from the Greek 'opion'.[26] The Perso-Arabic terms, in turn, engendered the word 'afeem', widely used across the Indian subcontinent, and Chinese terms like 'afyon' and 'yapian'.[27] Even after its introduction to the Middle East, opium continued to be used largely for medicinal purposes.

In the Indian subcontinent the cultivation of poppies probably began towards the end of the first millennium of the common era. The first references to opium in Sanskrit date back to the eighth century, at about the time of the Arab conquest of Sind. This, along with the Perso-Arabic derivations of many Indian words for opium, suggests that the commercial cultivation of the poppy was introduced in the region by way of Iran and the Arab world.[28]

A useful analogy in thinking of the social history of opium is that of an opportunistic pathogen, one that goes through long periods of dormancy, affecting very small numbers of people.[29] But when social processes and historical events provide the pathogen with an opportunity, it bursts out to rapidly expand its circulation. Often, when these outbreaks happen, the pathogen undergoes a mutation, which allows it to elude human immune systems. In opioid outbreaks too the drug mutates and begins to be consumed in newer, more powerfully addictive forms.

In the case of opium the earliest opportunities for propagation were provided by the Mongols, around the fourteenth century, when their contiguous territories stretched from China to northern India, Iran, the Levant and Anatolia. The oral consumption of opium in various forms was popular among Mongol rulers and in their courts, and the practice was then passed on to their successors, the Ottoman, Safavid and Mughal empires. The ruling dynasties of these empires were, variously, Shia and Sunni Muslims, but their territories were contiguous—sprawling over a huge swath of Eurasia and north Africa—and they had a significant degree of communication with each other.

It was in these empires that the use of opium went through a second phase of expansion in the fifteenth and sixteenth centuries. The characteristic form in which opium was used also underwent a change at this time. Its potency was enhanced by mixing it with other psychoactives like cannabis, and the mixtures were consumed either as a beverage or a comestible.[30]

Since the people of these parts of Asia were introduced to opium at a time when supplies were limited, their exposure to it was slow and gradual. This afforded them time to develop social customs and usages for limiting the use of opium to certain contexts, much as Europeans did with alcohol.[31] This process is, of course, analogous to the way in which populations develop immunities to pathogens, except in this case the resistances were social rather than biological. The fact that other psychoactive substances, like cannabis and betel nut, were widely used in the Indian subcontinent probably also helped to limit the spread of opium locally. Moreover, even though opium was a major feature of courtly life in Mughal India, the drug was not an instrument of state policy, or a major source of revenue. Thus, the Mughal Empire had no financial incentive to encourage opium use or expand the industry.[32]

Over time, in the Indian subcontinent and Persia, the use of opium came to be socially acceptable so long as it was consumed orally, in the form of pills and tonics—but there was a powerful taboo against the smoking of opium, which is a much more addictive method of consumption. When drunk or eaten, opium, in the minimally pro-cessed forms in which it circulated in India, did not typically produce a 'high': it acted more in the manner of a soporific or analgesic. Hence, swallowing opium was seen in the same light as taking a medicine, whereas smoking the drug was considered a recreational activity, and hence 'a perversion'.[33] A similar pattern of opioid use emerged also in Europe and America. Even though various opioid-based tinctures and tonics were widely consumed in the West, through much of the nineteenth century, the recreational smoking of opium was strongly frowned upon: it was perceived as being characteristic of 'degenerate races' and was considered 'detestable'.[34]

In short, social conventions that had developed through centuries of exposure to opium may have helped to protect some parts of Eurasia from highly addictive forms of opioid use. It needs to be noted, however, that social resistances to addictive substances do not last forever, and can crumble quite quickly when drugs are synthesized into more addictive forms. Iran, for example, developed a major heroin-addiction problem in the early twentieth century, as did India with cocaine, which began to be mixed into the paste that is applied on betel leaves, to make paan.[35] And today parts of India, Pakistan and Afghanistan are once again in the grip of rapidly spreading opioid epidemics.

It is clear from many European travel narratives that by the 1500s, opium was circulating widely among the courtly elites of northern India, Afghanistan and Central Asia. In this period it was usually consumed in a form known as ma'jûn, a compound made of opium paste and some other substances. Ma'jûn was generally rolled into pellets and eaten, or mixed into beverages and drunk.[36] The first Mughal Emperor of India, Babur, refers to ma'jûn frequently in his autobiography.[37] His son Emperor Humayun was an even greater enthusiast.[38] Humayun's son Emperor Akbar also used opium, as did his grandson Jahangir, who is reported to have taken 'six draughts of alcohol each evening and a pill of opium'.[39] Opium use was also widespread in the courts of Rajput rulers, and the substance was even incorporated into some of their rituals, such as weddings.

But the indulgences of kings and emperors are rarely within the reach of ordinary people. The impressions conveyed by travel narratives and historical sources are probably skewed because of a disproportionate focus on elite practices: European travellers and merchants generally tended to attach themselves to royal entourages, and court chronicles were also largely written by people connected with ruling elites. In reality it is unlikely that even a small percentage of the general population would have been able to find, much less buy, opium, even if they had wanted to.

In pre-colonial India, opium poppies were cultivated in two regions of the subcontinent. The eastern and more important opium-producing region was in the Gangetic plain, around Patna, in modern-day Bihar, while the second was in an area known as Malwa, in west-central India. The total quantity of opium produced in Bihar through the seventeenth and eighteenth centuries was less than 5,000 chests, while Malwa probably produced around 4,000 chests. Since half the supply was exported,[40] the amount of opium available, on a per capita basis, to the 150–200 million inhabitants of the Indian subcontinent in this period was at most 1 or 2 grams per *year*, a minuscule amount.[41] According to Hans Derks's calculations, opium was used in small quantities even by the upper classes, a fraction of a gram per day.[42] The amounts are so small that they suggest that only a tiny minority, consisting mainly of rulers and noblemen, consumed opium in substantial quantities. The vast majority of the population of pre-colonial India clearly used the drug mostly for medicinal purposes if at all.

In the nineteenth century, British colonial writers and officials often conveyed the impression that opium was a traditional Indian drug, widely consumed by people of all classes. But it takes only a cursory glance at the figures to see that this could not possibly have been the case. While the knowledge of opium may have been widespread, as in Europe, its actual use was obviously quite limited. Opium use did indeed become common in the subcontinent in the late nineteenth century, when India was exporting as much as 100,000 chests of opium in some years.[43] But this phenomenal growth was not caused by 'tradition'—it came about, rather, because the drug was instrumental in the creation of a certain kind of colonial modernity.

FOUR

Frenemies

Poppies are a thirsty, labour-intensive crop, difficult to cultivate for small farmers.[1] It is estimated that even today, a peasant family growing poppies under optimal conditions would not be able to harvest more than 12 kilograms of opium in a year.[2] In pre-colonial times Bihari farmers would have produced far less than that: their poppies were generally grown on small strips of land along the borders of the crops they depended on for their sustenance. The raw opium was sold to middlemen who transported the drug to Patna, where it was processed and marketed to buyers from many parts of the Indian subcontinent, and indeed the world.[3]

These patterns began to change when Europeans became a powerful new force in the political economy of the Indian Ocean.[4] It was the Portuguese who discovered that opium could serve a useful diplomatic function as an item to be included in the gifts that they gave to local rulers to lubricate the flow of trade with their own country.[5] So it happened that the nexus between state power and trade, so characteristic of mercantilist Europe, slowly but surely turned opium into something that it had never been before—an instrument of state policy.

When the Dutch replaced the Portuguese as the dominant power in the Indian Ocean, they expanded the practice of gifting opium by incorporating it into their relentless quest for monopolies over Asian trade commodities, like nutmeg, mace and cloves.[6] Having succeeded in cornering the market in several other spices, they then set their sights on pepper, which, in terms of quantity and value, was by far the most important component of the spice trade. But pepper was a more difficult proposition than cloves, nutmeg and mace because it grew in several regions. Of these the most important were the kingdoms and principalities of the Malabar Coast, where it was traded for either silver or other goods. Historically, opium had played no part in the trade, but once Europeans began to distribute it as a gift, the demand for the drug grew so quickly that the Dutch traders were able to use it as a currency, to acquire pepper on the Malabar Coast.[7] The Dutch were thus the first to discover that the demand for opium and opiates can grow almost unstoppably once supplies are made easily available.

The Malay-speaking regions of pre-colonial Southeast Asia were relative latecomers to opium. In the sixteenth century many European travellers compiled lists of Javanese and Malay words, but opium did not figure in even one of them, which suggests that very little opium was in circulation in the region at the time.[8] When the Dutch started bringing Indian opium into the archipelago, many native rulers tried to stop the inflow and 'did what they could, and often in a very radical manner, to protect their subjects against the baneful drug'.[9] Some of the Sultans of Java and the Radjah of Lombok enacted stern prohibitions on opium within their territories.[10] But these prohibitions became increasingly ineffective as the Dutch grip on the archipelago tightened. From around 1640, when they first started procuring large amounts of opium in India, in a mere forty years the Dutch were able to create a seventeen-fold expansion in the market in Java and Madura.[11]

Through the seventeenth and early eighteenth centuries the insatiable demand on the part of European trading companies led to a huge surge in the production of opium in eastern India. Although they had stiff competition from English, Portuguese and Spanish merchants, the Dutch were the major buyers of opium in the region, and much of what they bought was sold in the East Indies. Over the eighteenth century they are estimated to have sold nearly 50,00,000 kilograms of opium in the Indonesian archipelago.[12]

The Dutch East India Company, generally known as the VOC (Vereenigde Oostindische Compagnie), gradually extended the practice of using opium as a trade currency throughout the East Indies, leveraging it to impose monopolies as well as monopsonies (where sellers could sell to only one buyer).[13] They would offer opium to local rulers in exchange for exclusive access to their products while insisting, at the same time, that they be the sole supplier of the drug to their kingdoms. In this way, as far back as the seventeenth century, the VOC established a complete monopoly over the selling of opium in the East Indies: it alone had the right to ship opium from eastern India to its territories, where it was auctioned off by its officials to opium 'farmers' or retailers, who then arranged for its sale to consumers. The system worked so well that the market for opium in the East Indies grew rapidly over the seventeenth century.[14] By the mid-eighteenth century opium from eastern India was among the most important items of trade in ports like Batavia (Jakarta) and Riau. In this period '[p]ractically the entire exports of Bengal opium were directed at the Indonesian archipelago'.[15] This continued to be the case for a long time afterwards.[16]

As more and more Indian opium flowed into the Dutch-controlled ports of Java, small quantities of the drug also began to travel eastwards, carried by diasporic Chinese merchants to Taiwan and the ports of the Fujian province.[17] The merchants brought with them also the habit of smoking opium, which had caught on among the Chinese of Batavia around 1617.[18] The practice was still in its infancy then, and the substance that was smoked was actually tobacco dipped in a solution of liquid opium.[19] The mixture was smoked in a pipe, like regular tobacco, and it produced only a tiny amount of morphia, 0.2 per cent by weight. Within a few years elite Chinese literati were also smoking opium in this form, and the technique gained ground quickly because tobacco was then already ubiquitous in China.[20] The ensuing spread of opium caused enough concern that the Qing state passed a ban on it as early as 1729, when the total annual importation was only 200 chests.[21] The ban penalized the dealers who ran opium dens but not the smokers themselves, 'who were thought to suffer badly enough from the effects of addiction'.[22]

Over the next decades the practice went through a complete transformation with the development of a technique for refining crude opium to create a substance known as chandu, or 'smoking opium' (in the words of the eminent historian of narcotics David Courtwright).[23] Although this kind of opioid was often lumped together with the type of opium that was used in medications, it was, in fact, a completely different substance. 'Smoking opium' did not need to be mixed with tobacco: it delivered a much more powerful high on its own, with a yield between 9 and 10 per cent morphia.[24] The high yields of morphia made this a significantly more addictive practice, and around the 1760s it became the preferred method of opium consumption in China and Indonesia. Inevitably there was a huge acceleration in the rate of addiction.

In effect, like a mutated pathogen, this new, more addictive avatar of the drug found 'virgin soil' in Southeast Asia and China, and was, therefore, able to expand its circulation with unprecedented rapidity, much like the epidemic diseases that were then decimating the indigenous peoples of the Americas. Just as the spread of deadly pathogens was often aided by European colonizers in the Americas, so too was the proliferation in the circulation of opium in Southeast Asia and China actively abetted by European empires.

The Chinese, for their part, were well aware of the European role in the rapid spread of opium in Asia. In 1791, the Chinese traveller Ong Tae-hae had this to say about the Javanese:

[C]oveting the wealth of Europeans, [they] have gradually fallen into their snare; but who could have calculated on the conquerors proceeding to invent the black fumes of opium, to tempt and delude the natives; urging them to consume this drug as a luxury, until they became so weak and emaciated, so dispirited and exhausted, that they could no longer think of regaining their land, nor conceive the idea of revenging their wrongs. The Javanese . . . were readily overcome by this poison, and lost all care for themselves; but we Chinese, of the central flowery land, have also been deluded by them; for no sooner do we partake of this substance, than we lose all anxieties about our native land, have no further concern for father or mother, wife or children, and are plunged into unspeakable misery.

He continues:

How is it then that we Chinese, together with the Javanese are so thoughtless as to fall into this snare? In this scheme of the Europeans they seem to have laid a foundation not to be rooted up for a myriad of years; having done which, they live at their ease, without dread of danger, while they give themselves up to the work of fleecing the people.[25]

The Dutch opium regime in the East Indies underwent many changes between the seventeenth and nineteenth centuries, but what remained constant was that every new measure invariably had the effect of expanding the market for the drug.[26] When faced with criticism, Dutch officials would argue that they were merely meeting a demand that was rooted in the inherent infirmities of the natives, and that if they did not provide a supply, others would. This pattern of disavowal, or 'denial', too would leave an enduring legacy: arguments like these were later adopted not only by other European narco-states, but also by twenty-first-century marketers of opiates.

Several Southeast Asian rulers tried to restrict the inflow of the drug to their domains, only to have their efforts pit them against the VOC, which depended on its monopoly of opium for a large part of its revenue. This meant that the VOC had to fight innumerable small but brutal 'opium wars' to prevent local rulers from limiting the circulation of opium in their territories.[27] This pattern would later be replicated, on a much larger scale, by Britain in China. In other words, the Dutch created a template in the seventeenth century that ensured, as Hans Derks notes, that 'almost all Asiatic wars' would henceforth have 'a strong narco-character through to the present, including the Vietnam and Afghanistan wars'.[28]

The VOC's opium monopoly in the Indonesian archipelago was constantly threatened by shippers of many stripes, English and American, Asian and European. Since the East Indies lay athwart the main trade route between India and China, innumerable opium-laden ships plied those waters and more than a few took advantage of opportunities to dispose of their cargoes where they could.[29] Keeping those ships out of the labyrinthine waterways of the Indonesian archipelago was a Herculean task, and the VOC seldom succeeded, despite waging a never-ending campaign against those it described as 'smugglers' and 'pirates'.[30] At the same time, the Dutch colonial regime also had to defend its opium monopoly against independent kingdoms that were trying to profit from the opium trade: a series of such conflicts ultimately led to the annexation of Bali.[31]

A notable aspect of the centuries-long Dutch involvement in the opium trade was that the colonial authorities consistently chose to buy the bulk of their supplies of opium from eastern India (although they sometimes added supplementary quantities from Turkey and Persia). However, they never attempted to cultivate poppies in their own colonial territories as they did with coca in the late nineteenth century. This was because of characteristically shrewd decisions, based on commercial as well as political considerations: they realized early on that if opium poppies were to be grown widely in the East Indies, not only would the price of the drug decline steeply, but the local rulers and chieftains would no longer depend on the Dutch for its supply. In other words, the profitability of the Dutch opium monopoly depended on the importation of the drug from India because it propped up prices. So when a nineteenth-century Dutch official mooted the idea of growing poppies in northern Sulawesi, his seniors silenced him by asking: 'Is it clever to inform the population about a product which can be grown so easy and cheap, but which is so expensive to buy . . . ?'[32]

The VOC's monopoly on opium was a golden goose for Dutch officials and private traders. Some of them profited on a scale that is almost unimaginable: in 1709, one Governor General went back to Holland with 10 million guilders—a '"Bill Gates fortune" at present value'.[33] In 1745 some senior officials of the VOC formed a club called the Amphioen (or Opium) Society, and negotiated special privileges in buying and disposing of opium.[34] This was crony capitalism at its most advanced and ingenious form: the Amphioen Society cannily protected itself by giving shares to powerful people in the colonies and in Holland. William IV, Prince of Orange, himself received a substantial number of shares from which he and his progeny reaped enormous profits.[35]

Nor was this the only link between the opium trade and the royal house of the Netherlands. In 1815, the newly crowned Dutch monarch, formerly Prince Willem Frederik of Orange-Nassau, founded an enterprise called the Royal Dutch Trading Company (Koninklijke Nederlandsche Handel-Maatschappij or NHM). Due to its royal sponsorship, the company became so powerful in the Dutch East Indies that it was able to take over the colonial opium monopoly.[36] The practices of the Royal Dutch Trading Company were so harsh that they became the target of a passionate denunciation in the novel *Max Havelaar* by the Dutch writer Eduard Douwes Dekker, better known as Multatuli.[37] While the company no longer exists today, its legacy lives on, as is the case with many other enterprises that profited from the opium trade. Its offshoots include an energy giant that has worked hard to promote denialism regarding fossil fuels and climate change: Royal Dutch/Shell.[38]

Although many of the company's other ventures failed at the time, its opium business was consistently profitable and earned vast sums of money for the royal family: 'the billions of the private fortune of the present House of Orange originate partly from this source.'[39]

Nor did these ventures slake the appetites of the House of Orange. In the late nineteenth century powerful members of the royal family established a tin-mining company on the Sumatran island of Billiton (Belitung) as a private undertaking. Through the influence of its royal patrons, the company also acquired the license to sell opium to its overworked and much-abused labour force, most of which was Chinese. That company is now one of the most important mining enterprises in the world—BHP Billiton (BHP Group Limited).[40]

In sum, it was the Dutch who led the way in enmeshing opium with colonialism, and in creating the first imperial narco-state, heavily dependent on drug revenues. But it was in India that the model of the colonial narco-state was perfected by the British.[41]

Throughout the 1600s and even afterwards, the Dutch and the English were the most intimate of enemies. From North America to the farthest reaches of the Indian Ocean, they competed ferociously, and often violently, for markets and colonies. In Europe, they fought a series of wars, one of which ended in a decisive defeat for Britain in 1667. Yet, at the same time, the two 'frenemies' also learnt from each other, copied each other and served in each other's armies, navies, businesses and universities. As for the royal families, they were so closely connected that William III, Prince of Orange-Nassau, and his wife, Queen Mary, were enthroned as the rulers of England in 1689.

This dynamic of intimate enmity also governed Anglo-Dutch relations in the Indian Ocean. Although the Dutch had a lead of a few decades in the East Indies, the English were constantly snapping at their heels. In 1623, the rivalry culminated in the execution of ten Englishmen—along with nine Japanese ronin and one Eurasian—in Amboyna (now Ambon), the Dutch capital in the Moluccas.[42] It was only after this that English territorial ambitions moved away from the East Indies and came to be focused on the Indian subcontinent.

The British East India Company's first permanent settlement in India was founded just four years after the Amboyna incident, near the city of Madras (now Chennai). In the decades that followed the Company would acquire Bombay, and also establish the city of Calcutta. It was the latter that became the launching pad for the East India Company's expansion into the Gangetic plain, the heartland of northern India. This region was known historically as Purvanchal ('eastern region'): its people were the Purbiyas ('easterners') and its principal language was Bhojpuri, which is now considered a dialect of Hindi.[43]

Purvanchal was rich not only in crafts, industries and agricultural products, but also in surplus labour, much of which was absorbed by the subcontinent's many competing armies. Over time a thriving market in military labour came into being in the Gangetic plain, and men of diverse castes and tribes resorted to it for employment. The military labour market was vital to the economy of the region because, contrary to popular myth, pre-colonial India was neither sedentary nor unchanging: it was turbulent, unsettled and extremely dynamic, a land of adventurers, where soldiering and war-making were major industries that employed as much as a quarter of the population.[44] The military labour market was also, as the historian Dirk Kolff has shown, an important avenue of social mobility, through which people could change and re-invent their place in the caste hierarchy.[45] The market was, therefore, a critical strategic resource: any rising power that sought to expand into northern India had to be able to recruit sepoys and camp-followers from the Gangetic plain. The East India Company also drew on this region for its native troops: even before it annexed Bihar it was recruiting Purbiyas for its territorial armies in three different parts of the subcontinent. These Bihari sepoys tended to be largely upper-caste Hindus, mainly Brahmins and Rajputs.[46]

Equipped with English weaponry, the army of the Bengal Presidency marched steadily westward, at the expense of the increasingly enfeebled remnants of the Mughal Empire. In 1757 and 1764 the East India Company defeated the tottering indigenous powers in two decisive battles.[47] The territories that came with those victories were quickly incorporated into the Company's Bengal Presidency, which from then on extended deep into the Gangetic plain, well past the city of Patna. This meant that much of the hinterland of the military labour market, as well as most of the opium-producing region of Bihar, was now in English hands; both would prove strategically crucial to the fortunes of the East India Company.

The English, like the Dutch and the French, had long maintained a 'factory' or trading station in Patna, so its officials were intimately familiar with the workings of the opium business. For a few years after the British conquest, the Europeans competed against each other in procuring opium, with the result that the acreage under poppy cultivation in the region soared from 283,000 hectares to 303,500 hectares in just one year. 'This large-scale conversion of paddy fields into poppy cultivation,' writes the historian Emdad-ul Haq, 'contributed to a famine in Bengal in 1770. This famine caused the death of 10 million people in an area that had been traditionally known as the "Golden Bengal" due to its natural resources.'[48]

In 1772, the Governor General of India, Warren Hastings, resolved the matter by placing Bihar's opium production wholly under the control of the East India Company. From then on farmers could sell their opium only to the Company's designated agents; local merchants who bought or sold the drug were deemed smugglers.[49] This shut French and Dutch merchants out of the trade, much to the detriment of Bihari farmers, who actually preferred to do business with other Europeans since they paid better than the English.[50]

For the colonial regime the opium market was a windfall and it could not have come at a better time: this was exactly the period when the taxes on Chinese tea were becoming increasingly indispensable sources of revenue, both for Britain and for the East India Company. At the same time Chinese tea was becoming increasingly difficult to acquire because of the dwindling supplies of silver from the Americas.[51] British officials were well aware, of course, of how their Dutch frenemies had expanded the demand for opium in the East Indies.[52] While some members of the Company doubted that the Chinese market could be enlarged in the same way, there were others who were confident that it was possible.[53]

The story goes that it was in 1767 that one Colonel Watson, a shipbuilder, formally proposed that the East India Company increase its opium shipments to China, during a meeting of a council of Company representatives in Calcutta.[54] The proposal was supported by 'an officer and an influential member of the company' called Mr Wheeler, 'and after being favorably entertained, it was adopted as a happy expedient towards raising a revenue for supporting government.'[55]

The Company's higher-ups in London were well aware that opium had been banned in China since 1729, and were not initially convinced that the expedient was indeed a happy one. At one point they even sent a stern admonition to Calcutta: '[I]t is beneath the Company to be engaged in such a clandestine trade; we therefore, hereby positively prohibit any more opium being sent to China on the Company's account.'[56] But these compunctions were erased by the prospect of profits. Not the least of the gainers was Colonel Watson himself, who began to specialize in building ships for the opium trade.[57]

Colonel Watson's name appears to have lived on within the British merchant community for a long time afterwards, which suggests that his compatriots fully appreciated the historic nature of the decision taken at that meeting in Calcutta in 1767.[58] But the idea itself—of using opium to finance trade in other commodities—was not really Colonel Watson's brainchild. The decision did not come about by accident, or because the Colonel had a eureka moment in 1767. By the time the East India Company's council in Calcutta decided to increase opium exports with a view to growing the Chinese market, the practice of using opium as a currency had acquired a lengthy pedigree in European colonial practices, and all the elements of the emergent system had already been in place for almost a century.

Europeans did not, by any means, invent the opium trade. Rather, as with the traffic in human beings on the Atlantic Coast, they took certain pre-existing, small-scale practices and transformed them while also expanding them by orders of magnitude.

From the time the Company took control of opium production in Bihar, British colonizers would claim that their opium monopoly was merely an extension of a pre-existing indigenous practice, and that the Mughal Empire had also maintained a monopoly on opium.[59] Over time, through repetition, this story came to be so thoroughly engraved on the historical record that it is often repeated even today. Yet, historians have been unable to turn up any evidence of a pre-colonial monopoly: under the Mughals, opium was taxed like other agricultural products, and the output may have been controlled, from time to time, by individual merchants or cartels, but the system does not appear to have been managed by the state.[60] While Mughal rulers and their courts did indeed use opium recreationally, their supplies were obtained not through a state monopoly but from private traders, including the Dutch.[61]

Thus, the story of a Mughal opium monopoly is but another instance of the British Empire's remarkable talents in self-exculpatory myth-making.[62] This is indeed one of the most astonishing aspects of the West's involvement with opium in Asia. Not only did Western colonizers succeed in using opium to extract incalculable wealth from Asians, but they were successful also in obscuring their own role in the trade by claiming that it had existed from time immemorial because non-white people were by nature prone to addiction and depravity.

The most effective weapons in this campaign of obfuscation were certain modes of thought that were then taking root in the West. Among the most powerful of these was the idea that there existed certain abstract forces and universal mechanisms that humans were powerless to control. So, for example, the devastation that was then being inflicted on Native Americans by colonizers was often said to be the work of laws of nature that operated independently of human agency.[63] Similarly, in this period many Westerners, especially the elites of the Anglosphere, came to be convinced that trade and commerce were also governed by laws that were impervious to human intervention, so that all efforts to curtail the free circulation of goods, opium included, were doomed to failure. Many colonial officials and merchants seem to have genuinely believed that Free Trade was a kind of natural, quasi-divine law, and that it was futile, even perverse, for any state to attempt to regulate the flow of opium—even though they knew perfectly well that it was armed force, rather than the abstract laws of Free Trade, that ensured the ever-expanding circulation of opium in Asia.

Equally significant in the concealment of the role of opium in European colonialism was the idea of 'History' as it developed in eighteenth- and nineteenth-century Europe. This too was another Enlightenment concept that played a powerful part in moulding the Western self-image: 'history' in this view was fundamentally a narrative of progress, evolving towards certain transcendent ends. As the historian Priya Satia has shown, the ideology of British imperialism was founded on a conception of time, and of history, as a narrative of ever-ascending Progress.[64] Hence the history of the eighteenth century was seen as a story of Man's natural rights, and of liberation and emancipation: the concurrent histories of genocide and slavery that were unfolding in the same period were either obscured or presented as unfortunate deviations from this narrative. Instead, the preferred story of the nineteenth century was one that foregrounded the Industrial Revolution, which was said to have been brought about by the scientific discoveries and technological innovations of lone geniuses. That many of the key innovations came from an armaments industry that had been supercharged by British colonial wars, and that much of the capital for industrialization was extracted by means of slave labour, and the drug trade, were relegated to irrelevance, simply because they did not fit the narrative of Progress.[65]

The idea of history as a purposive journey is so deeply entrenched in the contemporary imagination that it would probably have remained unshaken long into the future, if not for ongoing contemporary disasters, like America's current opioid crisis, and, even more significantly, the catastrophic impacts of climate change. It is as if history has itself intervened to expose the contradictions of the teleology of Progress.

FIVE

The Opium Department

In 2005, when I started writing *Sea of Poppies*, it was difficult to get a granular sense of how opium was produced in Bihar in the early nineteenth century. Since that time there has been a dramatic change: the literature on the colonial opium industry is now growing so fast that it is difficult to stay abreast of it. It appears that this upsurge of interest may have been stimulated in some part by the publication of the Ibis Trilogy: at least two important recent publications seem to suggest so, which is a matter of no little satisfaction to me since it is vanishingly rare for the circular pathways between historical fiction and academic historiography to be publicly acknowledged.[1]

In years to come the literature on the colonial opium industry may well continue to grow at an even faster pace. I know from my own work that the British Library's archives on opium are close to inexhaustible; documents relevant to the subject are so widely dispersed that previously untapped files and folders will probably continue to surface for a long time to come.[2] As for the private papers of Indian merchants and traders, research on them has barely begun even though many such collections are known to exist.

Because of the recent burgeoning of interest in the subject, much more is known today about the circumstances under which Bihari farmers were made to produce opium than was the case when I started writing *Sea of Poppies*. The credit for this goes in large part to two talented young scholars: the first is the Austrian historian Rolf Bauer, whose book *The Peasant Production of Opium in Nineteenth-Century India* was published in 2019. The second is Matthew Wormer, an American, whose dissertation, titled 'Opium, Economic Thought, and the Making of Britain's Free Trade Empire, 1773–1839', earned him a PhD in history from Stanford in 2022. The two studies complement each other nicely because Wormer's research is focused on the period before the First Opium War, while Bauer devotes more attention to the subsequent decades. Both are fine-grained, nuanced studies, filled with interesting observations and telling anecdotes. Together they tell a fascinating story of a complex set of conditions that mutated over time, while staying essentially stable for more than a century.

The first pivotal moment in the story consists of the East India Company's takeover of the opium industry in Bihar in 1772. The second big move occurred in 1799, when the Company's leadership decided to set up a bureaucracy that was devoted entirely to the production of the drug.[3] In the decades between those two crucial dates, there was much turmoil in the industry, pitting farmers, merchants and contractors against each other: the new opium bureaucracy's mission was to remedy the situation by stabilizing production while keeping the output fixed at around 4,800 chests per year, almost all of which was to be exported to the Dutch East Indies and China.[4]

Under the new regulations, the Opium Department was to oversee every aspect of the production and distribution of the drug, from the planting of poppies to the auctioning of the product in Calcutta. From then on it was the East India Company's employees who determined which farmers could grow poppies, how much they could plant and what they would be paid for their harvest, the entirety of which was to be surrendered to the Opium Department for processing in its own facilities.[5]

In the beginning, the territories within the Opium Department's jurisdiction consisted only of the central stretch of the Gangetic plain, extending from Patna in the east to Benares in the west. But in the years after 1830, when production started rising steeply, the Department's territories grew in proportion, eventually becoming a kingdom within an empire, extending all the way across Purvanchal, from the vicinity of Agra, in the west, to the borders of Bengal, in the east. Here, by the second half of the nineteenth century, roughly half a million acres came to be sown with poppies.

Cultivating this land required the labour of more than a million peasant households, probably some 5–7 million people altogether. The concentration of poppy farmers varied over this territory, being lighter in the west and heavier in the east, but in the most intensively farmed stretches of Bihar, Bauer estimates that well over half the population lived in households that cultivated poppies in the winter growing season.[6]

From the time of the Opium Department's founding, the bureaucracy that managed this millions-strong labour force was split geographically into two agencies, the Benares Agency in the west and the Patna Agency in the east.[7] Each agency was presided over by a British official known as the Opium Agent, a deceptively humble title since this was actually one of the most highly paid and most coveted posts within the colonial regime: not only did it come with a hefty salary and many perks, but it also did not require much work. In fact some Opium Agents spent more time socializing than attending to their official duties. Of one of them, John Wilton, who was the Patna Agent from 1803 to 1812, it was said that 'no one seemed to know that he had any other duty than that of entertaining his guests!'[8]

A major perk of the Agent's post was a palatial residence. John Wilton, for instance, lived in an 'elegant English-style house . . . complete with a billiard room and "the finest collection of paintings in India"'.[9] Decades later Sir John Henry Rivett-Carnac, the third baronet of Derby, who was head of the Benares Opium Agency from 1876 to 1895, described his official residence as 'a quite magnificent house on the Ganges at Ghazipur, surrounded by a good garden and fine grounds'.[10]

Another perk of the job was that the Agent was permitted to escape to the hills when the hot weather arrived, at the colonial regime's expense, with his family and staff. He would return at the start of the poppy-growing season, as the cold weather was setting in, around November. Then he, his family and his entourage would set off on a tour of inspection that would carry them across the Agency's vast domain. These tours were grand affairs, where the Agent and his wife travelled some 13 kilometres each day, in a landau, spending the night at a luxurious camp that had already been prepared ahead of their arrival. In his memoirs Rivett-Carnac writes,

[T]here were handsome double-poled tents to be used for reception, drawing-room, and dining-room. Then there was the Agent's office-tent, and a bedroom and dressing-room tent, and one for the English maid, when with us in camp. Then the Personal Assistant, or Private Secretary, who always accompanied the Agent, had his own tents. And there were tents for servants and horses, and for the guard which marched with the carts and posted sentries day and night. The Opium Officer of the district and his assistant generally marched with the camp, adding his tents to the line. All, or nearly all, the tents were in duplicate, so one was carried ahead and pitched ready for your arrival, whilst you slept peacefully in his twin brother. The camp would be pitched by the roadside, in a grove of mango-trees, the main routes being rich in these pleasing adjuncts to camp-life.[11]

At leisurely intervals the Agent and his entourage would head off 'for a shooting expedition, or a visit to a bazaar, or some place of note in the neighbourhood, which in these districts were plentiful, and often of great merit—old temples, ruins of great cities, celebrated shrines, and points of historical interest'.[12]

That Rivett-Carnac came across so many celebrated monuments was no coincidence, since Purvanchal was, historically, one of the richest, most fertile and most culturally creative parts of the Indian subcontinent—indeed the world. Yet, by the time of Rivett-Carnac's tours, the region had already fallen into the besetting poverty and stagnation that haunt it to this day. To glimpse those monuments through the Opium Agent's descriptions is thus to be reminded that Purvanchal's present condition is a historical anomaly, one that dates back to the very time when it began to supply the East India Company with the two vital resources it needed for its growth—sepoys and drugs.

Ranked below the two Agents was a small core group of white, mainly British officials who were lifetime employees of the Opium Department, occupying regular posts within the bureaucracy.[13] Over time, as the Department's territories expanded, this cadre grew to some six dozen officers with job titles like 'Assistant Sub-Deputy Opium Agent' and 'Sub-Deputy Opium Agent'. By the standards of British civil servants in India, the jobs were not well-paid, and promotions occurred at a glacially slow pace. In the 1870s a boy of seventeen would start as an Assistant Sub-Deputy Opium Agent at 200 pounds per annum; if he did well, he might, after many years, rise to the rank of a Fifth Grade Sub-Deputy Opium Agent. If he had the good fortune to rise four more grades, then he might end his career as a fully fledged Sub-Deputy Opium Agent, with a salary of 1,200 pounds sterling a year, followed by a pension of 500 pounds upon retirement.

Yet, the jobs were much sought-after because of a feature that made them attractive to white families who could not afford to educate large broods of sons: in contrast to other branches of the colonial bureaucracy, entry into the Opium Department was easy because it did not require clearing an examination.[14] The jobs were handed out to the young men on whom Opium Agents like Rivett-Carnac and other higher-ups chose to confer their patronage. By currying favour with these officials, any white family could provide a life of respectability for their male offspring, no matter how shiftless or improvident: '[T]here were many who could not resist the temptation of thus disposing of a son, and relieving themselves of the expenses and anxiety of further education.'[15]

But the life of a junior opium officer was not an easy one. Starting in their late teens or early twenties, assistants and sub-deputies would spend their initial years either in the villages where the Opium Department had its kothis (local offices) or in the small towns where its twenty-seven 'divisional headquarters' were located.[16] In these outposts they generally lived in 'chummeries', with two or three other white officers, all of them single men because the 'circumstances of the Department work were such that no young assistant could possibly move about in camp and do his work in a satisfactory manner if encumbered with a wife or female relations'.[17]

Yet, some officers did marry and bring their wives out to live with them in the small moffusil towns of Purvanchal. But this was not necessarily a guarantee of contentment. One thirty-six-year-old officer by the name of Henry Osborne got married while on leave in England in 1876, and brought his bride back to live with him in a village called Dhava, in Bihar, where he was posted as a Fifth Grade Sub-Deputy Opium Agent. In his diary Osborne notes that he slept with a pistol under his mattress, and suffered from frequent bouts of depression, some of them brought on by his wife's singing.[18] His relations with Rivett-Carnac were none too good either: the baronet refused to transfer him to a better post and did not see eye to eye with him on a matter regarding 'arrears of pay'.[19]

It so happened that Osborne had a colleague called Richard W. Blair who also brought his family to live in a small town in Bihar, where he was posted as Sub-Deputy Opium Agent. It was there, in Motihari, near the Nepal border, that Eric Blair, who later took the name George Orwell, was born in 1903. Orwell was still an infant when his mother, prompted by concerns about her children's education, left for England with him and his sisters. But a Sub-Deputy Opium Agent's salary was hardly adequate for a good school, and even though the boy did succeed in gaining entry into a 'snobbish and expensive' preparatory school, he was haunted throughout his life by memories of his straitened childhood.[20]

Later, as an officer with the Indian Imperial Police in Burma, Orwell probably smoked opium himself. 'What are the pleasures of opium?' he once wrote. 'Like other pleasures, they are, unfortunately, indescribable.'[21]

While the higher ranks of the Opium Department were strictly reserved for British or Euro-descended men, the vast majority of its staff consisted of low-paid Indians—clerks, secretaries and overseers, with titles like moharrir, mootsuddy and gomasta.[22] The Department also employed a large number of guards (burkandazes) and patrol officers (zilladars) who served as enforcers. The ranks of Indians in the Department's employment grew from about 1,000 to 2,400 in the 1870s. At that point there were over thirty times more Indian than British employees on the Department's payrolls: yet the salaries of all the Indians together amounted to less than half that of the seventy-five white staff.[23]

The huge disparity in remuneration was a constant feature of the Opium Department right from the start. One reason the British were paid more was to discourage corruption, but skimming and embezzlement were common even at the highest levels of the Department.[24] As for the Indians, their wages were so low as to ensure that they would exploit every opportunity to line their pockets. As Wormer notes: 'The yawning gap between the vast revenues earned from opium and the minimal outlay on labor costs invited fraud and corruption as inequalities widened year by year.'[25]

Opportunities for extortion and exploitation were plentiful for the Opium Department's Indian employees, most of whom were dispersed across the dense web of kothis that dotted the countryside. Humble though their status may have been within the ranks of the Opium Department, these petty officials wielded seigneurial powers in the villages where they were posted: they could break open doors, raid houses and arrest farmers almost at will. Nor was it easy to escape the eyes of the Opium Department's enforcers: from central Uttar Pradesh to eastern Bihar, the region was so heavily blanketed with the Department's outposts that no farmer was more than 16 kilometres from the nearest kothi. Moreover, the Department employed large numbers of spies and informants, who were rewarded with sizeable sums of money when they informed on their neighbours. Inevitably, accusations and counter-accusations abounded.

The Opium Department's functionaries were, in principle, responsible for drawing up the licenses and contracts that poppy farmers needed in order to get cash advances. But in practice these petty officials did not deal directly with ordinary farmers; instead, they exerted their power through a class of mainly upper-caste landlords or khatadars (bookkeepers), who were appointed by the Opium Department to serve as middlemen. Each of these bookkeepers was in charge of a group of a few dozen, mostly illiterate, farmers on whose behalf they signed licenses and contracts. So, while the farmers were theoretically free to reject contracts and advances, in practice they had little choice, since the Opium Department's functionaries wielded almost unlimited power over them: the threat of violence from burkandazes and zilladars was ever-present.

> Advances are made [wrote an early nineteenth century observer] by the govt, through its native servants, and if a *ryot* [farmer] refuses the advances, the simple plan of throwing the rupees into his house is adopted; should he attempt to abscond, the peons seize him, tie the advance up in his clothes, and push him into his house. The business being now settled, and there being no remedy, he applies himself, as he may, to the fulfilment of his contract.[26]

From time to time the colonial regime would introduce 'reforms' in the system, purportedly to ensure that the farmers who cultivated opium did so of their own choice. The problem was that left to themselves the farmers would have preferred to plant other, more remunerative crops, like sugar cane, cotton and tobacco. This meant that the regulations always had to leave some loopholes for various kinds of compulsion: 'Normalizing these coercive practices,' notes Wormer, 'was the task of bureaucratic reform.'[27]

One such loophole was a rule that prohibited farmers from appealing to the law without going through the British Opium Agent, which effectively ensured that their complaints never reached the courts. In an incident recorded in 1807:

> [O]ne desperate group of cultivators from Saran, Bihar's largest poppy district, traveled all the way to Calcutta to lay their grievances before the Governor General after the agent at Patna, John Wilton, had purportedly had them flogged upon seeking redress for mistreatment by their *gomastah*.

Their hopes that his 'Excellency in Council' would end these injustices and 'secure them the full price of [their] opium' met with indifference: the Governor General promptly referred their petition back to the Opium Agency, where it disappeared for good.[28] [John Wilton was none other than the high-living Agent who spent much of his time entertaining guests and collecting paintings.]

The farmers' contracts stipulated that they were to transport their harvest, in its entirety and at their own cost, to an official collection centre, where, after weighing and quality control, they were, in principle, meant to be paid the price set by the Opium Department.[29] This rate remained stagnant at Rs 3.50 for a seer (a little more than a kilogram) of raw opium through much of the early nineteenth century and rose only slightly thereafter. So low was the rate that it did not even cover the farmers' expenses. Poppies were a capital- and labour-intensive crop that required manure, hired workers, transportation and so on. On top of that, farmers had to pay bribes to various middlemen: '[T]hese bribes were theoretically illegal [but] their existence was widely recognized.'[30] In calculating the financial outlays that were required to grow opium, both Wormer and Bauer conclude that the costs of cultivation for farmers far exceeded what they were paid by the Opium Department.[31] In other words the price paid by the Department 'for crude opium was too low to even cover the costs of cultivation'.[32]

So, far from making any money by growing this hugely valuable commodity, the poppy farmers of eastern India actually made significant losses on their harvest.[33] Why, then, did they grow this crop? The reason was succinctly explained in a petition signed by hundreds of farmers: 'We cultivate the poppy under pressure from Government, otherwise we would not do it, and our prayer is that we may be released from this trouble.'[34]

The system was, therefore, coercive to its core: not only did farmers have to deal with the ever-looming threat of violence, but they also had no choice other than to plant poppies because the Opium Department stipulated that nothing else could be grown on land that had been earmarked for that purpose.[35] Farmers could be evicted if they planted any other crop, and since most poppy growers were 'tenants at will', they were in constant danger of losing their land.[36] So strict and punitive were the laws of the Opium Department that farmers were essentially trapped within a net of legal obligations and debt bondage. Even in times of famine, they had no recourse but to grow poppies in order to slake the British Empire's inexhaustible appetite for opium.[37]

Although opium was not grown on plantations, like indigo and some other crops, the Opium Department's regime of production was by no means lighter or more benevolent—to the contrary. The difference between the systems, as Bauer points out, is that plantations were owned by individual planters, while the Opium Department was an arm of the regime itself and was, therefore, empowered to make up its own laws as it pleased. Indeed, there is no more telling commentary on the oppressiveness of the official regime of opium cultivation than that it was envied by white plantation owners in India, who argued that they too should be allowed to use similar laws and coercive measures. However, the planters' pleas were sternly rebuffed by the colonial authorities, who asserted that poppies were an exception and had to be cultivated under an unusually severe regime because 'the opium business was a matter of public interests rather than a mere commercial activity'.[38] In other words, unlike indigo, opium had the status of a strategic resource.

The contracts that were forced upon farmers were binding, and those who failed to fulfil their quotas were suspected of having sold some of their product on the sly to private traders—for the East India

Company's monopoly had brought into being, as monopolies are apt to, a thriving 'black market'. By selling to this underground economy, farmers could earn many times more than the price offered by the Opium Department—a powerful lure for impoverished rural folk.[39] The official prices were so low that inevitably, many farmers did indeed succumb to temptation, which meant that criminality became widespread in the region, with substantial amounts of opium being smuggled out by organized networks.[40] This, in turn, caused the Opium Department to invest heavily in policing and in maintaining armies of spies and informers.[41]

Farmers who were unable to meet their quotas were also often suspected of keeping back some opium for their own use—for, over time, many poppy growers became accustomed to using the drug themselves (according to one British official, the consumption of opium increased one-hundred-fold in districts where poppies were cultivated).[42] In order to counter this the Opium Department began keeping ever-more-detailed records of exactly how much each poppy field yielded, down to the last chittack. The name of every farmer whose yields were 'suspiciously low or below those of the other men of the same license or village' was entered into a register, and he was watched carefully by spies and informers.[43] Thus the quotas assigned to farmers were by no means notional; they were strictly enforced, through the many instruments of compulsion that were available to the Department. A farmer who could not meet his quota would invite, in the first instance, the wrath of his bookkeeper, who, in turn, would have to answer to the functionaries of the Opium Department. Those who were found to have retained any of their own yield were fined heavily and punished.

These systems of punitive surveillance created an atmosphere of terror and secrecy in which farmers, and even passers-by, could be subjected to arbitrary punishments and fines. An Indian police officer told a British commission:

No person is allowed to pass by the places where the poppy
is grown. If a man passes by, he is accused of plucking off
the poppy buds . . . At the time when crop is ready, persons
charged with the office of measuring the poppy field use small
measurement and wrong weight in weighing. Sometimes
they play tricks with the cultivators by secretly throwing some
kachi afim [opium] in their houses through the help of the
policemen. In the same way they have to give a bribe to the
officers who make their contracts.[44]

Yet, despite all this, Rivett-Carnac had to admit: '[I]t is not pretended
that the department has yet succeeded, or is ever likely to succeed, in
preventing petty pilferings on the part of hundreds of thousands of
cultivators.'[45] Farmers did indeed find ingenious means of evading
and resisting the Opium Department: they secretly cultivated other
crops on lands earmarked for poppies; they bribed lower-level
officials; they adulterated their product and sold whatever they could
get away with to the underground market. All of this ensured not
only that substantial quantities of opium eluded the Department, but
also that the entire structure, from top to bottom, was ridden with
corruption and venality. For cultivators the difference may have been
only a matter of a few rupees, but for those who worked in the higher
levels of the bureaucracy, Indians included, there were opportunities
to skim off huge fortunes.[46]

While some British officials recognized that the abysmal prices
given to farmers and the low pay of local employees were the sources
of the Opium Department's problems, others came to be convinced
that corruption, apathy and 'utter disregard of moral principle' was
endemic to Indians as a race. This view was shared by the leadership
of the colonial regime: 'Calls from the agents in Bihar and Benares to
raise the pay of their Indian subordinates met with repeated dismissals
from the Opium Board in Calcutta, who justified their reluctance with

reference to the "moral turpitude" of the native population, whose "apathy and indolence . . . are proverbial."'[47]

Yet, in a broader sense, these were only minor problems. From the colonial regime's point of view, its drug-dealing enterprise was, on its own terms, extraordinarily lucrative. The acreage of land under poppy cultivation kept growing, and the production of opium increased phenomenally within a few decades.[48]

Through the first half of the eighteenth century exports of opium to China had seldom exceeded 200 chests, but by 1767 the number had increased to 1,000.[49] With the setting up of the Opium Department, the figure grew to 4,570 chests in 1800, and was stable at around 4,800 for a while.[50] But after 1830 exports grew rapidly, and opium soon became the keystone of the colonial economy: 'like the yeast in bread dough' it was the substance 'upon which the entire structure depended'.[51] Or, as an article in a journal published by the US National Defense University notes: 'English merchants, led by the British East India Company, from 1772 to 1850, established extensive opium supply chains . . . creating the world's first drug cartel.'[52]

This system was, therefore, on its own terms, one of the most successful commercial ventures in human history, producing immense profits for the British Empire for well over a hundred years. The opium trade was thus an essential element of an emerging capitalist system that was then spreading rapidly across the globe. Yet, far from being a free market, this system was firmly founded on colonialism and race; in that sense it was an instance of what Cedric J. Robinson called 'racial capitalism'.[53]

SIX

Big Brother

At the core of the Opium Department's finely spun web were the two Sudder ('Central') Opium Factories, where the drug was processed and packed. These factories were the twin capitals of the British Raj's opium empire, each serving as the hub for one of the Department's agencies. The factory of the Patna Agency was in the Gulzarbagh neighbourhood; the factory of the Benares Agency was in the town of Ghazipur, 'on the banks of the Ganges, forty miles below Benares as the crow flies'.[1]

Both factories were quasi-military, fortress-like establishments, surrounded by high, red-brick walls. The Patna factory was built in 1781, and the Ghazipur factory eight years later. The Ghazipur factory's first location was a small lot outside the town, but the East India Company's opium trading activities were expanding so fast in this period that the manufacturing unit could barely keep pace. In 1820 the Company set up a lavish new facility on a 43-acre site. A senior official described it in these words forty years later: 'The Factory occupies a large extent of ground, and contains several magnificent buildings, those of a late construction being all iron-roofed. Numerous trees, adjoining the place here and there, impart to it a quite picturesque appearance.'[2]

Ghazipur now became a company town: 10 per cent of its population of 40,000 worked in the opium factory, and over time a cluster of hamlets sprouted around its walls to house the workers' families. The factory's dependents did not, however, consist only of humans. Its trees were home to a troop of monkeys who loved to lap at the effluents that flowed out of the factory's drains. They were said to be the most contented and tranquil monkeys in all of Hindustan. The same was said also of the fish in the nearby stretch of river that received the effluents: fishermen liked to drop their nets there because the dazed fish were easy to haul up, and made for good eating.

So improbable do the words 'opium factory' sound today that it came as a surprise to me to learn that the Ghazipur factory is still up and running (the Patna factory was shuttered a long time ago). Nor is it a ghostly relic of the past—it is to this day one of the world's largest producers of legal opium, manufactured for medicinal use.[3] This confers on the Ghazipur Opium Factory the distinction of being one of the oldest continuously functioning industrial plants in the world. Even though its production processes were entirely manual, the factory's operations were thoroughly modern and rationalized, an early version of a Taylorite production line, with tasks broken down in minute detail.[4] And unlike most factories that date back hundreds of years, the Ghazipur factory was far from being a small-scale enterprise. The revenues that it has generated over the years are probably beyond computation: it was, after all, one of two factories that produced what was the British Empire's most lucrative article of trade, by weight, for a very long time.

Because of its historic factory, Ghazipur plays an important part in *Sea of Poppies*: the first few chapters are set in the outskirts of the city, and in one of the key scenes in the book, the character Deeti actually enters and walks around the compound of the Opium Factory. Given the importance of these settings, I wanted to visit the factory in person and assumed that this would be possible because many photographers and journalists had visited it in the 1970s and 1980s. But on making inquiries I discovered that the factory's regulations had been tightened in recent years and it was now all but impossible for outsiders to gain entry to it. That an institution which was once accessible to journalists should now be completely sealed off is but another instance of the ways in which opium seems to recede from view even as its impact upon the world continues to grow.

Things, however, were quite different in the nineteenth century. The Ghazipur and Patna opium factories were both extensively described and documented in print, and in paint and ink. In 1865, the head officer of the Ghazipur factory, J.W.S. MacArthur, even published a booklet called *Notes on an Opium Factory* for the edification of British tourists. 'Travellers passing through the station,' he writes, 'are recommended to pay a visit to the Opium Factory, and they will know more of the place and the work there carried on.'[5]

MacArthur's descriptions, and the maps and illustrations that accompany them, are so richly detailed that I found the experience of reading the booklet to be not unlike that of watching a documentary: this was indeed the principal source for the scenes in *Sea of Poppies* that are set inside the Ghazipur Opium Factory.

But MacArthur was by no means the Ghazipur Opium Factory's most illustrious chronicler; that honour goes to Rudyard Kipling, the second most quoted writer in the English language. Kipling's father, the artist John Lockwood Kipling, was a protégé of none other than the ubiquitous baronet Sir John Henry Rivett-Carnac. Rudyard ('Ruddy') was thus known to the baronet from his earliest childhood.

Kipling recorded his impressions of the Ghazipur factory in the essay 'In an Opium Factory', which was published in 1899. He was much struck by the factory's storage facilities: 'There are ranges and ranges of gigantic godowns, huge barns that can hold over half a million pounds' worth of opium. There are acres of bricked floor, regiments on regiments of chests; and yet more godowns and more godowns.'

Brief though it is, Kipling's essay is an outstanding example of the way in which the English language was often used to occlude and naturalize colonial practices and policies. Much of the essay is written in the passive voice; the opium factory simply exists, and produces vast wealth: 'At the beginning of the cold weather Ghazipur holds, locked up, a trifle, say, of three and a half millions sterling in opium' (a sum that would be worth more than half a billion US dollars today).

That the factory, and the elaborate organizational structure that supported it, was built by British colonizers elicits not a moment's thought; the responsibility for it is displaced, rather, on to the Chinese consumer. The factory does what it does, a manager explains, because 'of the China market. The C......n likes every inch of the stuff we send him, and uses it.' This was, of course, the common European understanding of the opium trade: imperial powers were merely seen to be meeting a demand that was asserted to have existed in China independently of Western colonialism.

Similarly, Kipling attributes the atmosphere of suspicion and surveillance that weighed upon the factory not to its white overseers but to the sticky hands of the natives who worked in it: '[S]pecial care is taken that none of the drug sticks to the hands of the coolies. Opium has a knack of doing this, and therefore coolies are searched at most inopportune moments. There are a good many Mahometans in Ghazipur, and they would all like a little opium.'

Kipling does occasionally wrinkle his nose at the factory's noxious fumes: 'The heart of the whole is the laboratory, which is full of the sick faint smell of an opium joint . . .' But everything untoward is ultimately irrelevant because it is all in the service of a greater cause— the Empire, for which the drug yields 'such a splendid income'.

What did the people of Ghazipur make of the massive new factory that quickly came to dominate their old and historic town?

It is impossible to say. As is so often the case with colonial India, there is very little to go on in terms of sources in Indian languages. Everything that is known about the Ghazipur Opium Factory comes from documents written in English; according to a leading contemporary expert nothing has ever been written about the two opium factories in Bhojpuri or Hindi: 'not even a short story'.[6]

This silence is largely due, no doubt, to the fact that the factories were even more intensely racialized than most British colonial institutions. As Wormer notes: 'Scientific standards of assessment, detailed paperwork, and rigorous bookkeeping requirements gave institutional form to a deepening distrust of the Indian officials who staffed the lower ranks of the colonial government.'[7]

The Indians who worked in the Opium Department's factories were under constant surveillance; and, as Kipling notes, they were subject to frequent searches. Indeed, the measures designed to prevent pilferage were so extreme that the workers were sometimes not only searched but also washed before they left the premises. This indignity was visited most often on the hundreds of young boys in the workforce: this was intended to prevent them from pinching opium by rubbing it on their bodies and then getting washed down at the bazaar, a method of pilferage that was said to fetch 4 annas per washing.[8]

This distrust of Indians would surely also have extended to local visitors, which is probably why there are no descriptions of the factory in Hindi or Bhojpuri.[9] White travellers, on the other hand, were not only welcomed but also encouraged to visit.[10] Over time the Patna and Ghazipur factory complexes even became a part of 'the Grand Tour of India' and were featured in many English guide books. A British MP who visited the Patna Opium Factory in 1889 wrote in a letter to his paper back home:

> [O]ur host met us at the station, and drove us to his bunga-low, picturesquely perched on the banks of the Ganges, near the Government Opium Factory, of which he is the engi-neer. After breakfast we visited the factory, and spent two hours in watching the various processes by which opium is finally reduced from the raw material, as it is sent in from the country, to square blocks for final consumption. In one yard we saw sufficient opium to have killed off in a single dose seven millions of strong men, and there was enough on the premises to have finished off the whole population of India.[11]

One Indian who could certainly have visited the Ghazipur Opium Factory was Kipling's contemporary and fellow Nobel Laureate, the poet Rabindranath Tagore, who spent six months in Ghazipur, living in a bungalow that had been found for him by a relative of his who worked in the factory.[12] During his stay, Tagore and his wife were visited by several relations, including his sister, the writer Swarnakumari Devi, who later composed a long piece about her stay in Ghazipur.[13] Their bungalow was close to the factory and through their relative the Tagores met many of the local Bengali residents, most of whom would have been employees of the Opium Department. The Tagores were dutiful tourists, going on walks and excursions every day, searching out every sight of interest in and around the town, including Lord Cornwallis's tomb. One day, finding themselves near an indigo factory, they almost went in but were repelled by the stench. The odour around the Opium Factory, they were told, was even worse.

Whether for this reason or not, the Tagores never visited the Opium Factory, even though, as Swarnakumari Devi notes, they could very well have done so. But evidently the factory inspired a kind of revulsion in them: seven years earlier, at the tender age of nineteen, Rabindranath Tagore had published a searing indictment of the colonial opium trade, titled 'The Death Traffic in China'.[14] He wrote:

> A whole nation, China, has been forced by Great Britain to accept the opium poison . . . When we read the history of unnatural and inhuman bloodshed in war, we have simply a feeling of horror mingled with that of wonder. But, in the Indo-China opium traffic, human nature itself sinks down to such a depth of despicable meanness, that it is hateful even to follow the story to its conclusion.[15]

The distaste that is evident in this passage probably derived from Tagore's guilty awareness that his own grandfather, Dwarkanath Tagore, had traded in opium, and had even petitioned the colonial government for a share of the reparations that China was forced to pay after the First Opium War. The poet would return to this subject again and again over his lifetime.

The contrast in the attitudes of Kipling and Tagore, two Nobel Laureates who were almost exact contemporaries, is itself a commentary on the differences in the perspectives of colonizer and colonized: on one side there is a smugly complacent acceptance of a manufacturing complex that produces enormous revenues for the colonial state, and on the other there is an aversion that seems to want to erase the factory by not referring to it in writing.

Fortunately, records of a different kind do exist and they present the divergent perceptions of colonizer and colonized even more vividly than would be the case with a written description. These records consist of three sets of images of the Patna Factory, one made by an Englishman and the others by Indians. By far the best known of these images is a set of six coloured lithographs made by an officer in the British colonial army, Captain Walter Stanhope Sherwill. The prints were displayed at an exhibition at London's Crystal Palace in 1851 and were later published as a bound volume, titled *Illustrations of the Mode of Preparing the Indian Opium Intended for the Chinese Market*.[16] They have since been widely reproduced, usually much reduced in size, and in black and white, rather than colour.[17]

Having long been familiar with the reproductions, I was taken by surprise when I first saw an original copy of Sherwill's prints.[18] They were much larger and more detailed than I had expected, and the colours were unexpectedly vivid.

The overall effect was startling: the prints gave the Patna factory the monumental dimensions of a cathedral, or an Egyptian temple, with towering ceilings, majestic columns and long shelves that converged upon perspective vanishing points. Among the human figures, those that were drawn to scale were mainly the white supervisors, who are shown to be leaning casually against the walls as they keep watch over the workers.

The Indian figures seem shrunken and gnome-like: bare-bodied men treading in vats of raw opium and boys scuttling between enor-

mous storage shelves. Yet, instead of producing an impression of veri-
similitude, the profusion of detail and the geometrical lines have quite
the opposite effect: they make the factory look like a stage-set, a fantasy (see insert images 2 and 3).

I thought, at first, that Sherwill's prints had been influenced by
the dreamlike portrayals of architecture that the eighteenth-century
Venetian artist Giovanni Battista Piranesi (1720–78) was famous for.

But I discovered later that Sherwill's primary interests did not
actually lie in the arts. A soldier by profession, he was also a surveyor
and economic geologist who spent a good deal of time scouring the
forests of central and eastern India for mineral resources. While
travelling he often sketched and drew, as colonial functionaries
with scientific interests were wont to do. As a naturalist he gained
enough recognition to be inducted into the Asiatic Society of
Bengal, one of the premier institutions of Western scholarship in
the Indian subcontinent.[19] At the same time he was actively involved
in the East India Company's military operations, particularly its
counter-insurgency campaigns. In the late 1850s he played a major
part in suppressing tribal revolts in the very forests that he had
mapped as a surveyor. In short, Sherwill was a member of a small
but immensely influential class of soldier-naturalists for whom
Science and Empire were refractions of each other, one requiring
the subjugation of Nature and the other necessitating the subduing
of 'brutes' and 'savages'.

These contexts also shaped Sherwill's practices as a maker of
images. For the most part his paintings are the standard fare of
amateur English artists, with flowing brushwork and soft edges. But
he also painted pictures that were intended to represent the colonial
regime's supposed success in implementing industrial policies in
India. This was the precise purpose behind his prints of the Opium
Factory, therefore the straight lines, sharp edges and geometrical
forms: it is as if the style itself were being used to evoke the rhetoric

of industrialism.[20] As the art historian Hope Childers observes, the prints were 'tailored to reassure metropolitan visitors at the Crystal Palace that industrial progress was being made in the colony'.[21]

'Progress' was indeed the god who reigned over the temple that Sherwill depicted in his prints of the Patna Opium Factory. The images were akin to votive offerings for the deity: a god for whom periodic exhibitions of industries and machinery served as festivals of adoration. Hence the imposing interiors and the suggestion of mechanized production, as in the textile factories of Birmingham and Manchester. Sherwill's prints were a kind of paean to the Industrial Revolution and the machinery that made it possible.[22]

The trouble, however, is that in the opium factories of Ghazipur and Patna machines were conspicuous by their absence. The processing of opium was done entirely by hand, and foot. Barefoot workers spent as much as ten hours a day tramping up and down long vats of raw opium. The fumes were so heavy that they often became sleepy and lethargic. Many visitors remarked on the powerful smells that pervaded the factories: '[T]he air is redolent with opium, not with the narcotic and purified odour of the finished drug, but with the odour of indescribable nastiness.'[23] Far from being clean, Euclidean spaces, the factory's interiors were crowded, hot and cramped, with hundreds of men and boys labouring under the eyes of their white overseers.

So striking was the lack of machinery that Kipling was moved to ask his tour guide: 'But has nobody found out any patent way of making these [opium] cakes and putting skins on them by machinery?' No, came the answer; the making of opium cakes required skilled human hands, for the finished product had to be so perfect that 'all the Celestials of the Middle Kingdom shall not be able to disprove that it weighs two seers one and three-quarter chittacks . . .'

The irony is that Sherwill, an aspiring scientist working with tools of representation that were intended to produce objective depictions, ended up creating images that were not just ideological but fantastically so. Through his visual language, he turned a grimy reality into a temple of Progress—a vengeful deity, who had to be appeased with sacrifices that involved the infliction of suffering on the benighted and the recalcitrant. And since the British Empire was the Church Militant of the cult of Progress, exacting these sacrifices from the colonized was considered inevitable, indeed a historical necessity. It is in this sense that the opium trade was also seen as a necessary evil in that it provided the British Empire with the funds that it needed in order to go about the business of converting its subject peoples to the worship of Progress.

China, on the other hand, was projected as decadent and degenerate, closed and backward, the very antithesis of all that was promised by Progress. The fact that it was the chief destination of the British Raj's opium was itself taken to be indicative of China's degradation—a perception underlined by the last words of the title of Sherwill's prints: *Opium Intended for the Chinese Market*. The implication is that the factory's opium (a substance widely perceived by Europeans as being incompatible with Progress) was not intended for distribution in British territories, but only in decadent China.

Like Sherwill's images, the title of his collection of prints was totally at odds with the reality of the Opium Department's factories. The opium produced in them was not, in fact, intended only for the Chinese market: a large part of its output was sold within British territories in India through an ever-expanding network of outlets that contributed very substantially to the revenues of the colonial regime. A considerable quantity of the factory's output was also meant for the Dutch East Indies—but this could not be acknowledged either since the Dutch were white Protestant Europeans, and their empire too was, by definition, an instrument of righteousness and Progress. The implication, in any case, was that Britain was overseeing the production and marketing of opium solely in order to meet the demands of retrograde Asiatics and their rulers.

This was entirely at odds with the reality. The only parts of Asia where opium was sponsored by ruling regimes were the colonies run by Europeans—the Dutch East Indies, India, the Philippines and, later, French Indo-China. In every part of Asia that enjoyed any kind of autonomy—Thailand, Japan and the kingdoms of Mandalay and Vietnam before their annexation—native rulers took early steps to ban or regulate opium.[24] In the eighteenth century, Siamese maritime inspectors 'expressed frequent suspicion over Dutch opium trafficking, leading to confrontations between Siamese patrols and Dutch defense actions and finally the withdrawal of the Dutch East India Company (VOC) from Siam in July 1740'.[25] King Rama III of Siam explicitly prohibited any trade in opium in an 1826 treaty with the British.[26] But British private traders paid little heed, and the drug became a frequent cause of friction between the East India Company and the Siamese: after the First Opium War the Siamese government stepped up its opium prohibition to include the death penalty.[27] It did not change course until forced to, by Western powers.

Similarly, in Vietnam, in 1820, the emperor imposed a strict ban on opium under which 'even sons and younger brothers of addicts were required to turn the offenders over to the authorities'.[28] But all of this was to no avail because British and French naval power ensured that foreign opium ships could not be seized, and smugglers could not be punished under local laws. Eventually Siam and other Southeast Asian powers were left with no option but to accept the British and French colonial models, in which opium was subjected to taxation and treated as a source of revenue. In Vietnam, after colonization, the French established an opium franchise that became one of the economic pillars of their colonial regime.[29]

This pattern was repeated through much of Asia, Japan being the rare exception where the country's rulers were able to enact and maintain a strict ban on opium. Japan was fortunate in that unlike China, its exports were not essential to the British economy, and so it was able to slip under the radar as it were. Additionally, the widespread understanding that opium had been the undoing of China ensured that the ban had extensive popular support. As an American official attested in 1905: 'No surer testimony to the reality of the evil effects of opium can be found than the horror with which China's next-door neighbor views it.'[30]

Of course, China too had acted early to ban the importation of opium, and the laws passed in 1729 were re-enacted twice more, once in the late eighteenth century and then again in the early nineteenth century.[31] Because of these bans, the East India Company could not formally or explicitly acknowledge that its opium was intended for the Chinese market: doing so would have meant the loss of its trading rights and the end of its immensely lucrative tea business. So, in order to preserve its commercial privileges, the Company created an ingenious subterfuge. Opium from the Ghazipur and Patna factories was loaded on to heavily guarded fleets and sent to Calcutta, where it was auctioned to 'private traders'.[32] Thereafter the Company disclaimed all responsibility for its product, which was then transported by these traders to Whampoa (Huangpu) on the Pearl River, where they would sell the drug to Chinese smugglers.[33] When the Chinese authorities clamped down on Whampoa's smuggling networks, the traffickers moved upriver to Lintin Island, at the mouth of the river, where they set up receiving boats to facilitate the distribution of opium.[34] From there, Chinese smugglers would whisk the drug away to the mainland, in speedy many-oared rowboats known as 'fast crabs' or 'scrambling dragons'.[35]

This meant that the traders' ships were empty of opium when they reached the first Chinese customs post and they could plausibly claim that they were trading only in legal goods.[36] They would then proceed upriver to the East India Company's factory, in Guangzhou's Foreign Enclave, where they would hand over their silver in exchange for a 'bill', or promissory note, that could be redeemed in London and some other major cities.[37] This ingenious system thus transformed a plant product, forcibly extracted from Indian peasants, into an item whose value kept multiplying as it was siphoned through China towards the West.[38] The bills issued by the Company, and by banks like Baring Brothers in London, were the crucial instrument that tied together the entire system of commodity trade, ranging from cotton produced by enslaved African Americans to opium supplied by Indian peasants. The functioning of this system of purportedly free trade thus depended crucially on enslavement, coerced labour, smuggling and black markets.[39]

Since this so-called 'Triangular Trade', through which Indian opium was exchanged for Chinese tea and bills on British banks, was founded on smuggling and carried out in open defiance of Qing law, the East India Company was always careful to claim, when dealing with Chinese officials, that its opium was *not* especially intended for China. But for its English audience, in India and Britain, it constantly asserted exactly the opposite, believing that the Chinese would never find out. Hence the title of Sherwill's prints, which derives directly from the lies and dissimulations that were spun around the opium trade in order to preserve the myth of the British Empire as a church of Progress.

It is perhaps no accident that state-sponsored spin of this kind is now often described as 'Orwellian'. The word is, of course, generally used in relation to science-fictional depictions of future dystopias. But George Orwell, as the son of an opium agent and an imperial police officer himself, would have been in a good position to know that the dystopia that he had projected into the future had many analogues in colonial practices as well.

By the late 1830s, the period in which the Ibis Trilogy is set, swelling streams of opium were flowing from India to China. The Qing state tried repeatedly to curb the flow by prohibiting the opium trade and by cracking down on traffickers. But these measures had little effect, so the Daoguang Emperor ultimately commanded his senior officials to write reports ('memorials') on how drug trafficking might be brought under control. Many measures were considered, including legalization, but the Emperor ultimately decided that the state had no recourse but to suppress the traffic. To that end the Emperor sent Lin Zexu, one of China's most able and honest civil servants, to Guangzhou as a high commissioner with special powers.

Arriving in Guangzhou in January 1839, Lin Zexu acted quickly, issuing proclamations that not only banned the opium trade, but also demanded that foreign merchants surrender all their stocks of opium.[40] When they refused, he put them under house arrest in the Foreign Enclave.[41] This induced them to change their minds, and they surrendered a total of 10,75,000 kilograms of opium, all of which was destroyed in an operation that was personally overseen by Lin Zexu himself.[42]

For the British government, the merchants' losses became the casus belli for war: it launched its attack on China in 1840, initiating the conflict known as the First Opium War—a war that needed to be fought, as one British opium trader matter-of-factly explained, because '6 millions [pounds] sterling are actually at stake, being nearly one-tenth part of the entire revenues of Great Britain and her Indian empire'.[43]

After suffering several catastrophic defeats, the Qing state signed the Treaty of Nanjing in 1842, whereby it was forced to compensate foreign opium traffickers to the tune of 6 million silver dollars. The other conditions included the opening of four other ports to foreign traders (and smugglers) and ceding the island of Hong Kong to the British as a colony. The island thereafter became the main hub of opium smuggling in China. 'Early Hong Kong,' writes historian Christopher Munn, 'served as "the central warehouse" for "British Indian produce" and had little other trade to sustain it. By the late 1840s it was estimated, three-quarters of the entire Indian opium crop passed through Hong Kong.'[44]

The outcome of the First Opium War guaranteed that the acreage under poppies in Bihar would continue to grow at a staggering rate, and so it did, increasing almost six-fold in twenty-five years.[45]

SEVEN

Visions

The two Indian artists who painted the Patna Opium Factory both belonged to a gharana, or school, that originated in the district of Pratapgarh in Rajasthan. As was often the case with musicians and artisans in India, the artists were members of inter-linked families of a single caste—they were Kayasthas, who traditionally placed great store by literacy, and were often employed by princely courts as scribes, bookkeepers and chroniclers. It was probably through this route that the artists of Pratapgarh entered their trade, by finding employment in one of the many ateliers maintained by the rajas and maharajas of Rajasthan.

Like musicians, artists tended to migrate to places where they could find patronage. In the seventeenth century some members of the Pratapgarh school settled in the court cities of the Mughal Empire, where they remained for over a century, producing works in the style of the Mughal ateliers. When the empire fell into decline in the early eighteenth century, they began to move farther east, towards the territories of the East India Company in Bengal.

It was probably in the city of Murshidabad, in Bengal, that the artist known as Sita Ram learnt to paint. Unfortunately very little is known about Sita Ram except that he was active in the first decades of the nineteenth century. His work disappeared from view soon after his lifetime and did not resurface again until the 1970s. But it was not until 1995, when the British Library acquired a large collection of his paintings, that Sita Ram came to be recognized as one of the greatest Indian artists of the nineteenth century.

The obscurity that shrouded Sita Ram's work for so long was due, in large part, to the fact that his paintings were entombed for a century and a half in the family archives of his chief patron: Lord Moira (later the Marquess of Hastings).[1] A battle-hardened veteran of the American Revolutionary War, Moira served as Governor General of India from 1813 to 1823. A major event in his eventful career was a tour of inspection that lasted eighteen months, between 1814 and 1815: it took him from Calcutta to Patna, Kanpur, Lucknow and to the gates of Delhi. Sita Ram accompanied the Governor General on this tour as a member of his entourage, which included some 10,000 troops and officials. Tasked with creating a pictorial record of the Governor General's travels, Sita Ram produced eighty large watercolours, which were later reproduced in two volumes. These volumes have recently been reprinted under the title *Sita Ram's Painted Views of India*. [2]

Sita Ram's paintings are, in fact, far more than a record of a journey; they bear witness to a strikingly original vision, one that is notable, most of all, for the way in which the artist plays with pictorial conventions, both Indian and European. Sita Ram's two paintings of the Patna Opium Factory are good examples of this. One of these is, quite literally, a bird's-eye view of the factory and its vast compound: the artist's eye takes wing, as it were, and rises to such a height that it can perceive the curvature of the earth in the distance. In the foreground is the artist himself, seated on a terrace, hard at work on a painting (see insert image 4).

As with Sherwill's prints, Sita Ram's watercolours were meant
to be seen primarily by viewers in England: he too clearly intended
to present the factory in the best possible light. But in contrast to
Sherwill, Sita Ram did so by drawing on the traditions of Indian
miniature painting. He flattered the factory by turning it into a
version of a Mughal or Rajput palace, complete with terraces,
gardens, walkways and river views. Like the grounds of a palace,
the complex is clean, verdant, well-ordered and dotted with only
a few figures. The same magical flight of fancy that allows Sita
Ram's eye to rise into the sky also permits him to conjure away the
factory's incessant activity, and to empty it of its thousands-strong
workforce.

Sita Ram's second painting of the Patna factory is, to my mind,
even more remarkable, a playful masterpiece that blends European
and Indian pictorial traditions with striking verve and originality.

The picture is of the interior of a godown, which Sita Ram presents
as a collage of forms, shapes and volumes, unfolding into each other
in a fashion that recalls the spatial grammar of Indian miniatures,
where exteriors and interiors are often juxtaposed to create a
continuity of narrative. The image also evokes one of Piranesi's most
famous etchings, *The Round Tower*—so much so that I am convinced
that Sita Ram fully intended to place his own picture in dialogue with
Piranesi's widely reproduced etching, which he may have seen in an
English home in Calcutta (see insert images 5 and 6).

In essence, both Sita Ram and Sherwill were trying to fit an
inconvenient Indian reality into a European mould, except that one did
so through the idiom of modernity while the other did so by appealing
to Western conceptions of the Orient, and of classical antiquity.

Piranesi is thus responsible for one of the uncanny echoes that
reverberate through the history of opioids. The artist's work was
of great interest to Arthur M. Sackler, the patriarch of the dynasty
behind America's twenty-first-century opioid epidemic. Sackler

assembled one of the most important collections of the artist's work, noting: 'Piranesi's genius will long be celebrated. His was an epochal achievement, a unique vision of what was to come . . .'[3]

A generation later the Patna Opium Factory was painted again by another descendant of the Kayastha artists of Rajasthan: a painter by the name of Shiva Lal, whose ancestors had moved from Murshidabad to Patna around the time the city was incorporated into the East India Company's Bengal Presidency. Patna's growing British population offered a ready market for the city's artists, who proved just as adept in catering to these new patrons as their ancestors had been with Rajasthani maharajas and Mughal grandees. These painters quickly developed a technique that blended elements of Indian and Western art: along with other styles that were then being developed in colonial settlements, their work would later come to be known, somewhat disparagingly, as 'Company Art'.

The name is misleading because the Company did not maintain ateliers or provide formal instruction to Indian artists: that was left to individual mentors and patrons.[4] In Patna, as elsewhere, there were many such, because amateur artists abounded among English colonizers in India, this being a time when a talent for drawing and painting was regarded as a social asset for women, and a valuable skill for soldiers and officials.[5] The colonizers were also eager buyers of artworks of different kinds. There was a great demand for portraits, for instance, which the Patna artists could provide for a fraction of what they would have cost in England. Souvenirs too were much sought after, particularly painted depictions of Indian landscapes and scenes of everyday life. An especially popular variety of souvenir was a genre of paintings known as 'firqa', which showed Indians doing 'typical' kinds of work.

Shiva Lal, who was active from around 1837 to 1887, was proficient in all these genres, and a successful businessman to boot. His grandson, who was the last practising artist of the Patna School, was interviewed at length by the art historian Mildred Archer in the 1940s.[6] He recalled that Shiva Lal was famous for being able to draw a portrait in one hour for a price of two gold coins. He also ran a studio and sometimes personally sold his paintings from the back of a bullock cart.[7]

One of Shiva Lal's patrons was the Opium Agent in charge of the Patna Factory, Robert Lyell: it was through this connection that Shiva Lal was invited into the Opium Factory's closely guarded precincts to paint the workers. There are nineteen such paintings and they are now in the collection of the Victoria and Albert Museum, in London. Unlike Sita Ram's watercolours, they are all painted in natural pigments (gouache) on mica, a material that artists of the Patna and Murshidabad schools often used to decorate lanterns for public occasions like the Muharram procession.

Lyell appears to have commissioned Shiva Lal to paint murals on the walls of the opium factory, perhaps for the edification of British tourists.[8] But those plans were upended in 1857 after a massive anti-colonial war broke out across the Gangetic plain. The disaffection was greatest in the poppy-growing areas of Purvanchal, which had long been seething under the coercive regime of the Opium Department.[9] Patna was one of the hotbeds of the conflict and the Opium Factory was one of the first British facilities to come under attack. Lyell was drawn into a melee and was killed by a gunshot. His death is said to have moved Shiva Lal to tears.

The war of 1857 was extremely violent and many British civilians, including women and children, were massacred by Indian soldiers. After the defeat of the Indian forces, British reprisals were also savage: troops were shot from the mouths of cannon and the roads to Delhi were lined with impaled corpses.[10] Nowhere was the defeat, and the repression and terror that followed, felt more strongly than in the epicentres of the war, many of which were in the Gangetic heartland.

Shiva Lal's paintings were made the year the war began and they reflect the intense polarization of the country's atmosphere in several ways. The most noticeable aspect is that none of the pictures contain any British figures, although the artist is known to have included some in his early drafts. Their excision is perhaps a sign of the sudden broadening of the gulf between colonizer and colonized.

The war may also have played a part in imparting something else to Shiva Lal's images: a subtle, almost involuntary, subversiveness that is strangely incongruent with the intense colonial loyalties that he is said to have displayed in 1857. Whereas both Sherwill and Sita Ram had, each in their own way, portrayed the Opium Factory as a testament to Empire, highlighting the buildings and their monumentality, Shiva Lal's focus is almost exclusively on the workers and the tasks they perform (see insert images 7 and 8). The built environment seems scarcely to exist, apart from a few walls and doorways in the background. Much of the factory's work seems to be happening out of doors, in conditions that are all too grimly familiar in India.

Unlike Sherwill and Sita Ram, Shiva Lal is also attentive to the surveillance that was ever-present in the factory: one of his paintings shows workers being checked as they leave the factory. Even more subversive, perhaps, are his depictions of Indians working in the factory's chemical laboratories. As Childers points out in her insightful article, to portray Indians as skilled technicians working in a laboratory was to flout colonial conventions, which typically represented natives as technologically inept. This was even more pointedly true of opium factories, where chemical tests had a specifically racial dimension in that they were intended to prevent underpaid Indians from adulterating the product. The success of the tests was thus held to be entirely dependent on 'strict European superintendence' because Indians 'could not altogether be relied upon'.[11]

In their simplicity Shiva Lal's compositions are representative of the firqa genre; in no sense do they aspire to the perspectival grandeur or pictorial complexity of Sherwill's and Sita Ram's paintings, even though the artist was by no means lacking in technical proficiency. Yet, it is instructive to compare Shiva Lal's pictures with later images of the Patna and Ghazipur opium factories.

There are several such photographs dating from the late nineteenth century to the 1970s.[12] They mainly show the workers labouring outdoors in grimy, crowded conditions, bare-bodied and clad in dhotis, just as they are in Shiva Lal's pictures. The buildings that are visible in the background are by no means monumental: they look like low sheds, of the kind that can be seen in any workshop or mill in India. Stranger still, even in the most recent photographs, the processes of production seem to be much like they were back when Shiva Lal painted them.

In short, Shiva Lal's images may have been exceedingly simple but they were more true to their subject than the highly sophisticated pictures produced by Sherwill and Sita Ram.

To look at Shiva Lal's pictures, or at photographs of the factories, is to be astonished, all over again, by the fact that the people who were producing incalculable amounts of capital for rapidly industrializing countries like Britain and the United States were actually legions of underpaid workers, whose labour, far from bringing any advancement to their homelands, would eventually turn those once-prosperous lands into regions marked by poverty and strife.

And that was indeed the fate that opium brought upon the regions that were unfortunate enough to be chosen by the Opium Department for growing poppy. In a rigorous study of the historical consequences of opium cultivation in British India, the economist

Jonathan Lehne has shown that districts that were officially designated poppy-growing areas have had significantly worse long-term social and economic outcomes than other neighbouring districts.[13] These long-term effects persist to this day: even now areas where poppies were cultivated in the past have distinctly lower levels of literacy, and fewer primary schools and healthcare facilities.

Lehne attributes this to the fact that in opium-growing areas British administrative officials also held concurrent positions in the Opium Department. As a result their attention was largely focused on meeting revenue targets and on the prevention of pilferage and smuggling. Hence, expenditure on healthcare and education, woefully inadequate in any case, was even more paltry in opium-growing areas. What little money there was for public investment was spent, rather, on paying for policing and in rewarding spies and informants.

These long-term effects are comparable, Lehne argues, to those that are typically associated with the 'resource curse' that often results from the intensive mining of precious metals and minerals. The analogy is apt but also inadequate, since gold and silver mines do not produce a renewable resource and are usually worked to exhaustion within a few decades. The British opium regime, on the other hand, endured for more than a century and a half: the sheer longevity, as much as the oppressiveness of the system, ensured that it would have deep and lasting effects.

Moreover, a gold mine can, after all, be spatially segregated from its surroundings, and the miners who work in it can be body-searched as they enter and exit the premises. But in poppy-growing areas a precious commodity was being produced in open fields with family labour: neither the sites nor the people who worked on them could be segregated from the rest of the population. The very fact that a substance of great value was being produced at a loss by increasingly impoverished farmers was a guarantee of lawlessness.[14] And criminality was indeed rife in those areas. Thus, it wasn't just those who worked in opium factories who were kept under constant watch: in poppy-growing areas everybody who had access to the fields, or to poppy gum, was treated as a potential criminal. The apparatus of spying and surveillance bore down on a large part of the population, including farmers, bazaar merchants, petty traders, bullock cart drivers and so on. In effect, a large part of the population was either criminalized or regarded as being borderline delinquent. The long-term effects of this system of surveillance and criminalization continue to manifest themselves in the discord and lack of social trust that plague much of Bihar, Uttar Pradesh and Jharkhand to this day.

'Colonial opium production,' writes Lehne, 'might therefore be considered an example of a historical resource curse. Its adverse effects on the wider economy have persisted long after the opium agencies were closed.'[15]

But opium was not the only resource the Gangetic heartland provided for the colonial state: its true tragedy lay in the fact that it also contributed, in abundant measure, another vital resource—manpower for colonial armies, especially in the critical years of the British Empire, between the mid-eighteenth and early nineteenth centuries.[16] The most important military victories of the East India Company in the period of its ascendancy were won by men from Purvanchal, many of whom hailed from the very districts where opium was grown at considerable cost to farmers. That those regions became the epicentres of the war of 1857 was, of course, by no means a coincidence.

At the end of the war, the victors exacted revenge in many ways: mass shootings and hangings were only the most visible reprisals; far more damaging long-term consequences resulted from a measure of a different kind. After 1857 the colonial regime rebalanced the ethnic composition of its army, drastically reducing its intake of soldiers from the Gangetic heartland: before, Purbiyas had constituted almost half the army; within a few decades their numbers were reduced to less than 11 per cent.[17] Thus Purbiyas, who had served in the most critical wars and battles fought by the British in India when the Company's position was still tenuous, came to be almost excluded from military service, while groups that had joined the colonial forces when British power was already paramount, globally, came to reap the rewards handed out by a victorious Empire.[18]

One of the reasons why the British were able to win the war of 1857 was that a new source of military manpower had opened up for them in the Punjab, which, ironically, they had conquered a short while before with the support of battalions of Purbiyas. The animosities generated by the Purbiya role in the defeat of the Sikh kingdom played no small part in causing Sikh Punjabis to side with the British in 1857.[19] Thereafter the Punjab became a major recruiting ground, and in order to retain the loyalty of Punjabi troops the colonial regime invested heavily in the region, over decades, launching massive irrigation and land reclamation projects. The British embrace of the Punjab had other, more subtle, effects as well, providing better access to education and promoting other sectors of the economy, like construction, war provisioning and so on. As a result, the area that constituted the Punjab before 1947 remains, to this day, probably the single most prosperous region of the subcontinent. The lopsided and uneven development of the Indian subcontinent is thus directly traceable to colonial policies, as is the disproportionate weightage of Punjabis in the Indian and Pakistani armies, even today.

The long-term fallout of these developments were catastrophic for the Gangetic heartland. In India military service was not just a vital source of employment; it was also the principal avenue of social mobility. This portal was now slammed shut in the faces of those who had depended on it the most. At the same time the farmers of the region were compelled to continue producing opium at considerable loss to themselves, and with no commensurate investment from the colonial authorities. It is scarcely surprising then that this is now the poorest region in India, often derided as the 'sick' (bimaru) part of the country. Nor is it surprising that it is the region where social hierarchies are most entrenched and oppressive. As the Nobel prize–winning economist Abhijit Banerjee and his colleague Lakshmi Iyer have shown, divergent colonial policies, implemented 150 years ago, have continued to influence regional differences in India in relation to inequality, health and educational outcomes, and levels of violent crime to this day.[20]

That effects such as these should persist over centuries may seem unlikely to those who believe that the lingering effects of history can be erased by legislation or by increasing technological acceleration ('Progress'!). Nowhere is this belief more fervently subscribed to than in the United States, yet even there it is now clear that some of the legacies of colonial practices, such as slavery and the dispossession of Native Americans, have endured over centuries to the present day, imprinting certain pervasive patterns of structural racism on the United States.

The stamp of the past sometimes sinks so deep into the fabric of everyday life that its traces are difficult, if not impossible, to erase.

EIGHT

Family Story

For me the strangest, most unexpected result of writing the Ibis Trilogy was the discovery that a plant, the opium poppy, had to a significant degree, and without my being aware of it, moulded the history of my own family. This discovery, in turn, took the Trilogy in a direction that I had not anticipated when I began working on it.

When I started writing *Sea of Poppies* my interest lay primarily in the stories of the indentured workers who left India in the nineteenth century and went to work on plantations in Mauritius, Fiji, Guyana and elsewhere. Many, if not most, of these workers were Purbiyas, and a large number were from a part of Bihar with which I have an ancestral connection: Saran district, the headquarters of which is a city called Chhapra. This was home to my father's family for more than 100 years, although they were not themselves ethnically Bihari. They were Bengali migrants whose origins lay a long way to the east, in what is now Bangladesh. The story goes that the family was displaced from their ancestral village by a catastrophic flood in the mid-nineteenth century, after which they began to move westwards until, at last, they came to rest in Chhapra.

Chhapra is not well known outside the region, but for speakers of Bhojpuri, who number well over 50 million worldwide, it is a place of considerable cultural significance.[1] One notable aspect of Bhojpuri culture is its remarkable gift for assimilation. In Mauritius, for example, many indentured migrants were ethnically Bengali, but within a generation or two of their arrival they were completely absorbed into Bhojpuri culture. Bhojpuri even became the first language of some Chinese–Mauritian families.

In the case of my father and his siblings too, the assimilative powers of Bhojpuri prevailed over Bengali linguistic parochialism: it was the language they spoke with each other when they were growing up in Chhapra, and even later, after they had left Bihar and re settled elsewhere, mainly in West Bengal. I myself was born in Calcutta and have no connection with Bihar except through my father's family. Yet, Bhojpuri left a mark on me too: I grew up hearing my father speak it with my uncles and aunts, and came to love its earthy cadences. Even though I never learnt to speak Bhojpuri myself, its rhythms and my father's stories of growing up in Chhapra were my principal links with Bihar. That, in turn, sparked my interest in the music and culture of the indentured diaspora, which is suffused with the rhythms of Bhojpuri.

In my father's stories, Chhapra was always encircled by a nostalgic halo. His own father, my grandfather, was an advocate in the district courts, and he and his relatives, along with other educated, professional families, many of whom were also Bengalis, were part of a relatively privileged circle. My father loved to tell stories about how he and his brothers would roam the town's streets, and of festive occasions when they would cook huge pots of food in their courtyard. My grandfather, who died long before I was born, was said to be a man of refined tastes who liked to plant exotic trees and flowers in his garden. He would also host musical evenings featuring some of Chhapra's famous singers and dancers, like the legendary Rasoolan Bai. This particular set of stories intrigued me because they dated back to a time when singers and dancers were usually tawaifs, or courtesans; my father's family was so intensely conservative that I found it hard to believe that my grandfather, who was known to be a fiercely puritanical patriarch, had entertained courtesans in his own home.

Another reason why I was intrigued by the nostalgic, rosy-hued tales of my father's childhood was that they were completely at odds with the images of Bihar that were prevalent in India when I was coming of age. In the 1970s, Bihar's image was largely negative; when it figured in the news it was almost always because of clashes between caste or religious groups, or because of floods and other natural disasters.

Bihar's reputation was not, of course, entirely undeserved: the state was, and still is, one of the poorest in the country, with the lowest per capita income and persistently low levels of literacy, nutrition, life expectancy, access to healthcare and so on.[2] But at the same time Bihar wields enormous demographic clout; its population, of 99 million, is almost equal to that of Egypt. As a result, the state exercises disproportionate influence on Indian politics; many commentators reflexively blame Bihar for India's perennially abysmal scores in indexes of economic and social well-being.

In short, since the nineteenth century Bihar has been regarded as benighted, poor and lacking in opportunities. This being the case, why had my ancestors decided, I often wondered, to settle in Chhapra of all places? Surely, having travelled this far from their homeland they could have continued further, in the direction of Bombay, or Delhi, or some other more promising place? After all, in the nineteenth century, hundreds of thousands of people were choosing to indenture themselves rather than remain at home in Bihar. Why, then, would my forebears, who were also from the Kayastha caste, and whose hereditary occupations were scribe, clerk and bookkeeper, choose to make that impoverished region their destination? Was it perhaps because they had found jobs in the growing industry that was transporting thousands of indentured workers *out* of Bihar? Many Bengali clerical workers were indeed employed in the colonial offices that managed the process of emigration, and some of them—as I would find out later in Mauritius—have left their mark on that story.

Lovingly preserved in the archives of the Mahatma Gandhi Institute in Mauritius is a large collection of the emigration certificates that were issued to indentured workers when they departed from India.[3] The certificates were divided into ten columns that recorded each migrant's name, age, height, caste, village and marks of identification, such as uneven teeth, moles, pierced ears and so on. The English spellings of the migrants' names often appear strangely mangled, maybe because the clerks who recorded them did not understand some of the tongues—Angika, Magahi, Tharu—spoken by the recruits.[4] Or it could be that the recruits themselves were too terrified to speak out loud, not only because of the overbearing demeanour of the clerks behind the desks, but also because entering their names into governmental records was itself traumatic for people who were accustomed to doing their utmost to elude the predatory gaze of the state. These yellowing and tattered slips of paper have an aura of sacredness about them, as well they should, being testaments to the existence of people who might otherwise have been totally effaced from history. There is something deeply moving about these flimsy pieces of paper with their ragged folds and water stains: every crease and mark is evidence of how fiercely they were guarded during those interminable voyages in the cramped holds of vessels that were often former slave ships (like the *Ibis*). Some of the later certificates of emigration include photographs of the migrants. These images too are often heartrending: the people in them appear impossibly young, just children, their eyes clouded with confusion, suspicion and hurt. It is hard to imagine the courage it must have taken for them to embark on journeys to unknown destinations.

Long ago, while translating the letters of the twelfth-century Jewish merchant Abraham Ben Yiju, I had learnt that some surprising nuggets of information can sometimes be hidden on the flip side of pieces of paper.[5] And sure enough, when I turned over those certificates of emigration I discovered something that I had never seen mentioned in the literature, possibly because no one had thought to look there: the backs of some of the certificates had been scrawled on in Bengali script! The scribbles were mainly notes that listed the name of the recruiter (duffadar) responsible for bringing in the prospective migrant, probably because the recruiter had to be paid a fee (from which the clerk, no doubt, took a cut).[6] It was a strangely unsettling feeling to think that some of those scribbles might have been penned by my own forefathers.

I had gone to Mauritius believing that it was the industry of indenture that had drawn my forebears to Chhapra. But as I dug deeper into the research for Sea of Poppies, I came to realize that I had been barking up the wrong tree. I learnt that the area around Chhapra was one of the most intensively farmed opium-producing districts in the Gangetic plain. The management and adjudication of poppy-growing was thus the chief business of the town's courts and of the local administration. The district's most senior British officer was a representative of the Opium Department, and was armed with a panoply of dictatorial powers. The town was also a major port of call for the fleets of river vessels that transported opium down the Ganges to Calcutta. In short, the crucial detail that my father had excluded from his glowing accounts of Chhapra was that the town's chief business in the mid-nineteenth century, when our ancestors settled there, was opium.

This shadowy reality forms the background of an unusual literary work by a Bhojpuri writer called Pandey Kapil, who was born in Chhapra in 1930, nine years after my father. The book is called *Phoolsunghi* and it is said to be 'the most loved of all Bhojpuri novels'. *Phoolsunghi* was first published in Bhojpuri in the mid-1970s and has only recently appeared in English, in a fine translation by Dr Gautam Choubey.[7]

At the time when *Phoolsunghi* was written, Bihar was in the throes of a Maoist insurgency, and India was going through the period of authoritarian rule known as the Emergency. But these events cast no shadow on the book: *Phoolsunghi* is a historical novel that covers a period of ninety years, starting in the 1830s. In other words, the book is set in precisely that period when opium production was at its peak in Bihar. Indeed, it is the only Indian novel that I know of in which opium is a pervasive presence. However, Pandey Kapil himself could not have had any personal experience of the colonial opium regime: poppy cultivation in Bihar was greatly reduced by the time he came of age, so his book must have been largely based on the memories of others. Indeed, it is evident, from various errors of nomenclature in relation to opium officials, that the author's depiction of the local opium trade was based on hearsay and legend.

This makes the overwhelming presence of opium in the novel all the more striking. The story is a kind of romance, and much of the action takes place in the opulent bungalow of the British Opium Agent (who would actually have been the Sub-Deputy Opium Agent). Not only is every character in the book connected with opium in some way, but also it is often their proximity to the drug that decides their fate.

At the centre of the novel is a character called Haliwant Sahay, a Kayastha, who enters the story as a 'bashful' fifteen-year-old orphan and soon endears himself to Henry Revel, a recently widowed and childless English Opium Agent. Revel adopts the boy and hands him the keys to the kingdom of opium, so to speak, after which the Englishman's story veers off in a direction that was not uncommon in Indian narratives of the colonial encounter: he abandons his Englishness and becomes the beloved local saint Revel Baba, a world-renouncing sadhu-like figure. Haliwant Sahay, by contrast, travels in the other direction, adopting English ways, taking over the management of the opium trade and acquiring a zamindari to boot. As his power grows he sets his sights on a famous courtesan and turns her into a caged 'flowerpecker bird' (*phoolsunghi*), thereby breaking the heart of a legendary musician who is besotted with her. Music and the many kinds of intoxication that go into its making are among the novel's core themes.

Considering that *Phoolsunghi* was written long after the end of the colonial poppy-growing era, the role that opium plays in the novel is an indication of the magnitude of the drug's presence, not only in the economic but also in the cultural and imaginative life of Bihar. As the translator notes, everybody in the novel lives in a moral universe created by the Opium Agent, who is a lofty, godlike figure even before he becomes a saint. In time Sahay too comes to share in the deification: 'Like a true sahib, he always soared in the sky, distant from earthbound mortals. With his mere gaze, he could set things aflame and unnerve people, as the sahibs were known to do.' Sahay was thus following in the footsteps of Sir Charles D'Oyly, who was the Opium Agent in Patna from 1821 to 1831; a witty socialite and accomplished artist, D'Oyly was also a figure of terror who, in the words of a Telegu traveller, 'tours the country with a posse of armed men to collect [opium] even by force'.[8]

Opium was thus no ordinary crop: it actually created a new class of all-powerful, godlike beings, 'distant from earthbound mortals'. It is a testament to the powers of the opium poppy that in the 150 years of the colonial poppy-growing era, the plant succeeded in transforming the culture as well as the political economy of the region.

For me, *Phoolsunghi* was revelatory also in that it provided the context that I had long needed for my father's stories of Chhapra. I understood, for instance, why my puritanical grandfather would have hosted courtesans at his house: he evidently belonged to a circle where this was a social necessity. I understood why he collected unusual trees and plants: he was probably emulating the practices of Opium Agents, among whom gardening appears to have been a popular pursuit. The book describes the Opium Agent thus: 'Revel Sahib was a man of exquisite taste . . . The sprawling compound in front of his bungalow was bedecked with oak and bottle trees. Its carpet-like grass was mowed with such loving care that one shrank from stepping on it.'[9]

But most of all, *Phoolsunghi* confirmed for me what my research for the Ibis Trilogy had already led me to suspect: it was the colonial opium industry that had brought my ancestors to Chhapra and kept them there. Bengalis played so important a role in the Opium Department that there were complaints about their keeping accounts 'in Bengallee, instead of the language familiar to the inhabitants of the province'.[10] Being literate in that language, my ancestors would probably not have had too much trouble in finding employment somewhere within the Opium Department. Although they were not among the handful of Bengali opium dewans who are known to have amassed fortunes, they did well enough that my grandfather was able to study law and start a practice as an advocate in Chhapra. Yet, even as a lawyer, my grandfather's work would have been inextricably tied to opium: many, if not most, of his cases would have concerned disputes over poppy-growing land, and the like. In this light, it is easy to see how a form of production that impoverished vast numbers of peasants, to the point of pushing them to indenture themselves, was also able to provide comfortable niches to a handful of people who possessed the skills to take advantage of the system.

That Bihar is now often described as being steeped in tradition and backwardness is a complete reversal of the reality. What the region is actually mired in, as *Phoolsunghi* so brilliantly shows, is not 'tradition' but rather a particular iteration of colonial modernity, one that followed the imposition of an entirely new and thoroughly modern industrial system centred upon the production of opium.[11]

What is truly staggering to contemplate, however, is that the upheavals caused by the opium regime, which profoundly altered the lives of millions of people, and shaped my family's destiny, were not dictated by any local or regional imperatives. They were rather the unintended consequences of the ongoing, centuries-long relationship of conflict and competition between two foreign powers located at the far ends of the Eurasian landmass—Great Britain and China.

NINE
Malwa

A love of pilgrimages ran very deep in my father's family, even more so than is usually the case in Indian households. This may have played some part in inducing my ancestors to settle in Chhapra, which is conveniently located between two of the most important Hindu sites of pilgrimage: Benares and Gaya.

Benares, the most sacred of cities for Hindus, lies about 200 kilometres upriver from Chhapra, a journey that would have taken three or four days by boat. An especially important day of observance in Benares is Maha Shivaratri (literally, the 'Great Night of Shiva'), which honours the god who is most closely associated with the city. If there was any day of the year when my forebears would have wanted to be in Benares, that would have been it.

As it happens, Maha Shivaratri usually falls in late winter, around the end of February or the beginning of March, at exactly the time when poppy flowers would have been in bloom. Travelling to and from Benares, my great-great-grandparents would have found themselves passing through a landscape that was blanketed with snowdrifts of white flowers.

In the production of opium, as with many other botanical goods, the colonial preference was always for standardized monocultures, so the poppies grown on the Opium Department's territories were uniformly of the same colour: white. The Department's officials clung resolutely to the belief that white poppies produced the best opium, so this was the variety planted throughout the region (the opium poppies cultivated around Ghazipur are of this variety even today).

This was not the case elsewhere, however, as my forebears would have discovered had their passion for pilgrimages taken them farther afield, perhaps to the great Shiva temple of Omkareshwar on the banks of another sacred river, the Narmada, in central India. These territories were not directly administered by the colonial state, but poppies were grown there too, under conditions that were markedly different from those of Bihar. Here the poppy fields were as riotously coloured as the clothes of revellers on Holi, strewn with red, pink and purple flowers.[1]

The sight of these vibrant hues would have come as a surprise to anyone accustomed to the uniformity of Bihar's snow-white poppy fields.[2] Bihar-based travellers might even have scoffed at the farmers of the Narmada valley, believing them to be ignorant yokels who would have done better to plant the white poppies that colonial experts believed to be superior. But they would have been wrong: the exceptional quality of the Company's opium was due not to its preferred variety of flower but rather to its standardized manufacturing processes and testing procedures, which guaranteed a higher grade of product than that produced in central India. In fact the Opium Department's own scientists had determined, through rigorous tests, that the coloured poppies of central and western India produced a finer grade of opium than the white variety (this perhaps is why poppy farmers in today's Afghanistan prefer the coloured variety).[3] The Opium Department's attachment to its chosen strain was perhaps born out of nothing more than a deep-rooted belief in the virtues of whiteness.

The colour of the flowers would not have been the only surprise that the patterns of poppy cultivation in the Narmada valley would have held for travellers from the east. They would have also seen poppies being cultivated not as a primary crop, but in patches along the borders of fields of sugar cane and other winter crops. They would have learnt, moreover, that the poppy farmers of the region were not bound by law to sell their harvest to the Opium Department or any other colonial agency; their product was sold instead to local merchants, who processed and packaged the opium in their own small workshops. 'Here,' wrote a nineteenth-century British chronicler of the opium trade, 'the poppy is cultivated, and opium is manufactured as freely as rice and wheat are cultivated, without any restraint or interference on the part of government agents. The question with the farmers, therefore, is simply one of profit, whether they will raise a crop of the poppy, or of rice or wheat.'[4]

Had eastern travellers entered the home of a poppy farmer, they would have noticed, to their further surprise, that in this region, the harvested poppy latex was stored not in pots of water, as was the practice in the east, but in containers filled with linseed oil.[5] Had curiosity compelled them to visit a production facility, they would have been astonished to find themselves not in a huge fortress of a factory, like those of Patna or Ghazipur, but in a small shed, filled with flat cakes laid out to dry in the shade. They would have discovered that it took a year or more for the product to be ready, and as much as two years for it be sent overseas. All of this would have seemed strange, even startling, to anyone accustomed to the procedures of the Opium Department.

What would not have been apparent, however, to any but the most perceptive traveller is that the differences in the two patterns of production would have profound and long-lasting consequences for their respective regions.

These differences can all be traced back, ultimately, to the fact that the British expanded their territories in eastern India much earlier than they did in the west. By 1765, when the East India Company was already in control of most of the Gangetic plain, its holdings on the west coast consisted of little more than the port of Bombay. This was a mere foothold compared even to the Portuguese territories along the coast, which included not only Goa but also the strategically located colonies of Daman and Diu in the Gulf of Cambay.

The hinterlands of Bombay were then controlled by a set of powerful Maratha principalities. These states, the most important of which had their capitals in Gwalior, Baroda, Indore and Nagpur, were founded after the region was wrested away from the Mughal Empire in the seventeenth century by the Maratha leader Shivaji Bhosale. Following his death his realm was divided up between several energetic Maratha dynasties. Unlike the kingdoms of the Gangetic plain, the major Maratha states were well able to hold their own against the East India Company's armies.[6] In tactics, as in armaments, the Maratha dynasties went to great lengths to keep pace with the innovations of the day, and in some regards their military doctrines were actually in advance of those of the British.[7]

The military historian Randolf Cooper writes:

> The memoirs of the British officers who witnessed the Maratha artillery in action leave no doubt about its level of sophistication. At the time of the Second Maratha War [1803], France was considered to have the finest artillery in the world. When British officers saw the volume of fire produced by the Maratha guns, some asserted incorrectly that they were manned by Frenchmen but all agreed the

effect was devastating. Another false assumption was that Frenchmen were responsible for the production of artillery and its accoutrements in India, when in fact the French merely provided the most modern example to be copied.[8]

Another reason that the British were slow to expand in western and central India was that their main base in the region, Bombay, was hemmed in by a steep range of mountains and a rugged plateau.[9] Unlike the wide, flat plains of Bengal, so perfect for infantry manoeuvres, the terrain beyond Bombay was better suited to guerrilla-style resistance. It was precisely by taking advantage of the lay of the land that Shivaji's Maratha warriors had defeated the forces of the Mughals.

The upshot was that at a time when the British had succeeded in eliminating all opposition in the Gangetic plain, they still faced formidable challenges in western and central India, especially in Malwa, a region that covered much of present-day Madhya Pradesh, as well as parts of Maharashtra, Gujarat and Rajasthan.[10]

In Malwa too the cultivation of poppies had grown steadily since the sixteenth century. Over time opium became an important article of commerce for the merchants of the surrounding regions, whose networks reached all the way from the coast into the deepest fastnesses of Malwa. These included enterprising business communities from several different religions—Hindus, Jains and many Muslim sects—which had for centuries traded and speculated in agricultural commodities such as wheat, cotton, sugar cane and so on.[11] As the cultivation of poppies expanded, opium too became an important commodity for trade and speculation for Jains and Marwaris, Bohras and Ismailis.

The seths and sahukars who dominated the commercial worlds of western and central India were symbiotically linked to the region's rajas, nawabs and maharajas, who depended on them for credit and financing. So, whereas in Bengal it was the East India Company that took advantage of indigenous banking systems, in Malwa and Gujarat it was the native states that benefited from the support of local mercantile networks, which provided them with the wherewithal to maintain well-equipped standing armies. As a result, despite their internal rivalries and conflicts, these states were able to muster enough strength and military expertise to inflict several defeats on the East India Company in the last quarter of the eighteenth century.

It wasn't till the dawn of the nineteenth century that the leadership of the East India Company realized that the states of western and central India, apart from constituting a strategic threat, might also become economic rivals. In 1800, just as an increase in the value of Bengal opium was bringing huge profits into the Company's coffers, its officials woke to the disturbing realization that their efforts to expand the drug market in China had not escaped the notice of the canny merchants of the west coast: between 1800 and 1803 over 63,500 kilograms of opium had been exported to China by private traders, through the Company's own port, Bombay![12] Nor was this all: opium was also being exported from a number of other ports on the west coast, including the Portuguese colonies of Goa, Daman and Diu. Western India's opium industry was thus fully on track to match, and even outpace, the Company's own rapidly growing drug-running operation.[13]

At this time the Company's leaders believed that the market for opium in China and Southeast Asia was a limited one, and that an increase in supply would lead to a crash in prices.[14] From this perspective the growth in opium exports from Malwa represented a serious threat to the Company's profits.

The Governor General in Calcutta at the time was Lord Wellesley, older brother of Arthur Wellesley, the future duke of Wellington. Believing that the growth of Malwa exports would have 'detrimental consequences' for the revenues from the Bengal opium monopoly, Lord Wellesley ordered the Company's Bombay officials to take the strongest possible measures for 'the prevention of the growth of that Commerce and for its ultimate annihilation'.[15]

As it happened, even as the Governor General was writing this letter, his brother Arthur Wellesley, then thirty-four years old, was heading into western India on a campaign that would culminate in a battle that he would cite, to the end of his days, as the most important military achievement of his life. In September 1803, in Assaye, in present-day Maharashtra, the future Iron Duke narrowly defeated a much larger allied Maratha force led by the Scindias. Later, writing to a correspondent, Wellesley commented: 'Their infantry is the best I have seen in India, excepting our own . . . I assure you that their fire was so heavy, that I much doubted at one time whether I should be able to prevail upon our troops to advance.'[16]

Six weeks later, in Laswari, near Delhi, another Scindia army was narrowly defeated by a British force led by General Gerard Lake. 'In forty years of soldiering,' writes Randolf Cooper, 'Lake had faced death many times on foreign battlefields. Not even the pounding he took at Yorktown could measure up to what he endured at the hands of Scindia's battalions.'

In a letter to the Governor General, Lake, who lost his son on the battlefield, wrote:

These [Maratha] battalions are most uncommonly well appointed, have a most numerous artillery, as well served as they possibly can be, the gunners standing to their guns until killed by the bayonet. All the sepoys of the enemy behaved exceedingly well . . . I never was in so severe a business in my life and pray God I never may be in such a situation again. Their army is better appointed than ours; no expense is spared whatever, and they have three times the number of men to a gun we have . . . These fellows fought like devils, or rather heroes . . . I verily believe, from the position they had taken, we might have failed.'[17]

In other words the Maratha armies came within a hair's breadth of defeating the Company, and might well have done so if not for the treachery of European mercenaries who switched sides late in the game. A victory at that point would likely not have affected the outcome in the long run, because by then the British appetite for conquest had become so insatiable that they would surely have attacked again and again, and with their immense financial resources would probably have prevailed eventually. But even though the Marathas ultimately failed to hold off the Company, the time they purchased, with their dogged resistance, made an enormous difference to the destiny of western India.[18]

The year 1803 thus marked a critical moment in India's colonial history in that it finally gave the British a decisive military advantage over the Marathas. Here at last was a golden opportunity to enhance the value of the Company's Bengal monopoly by 'annihilating' the Malwa opium industry! As instructed by Lord Wellesley, the Company's Bombay officials quickly issued orders banning the export of opium from Bombay and prohibiting the cultivation of poppies on its newly annexed territories.[19]

But this was easier said than done. Even after their defeat, the Maratha states were by no means crippled: they still controlled large tracts of land and continued to maintain formidable armies. They were thus powerful enough to make it unfeasible for the Company to think of incorporating their realms into the territories that it administered directly. Instead, the Company opted to place them under a form of indirect rule, whereby the colonial regime maintained overall control but did not involve itself in administrative, financial and judicial matters: this meant that it had no direct control over patterns of cultivation, since it did not collect revenues. For the mercantile networks of the region this was a boon, for it provided them enough cover to continue to trade in opium and send caravans clandestinely to the ports along the coast, from where the drug could be whisked away to Southeast Asia and China. When the British tried to stop the flow out of one port, the merchants merely switched directions and sent their produce to another.[20]

The predicament the East India Company now faced was one that had also bedevilled its rival, the Dutch VOC, in the preceding century, when it sought to impose monopolies on spices like cloves and nutmeg. The trouble with trying to monopolize a botanical commodity is that it is difficult, if not impossible, to restrict a species to any determinate region, especially if those plants also happen to generate huge profits. The Dutch, in the eighteenth century, had tried to restrict the cultivation of clove and nutmeg trees to certain specifically designated islands. However, the policy was undermined not only by indigenous resistance, but also by the trees themselves: they grew in such abundance in the forests of Maluku that they were impossible to extirpate.[21] A similar scenario unfolded in western and central India in the first decades of the nineteenth century, with the Company trying to force treaties banning poppy cultivation on indigenous states. A key figure in the implementation of this policy was another Wellesley, Gerald, son of the (by then) former Governor General, and nephew of the Iron Duke. He spent several years living in Indore, where he had three children with a local woman whose name was recorded as 'Culoo'.[22]

During his stay in Indore, where he was the British representative ('Resident'), Wellesley held protracted negotiations with the ruling Holkars and other princely families, offering them compensation in

exchange for signing treaties that banned the opium trade.[23] Many
of the princes had no alternative but to sign, though the most
powerful of them, the Maharaja of Gwalior, flatly refused. But the
Holkars of Indore, like some of the other royals, chose the path of
least resistance and signed a treaty that was quite unequivocal in its
language: it gave the British the power to stop and 'appropriate any
opium herein prohibited which they may discover passing to and fro
in the Maharajah's territories'.[24]

The severity of the treaty's tone actually masked a very weak
hand: Wellesley simply did not have the personnel to keep track of all
the opium that was 'passing to and fro in the Maharajah's territories'.
Nor did the Maharaja, or any of his fellow princes, have any intention
of enforcing the treaty: they not only allowed the trade to continue
more or less unhindered, but also conspired with mercantile networks
to keep it hidden from the British.

As for the merchants of Malwa, the drug had become a major
source of revenue for them by this time. Their profits from other
goods had been eroded because of competition from the British, so
opium, correspondingly, had become crucial to their fortunes. So,
despite the Company's best efforts at suppressing the cultivation
of poppies, the crop continued to flourish in regions not directly
administered by the British.

Along with applying political pressure on local rajas, nawabs and
maharajas, the Company also tried to take control of the Malwa opium
industry by becoming the biggest buyer on the market. But in this too
they were thwarted by the commercial networks of the region. The
Company's officials quickly discovered that Malwa opium was not
available for sale to all comers even if they had the money to pay for
it. The supplies were controlled by a syndicate, which had the power

to choose their buyers and to withhold the goods from the market. The material attributes of opium were instrumental in this: not only was it a commodity that was high in value and low in bulk, but it was also believed to improve in quality over time, which actually gave merchants an incentive to hold on to their reserves.[25] Buying directly from poppy farmers was also not an option because their entire crop was usually bought up a year ahead by speculators. Moreover, the Company simply couldn't afford to speculate in opium futures on the scale that would have been necessary to corner the market. It didn't help either that Gerald Wellesley managed to alienate some of the most important dealers with his high-handed ways. 'He has abused and affronted us so much,' they wrote in a letter, 'that we nearly thought that [he] would rob us.'[26]

In effect, as historian Amar Farooqui notes,

Indian merchants thwarted attempts of the British Indian government to establish a monopoly of the Bengal type over opium in western India . . . They were encouraged in their truculence by the tacit or active support of numerous other indigenous groups ranging from Indian rulers in the region with their truncated authority to armed 'bandits'. What we encounter here is . . . a serious conflict between colonialism and Indian capitalists, wherein indigenous merchants were able to engage in a contest at various levels including in that crucial arena, the market.[27]

Essentially the colonial regime was hoist with its own petard: in resisting the East India Company's attempts to control the trade, the Malwa networks were doing to the British something similar to what they themselves were doing to the Qing Empire. Just as the Company was using every conceivable dodge to circumvent Chinese efforts to stop the inflow of opium, so too were the merchants, rulers and peasants of Malwa employing every possible subterfuge to preserve their profits and thwart British efforts to impose a monopoly on the trade.

Yet, there was also a crucial difference. The British were militarily so powerful that they could—and eventually did—force the Qing to legitimize what was essentially a trade steeped in criminality. However, no such avenue was open to the rulers and merchants of Malwa, who were much weaker than the colonizers. Faced with an overwhelming asymmetry in military power, there were very few weapons that the colonized could resort to: the clandestine opium trade thus became an instrument of resistance, a means of preventing the colonial power from appropriating a vitally important source of income. As Farooqui shows in his aptly titled book *Smuggling as Subversion*, Malwa opium evolved into a 'weapon of the weak', used by local rulers and mercantile networks to retain their hold on a lucrative stream of revenue. It needs to be noted, however, that their motives in doing so were largely opportunistic and self-interested.[28]

In this too the history of opium in western India was brimful of portents for the following centuries, in which drugs would increasingly ensure the survival of insurgent groups in the face of overwhelming military force, as exemplified, most recently, by the Taliban in Afghanistan.[29] Indeed, there are some uncanny similarities between the nineteenth-century opium industry of Malwa and that of present-day Afghanistan. Just as in Malwa, cash advances from landowners and moneylenders played a large part in the expansion of poppy farming in Afghanistan after 1980; there too crops were often bought up a year in advance by cartels; and there too the opium economy has been an important source of income and employment in uncertain times.[30] As a result, the US military's attempts to eradicate the industry created enormous resentment against the US-backed government that was put in place after 2001, and ultimately caused its downfall.[31]

The brute fact is that it was a flower that defeated the mightiest military power in human history: the opium poppy may be humble in appearance, but it is one of the most powerful Beings that humans have encountered in their time on earth. To be sure, tea, sugarcane, tobacco, rubber, cotton, *Yersinia pestis*, and many other plants and pathogens have played major roles in human history, some of them over several centuries. But today they are all much diminished in their influence, while the opium poppy is mightier than ever.

The continuing challenge of the Malwa networks, along with internal debates within the Company, ultimately prompted British officials to reconsider the very nature of the drug trade. Abandoning the idea that opium was a luxury good with a limited market, they began to think of it as a mass commodity that could generate potentially limitless profits.[32] This resulted in an abrupt change of policy in 1830: the colonial regime annulled its opium treaties with the Malwa states, and removed all restrictions on the cultivation of poppies. Their plan now was to make the best of the situation by earning revenues from the growing trade in Malwa opium, so it was decreed that any amount of the drug could now be shipped out of Bombay, so long as a transit duty was paid.[33]

The duty amount was initially pegged low enough to make it more profitable to ship opium from Bombay than other ports. But this did not stop the outflow of opium from Karachi, in Sind, and from the Portuguese colonies of Goa and Daman.[34] Not much could be done about the latter since the Portuguese were an important ally in Britain's global struggle against the French, and could not, therefore, be cut out of a hugely lucrative commerce.[35] But Karachi was another matter: the competition from the city was bothersome enough that the Company eventually invaded Sind and took control of the port.[36]

This not only ensured Bombay's hold on the opium trade, but also allowed the Company to jack up the transit duties to 50 and even 70 per cent of the value of each chest of opium.[37] Within six years of the conquest of Sind, British revenues from Malwa opium had increased almost four-fold.[38]

The result was an enormous windfall for the colonial regime, as well as a huge increase in the volume of opium that was being shipped from India to China. The annual average of exported Malwa opium increased almost three-fold in the decade after 1830, soon amounting to more than double the volume that was being shipped from Calcutta. This, in turn, sparked off a race between western and eastern India, with the Opium Department ramping up production in its own territories in the Gangetic plain.[39] This huge increase in supply did nothing to depress demand—far from it.

As Wormer notes, after the 1830s opium was the colonial regime's 'principal export, averaging twenty to thirty percent of the annual total into the 1880s. During the general depression at mid-century it became almost the sole article of overseas commerce, peaking at half of all exports in 1846-47. Production soared from four thousand chests per year in 1820 to over ninety thousand chests in the 1870s, making it "probably the largest commerce of the time in any single commodity."'[40]

Malwa and Purvanchal thus became the two wellsprings of the rivers of opium that were flowing into China in the years before the First Opium War. The key difference between the revenues the British derived from these two regions was that in the east it was the sole beneficiary of its opium sales, whereas in the west its gains came only from transit duties. This does not mean, however, that Malwa opium was any less lucrative for the colonizers. On the contrary, the Malwa product was even more profitable than Bengal opium, which required the maintenance of a huge and costly bureaucratic establishment. Bauer estimates that the costs of producing opium in eastern India amounted to more than a third of the gross revenue that the British earned from it, while the costs of administering the transit tax in the west came to a mere 0.17 per cent. So, for the colonial regime the revenue per chest was the same for Malwa and Bengal opium.[41]

Why then did the colonizers continue to maintain the monopoly system in Bengal, with all its administrative costs? Why didn't they do away with the huge bureaucracy and allow local merchants to run the trade, as in Malwa, while collecting similarly lucrative duties and taxes? The reasons that Bauer cites are these: The Opium Department's bureaucracy was a massive vested interest that would not allow itself to be easily done away with. Moreover, its production processes were instrumental in setting certain standards of quality. Its product was consistently of a higher grade than Malwa opium, which was often adulterated and, therefore, fetched a lower price in China.[42] But the most important reason was that the Opium Department's tight hold on Benares and Patna opium allowed it to increase production as needed, especially after 1830, when the British Empire began to flood China with opium.[43]

But of course, not all of India's opium was exported. As the supply grew there was a huge increase also in domestic opium use, particularly in certain rural areas in present-day Andhra Pradesh, Odisha, Sind, Gujarat, central Punjab and particularly Assam, where opium was smoked rather than ingested orally.[44] Remarking on 'the universal prevalence of the use of opium among the wretched inhabitants of Assam', a British journal noted: '[I]f the introduction of the poisonous drug into China were productive of the same effects as it is stated to have had in Assam, we need not wonder at the determination evinced by the emperor to put it down at all hazards, and we cannot sufficiently admire the paternal feeling which actuated him on the occasion, and for which the Chinese nation owes him a debt of immeasurable gratitude.'[45]

For Bombay, Malwa opium was a blessing, a boon. As Farooqui has shown, Bombay was on the verge of being abandoned by the British in the late eighteenth century because it produced very little revenue for the East India Company.[46] In 1788, the Governor General, Lord Cornwallis, even wrote to the British Prime Minister, William Pitt, recommending that Bombay be scaled down to a small outpost. 'I have reflected most sincerely,' writes Cornwallis, 'and have conversed with the most sensible men in this country, on the utility of the civil establishment in Bombay and I am perfectly convinced that the Company derive no benefit from it.'[47]

At that time Bombay's expenses so far exceeded its revenues that it had to be heavily subsidised by Calcutta and Madras.[48] It was Malwa opium that solved Bombay's revenue problem: the transit tax charged by the British was a cash cow of the best sort, yielding funds aplenty at very little administrative cost. In effect the islands of Bombay were kept afloat by Malwa's growing reservoirs of opium.[49]

But Malwa's opium benefited many others as well, primarily because it was produced under circumstances that were markedly different from those in eastern India. The most important difference was that the profits of the Malwa opium industry were distributed much more evenly than those generated from the official, colonial monopoly of eastern India. What remained of the gains from Malwa opium, after the colonial regime had taken its cut, stayed in the hands of Indians, at various levels of the social hierarchy: while the nawabs and maharajas, seths and sahukars undoubtedly profited the most, some benefits trickled down to petty traders and farmers too. In other words, decades of dogged opposition to English rule, which first took the form of military resistance and then changed into a fightback through market mechanisms and clandestine trade, succeeded in keeping a significant part of the gains of the opium trade out of British hands.

The fact that poppy cultivation in Malwa began as a clandestine industry ensured that it would remain forever shrouded in secrecy. 'The success of the venture lay in keeping it out of view,' writes Farooqui. 'Since indigenous groups engaged in it were excessively secretive, documentary evidence originating from the Indian side is not easily forthcoming.'[50] What this means is that opium became the proverbial elephant in the room in western India, rendered invisible by common consent: it was, and was known to be, the main driver of the economy, but it left even fewer traces in public memory than the opium industry of eastern India. There are no paintings or drawings, for instance, of the workshops in Malwa where the drug was processed and packed. Indeed, I have not been able to find a single image related to opium in the Malwa region.

Today it is largely forgotten that opium once played a crucial part in the economy of western India; the fact that the drug had a recognized role in certain rituals has also been rigorously repressed. The intensity of the taboo was illustrated by an incident that occurred while I was writing *Sea of Poppies*. It involved a prominent political figure of the time: Jaswant Singh, a stalwart of the BJP who had served as minister in the defence, foreign affairs and finance ministries. In 2007, it was alleged that a ritual libation, containing a small quantity of opium, had been served at the wedding of Jaswant Singh's son (as was common within their Rajput community). The custom was for a very dilute solution of opium to be splashed into the outspread palms of those present, almost like holy water. Of all the many ways of consuming opium this is perhaps the only one that can be considered an act of homage, honouring the poppy's extraordinary ability to both assuage and destroy.

However, the allegation that the custom had been observed by a minister caused an explosion of outrage across India; politicians of every hue claimed to be utterly scandalized; lawsuits were filed and there were calls for Jaswant Singh's resignation as a Member of Parliament. For a while it seemed that the incident might end a distinguished political career. Nobody cared to remember that certain preparations of opium have been used in Indian rituals for centuries. It was as though opium were something utterly unknown and alien, an unspeakable thing whose very mention was a desecration of India's self-image as a nation of pious abstainers (even though the country is home to two of the world's largest opium-processing plants).

But this wilful amnesia cannot disguise the fact that the fortunes of modern Mumbai were largely shaped by opium, and by China. As Farooqui notes: '[T]he destiny of Bombay as a great commercial and industrial center was born of its becoming an accomplice in the drugging of countless Chinese with opium, a venture in which the Indian business class showed great zeal alongside the East India Company. This is the sordid underside of Bombay's colonial past.'[51]

Today, at a time when 'the economy' and 'business' are thought to be insulated spheres that function according to their own laws, it has become customary to lionize merchants and businessmen for their shrewdness and entrepreneurialism. But the real lesson to be learnt from the commercial world of western India is that political and military support have always been crucial to the flourishing of business and enterprise in the modern era. If private enterprise was able to thrive in western India, but not in the east, it was ultimately because the Maratha kingdoms were able to fight off the predatory colonial power for much longer than the states of the Gangetic plain. The credit for western India's entrepreneurial prowess is ultimately due not only to the financial acumen of its businessmen but also to the foresight and acuity of the political and military leadership of the Maratha states. The years in which they held back the inexorable British advance eventually made an enormous difference to their region.

The critical value of military power in relation to capitalist enterprise was perfectly well understood by the British, who, despite their ceaseless trumpeting of the virtues of 'Free Trade', constantly used their armed forces to create business opportunities and to crush competitors.[52] These practices have remained essential to the functioning of modern imperialism to the present day. Not for nothing did one of the founders of the contemporary global economy, the Dutch colonizer Jan Pieterszoon Coen, utter the famous words: 'There can be no trade without war, and no war without trade.'

TEN

East and West

Because of their divergent histories, the opium industries in eastern and western India evolved in completely different directions—with long-lasting consequences for the two regions. In western and central India, as John F. Richards, one of the most eminent historians of opium, notes, opium 'offered reliable profits to numerous brokers, traders, and commission agents'. In eastern India, by contrast, 'the multiplier effect from the profits of Bengal opium was constricted'.[1]

In other words, the money generated by Malwa's opium industry trickled down much deeper, with a larger share of the profits remaining in indigenous hands. The benefits were felt all the way across the social spectrum. Some of Malwa's poppy farmers, for instance, made two, sometimes even three, times as much as their eastern counterparts.[2] Moreover they were spared the draconian surveillance regime of the Opium Department with all its corrosive effects.

Petty merchants and rural moneylenders, on the other hand, gained a great deal from processing and selling opium, although not as much, of course, as those who sat atop the social pyramid—that is to say the rajas, nawabs and maharajas of central and western India. A staggering number of 'princely states' were sustained by revenues from opium. 'By the end of the nineteenth century,' writes Richards, 'some ninety states engaged in opium production. These ranged in size from the largest in territory and population such as Indore, Mewar, Bhopal, Jaipur, Marwar, Gwalior, Alwar, and Bikaner, to smaller states that dwindled to the size of Sitamau in Malwa with its few thousand inhabitants and one principal town.'[3]

The splendid nineteenth-century palaces that dot the landscapes of Madhya Pradesh, Rajasthan and Gujarat bear witness to the enormous profits that the potentates of the region earned from opium. It is perhaps appropriate that many of those palaces have now been turned into luxury hotels where foreign tourists can be transported into the realm of fantasy that is now marketed as 'Incredible India'.

For India's rajas and nawabs, however, the industry that had been fostered initially by an attitude of resistance ultimately became a pathway to hopeless dependency on the colonial state. Opium revenues slowly turned into a payoff for the princes' acquiescence in British rule. In the 1920s and 1930s, as anti-imperialist movements of various kinds gathered steam across the subcontinent, the princes of India, as a class, came to be seen as the most loyal allies of the British Raj (although there were many who sympathized with, and even financed, the anti-colonial struggle). This perception served to alienate their compatriots to such a degree that animosity towards their ruling dynasties persisted long after the states had been incorporated into independent India. In 1971, when Indira Gandhi abolished the annual payments that had been promised to the princes in exchange for their accession to independent India, the move was greeted with acclaim in much of the country.

Such was the prevailing hostility to the princely states that their actual record of governance did not receive fair scrutiny in the decades after Independence. The Indian intelligentsia was all-too-willing to believe that indigenous rulers were uniformly decadent, backward and corrupt. This narrative was eagerly promoted by the British, who liked to present themselves as the sole agents of 'Progress' in the subcontinent. But in reality, as is now increasingly acknowledged, many Indian rulers were much more interested in public welfare than were the colonizers, whose main interest lay in siphoning off revenue.[4] The economist Lakshmi Iyer, for instance, has shown, in a detailed statistical analysis, that some native states made much bigger investments in 'public goods' than British colonizers did in the areas that they ruled directly: 'For instance, the native state of Mysore carried out smallpox vaccination as early as 1806. The state of Travancore announced a policy of free primary education in 1817 . . . The state of Baroda was probably the first to introduce compulsory primary education in 1892, while the British passed a compulsory education act in the nearby Central Provinces only in 1920.'[5]

The colonial regime's claim to being the prime agent of 'Progress' in the subcontinent was, therefore, completely without foundation.

Of all the beneficiaries of the Malwa opium trade, none gained more than the mercantile networks of western India. 'There can be no doubt,' writes Farooqui, 'that opium was the main source of capital accumulation for indigenous merchants and bankers in western India during the first half of the nineteenth century.'[6]

Opium was, of course, a key source of capital not just for Indians, but also for many British, American and European businessmen. Western entrepreneurs, though, were fortunate to have access to many other sources of capital, whereas the constrained circumstances of a colonial economy left Indian businessmen with little choice: it was opium or bust. The trading communities of central and western

India understood this very well, and irrespective of their differences in religion and caste, they all leapt into the drug trade as best they could.

That businessmen of every religious group were involved in the opium trade is evident from even a cursory glance at the names that crop up in historical records. So, for instance, Appa Gangadhar, a powerful courtly figure who controlled vast swathes of poppy-growing lands, was a Maratha Hindu. Two of the best-known insurance brokers of Indore, Poonasah Man Singh and Chaman Singh Hurruckchand, were also Hindus, as were Seth Karamchand Dhongershee, a leading Gujarati opium agent, and Seth Naomal Hotchand of Karachi. The Ahmedabad-based firm of the Hindu seth Kessresing Khooshalchund was the second most important opium-trading concern in the entire Malwa region.[7] On the other hand, Sir Roger de Faria, one of the most famous opium traders of the west coast, was a Goan Catholic, while the speculator who was sometimes described as 'the Rothschild of opium', Seth Bahadur Mal, was a Marwari Hindu based in Kota.[8] The major opium-trading ventures of Malwa were similarly diverse: they included, for instance, a firm known as Birdman (Vardhaman) & Mansaram, as well as a European company called Gilder & De Souza. Gujarati and Marwari Hindus with names like Madowdass Ransordass, Motichand Amichand and Ameechand Sukurchand played significant roles in the Malwa opium trade, as did Muslims from the Bohra and Memon sects, like Agha Mohammad Suastry and Mohammad Ali Rogay. The most visible figures in the trade, however, were Parsi merchant princes, like the scions of the Wadia family and Sir Jamsetjee Jejeebhoy, the first Indian baronet (see insert image 9). But the idea that Parsis controlled the opium trade is a myth.[9] 'Of the 120 Indian-controlled companies dealing in opium between around 1803–1830,' writes the historian Jenny Rose, 'only 49 were owned by Parsis.'[10] And towards the later years of the nineteenth century, the opium trade in western India would come to be dominated by a family of Baghdadi Jews, the Sassoons.[11]

If the opium trade came to be identified with Parsi and Jewish merchants, it is largely because they were involved in the most conspicuous sector of the industry—overseas shipping. The inland flows of the drug, on the other hand, were generally hidden from the public eye, as were the Marwari, Gujarati, Sindhi and Bohra traders who held sway over this segment of the industry. Thus, in one way or another, opium was crucial to the success of businessmen from every trading community in western and central India: indeed, it can be said quite categorically that in this period there were very few business houses, trading families and commercial firms in this region that were *not* involved with opium in some way.

But capital was not all that opium provided to the business houses of western India; it also gave them many other benefits, quite a few of them intangible: the businessmen who participated acquired entrepreneurial skills and gained entry into far-flung networks of information and credit; they learnt about the vagaries of global trade and became adept at dealing with foreign currencies; they observed the emergence of new industries and grew accustomed to coping with, and adopting, new technologies. Malwa merchants were so well-versed in the international dimensions of the opium trade that by the 1830s Marwari seths, based deep in the heart of Rajasthan, came to possess a keen awareness of the Chinese market.[12] The greatest of the Malwa opium merchants, Seth Bahadur Mal, was based in Rajasthan, but his information channels stretched from Bombay and Calcutta all the way to China. In 1830 he even sent emissaries to Guangzhou in the hope of getting better prices for his opium.

Having bested the world's most powerful narco-state, the British Empire, at its own game, the merchants of western India acquired a sense of self-confidence that saved them from developing a psychological dependence on the colonial state.[13] In the words of the historian Marika Vicziany: '[I]n contrast to Calcutta, it was the good fortune of Bombay that the growing dominance of the European firms occurred after a long period during which the Indian merchants had participated in foreign trade. This experience enabled many of the most prominent Indian merchants to acquire the capital and commercial skills which facilitated the transfer of their ability from foreign trade to local industry.'[14]

If none of this is acknowledged or remembered today, it is because, as with everything to do with opium, these connections have been systematically suppressed over the years. Even now researchers often face difficulties in piercing the wall of silence that surrounds opium. This is how Asiya Siddiqi, a pioneering historian of Indian business, describes her own experience:

> Most of us do not know that this [opium] trade ever existed and many of us would rather not be reminded that it did. When I first started exploring it, the representative of a leading business house in Bombay said to me, 'Why do you want to dig up these facts?' The subject is a sensitive one on account of the millions of chests of opium that were shipped from Indian ports to China over the course of almost a century and a half.[15]

The legacies of the opium industry in eastern India were of an altogether different kind. Because of the Opium Department's monopoly, the rewards of the drug racket accrued first to the colonial regime, and then to a small number of speculators and merchants of whom very few were native to the region: most of those who benefited were expatriates, whether Indian or Westerner.[16] Even though Calcutta was the global hub of the trade, only a handful of native-born Bengalis from the city's most prominent families were able to buy and export significant quantities of opium for their own profit. They included merchant princes like Dwarkanath Tagore, Muttyloll Seal, Conielal Mullick and Ramdoolal Dey, who was the richest of them all with a fortune of a billion rupees.[17] But even these fabulously wealthy Bengali businessmen had to deal with headwinds that put them at a disadvantage in relation to their counterparts in western India. First, they did not have access to the supply chain of opium in their region, which was entirely in British hands. Nor could they access supplies from the west, since those were controlled by the Malwa trading networks. Second, they had to deal with a 'covert exclusion policy' designed to keep them in a role subsidiary to that of British private traders. When Bengali merchants bought opium at the Calcutta auctions, for example, they were denied the three-month grace period that was routinely extended to British private traders to cover their purchases: they had to pay upfront. They were also refused shipping insurance for the transportation of their opium to China. These mechanisms ensured that Bengali merchants were pushed to the margins of Calcutta's most important industry.[18] As Wormer notes:

> The independent strength of indigenous mercantile groups in western India at the turn of the nineteenth century made for a marked contrast with circumstances in Bengal. There both major banking houses and the local agents of British merchants, known as 'banians,' found themselves increasingly reduced to a subordinate role within the hierarchical, racially-stratified commercial order that began to take shape in the 1780s with the rise of a market for Company bills of exchange in Calcutta.[19]

As for the majority of ordinary Calcuttans, they knew nothing, either about the commerce that undergirded the city's economy, or of the commodity that made it a prime destination for foreign ships. Everything connected with opium was carefully screened from the gaze of the city's native population; very few were even aware of the comings and goings of the Opium Department's cargoes. Opium flowed through Calcutta like a ghostly river, unobserved by the local populace: every year, thousands of mango-wood chests, stamped with the seal of the Opium Department, were shipped downriver from the factories of Ghazipur and Patna in closely guarded flotillas of riverboats (and later, in special trains). On arriving in Calcutta, the chests of opium disappeared into fortress-like warehouses, where a select few merchants were invited to inspect them before they were put up for auction. After they had been bid upon and sold, they were transferred directly to the merchant vessels that would carry them to China and the East Indies.

In Bombay, by contrast, through much of the nineteenth century, the trade in opium was brisk and public. This is how Govind Narain, a nineteenth-century Marathi chronicler of Bombay, describes the city's opium bazaar: 'If one turns towards the East at Mumbadevi Square, one comes across the counting houses of the big moneylenders . . . Just a little ahead are the opium traders, mainly Marwadi and other kinds of Gujars, who conduct their noisy and boisterous trade on the streets.'[20]

From Bombay's opium bazaar it was a short walk to the bustling precincts of the Fort, where there were any number of shipping agents who regularly placed advertisements in the Gujarati press, announcing the departure of China-bound ships. All that an enterprising young trader needed to do was scrape together the money to buy passage.

This was exactly how a sixteen-year-old Parsi boy by the name of Nariman Karkaria set off for China in 1910. Having run away to Bombay from his home in Navsari, he happened to pick up a Parsi-run Gujarati newspaper, *Jame Jamshed*. He writes in his autobiography:

As luck would have it, my gaze fell on the advertisements while flipping the pages of the newspaper. The Rubatino Shipping Line Company's steamer *Capri* was scheduled to leave on Tuesday, the thirteenth of August 1910 for China. When I read this, a wild thought about going to China flashed in my mind. I had heard about the glories of China frequently and I had often seen the sethias from China with their *khobas*, large red-coloured *pagdis*.

Karkaria ended up in Hong Kong, where he found employment at various Parsi firms.[21]

In Calcutta, by contrast, opium was disposed of sight unseen at auctions conducted in high ceremonial style on the premises of the Board of Revenue in Dalhousie Square, very close to the seat of British power (the building is now, appropriately, occupied by the Hong Kong and Shanghai Banking Corporation).[22] These auctions were held on the eleventh day of every month and bidders had to hold special tickets in order to enter the auction room. The ticket holders were such a famously cosmopolitan group that British tourists would gather to gawk from a gallery that overlooked the auction room: 'Jews and Gentiles are wild in their manner; and Greeks, Armenians, Persians, mingled in with native Indians of many dialects; and Englishmen, and all the representatives of the continent of Europe, of Asia, and of Africa, are wrought up to the greatest possible excitement by the sharp bidding.'[23]

The excitement of the auctions hinged on the first few minutes, when the bidders were agog to learn whether 'any good or bad news from China may have led to an alteration in the value of opium subsequently to the last monthly sale'. All eyes were then fixed on the ultra-rich merchants who actually set the prices: 'The rival millionaires contend by a quiet nod to the auctioneer. The ruling price for the day is soon settled between them, as they well know to what limit they may safely go.' It was only after the big fish had feasted that the minnows had a chance to nibble at the remains. And so 'in the course of an hour the auction room is empty'.[24]

In short, Bombay's opium trade was conducted in the boisterous spirit of an Indian bazaar, and a good part of the gains trickled down into the pockets of petty traders, small businessmen and a host of others who were native to the region. In Calcutta, opium was bought and sold with the pompous ceremony of an art auction, and the gains went first to the colonial regime and then to wealthy merchants who were either from overseas or other parts of India.

Not far from the precincts of the Board of Revenue, in the crowded alleyways around Dalhousie Square, there existed another, very different, market in opium. In my novel *Flood of Fire*, it is in those lanes that the young American sailor, Zachary Reid, begins his initiation into the drug trade under the mentorship of the gender-fluid gomasta (business agent) Baboo Nob Kissin Pander.

The market takes Zachary by surprise because there are no saleable wares on display. What he sees instead is 'a small cluster of lamplit stalls' with turbaned men sitting cross-legged on cloth-covered counters, holding large ledgers in their laps. It falls to Baboo Nob Kissin to explain that this is not a bazaar for opium as such; it is a market in which people 'trade in something unseen and unknown: the prices that opium would fetch in the future, near or distant'. This was, in other words, a market where traders speculated in opium futures.

Trading in agricultural futures was an old business practice in India, predating the emergence of opium as a major commodity.

But as opium grew in commercial importance, speculators began to gamble huge sums of money on it. Since Calcutta's monthly auctions were instrumental in setting the countrywide market rate, they were eagerly followed by the big Malwa trading networks, which developed elaborate communications systems to obtain the information with the greatest possible dispatch. The moment the price was set in Calcutta, messengers would go hurtling off to send word to Kota, Ujjain and the other major trading hubs in central and western India.

Through their Calcutta agents, the Malwa merchants would also place large bets on the outcome of each auction. There were two market instruments through which bets were placed, both known as chitties (letters). The first kind was called tazi chittie (fresh letter) and it was intended for the bulls. The second kind was called mandi chittie (bazaar letter) and it was for the bears, to short the market. The bulls were known as taziwallahs and the bears were known as mandiwallahs.[25] The chitties could be written to cover any span of time, from a month to many years.

All in all, it was a remarkably modern marketplace, with its trading scrips and its proto-Bloombergian information systems. The market even had its own encryption system to ensure the secrecy of every transaction. For the uninitiated, the functioning of this system was a marvel to behold.

In *Flood of Fire*, Zachary watches in astonishment as Baboo Nob Kissin makes a deal with a futures trader:

[W]ithout saying a word aloud, both men began to make rapid gestures with their hands and fingers. All of a sudden, the Baboo thrust his hands under the shawl that lay draped over the broker's lap. The shawl began to bounce and writhe as their hidden fingers twined with each other, twisting and turning in a secret dance. Gradually these motions built to a climax and a shudder of understanding passed through both of them; then their hands fell inert under the shawl and they exchanged a quiet smile.[26]

The functioning of these informal markets often astounded Western visitors: 'Intuitively they [the Indian traders] understand all the clap-trap of the Stock Exchange; with astonishing cleverness they put the market up and down with as much ease as the most experienced bulls and bears of the West.'[27]

Of the vast sums of money generated by the opium futures market, very little found its way to Bengali or Bihari businessmen. Since the entire opium supply of eastern India was controlled by the colonial regime, the trading communities of the region had no supplies of their own to put into play, so to speak, and were effectively shut out of the futures market as well.

For the commercial networks of western and central India, on the other hand, the opium markets of Calcutta, formal and informal, were of such critical importance that it was necessary for them to maintain a significant presence there. Thus the opium poppy became the catalyst for another set of migratory movements: just as it had drawn Bengalis to Bihar, it also drew Marwaris to Bengal in increasing numbers.

'Opium,' writes the historian Thomas Timberg, 'was a natural commodity for Marwaris. They had been dealing with it in Malwa and their homelands, and especially in speculation in its price . . . The relative increase of the importance of Malwa over Bengal opium necessarily led to an increase in their importance as opium traders.'[28]

Over time Calcutta turned into a major hub for Marwaris, who became an integral part of the city's fabric, contributing richly to its cultural and social life. But because of the historical contingencies that moulded the economy of Bengal, the community also came to hold sway over the local economy to a degree that is without parallel in India. While Marwaris are leaders in commerce everywhere in the country, nowhere are they so completely dominant as in eastern India. Even in the south, local entrepreneurs figure prominently in the business world. Only in Bengal is this not the case.

Can all this be laid at the feet of the opium poppy? Of course not. The poppy played no part in establishing the Maratha kingdoms, for instance, and there were many pre-existing differences between the commercial worlds of eastern and western India. Yet, it is clear that the divergent patterns of the opium industries of eastern and western India 'laid the foundation for a much more dynamic economy in western India than in the east accounting for, to some extent, the current development of Bombay over Calcutta'.[29]

The tragedy, of course, is that it was Bihar, and its increasingly impoverished poppy farmers, that made it possible for the colonial regime to set up the drug-pushing racket that later became a gravy train for the opium industry of western India. Yet, sadly, in today's Mumbai, migrants from eastern UP and Bihar are often the targets of all manner of abuse and discrimination. In recent years, Bihari migrant workers in the city have even been physically assaulted by Marathi chauvinists for performing rituals for Chhath Puja, their most important religious observance of the year.[30] Yet, as Farooqui notes: 'Modern Bombay, in a sense, has its genesis in the poppy fields of Bihar.'[31]

Throughout the colonial era, Calcutta and Bombay defined the two opposed poles of India's political economy. Opium gave these two cities a major advantage over Madras, the oldest British settlement in India, which had once far exceeded Bombay in its commercial importance. But as Calcutta and Bombay flourished, Madras, lacking an opium-producing hinterland, gradually fell behind and became a 'backwater of Empire'.[32]

Of the three cities, Bombay was the upstart. In the early 1820s its exports amounted to less than a fourth of Calcutta's, but following the boom in the Malwa opium industry Bombay grew so rapidly that by mid-century it had caught up with Calcutta. After the Opium Wars, when all fetters were removed from the British Empire's drug-pushing racket, the value of Bombay's opium exports increased ten-fold. As the historian Claude Markovits observes: 'Before becoming the "Manchester of India", Bombay thus became its "Medellin".'[33]

But even though Calcutta and Bombay were both hubs of the opium trade, the ways in which business was conducted in the two cities were completely different. Calcutta was the capital of British India throughout the nineteenth century, and it had the largest number of white residents of any city in the country. Being the seat of British power its economy was largely controlled by the white business community, which was closely networked with colonial officials in India, many of whom invested their savings with them. There were further circles of exclusion even within the white business community, with a group of interconnected merchants of Scottish origin playing a dominant role. Race and community were thus central features of Calcutta's economic life, with a few Scottish firms exercising oligopolistic control over some parts of the business world. The Marwaris were their only significant competitors.

In Bombay, on the other hand, businessmen from many different backgrounds were able to operate on more equal terms. This was not a chance outcome: it was, rather, yet another legacy of the Marathas' protracted resistance to the British onslaught because of which 'Western India was conquered by the British at a later stage than Eastern India, thus escaping the period of unabashed exploitation which cost so dearly to indigenous merchants in Bengal'. As a result,

[T]he ethnic and communal diversity of Bombay's business
world was striking: it included merchants belonging to
many communities of Gujarat, including the Parsis, the
Hindu Vanias and Bhatias, the Muslim Bohras, Khojas and
Memons as well as businessmen from other provinces of
India (Sind, Marwar), Baghdadi Jews (the different branches
of the famous Sassoon family), non-British Europeans (the
Swiss firm of Volkarts), Japanese (Toyo Menka Kaisha) and
Britishers of various origins. The contrast was clear with the
increasingly polarized and oligopolistic world of Calcutta
where only two communities mattered: the Scots and the
Marwaris.[34]

The fact that the indigenous merchants of Bombay participated
directly in the export trade, spending long spells in China, also meant
that they had much more exposure to the outside world, so when
the explosive growth of the drug trade slowed down towards the
end of the nineteenth century, they were able to transition into other
industries, like textiles, yarn manufacturing, steel, cement, hotels and so
on. 'British Bombay, unlike Calcutta, was never essentially a colonial
city,' writes Gillian Tindall. 'The real life of Bombay was always lived
in . . . a more cosmopolitan and egalitarian setting; in warehouses . . . in
counting houses, in places where samples of raw cotton or opium or
silk or ivory or inlay-work were passed from hand to hand.'[35]

So while Bombay prospered, Calcutta's economy remained
quintessentially colonial, structured around racial and communal
hierarchies, and dependent on agricultural products like opium, jute
and tea, all wrung out of the soil by underpaid and ill-used workers.

These legacies have lived on. In today's Kolkata, the social lives of
businessmen and corporate executives still revolve around dowdy, old-
fashioned colonial clubs, which once catered largely, even exclusively,
to the city's white population. Even now the preferred garb at these

clubs is Western, and some of them will not permit kurtas and other Indian garments to be worn on the premises. Mumbai's businessmen are far flashier and more ostentatious than Kolkata's, but the city's social life is, in a curious way, strangely egalitarian, with billionaires and down-at-heel hucksters (and even writers) rubbing shoulders amicably at parties.

These differences in the two cities are not new. Rabindranath Tagore was struck by them as far back as 1939:

> I noticed one other thing in the city of Bombay. This was the wealth of the locals. How many Parsi, Muslim and Gujarati traders' names I saw emblazoned on the walls of mansions! So many names inscribed so prominently cannot be seen anywhere in Calcutta . . . The people of our region have not been able to experience wealth hence their miserliness is ugly, while their notion of extravagance is even more horrifying. It makes me happy to see that while the lifestyle of the rich people here is simple, they are liberal with their wealth.[36]

Such were the differences between the two cities that Mumbai became the country's economic and financial powerhouse, while Calcutta became the hotbed of India's radicalism, as well as a hub for the academic discipline of economics. Mumbai, it could be said, got the economy, while Calcutta got the economists.

As for radicalism, West Bengal's legacies of poverty and inequality ensured that communist ideologies would have a wide appeal in the region. And so it was that in the 1960s the state became the cradle of a long-lasting Maoist insurgency. Then in 1977 a communist-led coalition came to power in the state and went on to win election after election, until they were finally voted out in 2012. The hammer-and-sickle symbol was a common sight on the city's walls long after it had disappeared into museums elsewhere.

What gives Bengal's anti-capitalist tradition its depth and strength? I, personally, have no doubt that the peculiar conditions of eastern India's opium economy played some part in the gestation of this element of Bengal's culture. The fact that local traders and small businessmen were excluded from the region's most lucrative industry certainly meant that an indigenous capitalist class could not develop at the same pace as it had in the Bombay Presidency. To those who were shut out by the colonial opium monopoly it would have seemed self-evident that markets were always rigged, as such, and could not be trusted.

But these attitudes also nurtured another, quite different, set of beliefs: if it is in the nature of markets to be rigged, then it follows that all you have to do to make money is find players who know how to rig them. Thus Calcutta also became—and has long remained— the Ponzi scheme capital of India: the city's inhabitants seem to be drawn, like moths to a flame, to financial scams, which are known locally as 'chit funds'. Repeatedly, decade after decade, Bengalis have shown themselves to be peculiarly prone to squandering their life's savings on pyramid schemes started by hucksters who are usually also Bengalis. The inevitable collapse of these schemes has brought ruin upon hundreds of thousands of ordinary middle-class and lower-middle-class people, many of whom are otherwise quite worldly.

One such was my own father, a widely travelled World War II veteran. In retirement in Calcutta, swept along by one of the city's periodic waves of mass delusion, he put a large part of his savings in a chit fund called Sanchayita. Inevitably, the fund collapsed within a couple of years, ruining some 130,000 people and making things difficult for my family. Fortunately, my father had made another, perhaps equally risky, investment by gambling a large part of his modest earnings on giving me a schooling that was well beyond his means. Fortunately this gamble turned out better than his chit fund venture.

Looking back now, I realize that my father's decision to invest in my education probably owed a great deal to the experiences of his displaced forefathers. If there was anything they had learnt from the loss of their ancestral village, it was that the only sure hedge against floods and fires, the only thing that cannot be lost or taken away, is an education.

For the Indians involved in the opium trade, the fact that they were colluding in the smuggling of a substance that was illegal in China, and thereby bringing misery to millions of Chinese, seems to have been even less of a concern than it was to British and American opium traders. As Farooqui notes, no Indian merchants are known to have expressed any qualms about their activities. Yet, it was a Parsi, Dadabhai Naoroji, who became one of the earliest and most important Indian voices to speak out against the colonial opium trade. Born into a poor Parsi family in Navsari, Naoroji became a mathematician, scholar and public figure, both in India and Britain. He spent a good part of his life in London and was even elected to Parliament from 1892 to 1895.[37]

In his 1901 tract, *Poverty and Un-British Rule in India*, Naoroji writes:

What a spectacle [the opium trade] is to the world! In England no Statesman dares to propose that opium may be allowed to be sold in public houses at the corners of every street, in the same way as beer or spirits. On the contrary, Parliament, as representing the whole nation, distinctly enacts that 'opium and all preparations of opium or of "poppies," as "poison," be sold by certified chemists only, and every box, bottle, vessel, wrapper, or cover in which such poison is contained, be

distinctly labelled with the name of the article and the word
"poison," and with the name and address of the seller of the
poison.' And yet, at the other end of the world, this Christian,
highly civilised, and humane England forces a 'heathen' and
'barbarous' Power to take this 'poison,' and tempts a vast
human race to use it, and to degenerate and demoralise
themselves with this 'poison'! . . . It is wonderful how England
reconciles this to her conscience. This opium trade is a sin on
England's head, and a curse on India for her share in being the
instrument.[38]

Like Dadabhai Naoroji, many of the activists who campaigned
against the colonial opium trade were from Bombay's hinterlands,
most notably women like Pandita Ramabai and Soonderbai Powar.[39]
And it was an eminent public figure from western India, Gopal
Krishna Gokhale, who said, in 1907: 'I have always felt a sense of deep
humiliation at the thought of this [opium] revenue, derived as it is
practically from the degradation and moral ruin of the people of
China.'[40]

Indians would do well to remember these words every time they
are assailed by a sense of grievance in relation to China.

ELEVEN
Diasporas

The rationale for the colonial opium trade was provided by the ideology of free market capitalism, as embodied in the doctrine of Free Trade. It was in the name of this doctrine that Britain launched both its wars against China in the nineteenth century. And it is certainly a fact that the opium trade played a major part in laying the foundations of the globalized world market as we know it today. But this emergent marketplace, far from being an open arena in which individuals could compete freely based on their merits and abilities, was almost exactly the opposite: it was a closed, exclusive sphere, dominated by a variety of secretive and extremely clannish groups. No matter whether European or Asian, they were all held together by shared ethnicity, race or caste. Instead of being free, the operations of this marketplace were more like those of that spectral nether region that has always haunted capitalism: the underworld.

Among the many groups that formed this shadowy world, some of the most important were merchant communities that had been displaced from their native soil by war, persecution or political conflict. One such was the Armenian diaspora, whose dispersal from their homeland dates back to the conquest of the territory by the Seljuk Turks in the eleventh century.[1] Because of Armenia's geographical position athwart Eurasian trade routes, the region's merchants had an intimate understanding of the functioning of long-distance commerce. This enabled them to spread out widely along maritime and continental trade routes, establishing thriving settlements not only in major port cities like Amsterdam in the west and Guangzhou in the east, but also deep in the interior of Asia and Africa, in Tibet and Ethiopia.[2]

Some of the regions in which Armenian merchants were most active were the Ottoman, Safavid and Mughal Empires.[3] India was particularly welcoming of Armenians: the Emperor Akbar, one of whose wives, Mariam Begum Saheba, happened to be Armenian, personally invited them to settle in Agra, the Mughal capital. The first Armenian church there was established in 1562, and the community was quickly absorbed into the Mughal elite, serving as judges, governors and generals. In some parts of the Empire, such as Bengal, Armenians established thriving enclaves: the oldest Armenian grave in Calcutta dates back to 1630, many decades before the city was formally founded by the East India Company.[4] Indeed, Armenian intermediaries were instrumental in procuring the Mughal land grant that made it possible for the East India Company to establish a colony in Bengal.[5]

In short: the Armenian diaspora was active throughout those parts of Asia where the use of opium was spreading in the fifteenth and sixteenth centuries, and Armenians were also often members of the courtly elites who were beginning to use the drug at that time. This suggests that Armenian merchants were dealing in opium even before European colonial powers arrived in the Indian Ocean: they were probably among the many groups of traders and merchants who sold small quantities of opium, along with spices and other medicinal substances, not only in pre-colonial India but also across Southeast Asia.

By the time the British Empire began to ramp up its opium operation in Bihar, Armenian merchants were already an important presence in eastern India, so it was inevitable that they would be drawn into this enormously lucrative commerce. Like European and American 'private traders', Armenian merchants and shipowners were part of the clandestine conveyor belt that the East India Company relied on to smuggle its drugs into China and Southeast Asia. In the Dutch East Indies, especially in Java, there were many Armenian 'agency houses' that dealt in wholesale opium. 'Armenian firms with offices in Surabaya dominated this trade,' writes the historian James Rush. 'They purchased opium via agents in Turkey, India and Singapore for their Chinese clients and delivered it in Bali.'[6]

Armenian networks also often helped to subvert the Dutch regime's attempts to establish complete control over opium in the Indonesian archipelago. This dual role, of collusion and subversion (much like the smuggling activities of the Malwa trading networks), was a marked feature of the relationship between highly militarized and violence-prone colonial powers, like the Dutch and the British, and stateless merchant communities, like the Armenian diaspora, who had no armed forces or territorial ambitions of their own. The relationship was not a simple one of collaboration: Armenians themselves were often preyed upon by colonizers, who did not hesitate to seize their goods and ships.[7] As against the power of the colonizers, stateless diasporas also held some strong cards of their own, of which perhaps the most vital was their access to information: they were not only knowledgeable about the methods and institutions of Europeans, but were also intimately familiar with the practices of indigenous networks, and were often able to use this to their advantage.

Like the Armenians, but many centuries earlier, the Zoroastrian Parsis were also displaced from their ancestral homeland in Persia by war and conquest: from the eighth century onwards, groups of Parsis began to take refuge in Gujarat, and in the twelfth century they established what would become the historic heart of Parsi culture and religion in Navsari, near Surat. Hundreds of years later, when Surat became a major hub for European traders, Parsis, like Armenians, served as translators and intermediaries.

Merchant communities of every variety have much in common, and this was perhaps especially true of Parsis and Armenians, whose ancestral homelands had bordered on each other. They were alike also in sharing an interstitial position between colonized and colonizer— regarded by the British as essential intermediaries but also as potential rivals and competitors. The networks of the Armenian diaspora were, of course, older and more widespread, and they were well-versed in negotiating privileges with European powers, including the East India Company, with which they had concluded a special treaty as far back as 1688.

It is hardly surprising then that Armenians played an important role in opening new pathways for the Parsis, including, possibly, the route to China. Indeed, the first Parsi who is known to have travelled to China, a merchant by the name of Heerji Jeevanji Readymoney, actually sailed on an Armenian ship in 1756.[8] The connections between Parsis and Armenians would endure over many generations, into the twentieth century.

In the Ibis Trilogy too there is a close connection between an Armenian and a Parsi character: Bahram Modi's most intimate confidante is the Armenian watchmaker Zadig Karabedian.

In the Trilogy, Bahram Modi, like many Parsi notables, is a native son of Navsari, born into a once-prosperous family that has fallen upon hard times. But this chapter of his life is a distant backstory, far predating the timeline of the novels. This being the case, I did not feel it necessary to visit Navsari at the time of writing *River of Smoke*, the novel in which Bahram Modi makes his first appearance. Strangely it was the book itself that provided me with a passage to the town: soon after the novel's publication, in 2011, I was invited to speak at one of Navsari's most venerable Parsi institutions, the Meherjirana Library. Founded in 1872, the library is now a leading centre for scholarship on Zoroastrianism and Parsi history.

To speak at the Meherjirana Library to an audience that included many prominent Parsi historians and scholars was a daunting task, especially since my talk was intended to convey what a young Parsi merchant of the early nineteenth century might have made of Guangzhou. This was something I had given considerable thought to while writing *River of Smoke*, and there is a scene in the novel where Bahram Modi nostalgically recollects his youthful first impressions of a lavish banquet at a Chinese merchant's country estate:

[H]e recalled how he had stared, open-mouthed and unashamed, at the exquisite pavilions, the carved griffins, the terraced gardens and landscaped lakes—he had seen things whose very existence he could not have imagined. He remembered how eagerly he had attacked the food, delighting in the unknown aromas and unfamiliar tastes; he remembered the heady taste of the rice wine, and how it had seemed to him that he had stepped into some kind of waking dream: how was it possible that he, a penniless chokra from Navsari, had wandered into a place that seemed to belong in some legendary firdaus? It seemed to him now that he would gladly trade all his years of experience, all his knowledge of the world, to be granted once again an instant of such incandescent wonder—a moment in which, even in the midst of so many new and amazing things, nothing would seem more extraordinary than that he, a poor boy from a Gujarat village, had found his way into a Chinese garden.

While writing this passage I had assumed that in the early nineteenth century, when Parsi merchants were just beginning to travel eastwards in large numbers, a lad from Navsari would be completely unprepared for what he would encounter in China, that this experience would be absolutely new for the entire community and that young Bahram would not have heard stories about Malacca or Guangzhou from older relatives. But those assumptions crumbled when I went to visit the birthplaces of two real Navsari-born China traders who became titans in the commercial world of Bombay: Sir Jamsetjee Jejeebhoy (1783–1859) and Sir Jamsetji Tata (1839–1904), the founder of Tata Sons, now one of the largest corporate groups in the world.

The birthplaces of these two magnates, who were born almost half a century apart, are only a few hundred metres from each other, and both are now maintained as museums by family trusts. The dwellings are very alike: narrow-fronted row houses that would once have been flanked by similar structures on both sides. But they are now among the last remaining examples of their kind. The houses have roofs that are pitched from front to back, with two floors beneath. The upper floors are like attics or storage lofts, running the length of each home, and are connected to the lower floor by ladders, not staircases.

The ground floors of the two houses consist of a number of tiny rooms branching off corridors that stretch through the buildings, running past cramped little kitchens and water cisterns before opening out into small, white-walled courtyards where lie the outhouses. Both residences are so modest that it is impossible not to marvel at the thought that there lie the roots of some of the world's largest fortunes.

Yet, what was most striking about the houses, to me, was that their layout does not conform to any of the usual styles of Indian vernacular construction: they appear to have more in common, architecturally speaking, with the 'shophouses' of Malacca, Singapore and Guangzhou. This suggests that their design was influenced by the early maritime connections that once linked the coastal regions of the Indian Ocean, creating visual and structural continuities that caused those regions to have more in common with each other than with their hinterlands.

Since Sir Jamsetjee Jejeebhoy was born in 1783, this would mean that architectural influences from eastern Asia had already seeped into coastal Gujarat before his birth. For any enterprising young man growing up in these circumstances, venturing overseas, rather than deeper into the subcontinent, would probably have seemed the obvious choice even before the colonial opium traffic got fully under way. In other words, it is very likely that, contrary to my assumptions, a boy like Bahram Modi, growing up in Navsari in the early years of the nineteenth century, would have been sur-rounded by people who had stories to tell about China and South-east Asia.

Was I wrong, then, in my imagining of Bahram's youthful first impressions of Guangzhou? Not necessarily. The sense of wonder that we experience when we set our eyes upon a storied city is usually deepened by what we have heard about it. It is when we go to a place for which we have no imaginative context that we tend to be unmoved.

While all the commercial communities of western India were involved in the China trade, the Parsi role in it was, in one significant respect, different from that of the other groups. Generally speaking, the involvement of Indian merchants in dispatching goods to China did not extend beyond the coast: for some Hindu commercial castes, in fact, there were prohibitions on crossing the sea, and those who violated them would either lose caste or have to go through elaborate purification rituals. So, instead of travelling to China themselves, these merchants would consign their goods to agents or 'agency houses' with representatives in Guangzhou, who were experienced in conducting trade with the Chinese. The agents would carry the goods to China and bring back the returns in exchange for a percentage of the profits. This was known as the consignment system and the majority of Indian consignment agencies were run by Parsis, who generally charged less than the big British and American firms like Jardine Matheson & Co. or Russell & Co.[9] This allowed many small speculators in Bombay to participate in the opium trade: '[E]very cooks servant labourer speculating in this drug,' Jamsetjee Jejeebhoy complained in 1845, 'some of them making handsome profits'.[10]

So broad based was the participation in Bombay's opium trade that in 1842 no less than 163 individuals and firms petitioned the colonial government for a share of the reparations that China was forced to pay after the end of the First Opium War. Of these petitioners, as Madhavi Thampi and Shalini Saksena point out in their excellent study, *China and the Making of Bombay*, 'less than one-third were Parsis, while the rest, judging from the names, appear to be Jains or Marwaris and other Hindus'.[11]

The distinctiveness of the Parsi role in the opium trade, then, lay in the fact that they accounted for the majority of the non-Western merchants who were present in Guangzhou in the years before the First Opium War. At times they even outnumbered merchants of other nationalities. In 1831, for instance, there were forty-one Parsis in Guangzhou's Foreign Enclave, as against thirty-two English and twenty-one American merchants.[12] Thus, inasmuch as the Indo-Chinese relationship had a human face in the nineteenth century, that face belonged to the Parsis. This is why they are one of the few groups in the subcontinent to retain a vivid collective memory of the China connection.

However, the subcontinental contingent in Guangzhou's Foreign Enclave did not, by any means, consist only of merchants: among the forty-one Parsis present there in 1831, for instance, there were five clerks and fifteen servants. A great number of lascars also circulated through the city, and many of the accountants, servants, shroffs, guards and gatekeepers who staffed the British and other factories were also from Hindustan. Indeed, it is quite possible that, numerically speaking, Indians were the single largest group of foreigners in Guangzhou in the early nineteenth century.

Guangzhou in the period before the First Opium War was the strangest of entrepôts. It was the only Chinese port where foreigners were allowed to conduct trade, but the conditions that were imposed on them were extremely restrictive. Oddly enough, this worked to the advantage of the Parsi merchants.

The 'Canton system', as it has been called, evolved slowly over the early eighteenth century at a time when the Chinese were growing increasingly apprehensive of European intentions. Because of their connections with the Chinese diaspora in Southeast Asia, it was not unknown to Qing officials that the modus operandi of European colonizers was to first set up small, seemingly innocuous trading posts where they would take up residence with their wives and children. They would then gradually fortify the settlements and turn them into command centres for territorial conquest.[13]

The Dutch did, in fact, make an attempt to do this right on the Pearl River. When they first arrived in Guangzhou, in 1601, the Chinese trustingly gave them a small island opposite the city to use as a warehouse. But the Dutch tried to turn the island into a fortified base by smuggling in cannons hidden in barrels: the plot fell apart when one of the barrels broke and a cannon spilled out. They were then driven out by local officials, not by force, but by 'sanctions'—that is the withholding of food and water.[14]

The British too were sometimes so aggressive in their dealings with the Chinese that they left an impression 'of the proverbial bull entering the China shop'.[15] For example, in 1637, one Captain John Weddell forced his way up the Pearl River and even bombarded Guangzhou.[16]

These incidents were not forgotten, and Chinese officials took several steps to prevent such disruptions in the future. In 1757, the Qianlong Emperor, who ruled at the zenith of the Qing dynasty, decreed that foreign trade with China would be funnelled exclusively through Guangzhou, which is 100 kilometres inland from the South China Sea.[17] Even within Guangzhou, only a few licensed Chinese merchants, known as the Cohong guild, were authorized to do business with foreigners.[18] Moreover, aliens (often referred to as 'fan-qui') were permitted to reside only in a small enclave that was 180 metres outside the southwestern corner of Guangzhou's battlements, and was, therefore, not considered a part of the city itself. They were allowed to remain there only for the duration of the trading season (roughly September to March) and could not enter the city proper.[19] They were not allowed to keep weapons or use sedan chairs, and every foreigner was required to hire a local comprador to supply him with food, servants etc.[20] There were many other restrictions as well, but perhaps the most important among them was that foreigners could not bring their wives or children to Guangzhou—this measure was intended to prevent them from establishing a permanent presence. Although, in principle, the compradors were not allowed to provide the foreigners with 'boys or courtesans', many merchants (including Bahram Modi) had Chinese mistresses or wives.[21]

The physical constraints of the Foreign Enclave matched these legal restrictions.[22] The area consisted of a narrow strip of shore, a quarter of a mile in length and half that in breadth. This thin shelf of land was known as the Thirteen Factories, because it was the site of thirteen large buildings ('factories'), each of which was, in fact, a complex of houses that served both as residential quarters and premises of business.[23] In appearance, according to the eighteenth-century Chinese writer Shen Fu, they were 'just like . . . a foreign painting'.[24] Although the factories belonged, in principle, to the Cohong guild, most of them came to be associated, over time, with a particular flag—British, French, Danish, Austro-Hungarian, Swedish, American and so on (see insert image 10).[25] The Americans occupied the French factory for a while but were later largely accommodated in the Swedish factory.[26] Each of the factories had its own conventions and usages; the residents inevitably lived cheek by jowl and spent a lot of time together, often eating at the same table.

To live in Guangzhou, then, was like being confined within a luxurious, exclusively male seraglio—a 'Golden Ghetto', to borrow American historian Jacques M. Downs's memorable phrase.[27] This is how a young American trader, newly arrived in Guangzhou, described the factories in a letter to his brother in New York:

[They] are very large and commodious buildings, the dining room and parlours are on the 2nd floor, and very large and nicely furnished, and filled with handsome pictures, on the next floor the sleeping rooms . . . the Counting rooms are arranged in fine Style, the front one being for the partners and the back ones for the Clerk's, each one has a desk for himself, and if you want anything you have only to ring your bell, and your boy is at your Side.[28]

Life in this ghetto was exceedingly luxurious. Merchants would begin the day with an elaborate bath in a fancy tub; after that a stroll and breakfast, which consisted of rice, cakes, toast, curry, eggs and fish. At noon, a light lunch was offered in the dining room. Dinner, served at about six-thirty, was a great social occasion: there were always many courses, accompanied by several kinds of wine, beer and India ale, and the meals would end with brandy and long black Manila cheroots.[29]

Social life in the Thirteen Factories was a curious blend of conviviality and convention, boisterousness and reserve.[30] 'The Europeans at Canton do not associate together so freely as might be expected,' observed Major Samuel Shaw, the first American consul in Guangzhou, 'the gentlemen of the respective factories keeping much by themselves, and, excepting a few instances, observing a very ceremonious and reserved behaviour.'[31] But at the same time these merchants would also regularly dance with each other—a necessity imposed on them by the absence of women. In a sense it was this very lack that accounted for their adherence to convention. As one foreign merchant wrote: 'We are such a mixture of gentlemen, sailors, and all of us necessarily batchelors, while at Canton, a certain etiquette is quite necessary to keep us from becoming as the Chinese say many of us are—"half wild mans".'[32]

Like a tall-masted ship, the Foreign Enclave had its own rituals and hierarchies, and like most ocean-going vessels of that period, it too was presided over by Europeans—in this case by the British, who were at this time falling increasingly under the sway of racist ideologies. To imagine the challenges a subcontinental merchant would have faced in gaining a toehold in such a place is not difficult. Even the simplest aspects of life in the Foreign Enclave would have presented a problem. Where, for instance, was the Bombay merchant to live?[33] Despite the large number of Hindustanis in Guangzhou, there was no Indian factory. The story goes that in the early years of the trade, because of connections that stretched all the way back to seventeenth-century Surat, Parsis were given accommodation in the Dutch factory.[34] Later, as the number of Bombay merchants grew, they gravitated towards one particular factory, the Fungtai, that came to be known as the 'Chow-Chow' (or miscellaneous) factory.[35]

Although the Bombay merchants were at a disadvantage in some respects, they did hold one very powerful card: their access to indigenous trading networks, which gave them the ability to procure Malwa opium at the best possible prices.[36] This created symbiotic interests that overrode some formidable social barriers and laid the foundations of many lucrative partnerships: the relationship that developed between Jamsetjee Jejeebhoy and William Jardine of Jardine Matheson & Co. is but one example.[37]

Another factor that made it possible for Parsis to operate success-fully in Guangzhou was their relative freedom from many of the taboos and dietary restrictions that made socializing with foreigners difficult for orthodox Hindus and Muslims. Indeed, dietary prejudices may have long played an important, though largely unnoticed, role in creating barriers between Indians and Chinese people. Even though certain 'Indian Chinese' dishes are very popular in India today, some aspects of Chinese cuisine still evoke extreme aversion, especially among the upper-caste, often vegetarian, diplomats and bureaucrats who dominate India's policymaking circles. The writer Pallavi Aiyar has even suggested that the antipathy that many Indians feel towards China stems from the idea that 'they eat everything'.[38]

Attitudes of that kind would certainly have created insuperable barriers in Guangzhou's Foreign Enclave, where socializing over shared meals was essential to the conduct of business. Such meals would almost always have included meat, which in itself would have served to exclude conservative Hindu merchants, many of whom were vegetarian: for them even to enter a house where beef was served meant losing caste. Similar prohibitions would have applied to Muslim merchants in relation to pork, alcohol and many other items that were greatly relished by Westerners and Chinese alike.

Parsis, by contrast, were not subject to any such dietary restrictions and were able to participate wholeheartedly in the Foreign Enclave's rituals of commensality, such as the lavish feasts that were regularly thrown by British and American merchants, and the multi-course, hours-long banquets that the Cohong merchants liked to host at their country estates. Many Parsi traders were great hosts themselves: '[T]he Parsees are the most remarkable of any of the races in Canton,' wrote an American traveller. 'They give feasts, and drink wine, and cheer vociferously, and are a jolly set.'[39] As a result many Parsis were able to develop close partnerships with leading Chinese merchants. Sir Jamsetjee Jejeebhoy, for example, had a very good rapport with the most important of the Cohong merchants, Wu Bingjian (known as Howqua to foreigners), who was, at the time, possibly the richest man in the world.[40]

Yet, at the same time, the Parsi traders of South China were extremely insistent on maintaining their own distinctive identity. They always wore Parsi robes and headgear, for instance, which earned them the moniker 'White Hat Aliens'. Nor were their relations with their British and American counterparts always easy. Indeed, Parsis, like Jews and Armenians, were in a position that was at once privileged but also, in some respects, marginal. This made them extremely assertive, and even touchy, when they encountered white racism. At one social event, perhaps the most famous of its time, this almost led to a brawl.

The event was an enormous, riotous party, held just before the onset of the opium crisis of 1839: it was in honour of William Jardine, who was embarking for England armed with a huge slush fund collected by foreign merchants for the purpose of bribing British politicians and journalists to support a war against China (an enterprise in which Jardine succeeded beyond all measure).[41] Since Jardine's partnerships with Bombay merchants were essential to his business, several Parsis were among the invitees and they presented him with a princely gift: a silver dinner service valued at 1,000 guineas.[42] Many toasts were drunk over the course of the evening, and one of the toasters wished the guest of honour, who was then in his mid-fifties, good luck in finding a wife who was the 'fairest of the fair'. Jardine's response was that he very much doubted that a man of his age deserved 'the fairest of the fair', and that he would be content with 'some dame "fat, fair and forty"'.[43] This was greeted with loud huzzahs and the senior merchants rose to join the dancing, which was already under way. Jardine himself took the lead, waltzing with his close friend, William Wetmore, to music provided by a ship's band.[44]

At around 3 a.m., according to a letter that an American trader, Robert Bennet Forbes, wrote to his wife the next day, '[A] young Scotchman cried—"let us clear the table & send those d____d Parsees home & then we will have supper!!!"' This angered the Parsis so much that a fight would have broken out had Forbes not intervened and made them all shake hands: '[I]t was of course imperatively necessary then to have a parting glass by way of good fellowship and reconciliation'.[45]

Apart from Guangzhou, Parsis, like traders of other nationalities, also had a significant presence in Macao, where the first Parsi association was formed in 1822. So significant was the community's presence in the Pearl River Delta that Parsis had their own cemetery near Whampoa.[46] It was built around 1847 and was in use until 1923.[47] It now falls within the premises of a large shipping company, and obtaining permission to visit it is difficult. However, in 2011, the distinguished historian Tansen Sen, one of the leading experts on the connections between India and China, was able to make arrangements for us to visit the cemetery together.

The cemetery is tucked away at the top of an overgrown hillock with the shipyard's cranes looming over it: to get to it we had to fight our way through masses of luxuriant greenery. The graves are stately, flat-topped granite sepulchres, some of them inscribed with Gujarati as well as English letters, now so worn that they are hard to decipher. Among the more legible, there is one that reads: 'To the memory of Burjorjee Eduljee Kotwal, Parsee inhabitant of Bombay who departed this life at Canton on the 1st Day of August 1850, and the 9th day of the 11th Month of Yazdezerd 1219, in the 36th Year of his Age.'

In Hong Kong, Parsis had an even more significant presence, with an Agiary, or fire temple, that exists to this day, on Causeway Bay. The Parsi cemetery there was built in 1852, in Happy Valley, and is still a beautifully maintained haven of tranquillity amidst the frenetic bustle of the city.[48] The Parsis of Hong Kong lived mainly around Wyndham Street, which was once 'known as "Malacca" by the Chinese for its ubiquitous Indian presence'.[49] Even though Hong Kong's Parsi community has now dwindled to only about 200 members, Parsi names are scattered all over the city. A major road is named after Sir Hormusjee Naorojee Mody, a former opium auctioneer who became a real estate tycoon and philanthropist, helping to found Hong Kong University and many other important institutions. Sir Hormusjee's business partner was an Armenian from Calcutta, Sir Catchick Paul Chater, who became one of the wealthiest business magnates in Hong Kong. Long-time friends, Chater and Mody both had grand houses on Conduit Road and were responsible for reclaiming a part of the land the city now stands on. Another Parsi name that is often seen on the streets of Hong Kong is Kotewall, because of Sir Robert Hormus Kotewall, a prominent businessman and legislator. Although Sir Robert Kotewall's name came from his Parsi father, he was, in fact, a member of a somewhat different group: the Sino-Indian community of southern China. Many Parsi traders had Chinese mistresses, with whom they fathered children. Although this part of their lives was generally kept hidden from their families back home in Bombay, the merchants were by no means neglectful of their children. Many were taken into their firms and became an essential part of their business operations.

Over time the Sino-Indians of South China merged into the much larger Eurasian community that has done so much to make Hong Kong a vibrant and cosmopolitan city. Indeed (as I discovered while writing this), Sir Robert Kotewall's descendants include the Hollywood star Max Minghella, whose mother, Carolyn Jane Choa, is from Hong Kong, and whose father was the late Anthony Minghella, director of *The English Patient* and *The Talented Mr Ripley*.

While many Parsi merchants made enormous amounts of money in China, that was not necessarily the most valuable part of what they gained from their time there.[50] Through their connections with Western and Chinese businessmen they also learnt about the economic and industrial transformations that were then underway in Europe and America. This, in turn, gave them a considerable advantage over other Indian commercial communities when it came to branching out into new businesses, which they did with great gusto. The fact that many of them came back from China with plenty of capital allowed them to launch many new ventures. Parsi entrepreneurs thus became the pioneers of Indian industry and commerce, plunging into banking and insurance, and setting up textile mills, steel plants and many different kinds of factories and manufacturing units. They were also quick to embrace the fossil fuel economy, and became leaders in the use of steam in the timber, cotton and shipping industries. Parsis founded the Bombay Steam Navigation Company, which had a fleet of steamers that sailed all along the west coast of the subcontinent, from Karachi to Colombo.[51] And it was a Parsi who founded Hong Kong's iconic Star Ferries.

This Parsi tradition of innovation and entrepreneurship has left a lasting legacy, one that was made apparent during the COVID-19 pandemic, when it suddenly came to light that the world's largest manufacturer of AstraZeneca's Covishield vaccine was a little-known Parsi-owned company in Pune. For a while this company, the Serum Institute of India, founded by the Parsi entrepreneur Cyrus Poonawalla, seemed to hold the fate of a greater part of humanity in its hands.

Bombay and its hinterlands thus benefited from Malwa's opium in multiple ways. Not only did the wealth generated by the region's poppy farmers seep into the pockets of more people, but the returns on opium that were brought back from China also fostered a culture of innovation and entrepreneurship. The opium that was exported from Calcutta, on the other hand, brought no such gains to the city or its hinterland: the trade conferred its benefits instead on Britain, the United States and Europe.

It is tempting to attribute Bombay's success primarily to the commercial culture of western India. Yet, it must be remembered that it was ultimately the Maratha states' determined resistance to the British Empire that laid the groundwork for the success of the region's businessmen. Nor can it be forgotten that the burden of that success was borne by the opium users and addicts of Southeast Asia and China.

Of course, opium was not the only commodity that Bombay's merchants exported: cotton also played a very important role in their trade with China.[52] But opium was the 'keystone commodity' of their business, and what the historian Jacques M. Downs says of American traders in China applies no less to Indians: '. . . the entire China trade, was based on the opium traffic . . . Without opium it is difficult to see how the legitimate China trade could have developed.'[53]

Another diasporic group that became enormously important in the colonial opium trade was the community known as Baghdadi Jews. The name derives from the Babylonian (or Baghdadi) rites followed by most members of the community, not from their places of origin, which were, in fact, extremely diverse, ranging from many parts of the Middle East to North Africa and Central Asia.[54] But the community was always tiny, its numbers never amounting to more than 8,000.

The first Baghdadi Jews to come to India migrated in the 1700s, but it was not until the early nineteenth century that increasing Ottoman persecution forced many of them to move out. One such man, who became the patriarch of the community, was David Sassoon, a scion of a wealthy family who had actually served as the treasurer of Baghdad for twelve years before he arrived in Bombay in 1832, at the age of forty. Within a few decades David Sassoon was able to gain control of Malwa's opium sales, which he then used to dictate prices at the opium auctions in Calcutta. He did this so effectively that 'by 1871 Sassoons took control of the opium markets on both sides of India'.[55] The family firm, David Sassoon & Co., soon branched out along the transit routes for opium, with offices in Singapore, Hong Kong and Shanghai. While maintaining its monopoly on Indian opium, the firm also diversified into many other industries—a story that has been very well told in innumerable books.[56]

Known as the Rothschilds of the East, the Sassoons ultimately did marry into the famous banking dynasty—and into many other aristocratic families, eventually becoming completely assimilated into the British upper class. In Asia, the Sassoon name lives on today in every major hub of the opium trade, in the innumerable buildings, docks, libraries, factories, synagogues, hospitals and other institutions that the family founded in Bombay, Calcutta, Singapore, Hong Kong and Shanghai.[57]

Even though Parsi and Baghdadi opium traders were rivals and competitors, they also frequently collaborated in setting up new enterprises. Perhaps the most important, and certainly the longest-lived, of their partnerships was the Hong Kong and Shanghai Banking Corporation, which was set up in 1865. Of the fourteen members of the founding committee, three were Parsis and one was a representative of David Sassoon & Co.[58] Needless to add, the bank's rapid expansion owed a great deal to its funding of the opium trade.[59] The fact that this company, better known as HSBC, is today one of the world's largest banks is an indication of the extent to which the institutions of modern globalized capitalism are founded on opium.

Even more than Bombay, it was Singapore that was kept afloat by opium. As Carl Trocki puts it, Singapore's founding came about as a 'peripheral result of the India-China opium trade', so the city 'was born with opium in its very blood'.[60] But Singapore was also a free market experiment—there were no taxes on trade and no duties on imports or exports—made possible only because of opium, which generally provided about half the city's revenues. No less than 20 per cent of India's opium ended up in Singapore every year: although much of it was redistributed throughout the region, a large part was also consumed in the city. In effect, the 'rhythms of the opium trade more or less governed the economic development of nineteenth-century Singapore'.[61]

In Singapore, as in most of Southeast Asia, opium was administered through the so-called 'farm' system, wherein the right to import raw opium belonged solely to the colonial authorities; the rights to process and sell the drug were periodically auctioned off to local bidders. The merchant or, more commonly, the syndicate that put in the winning bid was known as the 'farmer', and the network of processing centres and dens where the raw opium was distilled into smokeable chandu was the 'farm'. There were many such farms in the British territories around Singapore. The island of Java also had many farms and farmers, and their bids 'yielded great sums of revenue for the island's Dutch administration'.[62] However, the official farms handled only a part of the opium that filtered through the region: powerful smuggling networks made sure that there was an active black market, which may, in fact, have controlled much more opium than the legal farms.[63]

Throughout Southeast Asia the opium farms were almost always run by diasporic Chinese merchants and syndicates.[64] In most of the region the consumers—usually plantation workers and miners—were also largely Chinese, but in some places, such as Java, opium was widely smoked by the indigenous population as well.[65] In Java there was a common saying among Dutch colonizers: 'The Javanese plows and sows. The Chinese gathers it in. And the European walks away with it.'[66]

Among the Chinese who ran the opium farms, many belonged to the Peranakan community, a diasporic group with deep roots in the region.[67] As with the Parsis and Armenians, countless early Chinese migrants in Southeast Asia were displaced by war, rebellion and political turmoil in their homeland, especially during the tumultuous transition between the Ming and Qing dynasties. Like Parsis in India, the Peranakan were gradually assimilated into Southeast Asian culture: not only did they, like Parsis, speak local languages and wear clothes that were adapted from local garments, but they, like Parsis, also evolved a hybrid and very highly refined cuisine. Many Peranakan men married Southeast Asian women; some also adopted the majority religion, Islam. At the same time, the Peranakan also held on to a distinctive identity and were careful to maintain their connections with their native regions in China. Again, like Parsis, the

Peranakan were culturally nimble and were able to adapt very well to the colonial regimes of the British, Dutch and French, for whom they served as essential interlocutors and intermediaries.

Across Southeast Asia, Peranakan merchants controlled many plantations and mines, in which thousands of poor Chinese migrants toiled under terrible conditions: for most of these workers opium was a necessity just to get through the day. 'In dulling their very real pain, opium made them insensitive to the long-term damage their exhausting labor was doing to their own bodies. They could literally work themselves to death without feeling much pain.'[68]

The dens and outlets from which the workers bought their opium were often run by the same merchants and syndicates who owned the mines or plantations.[69] In numerous instances, it was the opium farm, rather than a mine or a plantation, that generated the bulk of the owners' profits. Opium thus became a very important source of capital accumulation for diasporic Chinese elites in Southeast Asia.

Apart from the Peranakan, several other migrant Chinese groups, particularly the brotherhoods and syndicates known as the kongsi (or 'secret societies' as colonial authorities liked to label them), were able to work their way up the economic and social ladder through the farming system.[70] Opium was thus, in every way, crucial to the making of Southeast Asia's modern economy, providing not only sustenance for what is arguably the region's most important city, Singapore, but also the seed capital for entrepreneurs and industrialists. Most of the prominent and well-respected families in nineteenth-century Singapore were directly or indirectly linked to the opium farms: the names of the farmers are, in fact, a 'virtual who's who of Chinese in Singapore'.[71]

The farming system came to an end in much of Southeast Asia in the 1880s as European colonial powers grew in confidence and tightened their hold on local populations (Singapore, which retained its opium farm until 1910, was an exception).[72] The farms were replaced by state monopolies, which took over the processing as well as the retailing of the drug.[73] The rationale for these monopolies was that of restricting usage while increasing revenues, but so long as opium remained a major source of revenue for colonial regimes its officers were inevitably under pressure to show increased profits.[74] So 'official Dutch expressions of concern about the hazards of opium, however well meant in theory, [were] largely insincere in practice'.[75] What the official monopolies mainly succeeded in doing was actually increase the profits that colonial regimes reaped from opium.[76] As one Dutch official frankly admitted: 'In the system of the Opiumregie, there is no place to reduce the quantities which could be sold; it is necessary to help every buyer.'[77]

Although the end of the farming system was a loss for diasporic Chinese businessmen and syndicates, by the time of its abolition many of them had already begun to branch out into other industries. As with the Parsis in India, opium thus provided the seed capital for many modern Southeast Asian enterprises: the fortunes of most of the older Crazy Rich Southeast Asian families were seeded by opium.

The staggering reality is that many of the cities that are now pillars of the modern globalized economy—Mumbai, Singapore, Hong Kong and Shanghai—were initially sustained by opium. In other words, it wasn't Free Trade or the autonomous laws of the market that laid the foundations of globalized economy: it was a monopolistic trade in a drug produced under colonial auspices by poor Asian farmers, a substance that creates addiction, the very negation of freedom. This, as Trocki notes, was the fundamental paradox of the colonial system itself: 'A ruling power that took much pride in its laws and system of justice was dependent on an "illegal" and virtually totalitarian system of social control to maintain its tax base.'[78]

TWELVE
Boston Brahmins

After Britain, the country that benefited the most from the China trade—and, therefore, the global traffic in opium—was none other than the United States. And in the United States, unlike Britain, it is well-established that the beneficiaries included many of the pre-eminent families, institutions and individuals in the land.

This is not to imply that fewer British subjects benefited from opium; quite the contrary. As the prime mover behind the global drug traffic, Britain's involvement with opium was obviously on a much larger scale than that of the United States: not only was the British colonial apparatus in India overseeing the production and distribution of most of the world's opium, but Britain was also home to the single largest, and richest, group of 'private traders' involved in smuggling opium into China. It is possible that the pathways of fortunes that British traders brought back could be tracked in the same way the circulation of the wealth derived from slavery has been charted in recent years. But the task would not be an easy one because opium money seeped so deep into nineteenth-century Britain that it essentially became invisible through ubiquity. In any event, this exercise has not been undertaken, possibly because of its inherent difficulties, or because it would threaten cherished myths about Britain's imperial past, or because there exists no domestic constituency to press for such an investigation, as was done for slavery.

On the other hand, even though the United States' involvement with the nineteenth-century opium trade was on a far smaller scale than that of Britain, what became of the money that was brought back by American private traders has been tracked in considerable detail. The principal reason for this is probably that those funds had a much greater impact in the young, newly independent country because its economy was tiny compared to Britain's.

Such was the influence of the China trade on the United States that its place in American memory is very different from that in British or Indian memory. One sign of this is that while Britain possesses vast collections of Chinese objects, books and artworks, it does not, so far as I know, have any museums devoted solely to the China trade: its Chinese artefacts are mostly housed in institutions that are global in scope, such as the British Museum and the Victoria and Albert Museum. In America, by contrast, there exists a museum dedicated entirely to the China trade. Nor is this the only one; there are several others in which the China trade figures prominently, such as the impressive and well-funded Peabody Essex Museum in Salem, Massachusetts.

Another measure of the impact of the China trade on the United States is the sheer number of American towns and cities named 'Canton': there are more than thirty, twice as many as are named after London. Yet, while there are many American Cantons, there is not a single 'Guangzhou', or even 'Whampoa': those names would perhaps have made China's unseen presence within the country uncomfortably real. The word 'Canton' thus served to create a very particular niche within American memory, one in which China was domesticated and anglicized, and where the disconcerting realities of the opium trade were rendered palatable.

Those realities have been the subject of several excellent studies, including John R. Haddad's *America's First Adventure in China*, Dael A. Norwood's *Trading Freedom* and Jacques M. Downs's *The Golden Ghetto: The American Commercial Community at Canton and the Shaping of American China Policy, 1784–1844*. The latter was the outcome of a lifetime's work: Downs combed through the records of all the major traders, which together constitute an archive of monumental proportions, having been preserved by 'New Englanders and Philadelphians—people who never discard anything, be it documents, clothes, broken furniture, or outworn institutions'.[1] Yet, while massive in size, the archive does not necessarily provide a transparent window on the past: the traders were generally very careful to hide the real nature of their businesses, even warning their families back home not to make anything public of their letters.[2] In some instances the traders' descendants selectively destroyed papers that mentioned the buying and selling of opium.

Opium did not, by any means, account for the entirety of the traders' businesses, but their other ventures were entirely predicated on it: they used their earnings from the drug to fund their purchases of teas, porcelain, silk, artworks and much else. Thus, for example, in a letter written shortly after Commissioner Lin Zexu shut down the opium trade, Robert Bennet Forbes, a young Yankee trader, explains that no other part of the foreign merchants' business with China could function without opium: '[T]he Opium trade being cut off there is no money . . . thus does the Opium Trade affect every one trading here and us too . . . we cannot get money to buy tea & so we do not get our commissions.'[3]

Traders like Forbes and his brother John understood perfectly well, as Downs notes, that: 'the entire China trade, was based on the opium traffic'.[4] It is essential to remember, therefore, that America's

'China trade', as a legitimate commerce, existed for only about twenty years, from 1784 to 1804. When applied to later forms of the commerce, the expression 'China trade' is nothing other than a polite euphemism, much like calling Pablo Escobar's cocaine business the 'Andean Trade'.

The 'coupling' of the United States and China is not a new phenomenon, as many American pundits seem to believe. As the historian Dael A. Norwood explains in his book *Trading Freedom*, this link has existed since the earliest days of the republic. In America, as in Britain, it was tea that created initial connections. Americans too were enthusiastic drinkers of tea, which 'had a special place in the new nation's political imagination for its ties to the performance of gentility'.[5] But during the colonial period Americans were expressly forbidden to trade with China, that being the exclusive prerogative of the East India Company. As a result the tea that Americans drank had to be routed through Britain, which made it more expensive. The resentments generated by this exploded in 1773 with the Boston Tea Party, which helped light the fuse of the American War of Independence.[6]

At the end of the war in 1783, the new nation found itself independent but hemmed in: 'the child that had left its parents had nowhere to turn'.[7] With nearby British colonies shut off from trade, China was one of the few worthwhile destinations open to American ships, a potential lifeline for the country's merchants.[8] 'Send ships immediately to China,' John Adams told Congress in 1783, 'this trade is as open to us as to any nation.'[9] Adams got his wish soon enough: the first American vessel to set off for China, a diminutive sloop by the name of *Harriet*, hoisted sail the same year, within weeks of the departure of the British from New York. But the *Harriet* never reached China: its cargo, which consisted mainly of ginseng roots, was acquired at an unusually high price by the captain of an East India Company ship at the Cape of Good Hope.[10] This was probably done in the hope of dissuading the Americans from entering directly into the China trade—but the race was already on and there was no stopping it.

The *Harriet* was followed, two months later, by a much larger vessel, whose mission was announced by its name: *Empress of China*. The supercargo (business agent) was Samuel Shaw, a veteran of the Revolutionary War who would later become an ardent advocate for expanding America's trade relations with China.[11]

Six months after its departure from New York, the *Empress* became the first American ship to drop anchor at Whampoa, the last deep-water anchorage on the Pearl River.[12] The Americans were warmly welcomed by Chinese merchants, and the *Empress*'s cargo, which consisted of rum, furs and 'the largest quantity of ginseng ever brought to the Chinese market' was sold for good prices. On its way back the ship's holds were filled with tea, porcelain and textiles; it also carried some Shanghai roosters, which on being cross-bred with American strains produced a variety—the 'Bucks County Chicken'—that soon became immensely popular in the United States.[13] These imports earned the *Empress*'s owners $30,000, a solid 25 percent return on their investment. Word of the ship's successful voyage spread quickly along the eastern seaboard, and soon merchants and shipowners from Boston, Salem, Providence, New York and Baltimore were also outfitting vessels for the journey to China. Within a few years of the *Empress of China*'s voyage, dozens of American ships were visiting Guangzhou annually.[14]

But American merchants quickly ran into the same problem as others before them: they had to pay for Chinese tea with Spanish silver dollars, and there was little the Chinese wanted from them other than bullion.[15] Ginseng was one commodity for which there was some demand in China, but the American product was considered inferior, and there was only so much of it that the market could absorb.[16] What else? For a while the answer was furs and sealskins, and that was how two Massachusetts families—the Delanos and the Perkinses— were drawn into the China trade along with John Jacob Astor, America's most prominent vendor of furs.[17] However, despite their initial success in selling furs to the Chinese, they soon encountered an insurmountable challenge: there were only so many seals and sea otters that could be killed before their numbers dwindled to a point where it was no longer economical to hunt them. Sandalwood became the next solution and several Pacific islands were ransacked until they were thoroughly depleted of sandalwood trees; then it was the turn of the humble sea cucumber (bêche de mer)—and so on.[18] All the while there hung before the Americans the solution that had been fashioned by the British in the late eighteenth century: opium, a commodity which, unlike ginseng, did not obey the dictates of the supposed laws of supply and demand.[19]

Americans were at a disadvantage, however, because in the early years of the opium traffic they were shut out of the East India Company's auctions in Calcutta.[20] But the success of the British drug-running operation induced American merchants to look for other sources of opium, and they found a good one in Izmir (Smyrna), which was the outlet for Turkey's principal opium-growing region in the interior.[21]

The pioneers in the Turkish drug trade were the brothers James Smith Wilcocks and Benjamin Chew Wilcocks, from a prominent Philadelphia family.[22] The Wilcocks brothers travelled as supercargoes on the first American ship to carry Turkish opium, the *Pennsylvania*, in 1805. The ship disposed of its fifty chests of Izmir opium even before reaching China; the cargo was sold in Jakarta.[23] The success of this pioneering effort created something of an 'opium rush' among leading American merchants like John Jacob Astor of New

York, Joseph Peabody of Salem and Stephen Girard of Philadelphia.[24] Girard was a self-made man who had come to America from France as a cabin boy, and had eventually become an immensely wealthy enslaver, banker and shipping magnate. After learning of the Turkish opium route, he wrote urgently to his agents in the Mediterranean: 'I am very much in favor of investing heavily in opium.'[25] When Girard died in 1831, he was the wealthiest man in America, and is still counted among the richest Americans of all time; the same is true of Astor and Peabody.

Soon there were so many American merchants in Izmir that they were able to monopolize the shipping of Turkish opium to China.[26] But the output of the Turkish industry was not large, and the opportunities in India were simply too great to be missed. So even as they were setting up the traffic in Turkish opium, some Americans also began eyeing the East India Company's auctions in Bengal. In 1804 Charles Cabot, captain of a Boston-owned ship, declared, 'I intend to purchase Opium at the Company's sales & proceed to the eastward where I have no doubt of being first at market.'[27]

Those early attempts to tap the Indian market foundered initially because of the disruptions caused first by the Napoleonic Wars, and then by the British-American War of 1812.[28] But after the war ended in 1815, Americans began to expand their dealings in opium at a rapid rate.[29] John Jacob Astor even sent a ship into the Persian Gulf in an attempt at finding another source to supplement the supplies from Turkey.[30] Astor's speculations in opium in this period were large enough to send tremors down his rivals' spines. 'We know of no one but Astor we fear,' declared the Boston firm that then dominated the Turkish market.[31]

By 1818 Americans were, by some estimates, smuggling as much as a third of all the opium consumed in China, thereby posing a major challenge to the East India Company's domination of the market.[32] Indeed, competition from Americans, and their Turkish opium, was one of the reasons why the Company ramped up its production in Bihar soon after.

Meanwhile India continued to be by far the greatest source of profits in the opium trade, and American merchants remained eager to expand their reach into the Indian traffic: the fact that they were shut out of it only whetted their appetites. And it was not as if the Americans did not hold some winning cards of their own. Marketing Turkish opium in China had put them in a good position to act as agents for Indian businessmen; they knew the ins and outs of the trade, and had acquired extensive contacts within smuggling networks. They also had their own receiving ships at Lintin Island, on the Pearl River, where they could offer to store their partners' drug consignments at lower rates than those of the big British smuggling networks.[33] Moreover, their connections with the business worlds of Bombay and Calcutta went back a long way, to the years immediately following the formal recognition of American independence in 1783.

By the late 1780s several New England merchants had started to work with Parsi and Gujarati brokers in Bombay, because they offered better rates and more reliable service than English agents.[34] Bombay's major export then was cotton, while the American products that found a market there were gin, rum, iron and cordage.[35] At that time, British regulations made it difficult for Americans to carry Indian goods to China, but the rules changed after 1815, and that was when New England merchants plunged headlong into the trafficking of Malwa opium.[36]

Soon, several American merchants, mainly from Salem, were residing in Bombay, where their provisions and housing were taken care of by their Parsi partners.[37] While the Americans did find partners among the great Parsi merchant clans, like the Wadia, Dadiseth and Readymoney families, most of the bigger companies were already spoken for by the British behemoths like Jardine Matheson

& Co. and Dent & Co. Thus it was often the smaller Parsi firms that were more eager to work with them. Among the Gujarati firms that partnered with Americans, the most important was Ahmedabad's Hutheesing Khushalchand, one of the largest Malwa opium brokerages.

The indefatigable Benjamin Chew Wilcocks of Philadelphia was one of the pioneers in establishing American–Indian partnerships in opium. By 1824 Wilcocks was doing business to the tune of 100,000 silver dollars annually with Hormuzjee Dorabjee of Bombay, and this kept growing steadily until his retirement in 1827, when he passed his company to a relative, John R. Latimer, who further developed the firm's connection with Parsi merchants, most notably the Cowasjee, Framjee and Hormuzjee families.[38]

Following close on the heels of the Philadelphia merchants were the big opium-trading clans of Boston—the Perkins, Sturgis, Russell and Forbes families, who were all as intricately interrelated as the Mafia lineages of southern Italy. They called themselves 'the Boston Concern' and the eventual merger of their firms would make them the single biggest opium-trading network in China.[39] The wealth they gained from the opium trade would establish them as core members of the elite circle that Oliver Wendell Holmes called 'the Boston Brahmins', America's closest equivalent to an aristocracy.[40]

'Almost without exception,' writes Downs, 'Americans involved in opium during the last quarter century of the old China trade went home with fortunes after only a few years in the trade.'[41]

Who were these fortunate Americans? It is no accident that their names read like a litany of the Northeastern upper crust: Astor, Cabot, Peabody, Brown, Archer, Hathaway, Webster, Delano,

Coolidge, Forbes, Russell, Perkins, Bryant and so on. They were mostly from the more privileged ranks of white settler society, families of British origin that had long been settled in the north-east.[42] Many of them were educated in elite schools like the Boston Latin School, Milton Academy, Phillips Academy Andover, Phillips Exeter Academy and so on, and many went to universities like Harvard, Yale, the University of Pennsylvania and Brown (named after a prominent slave- and opium-trading family from Providence, Rhode Island).[43]

To belong to an upper-crust Northeastern family in the early nineteenth century was different from being a member of other white elites, such as those of Europe or even the American South. The Northeastern elite was not principally a landowning group but a largely professional and mercantile class, subject to the fluctuations of a young and erratic economy. Businesses failed so frequently that even the most well-connected families lived with a certain degree of precarity.

A case in point is the family of Washington Irving, author of *Rip Van Winkle*, *The Legend of Sleepy Hollow* and other classic American stories. The writer and his brothers belonged to one of the most well-connected families of the Northeast, with a circle of friends whose surnames are now emblazoned on streets across Manhattan and Brooklyn: Schermerhorn, Schuyler, Van Rensselaer, Livingston and so on. Their family home was at 3, Bridge Street, a prize location in the heart of lower Manhattan, and they also owned several country cottages between them. Yet, it is clear from the family's correspondence that the younger Irvings were constantly plagued by money worries. 'I have a terrible load of debts on my shoulders,' complained Theodore Irving, one of the writer's nephews, 'which must be paid before I can breathe freely.'[44] At times the young man's laments sound like those of single twenty-something New Yorkers today:

I used to sigh and say to myself after all there is no place like New York—but then the want of money never entered my head. Money—money—money!—worshipped by all in society here and none more than the lovelier part of creation. Yes—'tis a melancholy fact the women here make obeisance to the men with riches.[45]

It wasn't Theodore, however, but his younger brother William—Will to his relatives—who was chosen to go to Guangzhou to restore the family's fortunes: Washington Irving himself pulled strings to get his nephew a clerkship in the biggest American opium-trading firm in China, Russell & Co. Twenty-two-year-old Will set off for China in 1833 with another young man of the same age, Abiel Abbot Low, who was also on his way to Guangzhou to join Russell & Co. Abbot Low, as he was generally known to his friends, was from a Salem family that had recently resettled in Brooklyn. He and Will became good friends during the journey, and on reaching Guangzhou they bought a boat together and would often go sailing on the Pearl River.[46]

At around the same time as Irving and Low, another young American, by the name of Warren Delano Jr, also joined Russell & Co. All three men started off as clerks in the firm's offices in Guangzhou's Foreign Enclave, where Will was known to everyone as 'a nephew of Washington Irving'.[47] But while Low and Delano prospered, William Irving was not able to make much headway and began to despair of his prospects in the firm. His family did what they could to encourage him.

I don't like your being in low spirits, [wrote his brother Theodore] you *must cheer* up—consider the few years to come as a Purgatory leading to ease and opulence—for be your prospects what they may in the [firm], you can certainly

lay up something by speculating . . . I would join you there
tomorrow if money could be made—for alack a-day this
poverty is a dirty thing.[48]

But Will's gloom continued unabated, prompting his brother to
write, reassuringly: 'I have no wish that you should amass great wealth,
my hope is that you may pick up some 20 or 40 thousand dollars, and
be able to return to your native country while yet young—I would
not have you pass more than ten years away.'[49]

But even as Will was complaining about his own career, he was
also reporting back on the vast sums that other Americans were
making in Guangzhou. 'We may have been mistaken,' wrote his
father, 'in the expectations of your soon getting an interest in the
[firm], but from all we can learn from the frequent changes in
the partners we still think your prospects are good. You say that Mr
Heard leaves this spring having amassed $150,000 in *three years*.'[50]

Will seems to have come to the conclusion that his inability to
rise in Russell & Co. was due to the fact that, unlike Abbot Low and
Warren Delano Jr, he had no funds of his own to speculate on opium.
So he wrote to his relatives to raise money for him, which they very
obligingly did, creating a small family fund in which Washington
Irving, who appears to have been surprisingly well-informed about
opium dealings in Canton, also invested. '[Y]ou will have great
opportunities of speculating,' wrote brother Theodore, 'Uncle
Washington has commissioned father to advance monies, to allow
you to speculate.'[51]

Despite this, advancement still eluded William and the gloomy
letters continued. Theodore, as always, did his best to cheer him up:

Do you not go to Macao during the season when not busy?
Mrs Olyphant told us it was the custom. It will be quite a treat
to see the *women* again, and if the Portuguese girls there have

not degenerated from their mothers in Portugal, they will be goodly to gaze upon. Do write in your letters every little thing—you cannot imagine how deeply interesting everything is, touching that wild and almost unknown region. Tell me all about Macao and its women.[52]

But Will continued to flounder: perhaps he found drug-trading distasteful; or perhaps he had no head for business; or perhaps his failure to get ahead was due to the fact that unlike Delano and Low, both of whom were from Massachusetts families, he had no close relatives in the Boston firms that were Russell & Co.'s closest partners. As a last resort the Irving family placed their hopes for Will's future in the hands of another well-connected American, Joseph Coolidge.

A Yankee blueblood and Harvard graduate, Coolidge was married to Thomas Jefferson's favourite grand-daughter, Ellen Wayles Randolph. Jefferson himself presided over the wedding at Monticello. A few years before his marriage, Coolidge had gone on a Grand Tour of Europe and, while passing through Paris, had sought out Washington Irving, who was there at the time. The writer took a shine to the young man and introduced him to Lord Byron, who was then living in Ravenna. Coolidge went to see the poet and was gifted a copy of *Marino Faliero, Doge of Venice*, Byron's most recent work. The meeting made a tremendous impression on Coolidge; he must have talked about it for the rest of his life for it was even mentioned in his obituary, sixty years later: 'Comparatively few . . . were aware that we had here in Boston a gentleman who was personally acquainted with Lord Byron, and who had been on familiar and intimate terms with many of the most remarkable men of modern times.'[53]

It was probably through Washington Irving that Coolidge found his way into the opium trade. The writer seems to have done him another good turn by recommending him to the Boston Concern, possibly in the hope that Coolidge would help young Will with his career. But this was a big mistake: although charming and well-read, Coolidge was actually a quarrelsome and unreliable fellow, who in the course of his short career in Guangzhou managed to antagonize almost everyone who crossed his path.[54] Far from advancing Will's career, Coolidge actually ended it, by starting a nasty quarrel. What the dispute was about is not known but it was so ugly that Will left Guangzhou immediately, without even picking up his trunk or collecting his washing. His belongings were later forwarded to him, in Manila, by Abbot Low, who also disposed of the last of the opium that Will had bought with the funds his family had sent him. But that too did not turn out well because the sale was made at a loss.

Thus ended the ill-starred venture of William Irving, who returned to New York with very little to show for his pains: he was one of the rare Americans of his class who failed to make a fortune in Guangzhou.

William Irving's career may have diverged from the usual pattern, but he was entirely typical of American opium traffickers of this period in that he was a less affluent member of a privileged class. Many of the Yankees who established the American connection with China were, similarly, from the more penurious branches of the families of rich merchants: usually nephews of wealthy or influential men, their entry into the business came about through nepotism, in the exact sense.[55] This was true, for instance, of Samuel Russell, the founder of Russell & Co.: he started off in Middletown, Connecticut, as a 'half-orphaned' white boy with only an 'ordinary schooling'. But he had uncles in Providence who did business with China and it was they who initially sent him out to Guangzhou and helped him establish his company.[56] He could not have built his fortune without his family connections.[57] That he was believed to be a 'self-made man' is a sign of how the expression often conceals many kinds of privilege.

To go out to China at this time meant being away from one's home for years on end, so young men needed to be very hungry and highly motivated to make the journey. It is not surprising then that many of those who went were the poor relations of rich men, boys who had grown up in the orbit of wealth, chafing at their own straitened circumstances and longing for an opportunity to better their lot.[58] But to be merely intelligent, ambitious and white wasn't enough: a certain kind of class privilege was essential. To succeed in Guangzhou, a young American needed an education, as well as family connections to secure for him not just a clerkship in a good firm but also access to capital, which usually came, as in Will Irving's case, from relatives. A penniless white boy from the backwoods, no matter how intelligent, hard-working or ambitious, would have stood very little chance of finding a place at Russell & Co., let alone a Jew or a black man.

Youth was another attribute that many American China merchants had in common, and sometimes it worked to their advantage. As it did for John Perkins Cushing, an impoverished nephew of Thomas Handasyd Perkins, one of Boston's wealthiest merchants.[59] Thomas H. Perkins had himself made an early journey to Guangzhou, as a supercargo on his brother-in-law's ship, the Astrea, and had come back convinced that the future of American business lay in China.[60] In 1803 he sent a couple of representatives to Guangzhou to set up an office; one was a senior partner and the other was Perkins's sixteen-year-old nephew, John Cushing.[61] The older man fell ill and died soon after reaching Guangzhou, and the inexperienced teenage boy suddenly found himself alone, saddled with a huge responsibility. Fortunately for him, the wealthiest and most powerful member of the Cohong syndicate took him under his wing.[62] This was none other than the immensely wealthy Wu Bingjian (Howqua), a man of great intelligence and foresight.[63] Portraits of Wu Bingjian (of which there are many) depict him as a tall, frail man with a gentle smile and an avuncular glint in his eye (see insert image 12). At the time of his first meeting with John Cushing, Wu Bingjian was in his early thirties and had recently lost a sixteen-year-old son: it was perhaps this that caused him to look upon the boy's plight with sympathy. In any event, John Cushing soon became 'like a son' to Wu Bingjian, who guided the lad in setting up his business and gave him interest-free loans. With Wu Bingjian's help, the once-penurious Yankee boy became a millionaire and upon his return to Boston was regarded as one of the most eligible bachelors in the land. 'It was a token of the pair's great friendship that Cushing was sometimes called Mr Howqua in jest by other Bostonians.'[64]

After his departure from Guangzhou, John Cushing's place at Russell & Co. was taken by another impecunious Perkins relative, John Murray Forbes. Along with his brother Robert Bennet Forbes, John Murray made a fortune in China and became a great American tycoon, leaving a legacy so lasting that the family name is still an icon of American capitalism.[65]

John Forbes's path to success was very much like that of his uncle John Cushing's. He too grew up in straitened circumstances but in a family that had important commercial and educational connections: one of his uncles was Thomas Handasyd Perkins, the Boston merchant, and another was the head of Phillips Exeter Academy.[66] On arriving in Guangzhou in 1830, as a boy of seventeen, he was shoehorned into Russell & Co. by his family. Soon, he and his brother were also on quasi-familial terms with Wu Bingjian and his clan. Years later, John Forbes would write:

> Howqua, who never did anything by halves, at once took me as Mr Cushing's successor, and . . . gave me his entire confidence. All his foreign letters, some of which were of almost national importance, were handed to me to read, and to prepare such answers as he indicated . . . before I was eighteen years old it was not uncommon for him to order me to charter one or more entire ships at a time, and load them. The invoices were made out in my name, and the instructions as to sales and returns

given just as if the shipments were my own property, and at one time I had as much as half a million dollars thus afloat.[67]

The two Forbes brothers eventually became Wu Bingjian's investment managers in the United States. Through them the Wu clan invested hundreds of thousands of dollars in the mid-nineteenth-century American economy.[68] All of this was done on trust, without any written contracts, yet the families continued to honour their obligations to each other long after Wu Bingjian's death in 1843.

While many of the Americans merchants in Guangzhou were 'poor relations', there were some who were born to wealth. One such was Augustine Heard, the son of a leading merchant from Ipswich, Massachusetts. Heard attended school at Phillips Exeter before travelling to China, first as a supercargo, then as a ship's captain and finally as a member of Russell & Co. He was a senior partner at the start of the First Opium War, when British merchants withdrew from the city and boycotted the port. Charles Elliot, the most senior British official in China, tried to persuade the Americans to leave as well, with threats as well as entreaties, but they defied him. Fortunately, the gamble paid off handsomely: although their operations were occasionally disrupted by riots and other disturbances, many Americans made a killing at this time, because the demand for tea continued unabated in Europe and America, and they were the only traders who could provide a supply. Heard prospered even more than most, because his company began to handle the entire business of Jardine Matheson, amounting to 10 million dollars a year.

Soon, Heard was joined by another very privileged Bostonian, George Basil Dixwell, who came from a family that was descended from one of the three seventeenth-century judges who had condemned Charles I to death.[69] The Dixwells were successful in the academy as well as in commerce: one of George Dixwell's brothers was the headmaster of Boston's famous Latin School, the oldest still-existing school in the United States. George Dixwell himself was a gifted linguist, who learnt Bengali as well as Chinese. Dixwell eventually took over Heard's firm and built up a fleet of ships to transport and distribute Indian opium in China, thus becoming 'the principal architect of the Heard firm's immensely profitable commerce in opium'.[70]

Men like Heard, Dixwell, Cushing, the Forbes brothers and their many cousins and uncles may have been pioneers in a system that would come to be called capitalism, but in their social lives, and in their business operations, they were very much like any Indian commercial caste. They were, in Downs's words,

> wealthier and better educated than most American families of the time, they were generally in business or the professions, and the extended family operated as a unit. At least among the Boston families, there was a tendency to cluster. They often built houses on the same city block or in some small town, spent much of each day together, took trips and vacations jointly, joined the same political parties and social clubs, and attended the same schools and churches . . . The various family businesses were interwoven, and the young men tended to assume expected life roles within those firms. Marriage within their own local social set was more common than alliances outside of it, and there was no ban on the marriage of cousins.[71]

In this case, far from shattering 'the fetters of the extended family' (to quote Max Weber), the Protestant ethic actually reinforced those ties, creating solidarities akin to those of a Chinese commercial clan or an Indian trading caste.[72]

However, membership in this class was not a guarantee of success, as is evident from the case of William Irving. But given a modicum of ambition and competence, a man from that background could indeed prosper in Guangzhou. Many of these men were, no doubt, excellent businessmen, but of none of them could it be said that their success was due entirely to their entrepreneurial skills, or, as Max Weber would have it, to the 'unprecedented inner loneliness of the single individual'.[73]

THIRTEEN

American Stories

Americans were responsible for several important innovations in the nineteenth-century opium trade, including setting up a steady transportation channel between China and Turkey, and developing the system of using 'floating warehouses' at Lintin Island to facilitate the smuggling of opium.[1] Another was the design of a vessel that for a few decades played a very important role in the opium trade: the Baltimore clipper.[2]

The clipper was the contribution of a school of Baltimore shipbuilders who specialized in building small streamlined vessels that were fast enough to elude British warships.[3] These vessels were exceptionally agile and were much beloved by their skippers and crew. 'She swam like a duck and steered like a fish,' wrote the captain of the *Falcon*, an opium clipper. '"She can do everything but speak" was a common remark among the crew.'[4] Clippers could also, when needed, prey on merchant shipping, a useful quality for Baltimore's shipowners, for whom privateering (capturing ships of enemy nations) was a big business.[5]

Many Baltimore clippers were fore-and-aft rigged schooners, and the *Ibis*, after which my trilogy of novels is named, is one such. The vessel that features in the Trilogy is purportedly a creation of Baltimore's best-known shipbuilders, William and George Gardner, whose shipyard was at Fell's Point, on the harbour. Like many of the Gardner brothers' ships, the *Ibis* was originally built as a slave ship.

If the Gardner brothers are still remembered today it is not so much for their shipyards as for one of their workers: Frederick Douglass, who would go on to become one of the most famous African Americans of the nineteenth century. At the time, shipbuilding was one of the few industries where black men could find employment. But in the 1830s the influx of a number of working men from Britain and Ireland led to a sharpening of racial tensions, and one day in 1836—as Douglass vividly describes in his autobiography—he was beaten so viciously by a mob of white workers that he almost lost an eye.[6]

In *Sea of Poppies*, this incident is witnessed by Zachary Reid, the son of a white enslaver and an enslaved mother. A light-skinned freedman, Zachary realizes that he might be in danger, and runs away from Baltimore by joining the crew of the *Ibis*, which has just been acquired by a British merchant based in India: he signs up for the journey to Calcutta as the schooner's carpenter.

Journeys like Zachary's were not uncommon in the early nineteenth century because fast, streamlined ships, like Baltimore clippers, were much in demand for the transportation of opium from India to China. Before, ships would have to wait for the turning of the monsoon winds in order to sail that route. But schooner-rigged clippers were able to sail against the wind, and so the opium trade went from being a seasonal affair to a year-round commerce, in which speed was of the essence.[7] A ship that could get its cargo to the market before others would get a better price for its goods, and it could then turn around and head back to Bombay or Calcutta, usually with a cargo of bullion. Sometimes clippers would make the opium run between India and China two or even three times in a year.[8] Ships would frequently race against each other, and captains who made the journey in good time would be rewarded handsomely for their seamanship.

The larger opium-trading companies, like Jardine Matheson & Co. and Dent & Co., had dozens of ships continually in transit between India and China. The major American firms, like Russell & Co. and Augustine Heard & Co., also maintained sizeable fleets. Setting off from New York, Boston or Philadelphia, those ships would go to Bombay or Calcutta to sell their goods (which sometimes included ice from New England's ponds) before proceeding to China, with cargoes of opium.[9] Sometimes American-owned ships would shuttle back and forth between India and China for two or three years before heading back to the United States.

Baltimore schooners also happened to be very well-suited to another traffic that was gaining momentum in the 1830s. It was in this period, after the banning of slavery in the Empire, that transporting Indian indentured workers to British colonies was becoming a lucrative business for shipowners. A former slave ship like the *Ibis* was well-adapted to this purpose: even though the status of indentured workers was different from that of enslaved people, the physical conditions in which they were transported were quite similar.[10]

In *Sea of Poppies*, the *Ibis* leaves Baltimore with a foul-mouthed Boston Irishman as captain, and a crew of nineteen, of whom nine, including Zachary, are listed as black. The voyage quickly turns into a disaster, with many of the crewmen and officers falling ill or dying in accidents. Circumstances compel Zachary to step into the shoes of the second mate, even though he is a ship's carpenter rather than a seaman.

When the *Ibis* reaches Cape Town the crew melts away overnight, spreading word of 'a hell-afloat with pinch-gut pay'. No white seaman will sign on, so the captain is forced to take on a crew of lascars.

Zachary now discovers that lascars are not a tribe or nation, that 'they came from places that were far apart, and had nothing in common, except the Indian Ocean; among them were Chinese and East Africans, Arabs and Malays, Bengalis and Goans, Tamils and Arakanese'. To Zachary, the lascars seem ridiculous at first, with their bare feet and their sarongs and breechclouts. But he soon realizes that they are skilled seamen, well able to get the job done.

After leaving Cape Town, the *Ibis* sustains yet another loss: the captain succumbs to dysentery. Zachary, as the last American aboard, becomes the skipper by default. For the leader of the lascars, an Arakanese seaman by the name of Serang Ali, Zachary's sudden rise to eminence is a dream come true. In the early nineteenth century, experienced lascars perfectly capable of running a ship could not serve as ships' officers because of their race. Every Western-style merchant vessel, even those owned by Indian businessmen, had to be officered by white men, while the crewmen were overwhelmingly lascars. This racialized structure persisted, astonishingly, even through much of the twentieth century, with many, if not most, merchant ships being captained by Europeans and Americans, while the crews were largely South Asian or Filipino.

Lascars had a pecking order of their own: the most senior 'petty officers' were called serangs and tindals (the ranks still survive in the Indian Navy and merchant marine).[11] Serangs and tindals were often the most knowledgeable and competent men on board, yet they had to put up with a great deal of interference from callow or foul-mouthed white officers, some of whom were still in their teens. For Serang Ali, Zachary is a godsend because he is a light-complexioned American: since a ship must have a white captain, it may as well be someone who is as amiable, obliging and inexperienced as Zachary. So, in a kind of counterpoint to Herman Melville's novella *Benito Cereno*, in which a ship's white captain is turned into a figurehead by enslaved mutineers, Serang Ali and his crew of lascars slowly turn Zachary into a sahib and an officer, roles he comes increasingly to relish as he makes his way upwards in the opium trade.

Since opium was transported mainly by ship, it is not at all surprising that shipbuilding and carpentry became avenues through which many prominent families found their way into the trade. This was true, for instance, of the Wadias, a Parsi family that started off in Gujarat as shipbuilders.[12] It was from the deck of a Wadia-built ship, the *Minden*, that Francis Scott Key observed the bombardment of Baltimore on 13 September 1814, which inspired him to write the poem that became the United States' national anthem, 'The Star-Spangled Banner'.[13]

Among the many American families that found their way into the opium trade via shipbuilding and seafaring, there was one that would become exceptionally renowned: the Delano clan. Originally of Flemish origin, the founder of the American branch of the family, Philippe de Lannoy ('Delano' is thought to be a contraction of the name), settled in New England in 1621, aged nineteen, residing initially with an uncle who had arrived the year before on the *Mayflower*. He participated in the massacre of the Pequot tribe and acquired large tracts of land in New England. One of his descendants, a shipbuilder in Duxbury, Massachusetts, was the father of shipwright and master mariner Amasa Delano, who travelled to, and resided in, Guangzhou several times in the course of an extraordinarily eventful life. He was also the author of a noted maritime memoir based on his three circumnavigations of the earth: *A Narrative of Voyages and Travels in the Northern and Southern Hemisphere*.[14] It was in this memoir that Melville found the materials for *Benito Cereno*: the incident on which the story is based occurred in 1805, when Amasa Delano came upon a drifting Spanish slave ship, the *Tryal*, while transporting sealskins from Chile to China. Delano was none other than the story's real-life narrator.

It wasn't Amasa, however, but a Delano from a collateral branch who forged the family's connection with the opium trade: Warren Delano Jr, who arrived in Guangzhou the same year as Will Irving and quickly became the head of Russell & Co.'s offices in the city. He was joined there by his half-brother Edward, who also became a partner in the company. Together, the two Delano brothers held a majority stake in the biggest American opium-trading company for decades. Under Warren Delano Jr's leadership, Russell & Co. outdistanced every other American company in its opium holdings. Apart from being a sharp businessman, Delano was second to none in enjoying a good party. At William Jardine's legendary farewell dinner in January 1839, Delano was waltzing with a fellow merchant when he 'was *let go of* by his partner & tumbled headlong against a flower pot & cut a gash in his head an inch long'.[15] A few months later, when Lin Zexu forced the foreign traders to surrender their opium holdings, Russell & Co. contributed 93 per cent of the quantity handed over by Americans, one hundred times more than its closest American rival.

Through the First Opium War, Warren Delano served as the honorary consul of the United States in Guangzhou, a position he was well-equipped to fill not only because of his prominence as a merchant but also because he was not unsympathetic to the Chinese cause. In this Delano was not alone: many other Americans also disapproved of the British assault on China, and privately wished that the Chinese were better able to resist. Warren Delano Jr even helped the Chinese defence forces acquire their only Western ship, the *Cambridge*.[16] He, along with other members of Russell & Co., even aided Wu Bingjian's clan, warning them of attacks, tipping them off about when they needed to evacuate and protecting them from incurring losses on their cargoes.

But the Delano brothers were also among those who benefited the most from the Opium War, making windfall gains after the British withdrawal from Guangzhou.[17] And even though Russell & Co.

briefly abjured the opium trade at the insistence of Wu Bingjian, once the war was over they plunged right back into the drug-trafficking business. Like many of their fellow Americans, regardless of their private reservations, the Delano brothers were eager to take advantage of the conditions that the British had violently imposed on China. In the words of one such merchant: '[T]he opium trade is the branch of business which we should most encourage, it is by far the safest and most profitable.'[18]

Nor did the Delanos, or any of their compatriots, doubt that in relation to China—and the non-West in general—Americans and Europeans, whatever their internal differences, needed to act as essentially a single bloc. Even though Westerners were perennially at war with each other, they were entirely in agreement on the necessity of maintaining white supremacy at all costs.[19] The Chinese, for their part, understood very well the relationship between the two English-speaking countries and often referred to Americans as the 'younger brothers' of the British.

In 1843, after returning to the United States as an immensely wealthy man, Warren Delano Jr married Catherine Lyman, daughter of a distinguished Massachusetts family. The couple had many children, including a girl, Sara, whose only son, Franklin Delano Roosevelt, became the thirty-second President of the United States. Through his brothers and his children, Warren Delano Jr was related also to the Astors and many of America's most prominent families, including that of President Calvin Coolidge.

In 1857 Warren Delano Jr lost much of his wealth in a financial panic, so like many other American speculators before him, he returned to the opium trade and quickly rebuilt his fortune. It was at his palatial estate, Algonac, in New York, that Franklin and Eleanor Roosevelt were married.

Despite the great distance that separates the two countries, China was for the United States, as also for India, a gravitational force, exercising a largely unnoticed yet immensely powerful influence. This force even played a part in the territorial evolution of the United States. It has been argued, for instance, that a desire to expand trade with China was a significant consideration in Thomas Jefferson's acquisitions of territory, and in his sponsoring of the Lewis and Clark expedition to the west coast.[20] Meriwether Lewis explicitly acknowledges, in his reports, that a part of the expedition's mission was to explore overland routes that would make it easier to send furs, and other trade goods, to China.[21]

But long before Lewis and Clark reached the Pacific coast, the search for furs to trade with China had already brought a Boston seafarer, John Boit, to the mouth of the largest river in the Pacific Northwest. He named the river after his ship, the *Columbia*, in 1792. By the time Lewis and Clark reached the mouth of the river, in 1805, the indigenous people of the coast were already 'able to speak a bit of English thanks to the Canton fur trade'.[22] The voyage of the *Columbia* was one of the supplementary pieces of evidence that strengthened the United States' claim when the ownership of the Oregon Territory was disputed by Britain. Another point that buttressed the American claim was also related to the China trade: 'That was the settlement of Astoria, at the mouth of the Columbia, by John Jacob Astor. Astor had realized . . . that if furs were to be taken for the China trade and enough animals left to produce more furs, a permanent post would be necessary in the heart of the fur country.'[23]

A similar situation arose with the acquisition of Alaska in 1867. The purchase was strongly opposed by many Americans at the time, being widely derided as 'Seward's folly'. The argument that ultimately carried the day was that 'Alaska's proximity to China . . . would be reason enough to purchase it'.[24]

But above all, the means by which China made its mark on the
United States was the money that American opium traders brought
home. Many 'Canton graduates' (to use Downs's phrase) were in their
twenties when they returned from China: not only were they young
and vigorous, but also their experience of doing business in China had
given them a solid understanding of international trade and finance.
Many of them became successful entrepreneurs, ploughing their
opium money into every sector of the rapidly expanding American
economy.

One industry that profited greatly from opium money was
banking: Stephen Girard of Philadelphia founded one of America's
earliest banks, and the alumni of the Boston Concern also invested
heavily in fiscal and insurance companies.[25] But capital wasn't
China's only contribution to American banking; it also contributed
a key financial innovation that became a cornerstone of American,
and eventually global, banking systems: this was the institution of
bank deposit insurance, which today, through the Federal Deposit
Insurance Corporation (FDIC), underwrites the savings of the great
majority of Americans.

New York was the first state to enact a deposit insurance law, in
1829, and the legislator who was responsible for it, Joshua Forman,
explicitly based his proposal on Chinese precedents. 'The propriety of
making the banks liable for each other,' he told the state legislature,
'was suggested by the regulation of the Hong merchants in Canton,
where a number of men, each acting separately, have by the grant of
the government the exclusive right of trading with foreigners, and are
all made liable for the debts of each in case of failure.'[26]

In 1933 the century-old New York statute became the model for
national bank deposit insurance in the United States. 'Bank deposit
insurance,' writes the historian Frederick Delano Grant, 'has since
spread worldwide, and is now found in about one hundred nations.'[27]
But as with many other non-Western contributions to global business

and finance, bank deposit insurance is almost always described as an American financial innovation.

Another sector of the American economy that benefited greatly from opium money was the railroad industry. Thomas Handasyd Perkins built some of the earliest railroads in New England, possibly even the first. But it was his nephew John Murray Forbes who became one of the foremost railroad tycoons of his time. He returned from China in 1836, at the age of twenty-three, 'nearly bald' but in possession of a 'moderate competency' of his own as well as an enormous sum of money—500,000 dollars—that Wu Bingjian had given him to invest in American stocks.[28] While in China, Forbes had been sceptical of railways, and had asked his brother to avoid railway stocks: 'I have good reasons to believe, from all I can learn of the English railways, that ours will prove a failure after the first few years; the wear and tear proves ruinous. At any rate, keep clear of them.'[29]

But after returning to America, he changed his mind, possibly under the influence of his uncle John Cushing, who had already begun to invest Wu Bingjian's money in railroads.[30] Following suit, Forbes used the funds in his control to buy and complete the Michigan Central Railroad.[31] Among his partners in building and promoting railroads was a friend from his Guangzhou days, John Cleve Green, another alumnus of Russell & Co. who also became a railroad tycoon. Jacques Downs writes:

> There were several obvious reasons for the prominence of returned China traders in railroading. First they were rich, and they were searching for good domestic investments over which they could exercise a degree of prudent control. Second they had connections with both American and foreign capitalists (especially in Britain) and could draw upon resources not available to others. Third they were experienced in doing business at long distances and in delegating authority.[32]

It is well known that Chinese workers were instrumental in the building of America's railway infrastructure; that much of the capital that financed the railroads also came from China is a fact of which few are aware.[33] But that may be the reason why many of America's 'Cantons' are located close to railway lines.

Textiles, iron manufacturing, hoteliering and investment brokering were some of the other industries that benefited from opium money. 'Canton graduates,' writes Downs, 'went into all of these fields, becoming the seed corn of the economic revolution in America.'[34] Or, as Haddad puts it: 'Opium was really a way that America was able to transfer China's economic power to America's industrial revolution.'[35]

By investing in a wide range of industries, a small, tightly woven circle of upper-crust Yankees multiplied many times over the fortunes they had made in the opium trade. They then poured a part of their gains into an equally large variety of philanthropies, founding and funding universities, colleges, schools, hospitals, asylums, libraries, historical societies, churches and museums. One Canton graduate was responsible for an important innovation in American philanthropy: giving money on condition that matching amounts be raised from other sources.[36] John Cleve Green gave enormous sums of money to Princeton University, and is credited with having played a major part in the development of its science and engineering programmes.[37] Nor was he the only Canton graduate to pour money into the Ivy League: among the old and venerable institutions of north-eastern America, few indeed are those that have not, at some point or other, been endowed with funds that can be traced back to opium.

The connection between opium and philanthropy has endured till the present day. Members of the Sackler family, who owned Purdue Pharma and made billions of dollars from OxyContin and other prescription opioids, gave away so much money—to hospitals, universities and art museums across the world—that they were sometimes likened to the Medicis of Florence.[38] Ironically, one such institution is the Arthur M. Sackler Museum of Art and Archaeology at Peking University, named after the dynasty's patriarch, who was an obsessive collector of Chinese art and antiquities.[39] An even greater irony is that a section of the grounds of the Yuanming Yuan, the Qing Summer Palace, which was destroyed by British, French and Indian soldiers during the Second Opium War, is named after one of Arthur Sackler's wives.

Wealth derived from opium, going back to the early nineteenth century, has thus left a distinctive stamp on American architectural styles, modes of consumption, interior decor, philanthropy and forms of recreation. So showy and ostentatious were these merchants' houses that the Canton graduates could be said to have invented the enduring American fondness for residences that look like 'visible bank accounts'.[40]

Samuel Russell, the founder of Russell & Co., built himself a forty-four-room Greek Revival mansion that occupied an entire city block in Middletown, Connecticut: it now houses the philosophy department of Wesleyan University.[41] My son happened to be an undergraduate at Wesleyan while I was writing *Flood of Fire*, the last volume of the Ibis Trilogy. While visiting him I would often pass Russell House (as it is known on campus): it was always unsettling to recall that the mansion had been built with wealth generated by Indian poppy farmers and Chinese opium users.

Samuel Russell's mentor, Thomas Handasyd Perkins, owned a vast country estate as well as a four-storey townhouse with twenty-six fireplaces in Boston's Temple Place. But he was outdone by his nephew John Perkins Cushing, who bought up the entire city block around his mansion on Boston's Summer Street and surrounded it with a 'wall of porcelain' imported from Guangzhou. He also owned a 200-acre estate in Watertown, Massachusetts, with a deer park, a

20-acre lawn, and a mansion designed by one of the leading architects of the day, Andrew Jackson Downing.[42] The same architect would later remodel Warren Delano Jr's house, Algonac, adding Asian-style verandas and overhanging eaves.[43] John Murray Forbes owned a vast estate in Milton Massachusetts, and also 'bought the seven-mile-long island of Naushon next to Martha's Vineyard that is still privately held by his descendants'.[44]

Chinese-style design elements were common in the houses that the Canton graduates built, and are an indication that what China-returned merchants aspired to was not, in Downs's words, mere 'baronial splendor' or 'the comfort of the eighteenth century British squirearchy'.[45] Their aspirations were strongly influenced by memories of the luxurious lives that they had led in Guangzhou's Foreign Enclave, and by their observations of the country estates of wealthy Chinese merchants, with their collections of porcelain and artworks, and their landscaped gardens, which showcased the amazing botanical riches of the region's famous nurseries (see insert image 15). So they filled the interiors of their own houses with chinoiserie and artworks that they had collected in Guangzhou. John Cushing, for instance, decorated both his houses with 'Chinese wallpapers and porcelains so as to remind him of Canton'.[46] The prominent Pennsylvania merchant John Latimer made a fortune in the opium trade and built himself an opulent residence at 359, Walnut Street, Philadelphia. On entering, visitors immediately encountered a massive oil painting depicting a fire in Guangzhou's Foreign Enclave. In the library they saw:

> Chinese porcelain teacups, saucers, milk and teapots, sugar dish and stand, and a tea canister—each item with a colorful 'Canton' or 'Nanking' border. The pantry shelves bore a still larger assortment of willow-ware dinner sets, each piece showing an Oriental willow tree springing from a tiny river island. A fine corner cupboard in the dining room was reserved for ceramic

pieces decorated with the coats of arms and monograms of various Latimer family members. This room also exhibited large medallion-ware vases and two nests of intricately carved Chinese rosewood tables. In the dimly lit upper hallway, atop a washstand, one could perceive the glistening of Chinese lacquered toilet articles, in purple and gold.[47]

As is often the case, the tastes of the rich were emulated all the way down the American social ladder. It has been estimated that one-tenth to one-fifth of the effects in early nineteenth-century homes in major American port cities like Boston, Salem or Philadelphia were of Chinese origin. This does not pertain only to the wealthy. In fact: 'The majority of Chinese articles shipped to early Pennsylvania were found in poorer homes.'[48] Clippers returning from China typically carried substantial amounts of inferior porcelain that could be sold very cheaply in America.

It isn't only in today's America that dollar stores are filled with Chinese-made goods; shops that catered to poor Americans in the nineteenth century were also filled with Chinese objects. Nor were all these objects of identifiably Chinese origin. A great deal of 'Americana' then, as now, was also made in China. Many of the older portraits of George Washington that hang in American homes are actually copies, from the studios of Guangzhou. This is true also of many of the botanical water colours, landscapes and portraits that are to be found in America's antique stores, and on the walls of bed-and-breakfasts across the country.

The influence of Guangzhou and its Cohong merchants is evident also in the taste for horticulture that the Canton graduates brought back with them. Many of them created lavish and enormously expensive gardens, and encouraged their gardeners to experiment with breeding new varieties of flowers, as was the practice in the nurseries of Guangzhou. John Cushing once instructed his nephew

John Murray Forbes, who was then in Canton, 'to collect for me an assortment of the handsomest and rarest Japonicas and Peonies that are to be had in China together with any other rare and handsome flowers, plants or shrubs, and an assortment of flower Seed'.[49]

Even the recreational interests of the Canton graduates bore the stamp of Guangzhou. Sailing, yachting, rowing and regattas were among the few diversions that they had been permitted in Guangzhou, and on their return to America several of them became enthusiastic supporters of these pursuits. John Cushing's yacht *Sylph* won the first American yacht race in 1832. In these many ways 'retired China traders contributed much to the luxury and display of the lifestyle of the American rich'.[50]

Yet, despite their wealth, many Canton graduates never ceased to pine for the luxurious lives they had led in Guangzhou's Foreign Enclave.[51] Those lifestyles were impossible to reproduce in America no matter how much money they spent. Particularly vexing was the problem of staff: in America it was impossible to find servants and cooks who were as skilled as those of Guangzhou. Some Canton nabobs solved the problem by simply importing their servants from China.

In other words, these great American tycoons invented a lifestyle back home that could be described as a 'Cantonized' way of living. Because of their social eminence, elements of this style were widely copied and eventually seeped deep into the fabric of American social life.

The wider ripple effects of opium money on America are perhaps best illustrated by stories of individual traders and their families.

One particularly good example is Abbot Low—a historical figure with whom, despite the distance in time and circumstances, I feel a strange sense of connection. Abbot Low was a Brooklyn transplant, as am I, and he owned many properties on the street where my children went to school, in Brooklyn Heights. Another, perhaps more meaningful, link is a building that is named after Abbot Low: Columbia University's Low Library, around which I spent a lot of time in my first years in America.

Abbot Low was, of course, none other than the amiable young man who travelled to Guangzhou on the same ship as the unfortunate Will Irving. Given how valuable kinship was in the opium trade, it is hardly surprising that Abbot Low's career followed a completely different trajectory from that of his fellow traveller. He had an advantage over Will in that he hailed from a more powerful sub-caste: he was by origin a Massachusetts Yankee, born in Salem. His father was a merchant specializing in African and South American products, who moved his family to Brooklyn (40, Concord Street) in 1828, when 'Brooklyn was a village, and more like a big farm-yard; for the pigs ran about the streets in large numbers'.[52] As was the custom in upper-tier Salem families, Abbot Low went to Harvard and worked for a while as a clerk for an import–export firm in Salem. It was almost ordained that China would be the next step in Abbot Low's career because his uncle William H. Low was then the head of Russell & Co. in Guangzhou.

Unusually for the time, William Low had taken his wife, Abigail, to China with him. Since she was childless and in delicate health, he had also brought along his favourite niece, Harriet, Abbot Low's sister. Abigail and Harriet were the first American women ever to live in China. Their residence, however, was not in Guangzhou, which foreign women were forbidden to enter, but in Macao, where they were at the centre of a lively social circle that included the painter George Chinnery, who had spent many years in Calcutta before moving to South China (he had two sons with his Bengali mistress, one of whom, Robin Chinnery, is a major character in the Ibis Trilogy).[53] Chinnery and Harriet became good friends and he painted a fine portrait of her, with her smiling, rosy-cheeked face framed by ringlets and a book in her hands, highlighting her chief interest (see insert image 13).[54]

Harriet Low was a good writer herself: her diaries and correspondence chronicle the social lives of American and English expatriates in China in finely observed detail. Her adventurous spirit led to some notable escapades: she and her aunt once smuggled themselves into Guangzhou's Foreign Enclave, and even managed to spend a few days there before they were discovered and evicted by the Chinese authorities.[55] Their visit was not appreciated by the 'inveterate bachelors' of the Foreign Enclave either. 'What will Canton turn into, and where will bachelors find rest?' grumbled one merchant, while 'a crusty old fellow' was heard to remark: 'I hope we shall never be *bothered* with ladies in Canton again.'[56]

On another occasion, while trying to recover from a thwarted love affair, Harriet left Macao and moved into Russell & Co.'s opium-receiving ship at Lintin Island.[57] Although she avoids mentioning the drug in her papers, she was probably one of the few American women to observe the inner workings of the opium trade.

The later lives of both Abigail and Harriet were dogged by misfortune. Abigail Low's brothers, Frank and Joseph Knapp, were hanged in 1830 for their part in the murder of a prominent Salem shipowner and slave trader, Joseph White.[58] This was one of the most sensational crimes of nineteenth-century America and found mention in the works of Edgar Allan Poe and Nathaniel Hawthorne.[59] As for Harriet Low, she was prevented by her family from marrying her true love, and ended up married to a banker whose business failed within a few years. Having lost all her money, she was eventually provided for by her brother, Abbot Low, in Brooklyn.[60]

Abbot Low overlapped only briefly with his family in China, but he was soon very much at home in Russell & Co.: it is evident from his letters that he quickly became adept at selling opium at the best possible prices. Within five years of his arrival he was writing to a colleague: 'We have been doing well, exceedingly well, the past and present year and shall probably enter upon the next with flattering prospects . . . From India our consignments have been larger this season than any previous one since I have been here.'[61] These 'consignments' from India were, of course, shipments of opium.

But Low's views about his business seem to have undergone a change around the time Chinese attitudes towards opium smugglers began to harden. In 1839, after he and all the other opium traders in Guangzhou had been forced to surrender their drug stocks to Commissioner Lin Zexu, he wrote his sister Harriet a long letter about what had transpired.

> Of the whole quantity given up we [Russell & Co.] surrendered 1407 chests! Shortly before the Commissioner arrived we sent a consul to our friends declining to receive any further [opium] consignments; and for various reasons I am glad we are done irrevocably with a branch of business, that of late has seemed actually disreputable, a trade which has brought us into contact with the most degraded Chinese, and consequently served to sink us in the estimation of the better classes.[62]

The above passage leaves no doubt that Abbot Low, a deeply religious young Protestant, was dealing directly with the dregs of the Chinese underworld, and was perfectly well aware of that fact. Indeed the Canton graduates' involvement in opium smuggling was by no means indirect, or merely a matter of speculating in a commodity sight unseen: some of them spent extended periods on the receiving ships at Lintin and directly oversaw the sale of opium chests to Chinese smugglers. Robert Bennett Forbes spent so much time on a receiving ship that he fell ill because of 'the effluvia of opium'.[63]

Six years in China were enough for Abbot Low to make 'quite a good-sized fortune': two years before the end of his sojourn in

Guangzhou he wrote to his father announcing his decision to return
to the United States in 1840, come what may.[64] He kept to his plan and
left as intended, just before the British attacked China, thereby missing
out on the windfall profits that other American traders reaped during
the British boycott of Guangzhou. On reaching New York he sent a
wistful letter to Warren Delano Jr, who was then heading Russell &
Co. in Guangzhou:

> Sometimes when I think that if I had remained in Canton only
> a few months more I could have made as much as at any pre-
> vious time in the same number of years, there is a momen-
> tary feeling of regret; but it always yields to reflection . . . if I
> cannot keep a contented mind with what I have now, any sum
> of money would not secure it to me. I shall endeavor to carry
> out that rational plan of life which you doubtless give me the
> credit of having formed long ago, i.e., of taking a wife and set-
> tling down in a very quiet unpretending sort of way—more on
> the subject some months hence.[65]

Abbot Low followed the first part of his 'rational plan of life' to the
letter, marrying a 'sympathetic young Brooklyn lady', Miss Ellen
Dow, shortly after his return.[66] By that time he had already set up
his own firm, A.A. Low & Brothers, which soon became one of the
leading shipping companies in the United States, with a 'clipper fleet
consisting of sixteen vessels; clippers, barks and barkentines'.[67] One
of his first ships was named *Houqua*, after Wu Bingjian, and was
captained for many years by his brother Charles.

From shipping Abbot Low branched out into many other industries, investing in the first trans-Atlantic cable as well as the
Chesapeake and Ohio Railway. To house his expanding firm he also
constructed the building that is now the South Street Seaport Museum
in Manhattan.

So greatly did Abbot Low prosper that he was unable to keep to the second part of his 'rational plan of life'. Instead of 'settling down in a very quiet unpretending sort of way', he built himself an opulent palace at 3, Pierrepont Place in Brooklyn Heights, and moved in with his family in 1857. The house commands a sweeping view of New York's harbour, which would have allowed the family to watch the installation of the Statue of Liberty from their bedroom windows as it was happening. Abbot Low's mansion still exists, and in 2015 it came on the market at 40 million dollars, the most expensive listing ever in Brooklyn. Among those who are reported to have been interested in buying it were actor Matt Damon and his wife, Luciana Barroso.[68]

Living in their palatial Brooklyn mansion, the Lows put down deep roots in New York. One of Abbot Low's sons, Seth Low, became Mayor of Brooklyn, and then of greater New York. In between he also served as President of Columbia University: it was he who gifted the Low Library to the university, in his father's memory.

In one of those uncanny synchronicities that haunt the history of opium, it was in the Low Library's splendid rotunda, in 1962, that Brooklyn-born Arthur M. Sackler, the brain behind the marketing of the addictive and widely abused drug Valium, held the first major show of his collection of Chinese art and antiquities. Like many members of the Boston Concern, Arthur Sackler was a passionate collector of Chinese art.[69] His nephew Richard Sackler, who would become the force behind the launch and marketing of OxyContin, was a student at Columbia at that time, and proudly took his roommate to his uncle's show. The whole family, the roommate would later recall, had 'a thing about Asian art and Asian beauty'.[70] Years later, in Appalachia, pairing Valium with OxyContin would come to be known as 'the Cadillac High'.[71]

Another of Abbot Low's sons, Abbot Augustus 'Gus' Low, had an even more remarkable career. An inventor and industrialist, he at one time held more patents than any American, other than Thomas Edison. Apart from setting up industries based on his inventions, he also acquired an enormous tract of land, 46,000 acres—considerably larger than the duchy of Liechtenstein—in the Adirondacks, around St. Lawrence County in upstate New York (the county seat is called 'Canton'). There he built an empire of forest-related industries on land that he personally terraformed with dams. He also laid down railway lines to transport products like maple syrup and timber—but the venture didn't end well because sparks from the coal engines ignited disastrous forest fires. Still, Gus Low's signature remains imprinted on the landscape of the Adirondacks to this day. 'A.A. Low's wilderness dams have left a lasting legacy,' says the website of the Blue Mountain Lake Museum. 'Paddlers today enjoy more than three scenic miles of unencumbered flat water on the Bog River between the Lower and Upper dams.'[72]

These are just a few examples of the many ways in which money brought back from China grew and multiplied in America over generations, slowly seeping into the soil and even transforming the terrain.

The timescale over which the impacts of opium money were felt is illustrative of the workings of processes that are the exact inverse of the forms of discrimination that have locked many African Americans, Native Americans and working-class white Americans into patterns of structural, intergenerational poverty. The advantages of race, family, class and education that the Canton graduates enjoyed created the mirrored opposite of those processes, reinforcing patterns of structural, intergenerational wealth and privilege. And contrary to 'free market' mythologies, those fortunes were made possible ultimately by the structures of kinship, class and race that allowed the Canton graduates to monopolize the American share of the nineteenth-century opium trade.

The fact that the Canton graduates were largely successful in evading the stigma associated with opium peddling was also due to class and race. The idea that their activities were overlooked because 'mores were different then' in regard to drug dealing is completely unfounded. If anything, the social stigma on drug dealing was even more powerful then than it is now.[73] The stigma, and the silences it created, persisted over generations. Phyllis Forbes Kerr, great-great-great-granddaughter of Robert Bennet Forbes and editor of his papers, has spoken of dinners at the Forbes mansion in Milton, Massachusetts, when her uncles would tease her grandmother. 'We would sit at the table and she would say something about Forbes and they would say, "Oh, you mean the drug dealer," and she would get really mad.'[74]

What was truly different then was that it was not considered untoward for white men to inflict incalculable harm on other peoples, especially if it was done in faraway places. In a country where Native Americans were being dispossessed and slain en masse, and where millions of enslaved black people were toiling on plantations, selling opium to the distant Chinese probably did not appear particularly reprehensible.

The Canton graduates were protected also by the prevalent belief that a group of upper-crust white men from some of the nation's oldest Protestant families, men who had become titans of industry and pillars of their communities, simply could not have done anything blameworthy. These dynamics of race and class have not, by any means, ceased to operate even in twenty-first-century America. They resurfaced during the opioid epidemic, when the top executives of Purdue Pharma were often afforded preferential treatment by the legal system, merely because they were able to present themselves as respectable white businessmen who were 'temperamentally incapable of committing the kinds of crimes that should land a person in prison'.[75] And so, in 2019, the Mexican drug lord Joaquin 'El Chapo'

Guzman was sentenced to life in prison by a United States court, and was made to forfeit 12 billion dollars, while the managers of Purdue Pharma, despite being given three felony convictions, did not go to jail, and the Sacklers retained possession of most of their fortune.[76]

It also worked in favour of the Canton graduates that addiction was considered a moral failing, associated with people who were inherently weak-natured and naturally disposed to vice. These assumptions too remain powerfully embedded in contemporary American culture: the makers of prescription opioids took advantage of them by consistently presenting opioid addicts as people who were congenitally weak, incapable of self-restraint and prone to addiction.[77] The fact that these insinuations did not ultimately find general acceptance in today's America was probably due to the fact that the victims, in this case, were mainly white.

Although the story of the Canton graduates is unknown to most Americans, it is not a secret to the descendants of the great American opium magnates. When I was on book tours in the United States for the novels of the Ibis Trilogy, I often found that audiences in the West and Midwest would respond with surprise, and even shock, when I mentioned the names of the American institutions and families that benefited from the opium trade. However, this never happened in Massachusetts; there, audiences would, instead, nod and smile in wry agreement. Sometimes people would come up to me afterwards to say that they were related to the families I had mentioned; some even pointed me to the sources that I have used in writing this chapter.

One striking feature of the lives of the Canton graduates was that on their return to the United States they became the very souls of probity, 'almost distressingly genteel' in their ways.[78] Many, if not most, of them were demonstratively religious, and some were extremely generous in building and funding churches. Abbot Low, for instance, helped his family establish the still flourishing First Unitarian Church on Pierrepont Street in Brooklyn, New York.

In their business practices too, far from being swashbuckling entrepreneurs, the Canton graduates were cautious to a fault: 'they bore not the slightest resemblance to the caricatures of the grasping pirates of the Gilded Age'.[79] John Murray Forbes, for instance, was rigorously ethical in the management of his railroads, refusing 'to tolerate the slightest suggestion of stock watering'. Yet, as Downs notes, 'in their youthful days at Canton, these paragons of railroad virtue had, to the man, been opium traders'.[80]

The Canton graduates' yearning to be good citizens, and good Christians, is so patently evident that it is impossible not to ask how they reconciled their criminal dealings with their consciences. To be sure, this question could be asked of everyone who was dealing in drugs in Guangzhou at the time, but it is particularly pertinent in relation to the Yankee merchants for two reasons. First, many of the Americans insistently harped on the subject of conscience: 'Went to Church yesterday,' wrote Robert B. Forbes in 1839 as the opium crisis was intensifying, '& heard an exhilarating sermon from Mr Dickinson on the subject of conscience—I am glad that we have decent preaching here for nothing carries one home more than to meet in church & if we had not good preaching I should not go.'[81] And second, in 1844 the United States signed an 'unequal treaty' with the Qing state that explicitly banned the opium trade while giving American missionaries the right to build churches and hospitals in China.[82] (The American treaty differed from the one signed with the British in that the latter made no mention of churches and was silent on the opium issue—because the British government's strategy was to pressurize the Chinese into legalizing opium of their own accord.)[83]

This American insistence on the religious clauses shows that, more than any other foreign community, they were possessed with great missionary zeal. Yet, soon after 1844 the majority of American firms, led by Russell & Co., went back to trading in opium. There was, however, one very important exception: it so happened that the American community in Guangzhou also included a firm that was consistently and vocally opposed to opium smuggling. This was Olyphant & Co., a New York-based firm that prospered in the China trade even though it never dealt in opium. Founded by devout Christians, Olyphant & Co. was also a kinship group, its partners connected mainly through their wives. They were great benefactors to missionaries, financing their travel and stay in China. They never missed an opportunity to remind their fellow Americans of the indefensibility of opium smuggling.[84]

One particularly noteworthy partner of Olyphant & Co. was a merchant by the name of Charles W. King. A former student of Brown University, King was a teenager when he went to China, where he seems to have been something of a misfit from the start. Within the American community he was known as 'Miss King', evidently because there was something about his appearance that struck his compatriots as effeminate. 'King and Perit called this morning,' notes Harriet Low, in her journal entry for 21 June 1832. 'King looks more delicate than ever. P's a pretty boy about 18 I suppose.' Elsewhere she notes that King and two of his friends were known in Guangzhou's Foreign Enclave as 'the three ladies', 'from their fair complexion and some other things'.[85]

Whatever those 'other things' might have been, it is clear from these comments that Charles King was the target of various kinds of slurs within the community, and this might have played a part in hardening his attitudes towards his fellow merchants. In any event, he was absolutely unsparing in his denunciation of their smuggling activities, which is truly remarkable considering that this was a very close-knit and close-lipped community, where to be a dissident was to invite not only social opprobrium but also financial disaster.

In the late 1830s, when the opium crisis was intensifying, King tried repeatedly to get the foreign merchant community to take a public pledge:

> We, the undersigned, believing that the opium trade with China is fraught with evils, commercial, political, social and moral; that it gives just offence to the Government of this country; arrays the authorities and the people against the extension of our commerce and the liberty of our residence; and defers the hope of true Christian amelioration; do hereby declare that we will not take part in the purchase, transportation, or sale of the drug, either as principals or agents.[86]

Other than the partners of Olyphant and Co., not a single foreign merchant was willing to sign the pledge.[87] But that did not deter King: he appealed to the Canton Chamber of Commerce, submitted memorials, and even petitioned the United States Congress, though it was all to no avail. In 1839, when it became clear that the British were planning to treat Lin Zexu's seizure of contraband opium as a casus belli for war, King wrote an open letter that deserves to be treated as the *J'accuse* of the opium trade. Addressed to Charles Eliot, the British emissary, the letter points out that the opium traffic was entirely 'the creature of the East India Company', and goes on to list the harms that it was inflicting on China:

> For nearly forty years, the British merchants, led on by the East India Company, have been driving a trade, in violation of the highest laws, and the best interests of the Chinese empire. This course has been pushed so far, as to derange its currency, to corrupt its officers, and ruin multitudes of its people. The traffic has become associated in the politics of the country, with embarrassments and evil omens; in its penal code, with

the axe and the dungeon; in the breasts of men in private life,
with the wreck of property, virtue, honour, and happiness. All
ranks, from the Emperor on the throne, to the people of the
humblest hamlets, have felt its sting.[88]

Everything that Charles King said in his letter was common knowledge
among the foreign merchants of Guangzhou. None of it would have
come as a surprise to any of the outwardly pious young Americans
who were peddling drugs in China then: they were being told the
same things by Qing officials, by Christian preachers and, indeed, by
many anti-opium activists in England and America. In private, many
Yankee opium traffickers acknowledged that the opium trade was
causing great harm to China. Robert B. Forbes, for example, wrote to
his wife from Guangzhou, in 1839, frankly confessing that 'I made my
first fortune' in the opium trade, while also admitting that the trade
was 'demoralizing the minds, destroying the bodies, & draining the
country [China] of money'. But at the same time, he advised his wife
to be very discreet if the subject ever came up.[89]

This was of a piece with the Canton graduates' code of silence: as
Downs points out, 'whenever they were compelled to say anything
public about the traffic, they lied about it'.[90] The omertà was maintained
by their descendants, who were also careful to avoid mentioning how
their families' money had been made. Thomas Handasyd Perkins, for
instance, dominated the Turkish opium trade for years but 'opium is
not mentioned even once in a memoir compiled by his son-in-law and
published in 1856, two years after Perkins' death'.[91] Clearly, the Canton
graduates and their families had misgivings about the opium trade,
yet as Downs notes: 'It is remarkable, under the circumstances, that
there are so few expressions of guilt in the correspondence, especially
because the drug traders were often men of upright character.'[92]

One of the reasons why so many Americans of supposedly
'upright character' felt so few compunctions about their criminal

conduct was that for them Christian teachings actually played a very distant second fiddle to the gospel of Free Trade. As they saw it, their first duty was to make profits for their investors and stockholders. It was on exactly these grounds that Robert Bennet Forbes rejected British pleas to join in the evacuation of Guangzhou: his blunt reply to Charles Elliot was 'that his obligations to his owners took precedence over other considerations, whether of honor, patriotism, or the long-run benefit of the community'.[93] There could be no clearer summation of the most important accomplishment of the doctrine of Free Trade—the erasure of all ethical constraints in regard to profit-making.

In the post-Opium Wars period, these attitudes became even more strident. One merchant dismissed concerns about British and American drug dealing in Shanghai with these words:

> No doubt your anticipations of future evil have a certain foundation . . . But it is my business to make a fortune with the least possible loss of time . . . in two or three years, at farthest, I hope to realize a fortune and get away and what can it matter to me, if all Shanghai disappear afterwards, in fire or flood.[94]

This merchant's 'anticipations of future evil' were well-founded. It was with words very much like these that the managers of pharmaceutical companies justified the aggressive marketing of opiates to vulnerable Americans. It is with arguments like these also that the world's giant energy companies justify their suppression of the findings of their own climate scientists, even though they know that by doing so they are condemning all of humanity, including themselves and their families, to fire and flood. The predation that was once inflicted on distant lands and other races has slowly but surely turned the predators' claws on their own compatriots and their kin.

It is important to remember that no matter how genteel their manners, no matter how earnest their religious fervour, the British and American traders in Guangzhou belonged to an Anglo-American elite that had made a fine art of spouting pieties of various kinds while inflicting immeasurable harm on people around the world. The English in particular, with their endless moralizing, were often able to persuade people that anything they did was ipso facto respectable, no matter how indefensible it might appear. For Americans of British origin, who in that period regarded themselves as the junior partners of the English, the very fact that the East India Company had been promoting the opium trade for decades legitimized it in their eyes.[95] '[T]he [opium] trade has been carried on,' writes Robert B. Forbes in a letter home, 'by the most respectable merchants here & the great & honorable East India Company . . . has been the cultivator of the drug in India consequently there has been no moral feeling of indignation connected with the business.'[96] As Haddad notes: 'With these paragons of global trade [the EIC] casting their combined luminescence on the opium trade, could one really expect an impressionable young man to question the morality of the trade?'[97] This is perhaps the only persuasive extenuating circumstance that can be cited in favour of American, Parsi, Armenian and Baghdadi opium traders: they were merely following a path that had been charted, and was protected, by the world's paramount power, one that enforced its claims to moral ascendancy with overwhelming military and naval power.

American admiration of the British Empire only grew stronger over time. In a book published in 1920, the American writer Ellen Newbold La Motte wrote:

How . . . does it happen that we in America know nothing about Great Britain's Opium Monopoly? That the facts are new to us and come to us as a shock? One is because of our

admiration for Great Britain . . . Consequently England has
been able to rely upon those who know the facts to keep silent,
either through admiration or through fear.[98]

As the historian Priya Satia has shown, British colonialists in this
period developed a whole range of techniques for the 'management
of conscience', of which not the least important was the idea of
'history' as a trajectory of continuous progress. No doubt, many
Canton graduates also persuaded themselves that the opium trade
was a necessary evil, made justifiable by America's accelerating
industrial economy.

Nor should it be forgotten that American Canton graduates in
particular belonged to a country where many kinds of violence and
criminality were routinized in certain distinctive ways. Many of
them were descended from men who had participated personally
in exterminatory wars against the Native Americans of New England. Those wars were still raging, not far from New England, in
their own lifetimes. Slavery, similarly, was firmly entrenched in the
American South, and many New England shipowners continued
to covertly participate in the traffic in human beings, despite a rising tide of abolitionist sentiment in the Northeast. For young men
who had come of age in these circumstances, smuggling opium
into China may well have seemed like a relatively minor transgres-
sion. For them, Chinese addicts were just another set of expendable people.

Of course, none of this was ever publicly professed. Not only did
the Canton graduates go to great lengths to hide their connections
with the opium trade, but they also lied through their teeth, claiming
to have little or no connections with drug smuggling when the First
Opium War ignited controversies in the United States. These lies
were necessary, as Norwood notes, 'because Americans of all kinds
were well aware of opium's effects'.[99]

It is sometimes argued that Americans and Britons in this period did not look upon opium as illegal because it was not prohibited by law in their own countries. It is certainly true that many kinds of opium-based tonics and medications were widely consumed in Europe and America. But the ingredient in those medications was a low grade of opium, not the highly addictive substance that was in circulation in China and Southeast Asia: to conflate medicinal opium with the chandu-grade substance is like lumping codeine-based cough syrups with morphine.[100]

But more importantly, in the first half of the nineteenth century Anglo-American elites did not deem it necessary to ban opium because they did not believe that widespread opium addiction could ever pose a threat to their own countries. The reasons for this were, first, because there was very little chandu-grade opium in circulation in the United States and Britain. Second, the techniques for refining opium into chandu and smoking it in a pipe were extremely complex, and there was very little knowledge of them in the West. Third, there was a widespread belief in the West that a formal prohibition was unnecessary because white men were constitutionally disinclined to smoke opium.[101] Finally, instead of a legal ban, the practice of opium smoking was kept at bay in the United States and Britain by a racialized social stigma that was probably more effective than any law would have been. 'As Hogarth distinguished between beer and gin, the American practitioner distinguished between medicinal and smoking opium; the former was beneficial and indispensable, the latter dangerous and unnecessary.'[102]

As a result, between 1850 and the late 1860s in the United States, opium smoking was practised only by Chinese migrants. 'The first white man who smoked opium in America is said to have been a sporting character, named Clendenyn. This was in California in 1868.'[103] When the practice began to spread, bans were enacted locally, in San Francisco in 1875 and Virginia City in 1876. The Federal government also adopted various measures to keep the practice in check.[104]

In Britain, similarly, the opium that was in general circulation was a low grade of the drug, not 'smoking opium', and even this came to be strictly regulated as a 'poison', after the passage of the Pharmacy Act in 1868.[105] But just as in the United States, so too in Britain opium smoking was kept at bay by a powerful social stigma. And had it been the case that a group of foreign merchants had been engaged in smuggling large quantities of the drug into England, it certainly would have been banned.[106] This was one of the many questions that Lin Zexu posed in his undelivered letter to Queen Victoria: 'Let us suppose that foreigners came from another country, and brought opium into England, and seduced the people of your country to smoke it, would not you, the sovereign of the said country, look upon such a procedure with anger, and in your just indignation endeavor to get rid of it?'[107]

Hence the idea that Western merchants did not consider opium 'illegal' because there was no law against it is merely another disingenuous dodge. Those merchants were perfectly aware of China's laws, and they knew also that they would have been reviled by their families and peers if they had sold vast quantities of high-grade opium in their own countries.

Ultimately, what made it possible for the Canton graduates to get away with their lies, and their crimes, was that the burden was borne by non-white people in faraway countries. For white elites, at this time, it was completely normal to apply absolutely different standards to people of other races. The very fact of their racial difference meant that non-white people could be despoiled at will and their laws ignored.[108] Even though the Anglo-American drug smugglers of Guangzhou were heirs to both the Christian and Enlightenment ideas of the equality of all people, in practice their conduct followed a completely contrary logic. Instead, it fell to the Chinese, who were by no means egalitarian or universalist in their beliefs, to couch their admonitions of opium smugglers in the language of shared humanity. As Charles W. King pointed out in his letter to the British emissary, many of Commissioner Lin's moves were premised upon the conviction that 'those foreigners, though born and brought up beyond the pale of civilization, *have yet human hearts*'.[109]

After the two Opium Wars, when it became clear that China was completely helpless before the Western powers, the attitudes of Anglo-American merchants became even more stridently racist. In Guangzhou, for instance, foreign merchants moved their establishments to Shamian Island, from which Chinese people were excluded. The principle of judicial extraterritoriality that had been forced on China by the British ensured that white foreigners could not be tried under local laws, which meant that they could behave with impunity. 'We always make a practice,' said one British drug smuggler, 'of running over the Chinese fishing boats by night, for they will not get out of our way.'[110]

Essentially it was because colonialism had created a structure of power in which Euro-descended elites and their allies among Euro-adjacent diasporic groups enjoyed absolute dominance, that virtuous young Americans could commit their crimes in faraway countries and return with whitewashed hands to their homes to be celebrated as heroes for their role in building the American economy. In other words, it was the colonial world-system that allowed them to realize the aspiration that drug lords like Lucky Luciano and Pablo Escobar hankered after: of successfully going 'legit'.

The influence of America's Canton graduates extended far beyond their own lifetimes, ensuring a long afterlife for their practices. One such practice was that of collaborating with criminal networks: unbeknownst to themselves, Abbot Low and his American colleagues in Guangzhou were establishing a precedent that would ultimately

tea

IS 100% SWADESHI

INSERTED BY THE INDIAN TEA MARKET EXPANSION BO

1. Annada Munshi (1905–85) created a new context for the colonial practice of tea drinking by using the symbolism of the Indian national movement, such as a spinning wheel and a sari-clad figure that evokes 'Mother India'. As Gautam Bhadra notes, with this image 'tea was positioned within the idioms of Gandhian self-reliance and the nationalist movement'. (Gautam Bhadra, *From an Imperial Product to a National Drink*, 19.) It was through the imagery of advertising that tea was turned into chai, the quintessentially Indian beverage.

2. Towering racks and columns give the Patna Opium Factory's Stacking Room the stately dimensions of a cathedral. (W.S. Sherwill, courtesy Yale Center for British Art)

3. In *Sea of Poppies*, Deeti enters the Mixing Room of the Ghazipur Opium Factory to be met by a startling sight: '*[A] host of dark, legless torsos was circling around and around, like some enslaved tribe of demons. This vision— along with the overpowering fumes—made her groggy, and to keep herself from fainting she began to move slowly ahead. When her eyes had grown more accustomed to the gloom, she discovered the secret of those circling torsos: they were bare-bodied men, sunk waist-deep in tanks of opium, tramping around and around to soften the sludge. Their eyes were vacant, glazed, and yet somehow they managed to keep moving, as slow as ants in honey, tramping, treading.*' The mixing room of the Patna Factory would have been similar, but Sherwill has cleaned it up by removing the opium from the mixing vats. (W.S. Sherwill, courtesy Yale Center for British Art)

4. Sita Ram presents this view of the Patna Opium Godown as an exercise in perspective, knowing that his viewers would have no interest in the crowds of workers who would have been swarming all over the grounds. (Sita Ram, British Library, London, UK © British Library Board)

5 and 6. In the painting on the right, Sita Ram empties the godown of opium and turns the interior into an interesting play of volumes and shapes, putting the image in conversation with Piranesi's famous *Round Tower* (*left*). (Giovanni Battista Piranesi, courtesy Philadelphia Museum of Art, and Sita Ram, British Library, London, UK © British Library Board)

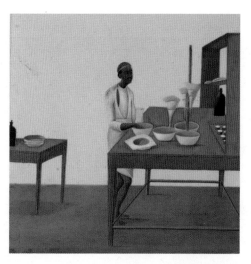

7. The Opium Department's British officials believed that their Indian employees were 'inherently untrustworthy and corrupt', and chemical tests were introduced partly to keep them in check (Wormer, 239). But Shiva Lal subverts those assumptions in this depiction of Indian technicians working in a laboratory. (Shiva Lal © Victoria and Albert Museum, London)

8. The manufacturing processes of the opium factories were like those of a rural cottage industry, with all the work being done manually. At the same time, the systems of surveillance and management, as well as the processes for assembling the product, were very much like those of the factories that came into being with the Industrial Revolution. This was a typically colonial iteration of modernity. (Shiva Lal © Victoria and Albert Museum, London)

9. Sir Jamsetjee Jejeebhoy by an unidentified Chinese artist. Of the many extant portraits of Sir Jamsetjee, this is the one that, to my mind, best captures the sitter's personality. (Courtesy Parsi-Times.com)

10. The grandest of the 'factories' in Guangzhou's Foreign Enclave was that of the East India Company, which had an extended portico and enclosed garden. Next to it was the Dutch Factory, which was only slightly less grand. In the eighteenth century, Parsi merchants were accommodated in the Dutch Factory. Many American merchants had their lodgings in the Swedish Factory. (William Daniell, courtesy Yale Center for British Art, Paul Mellon Collection)

11. The Thirteen Factories: in the foreground is the Floating City and Jackass Point, the Foreign Enclave's principal quay. Across the square, right next to the English Factory, is the Fungtai Factory, where Bahram Modi had his quarters. (Artists in Guangzhou, courtesy Peabody Essex Museum)

12. One of the wealthiest men in China in the nineteenth century, Wu Bingjian (Howqua) was known to have close ties with several founders of world-renowned companies, including Sir Jamsetjee Jejeebhoy, William Jardine, James Matheson and Abiel Abbot Low. (Courtesy Peabody Essex Museum)

13. Harriet Low's diaries and correspondence paint a vivid picture of the social circle of British and American merchants in southern China. The Lows were originally from Salem, Massachusetts, so it is entirely fitting that this portrait of the much-travelled Harriet Low has found its home at the Peabody Essex Museum. (George Chinnery, courtesy Peabody Essex Museum)

CANTON.

14. This view of Guangzhou shows the city's old double walls (they were torn down in the 1920s). The walls circle around the side of Mt Yuexiu (Yuexiushan, North Hill), converging upon the Zhenhai Tower. The Tower now houses the city museum of Guangzhou. The small fort occupied by Havildar Kesri Singh and the Bengal Volunteers battalion was situated on the far side of the Zhenhai Tower. The village of Sanyuanli is about halfway between the river on the left and the outermost city wall. (Courtesy Peabody Essex Museum)

15. Villas like this one, with their landscaped gardens, became a model for American, British and Parsi merchants. (Engraving by S. Bradshaw; photograph by Hulton Archive/Getty Images)

16. Chinese motifs on a Parsi gara sari, including a rickshaw in the foreground. (Photograph by author)

17. Guan Qiaochang was the most important artist in Guangzhou before the
First Opium War. (Courtesy Peabody Essex Museum)

18 and 19. The contrast in the styles of George Chinnery and Guan Qiaochang is nowhere more evident than in these two pictures. At the top is Chinnery's painting of Dr Thomas Colledge in his Ophthalmic Surgery. At the bottom is Guan Qiaochang's portrait of Dr Peter Parker. (Courtesy Peabody Essex Museum, and courtesy Wikipedia)

20. The Parsi building on Shamian Island, Guangzhou. The plaque at the corner reads: 'No. 2, 4, 6, 8, 10 South Shamian Street, Gazetted Building (B). Built during late Qing to Early Republican Period as the residence of Indian nationals.' (Photograph by author)

21. This is a good example of the portraits of sailors and ships' captains that Guangzhou's studios produced in abundance. Many of the nineteenth-century portraits that hang on the walls of British and American homes were actually 'Made in China'. (Spoilum, courtesy Peabody Essex Museum)

22. This exquisite Chinese sewing table led me to suspect that objects like these were the model for table-mounted Singer sewing machines, like the one my mother had. (Artists in Guangzhou, courtesy Peabody Essex Museum)

23. Chinese nodding-head dolls like these were probably the prototypes of the figures in my family's display case. (Artists in Guangzhou, courtesy Peabody Essex Museum)

come to haunt their own nation. Alfred W. McCoy has chronicled in minute detail how, through much of the twentieth century, the upper-crust, Ivy League Americans who ran the United States' intelligence services worked repeatedly with underworld opiate-peddling networks, first in parts of Europe like Sicily, southern France and Corsica, then in Southeast Asia and Latin America.[111] Those elite Americans believed, no doubt, that with their superior resources and acumen they would be able to control the drug underworld and use it for their own strategic purposes. What they did not understand was that they were colluding not only with human criminals but also with non-human entities that operate on a wholly different timescale. The unintended consequence of their collaborations was to empower the opium poppy and the coca plant—and the criminal cartels that trafficked them—to a point where they were able to establish a grip on the United States against which all human efforts have proved unavailing.

This grim story is presaged by a warning that Charles W. King included in his 1839 letter to the British emissary:

> Already, we are told, the use of the drug [opium] is insinu-ating itself into the habits of a morbid portion of Western society . . . Little, probably, is needed, particularly in com-munities where spirits are discountenanced, to bring in this more refined, more easily concealed substitute, and create a public taste for it. Such a taste once spread, and fixed, by trans-mission through one or two generations, and how shall it be eradicated?[112]

These words were all too prescient. It was precisely by actively creating a 'public taste' for opium, among 'discountenanced' and dispirited American communities, that the producers of prescription opioids addicted millions of people to prescription opiates. And, to a quite remarkable degree, those behind the opioid crisis—the rogue doctors, pharmacists, salesmen, executives and tycoons—were as indifferent to the suffering they had caused as their nineteenth-century predecessors. 'Those who bear responsibility for America's national nightmare,' writes Chris McGreal, 'show no . . . sense of guilt or torment. Even today, they shift responsibility for the epidemic onto those who fell victim to it.'[113] Like the upper-crust American opium traders of the nineteenth century, contemporary 'drug dealers in Armani suits' blamed the addicts. 'They get themselves addicted over and over again,' wrote Richard Sackler. 'They engage in it with full, criminal intent. Why should they be entitled to our sympathies?'[114] For them, the distressed rural folk who were worst affected by the opioid crisis were just as expendable as poor Asian addicts had been for their counterparts in the nineteenth century.

It is, to my mind, an entirely positive development that the current crisis has forced a reckoning with the extraordinary powers of the opium poppy, stirring up enormous outrage against the companies that reaped gargantuan profits from prescription opioids. It is notable, however, that it took a crisis that disproportionately affected white Americans to bring about this reckoning. Equally striking is the fact that the outrage against the manufacturers of prescription opioids has not led to a wider reckoning with the West's role in the promotion of opiates: this is a sign, I think, that narcotics are still being projected on to 'illegal aliens' and foreign countries in deeply misleading ways. If the story of the role that privileged, upper-class white Americans had played in the history of the opium trade were better known it would surely be more difficult, if not impossible, to impose xenophobic, anti-immigrant framings on issues concerning narcotics, as is still so often done in the United States.[115]

In 1997, on the eve of Hong Kong's return to China, *The New York Times* published a curious article on its editorial page titled 'The Opium War's Secret History: Some Awkward Truths for China and America'. The article, which attempts to walk a fine line between castigating China and atoning for America's involvement in the opium trade, mentions only one trader by name, Warren Delano Jr:

> The old China trader was close-mouthed about opium, as were his partners in Russell & Company. It is not clear how much F.D.R. knew about this source of his grandfather's wealth. But the President's recent biographer Geoffrey Ward rejects efforts by the Delano family to minimize Warren's involvement . . . The family's discomfort is understandable. We no longer believe that anything goes in the global marketplace, regardless of social consequences.[116]

The final sentence is deeply disingenuous in that it tries to explain away the opium trade by suggesting that it occurred at a time when it was generally believed that 'anything goes in the global marketplace, regardless of social consequences'. The Chinese certainly did not believe that profit trumped social consequences. This was precisely what Lin Zexu meant when he wrote in his (famously undelivered) letter to Queen Victoria that foreign opium traders, 'from their inordinate thirst after gain, are perfectly careless about the injuries they inflict upon us! And such being the case, we should like to ask what has become of that conscience which heaven has implanted in the breasts of all men?'[117]

What Lin Zexu was trying to underline in his letter to Queen Victoria, and in his pronouncements to the business communities of Guangzhou, was that the human hunger for profit can pose a grave danger to society if it is not constrained by certain ethical limits. This idea would once have seemed self-evident, which is why societies everywhere traditionally imposed certain customary restraints on commerce and on communities of traders. But that was precisely what was changing in the late eighteenth and early nineteenth centuries under the influence of Adam Smith, David Ricardo and advocates of the doctrine of Free Trade. The doctrine was radical not because it created new forms of commerce (market-oriented business ventures of many kinds long predated it); what was truly novel about it was that it invented abstract frames of reference, such as 'laws of the market', that served to eliminate all the ethical guardrails that had previously constrained trade and commerce. It is one of the great ironies of history that Adam Smith, a puritanical moral philosopher, unwittingly helped to construct a spurious moral calculus that would henceforth absolve businessmen of all responsibility for their actions by invoking an allegedly higher set of determinants—the laws of the market—which overrode every consideration of humanity, ethics and justice because humans were purportedly powerless to override them.

The idea that 'anything goes in the global marketplace' is, therefore, specifically a product of the ideologies of Free Trade that became dominant in the West, particularly in the Anglosphere, in the wake of the European 'Enlightenment', and it actually represents a radical break with what human beings believed before the modern era. This is not to suggest that greed and criminality did not exist before modern times. But the ideology of Free Trade capitalism sanctioned entirely new levels of depravity in the pursuit of profit, and the demons that were engendered as a result have now so viscerally taken hold of the world that they can probably never be exorcized.

Nor is it at all the case that the idea that 'anything goes in the global marketplace' is no longer current. As Naomi Oreskes and Erik Conway have shown in their book *The Big Myth*, corporations and right-wing think tanks have invested enormous amounts of money in promoting free market fundamentalism (which is nothing other than a modern iteration of the doctrine of Free Trade).[118] Thus, if anything, those ideas have an even firmer hold on the corporate world of today than they did among nineteenth-century British and American merchants. This is amply evident from all that giant energy corporations have done to spread disinformation about climate change. They have shown that they are literally willing to take 'anything goes' to the point of creating a catastrophe for all of humanity, just as opium traders were once willing to let millions of people fall into addiction on the pretext that there existed a law of the market that dictated it.

FOURTEEN
Guangzhou

To cross the 160 kilometres that separate Hong Kong from Guangzhou takes less than an hour in a high-speed train that hurtles through a landscape where elevated expressways loop and swirl between tall buildings like tangled ribbons of asphalt. For much of the way, the rail line cuts through Shenzhen, which became China's first Special Economic Zone in 1981. It was then a provincial town, but it grew so fast that it has now overtaken Guangzhou, the region's historic capital, as China's third biggest city. Today, Shenzhen is the world's fourth busiest port, and has the second largest number of skyscrapers of any city in the world and more billionaires than San Francisco.

On getting off the train in Guangzhou, the overwhelming impression is of having passed through a megalopolis that has sprung up overnight, erasing every trace of the past. But this is misleading: past and present intersect everywhere in Guangzhou, in the most unexpected ways—tucked between glittering skyscrapers and long stretches of urban redevelopment are thousand-year-old Buddhist temples, centuries-old gardens, a seventh-century mosque and neigh-bourhoods that have remained more or less intact since the eighteenth century.

On my first visit to the city, in September 2005, I stayed in a hotel on Shamian Island, the quarter that became Guangzhou's new Foreign Enclave after the Opium Wars. Originally a small sandbar, Shamian was leased, reclaimed and fortified by the British, who then auctioned off the lots to foreign merchants in 1861. Among the most enthusiastic bidders was a group of Parsis who succeeded in securing a prime corner lot by outbidding the richest British merchants (see insert image 20).[1]

The island's lots were laid out in a geometrical grid, with plenty of space for gardens, tennis courts, croquet lawns and walkways. It was designed to be an emphatically colonial outpost: whereas the architecture of the old Foreign Enclave had combined Chinese and European elements, Shamian's buildings were designed to be unmistakably Western in appearance.[2] On Shamian, China was held strictly at bay: Chinese people were allowed inside only if they were servants or service providers; otherwise, they were not permitted to live, or own property, or even spend the night on the island.[3] These rules were enforced by Shamian's own security forces, which consisted of guards and gunboats commanded by Western captains. These forces were often aggressive in their dealings with the citizenry of Guangzhou: in 1925, they opened fire on a crowd of protestors, killing fifty-two, in an event that has come to be known as the Shakee Massacre.[4]

Today, Shamian is known as Wenhua Cultural Park, and during my stay there, I observed a large foreign presence. This was because Guangzhou was then a popular destination for foreigners seeking to adopt Chinese babies: most of them stayed in hotels on Shamian Island.

In my journal I wrote:

The island's boulevards are beautifully planted with shade trees, and there are many parks and playgrounds that come boisterously to life in the evening. There are badminton and tennis courts everywhere, filled with people of all ages, all playing at a remarkably advanced level, and everywhere there are people exercising, many of them quite elderly. The streets around my hotel are filled with Westerners, mainly Americans with strollers. All around there are little stalls, advertising laundry services and strollers-for-hire. Everybody is friendly and helpful.

There is an elegant riverside park, with bright lights stretching away for miles: it overlooks the Pearl River where it flows into White Swan Lake. I had a beer at a café there and when I tried to tip the waiter he turned it down very firmly. No one expects tips here, not even the bellboy who carried up my suitcase. Strange to think that *cumshaw* [gratuities] figured in nineteenth-century Western accounts of China just as much as baksheesh did in accounts of India.

No trace remains today of the old Foreign Enclave where many of the events that precipitated the First Opium War occurred: it was burnt down during the war. The area of the shore where the Enclave once stood is now paved over with roads, embankments and a jetty. To imagine the site as it was in the early nineteenth century is all but impossible, not least because the most memorable feature of Guangzhou's riverfront, the sight that invariably flabbergasted foreign visitors, no longer exists: the 'floating city', which for centuries stretched all the way along the Pearl River to Whampoa and even beyond (see insert image 11).

This vast water-borne conurbation contained thousands of sampans and junks, moored so tightly together that they formed an extension of the shore. 'The river for a mile or two below Canton,' complained one eighteenth-century traveller, 'is covered with boats of various sizes from those of 100 tons down to a ferry boat all in motion and so close that it is with the utmost difficulty you can get past them.'⁵ Another was frankly amazed:

> Reader, imagine 84,000 boats, either at rest, or moving in all directions, inhabited by men, women and children, the infants having gourds tied to their back to buoy them in event of falling overboard, making up a floating population of not less than one hundred and fifty thousand; imagine this, and you will then have a very faint idea of the Pearl River, where it passes Canton.⁶

Yet, even in the absence of the floating city, when night falls on Guangzhou, today, no less than before, there is a subtle change of mood along the riverfront, evoking the words of the eighteenth-century Chinese writer Shen Fu: 'When we reached the river at Shamian the music and song were everywhere.'⁷

Today, as then, soon after sunset, pleasure boats sail lazily up the last stretch of the Pearl River, into White Swan Lake, where they circle around and around, with music spilling out of their windows and upper decks. It becomes much easier then to see the city through the eyes of the long-ago traveller who wrote that night is

> perhaps the best time for a stranger to approach Canton; for then the concourse of boats and vessels of various descriptions, all highly illuminated; the chop houses on shore bedecked with great numbers of globular oil-paper lamps; the din of the Chinese language on every side; the clamor of their gongs; the shrill notes of their music; and the glare of their fire-works; all combine to form a scene so novel and striking that the

impression which it leaves on one's memory can hardly ever be erased.[8]

Or, in the words of an American missionary who arrived in Guangzhou at night: 'The scene was more like magic than reality.'[9]

If anything remains of the old Thirteen Factories, it is the street that once marked the Enclave's northern boundary, Shishanhang Lu ('Thirteen Business Street'), known to Westerners as Thirteen Factory Street.[10] Back then it was narrow and crowded with people and conveyances of many kinds. 'Here we see men with flat baskets of fish hung at each end of a shoulder-staff; sedan chairs, which foreigners are not allowed to use; and some with umbrellas, all moving in opposite directions, and yet avoiding collision.'[11]

Today, the street is still known by the same name, Shishanhang Lu, but it now serves as a retail hub for Guangzhou's clothing industry. Although much wider now, the street is still a scene of frenetic activity—so much so that even I, despite having grown up in bustling cities, found myself gaping when I first set foot in it—but even to gape was not easy, because no matter where you stood, it was only a matter of seconds before you were in someone's way. It was not a charming sight, but its energy and industriousness did inspire a certain kind of awe.

As I stood at that street corner, among hurrying passers-by, 'all moving in opposite directions, and yet avoiding collision', I began to understand why nineteenth-century travellers were often overwhelmed with astonishment, awe and, at times, antipathy when they stepped into streets like this one: so intense is Guangzhou's industriousness that it makes visitors feel that they have been idle all their lives.

Shishanhang Lu was not the only street in Guangzhou that left me
with the impression that I was witnessing a contemporary version of
something that had existed for centuries. Indeed, this happened so
often that I began to think that despite all the highways, skyscrapers
and bright lights, Guangzhou has, in a sense, not changed at all: it is
still today what it has always been, a wellspring for the vast streams
of objects and entities through which China exercises its influence
upon the world.

Wandering around Guangzhou, I was constantly amazed by the
attention that was lavished on trees and plants. I wrote in my
journal:

> Everywhere in the city trees are marked with their botanical
> names, in Latin as well as Chinese. Many roads are shaded
> with ficus trees, with hanging aerial roots that flutter in the
> wind like ribbons. Everywhere you look there are plants,
> poking their heads out of grimy windows, luxuriating in
> cramped little terraces, pouring over the balconies of elegant
> apartments. It is as if everyone is a gardener here.

Later I would discover that this is another aspect of the city that has
not changed through the centuries. 'On the first view of the coast
of China,' wrote James Main, an English plant collector who visited
Guangzhou in the 1790s, 'the stranger concludes that the inhabitants
are a nation of gardeners.'[12] Main's mission was to look for unusual
flowers, and in this he was amply rewarded. 'Florimania,' he noted, 'is
even more prevalent in China than in Europe.' It was not uncommon
at that time for a wealthy Chinese merchant to pay the equivalent of
100 silver dollars for a rare or unusual plant.[13]

Flowers are indeed among China's greatest gifts to the world. In the words of the horticulturist Peter Valder, the garden plants of China

> eventually came to enrich gardens in much of the rest of the world . . . Amongst the best known of these plants are peaches, peonies, chrysanthemums, camellias, gardenias, azaleas, forsythias, wisteria, and crabapples, to mention but a few. And the development of the modern repeat-flowering roses would not have occurred had the so-called monthly roses not been brought to Europe from Chinese gardens.[14]

And for many years it was through Guangzhou that China's floral wonders were shared with the world. These flowers were not plants that grew in the wild: they were the products of careful craftsmanship, varieties created by expert breeding in specialized nurseries.

In the nineteenth century, the most important of Guangzhou's nurseries were located directly opposite the Foreign Enclave, across the Pearl River, on Honam (South Bank) Island.[15] Today the island is covered with forests of high-rises and expressways, but 200 years ago much of it was farmland.[16] The nurseries of Honam lay between the river and White Swan Lake, adjoining the country estates of their most generous patrons—the wealthy merchants of the Cohong guild.[17]

The Honam nurseries were collectively known as the Fa-ti (*Hua Di* or 'Flowery Land') Gardens, and the townsfolk would flock to them on holidays to buy azaleas, camellias, roses and other flowering plants. The number and variety of the plants in the nurseries surprised even learned Chinese visitors from the north. 'I had thought there were no flowers I did not know,' observed the eighteenth-century traveller Shen Fu, 'but here I only recognized six or seven out of every ten. I asked their names and found that some were not even entered in the *Handbook of Collected Fragrances*.'[18]

The Fa-ti nurseries were a favourite destination of foreign merchants; they even made a custom of celebrating Chinese New Year there.[19] Like so much else in Guangzhou, the nurseries of Fa-ti were unpretentious: their plants were displayed in earthen pots that were laid out in rows.[20] Some of the nurseries survived into the twentieth century and were turned into a horticultural commune after the revolution, although they were still known by the name Fa-ti or Hua Di. In 1981 a visiting British gardener published a photograph of one of them; they were evidently very much like the nurseries that can be seen in Chinese cities today.[21]

The pictures of Fa-ti are so unremarkable that it is hard to believe these modest establishments, on a stretch of shore that is now buried under glass-fronted towers, had a revolutionary impact on gardens around the world. From them came many of the flowers that to this day grace the planet's gardens, large and small, princely and humble.[22]

From the 1760s onwards, Guangzhou attracted a stream of British plant hunters. Some of the best known of them were sent out by Sir Joseph Banks, a figure who perfectly exemplifies the intersection of science and imperialism in this era: for forty-one years the president of the Royal Society, Sir Joseph was an avid collector of plants, and also a fervent advocate for the expansion of the British Empire.[23] Under his guidance, many East India Company employees in Guangzhou moonlighted as amateur plant hunters, among them John Reeves, famous for introducing the purple climbing wisteria (a variety that I planted in my backyard in Brooklyn while writing *River of Smoke* in which plant hunting is a major theme).[24]

Sir Joseph also dispatched a few English gardeners to Guangzhou to send plants back to Kew. One of them was William Kerr, whose stay in Guangzhou was not a happy one: although he did succeed in sending many plants to Sir Joseph, he was barely able to get by on his gardener's salary and took to drink.[25] Some of Kerr's introductions, like the Banks' rose and the tiger lily, are now favourites in gardens around the world.[26] One of Kerr's shipments to Kew was accompanied by a young Chinese gardener, Ah Fey, who attracted a great deal of attention during his stay in London (Ah Fey and William Kerr appear briefly in *River of Smoke*).[27]

In Guangzhou, plant hunters were actually more like 'plant-buyers' who went to Fa-ti, hat in hand, hoping to be sold, after much haggling, some new kind of bloom. Only after the British defeated the Qing in the Opium Wars were Western plant hunters able to roam across China and help themselves freely to the country's botanical and horticultural riches.[28] Many of these plants, as the garden historian Jane Kilpatrick notes, have now become so popular in Britain that 'their Chinese origins have been entirely forgotten and we have come to look upon them as our own'.[29]

That Guangzhou was the source of many of the world's most popular garden flowers is hard to reconcile with the city's gritty, far-from-flowery industriousness. This dichotomy was perhaps even more pronounced in the nineteenth century, when the city was at once a gateway for the export of rare flowers and the hub of a banned trade in the products of a very common flower, the opium poppy.

In *River of Smoke*, this dichotomy haunts Robin Chinnery, who, on the eve of the First Opium War, writes to his botanist friend Paulette: 'It is odd to think that this city, which has absorbed so much of the world's evil, has given, in return, so much beauty . . . One day all the rest will be forgotten . . . [but] the flowers will remain . . . The flowers of Canton are immortal and will bloom forever.'

Flowers were not all that Guangzhou contributed to the world's gardens. I woke to this while visiting Oxford soon after a trip to China that had taken me to the grounds of the Summer Palace in Beijing, as well as to Suzhou, home to many famous gardens, including the thousand-year-old 'Humble Administrator's Garden'.

I had been invited to Wolfson College, Oxford, by the noted biographer Dr Hermione Lee. I was sitting in her office, gazing at the college grounds, which adjoin a beautifully landscaped section of the Cherwell river. I remembered this stretch of the river well from my time as a graduate student at Oxford: dotted with weeping willows, it had seemed to me quintessentially English. But that day, as I sat there, staring, I realized suddenly that this ever-so-English garden was, in fact, of Chinese inspiration, with its drooping willows and its carefully crafted suggestion of 'nature in the wild'.[30]

I was not the first, by any means, to be struck by the resemblance between Chinese gardens and those that are regarded as typical of England. 'The English have derived their present taste in gardening from the Chinese,' wrote the Italian philosopher and art critic Count Francesco Algarotti in 1755, when the 'Landscape Movement' was transforming English gardens. 'The French regularity is now banished from all villas in England.'[31] Ten years later, a Frenchman declared, even more unequivocally: '[T]his taste, which, at present, prevails among the English in the manner of laying out their parks and gardens, is that of the Chinese.'[32] This taste soon spread to France as well, where the style was called *jardins Anglo-Chinois*. 'As the style was imitated further afield,' writes the historian Aldous Bertram, 'the Chinese association in its name and the numerous Chinese buildings favoured by the French spread from Paris across Europe.'[33]

Chinese influences on English (and, therefore, American) gardens are often traced back to a book on gardening that was published in 1692 by a former British ambassador to the Netherlands, Sir William Temple. Titled *Upon the Gardens of Epicurus*, the book paved the way for a break with the rigidly symmetrical, geometrical gardens that were then prevalent in Europe. That style of planting, Sir William noted, was scorned by the Chinese: instead 'their greatest reach of imagination is employed in contriving figures, where the beauty shall be great, and strike the eye, but without any order or disposition of parts that shall be commonly or easily observed'.[34]

Sir William Temple never travelled to China, so his knowledge of Chinese gardens probably came from members of one of the three Dutch embassies that were sent to the Qing court in the late 1600s.[35] By then information about Chinese gardens had already been circulating in Europe for a while, via Jesuit missionaries.[36] Most of it was based on the great gardens of northern China, but this changed in the late eighteenth century, when an Englishman by the name of William Chambers published two books on the gardens and architecture of China. Chambers had visited Guangzhou twice, and his material was mainly drawn from what he saw there.[37]

The gardens that Chambers would have seen in Guangzhou were generally enclosed within courtyards. This made them ideal models for copying by ordinary English gardeners, not only because they were small in size but also because they were perfect for highlighting the spectacular new blooms that were arriving in Europe via Guangzhou. Chambers is believed to be the first English gardener to have seen courtyard gardens of this sort, which belonged mainly to wealthy merchants of exactly the kind who patronized the nurseries of Fa-ti. 'Maintained in a state of often obsessive perfection, these gardens had been created within the high walls of wealthy houses across China for centuries, remaining largely hidden from European eyes.'[38]

Chambers's books had a revolutionary impact on British landscaping and garden architecture, introducing 'Chinese pavilions, zigzag bridges and serpentine paths'.[39] This influence extended into the heart of early America, even inspiring George Washington to lay down serpentine paths at Mt Vernon.[40] Thus, through Chambers and his books, the gardening culture of Guangzhou became 'an influential contribution to the idea that the English had copied the Chinese'.[41]

Of course, the idea that English gardens were 'nothing but an imitation of those of China' did not go down well in England, where over several centuries almost to the present day, fervent British garden-nationalists have vociferously disclaimed any foreign influence.[42] Some have proposed ingenious alternative genealogies, leading back to various parts of Europe, and even ancient Rome—anywhere, in fact, but China! But the last word deserves to go to the Cambridge historian who has taken this particular bull by the horns:

> How far English gardens differed from the real productions of China is irrelevant to the fact that . . . [they] were described by many observers as 'Chinese'. For at least sixty years, the idea of the Chinese garden managed to be an inspiration, a justifying precedent, an ideal model and a constantly adaptive canvas on which every changing fashion in England could be painted and reflected back into the English garden.[43]

Guangzhou and the nurseries of Fa-ti also had a profound impact on the visual landscape of the Indian subcontinent. Many of the flowers that travelled from China to Europe quickly became fixtures of Indian gardens as well. In some instances, British gardeners and botanists even cultivated Chinese plants in India before sending them on to Europe (some of these came to be mistakenly attributed to India, through the botanical appellation *Indica*).[44]

Of course, many plants that were indigenous to the Indian subcontinent—rhododendrons and camellias, for instance—were also taken to Europe. Yet, as with the tea bushes that were planted in Assam, Chinese plants seem to have held greater appeal for European gardeners in India than local ones: as a result, it was these varieties that colonized Indian gardens.

China's influence on colonial gardens in India was not restricted to plant varieties alone. Among the British in the late eighteenth and early nineteenth centuries, there was a widespread belief that Chinese groundsmen were better at gardening than Indians.[45] Through their role in the upkeep of colonial estates and properties, Chinese gardeners had a significant impact on the subcontinent and were probably responsible for introducing one of the most important features of contemporary Indian gardens. That is the extensive use of clay pots, often grouped together in large numbers, which serve as an analogue of a flower bed in the West.

In China, the use of clay pots in gardening goes back at least 1,500 years, to the Tang dynasty, and it is very likely that Chinese gardeners and nurserymen brought this practice with them from Guangzhou. The city's nurseries and gardens often consisted entirely of potted plants that could be arranged and rearranged within paved courtyards and enclosures—a practice that was clearly well suited to Indian conditions.[46]

Of course, Indian gardens borrowed from many cultures, but the flow of influences was always circular; it was not just a matter of 'subject peoples aping the ways of the British', as many colonizers believed.[47] Convictions like these gave rise to some strange delusions. For example, Virginia Woolf's sister-in-law Bella once voiced a sentiment that was shared by many homesick colonial ladies: 'It takes a primrose in the tropics to give one true nostalgia'.[48] But as it happens, many of the commonest primroses of the British garden were actually introductions from Asia.[49]

In that sense the contemporary Indian garden is a good example of the strangely occluded nature of the relationship between these two parts of Asia: a set of practices that has grown out of a complex pattern of circulatory exchanges has come to be regarded as a diffusion, brought from Europe to India.

There is no better illustration of the circular pathways of cultural influences than a craft that has had an important influence on India's arts and crafts: the technique of reverse glass painting.⁵⁰ This kind of painting presents interesting technical challenges because the picture is painted as a mirror image on the side of the glass that faces away from the viewer: this means that the order of painting is reversed— that is to say, the finishing touches must be applied first while the background has to be laid on last. In art historian Paul van Dongen's words, these paintings 'can also be viewed as puzzles composed of smaller and larger areas of colour and lines, which must accord with each other down to the smallest detail in form and colour and must fit into each other with the utmost precision.'⁵¹

In Europe, the technique was widely known in the sixteenth century but was practised largely as a folk art, and used to produce images of saints and holy sites. It was probably introduced to China by French and Italian Jesuits in the early seventeenth century and it caught on quickly. Within a few decades a great number of highly accomplished glass paintings were being produced in Guangzhou for the domestic as well as the foreign market.⁵²

From Guangzhou the technique made its way to other parts of Asia, including Java and India, in the late eighteenth century. In India, the technique was probably introduced by migrant Chinese glass painters who travelled there because they were attracted 'by the prospect of easy patronage from interested Indian (Mughal) aristocrats'.⁵³

The earliest Chinese practitioners of glass painting are said to have arrived in Surat, Gujarat, which was home to many Parsi merchants engaged in trading with China. It is possible that some may have come there at the behest of Parsi merchants, following a trail that was pioneered by Chinese silk weavers.

Something about reverse glass painting seems to have appealed to the Indian tastes—perhaps the translucence, or the brightness, or the element of glitter—and it became hugely popular. Some of the early paintings were ambitious and complex, but the technique was also quickly adapted to folk styles and was widely used for the production of religious images. It is possible that reverse glass painting was the progenitor of the calendar art that has so profoundly shaped the subcontinent's visual vocabulary.

Through Guangzhou, China also had a powerful impact on Indian textiles and clothing. Chinese elements were woven into the motifs of a style of textile that came to be identified with Parsis, a form of silk brocade known as the 'Garo' or 'Gara' sari. As Madhavi Thampi points out, this kind of sari represents 'a fascinating example of the fusion of Chinese and Indian cultural traditions'.[54]

Although these garments were woven as saris, the decorative motifs that figured on them were mainly Chinese (see insert image 16). 'Some of the motifs,' writes the historian Kalpana Desai, 'such as the sun, moon, flowery fowls, aquatic grass in sprays, grains of millet, are of ancient origin and were included in the list of twelve *chang* or "ornaments" with which the Chinese sacrificial robes used to be embroidered even prior to the Sung dynasty.'[55]

Through the Parsis, the influence of Chinese weaving extended deep into India, in ways that would have a tremendous impact on Indian textiles. The best example of this is a kind of sari known as the 'Tanchoi': these came to be so closely identified with the great weaving centre of Benares that they were known generically as 'Banarasi' saris. This is the kind of sari that my grandmother, mother and sister wore at their weddings; my wife wore one too at our wedding in Calcutta in 1990. In Bengal, as in many other parts of India, a Banarasi sari is indispensable for certain special occasions, even for families of modest means. However, this quintessentially Indian textile was not invented in India: as Madhavi Thampi explains, 'the art of *tanchoi* weaving . . . arrived in India from China via the west coast [of India]'.[56]

This is how Kalpana Desai tells the story:

Three weavers from the Joshi family of Surat left for Shanghai
to learn the art of Chinese silk weaving of a particular kind,
under the master weaver Chhoi sometime in the year 1856.
When they returned after acquiring a considerable command
over this art, they adopted the name of their master 'Chhoi',
and the material they wove was called by the people of Surat
'tanchoi' which simply meant the material made by the three
(*tan*) *chhois*.[57]

Dr Desai adds: '[*T*]*anchoi* weaving went out of vogue soon after the
first quarter of the twentieth century . . . As the market declined,
Surat ceased to manufacture *tanchois* and it was left to the Benares
weavers to revive the art.'[58]

The influence of Chinese textiles and garments extended beyond
materials and motifs: early Parsi garments suggest that Chinese
designs played an important part even in the evolution of such
characteristically 'Indian' articles of clothing as the blouse that is
worn with saris, a garment that is ubiquitous in the subcontinent.[59]

These too are marks left by the invisible hands that shaped the
visual language of Indian modernity.

Strangely for an unapologetically commercial city, Guangzhou was
also a great centre of art. One of the city's greatest attractions was
a set of studios on Old China Street in the Foreign Enclave. Every
visitor who could afford it, even sailors on day leave, would have their
'likenesses' painted there, a great luxury in an era when portraits
were out of reach for most ordinary people.[60] In Guangzhou, a
sailor could have a portrait made in an hour, while a sea captain or

a rich merchant could commission a large portrait of themselves from the city's most famous artists (see insert image 21). Canton graduates always brought back several such portraits with them when they returned; some of them can still be seen on the walls of their mansions.

Guangzhou's painters were as versatile as they were obliging. They would happily make multiple copies of portraits, in many sizes, down to miniatures that could be put into lockets—many of the miniatures that have been passed down in English, Dutch and American families were actually made in Guangzhou.[61] They were even willing to scale up miniatures to life-size portraits, a very convenient option, since lockets could be brought over easily in a sea captain's luggage. The one thing the painters would not do was flatter their sitters. When asked to do so, one painter is said to have answered: 'How can handsome face make, when handsome face no got?'[62]

Guangzhou's studios also produced many kinds of artworks for their Western patrons. These included expert reproductions of famous masterworks of European art, as well as vast quantities of souvenir paintings of 'typical' Chinese scenes. Pictures 'of the smutty kind' were another specialty because pornography was much in demand among young sailors and merchants.[63]

Some of the most influential specialties of Guangzhou's artists were 'natural history paintings', that is to say, illustrations of animals and plants.[64] Not only did those paintings have a profound impact on the techniques and style of Western botanical art, but they also often served to introduce European botanists to China's flowers.[65] Many of the pretty pictures of plants and birds that now hang on the walls of cosy bed-and-breakfasts in England and America were made in China, and even those that were not show the influence of Guangzhou's artists.[66]

One of the reasons why Guangzhou's studios could produce thousands of images of astonishing variety was that the artisans who worked there were not elite artists—that is to say, they were not highly refined scholars or literati of the kind who practised scroll painting and Chinese calligraphy. Many of Guangzhou's artists were descended from working-class families and had connections with porcelain kilns. Makers of Chinese porcelain were experienced in catering to European tastes, and skilled in using stencils to reproduce Western designs. Guangzhou's artists brought some of these very skills into their studios—there too stencils began to be used extensively; in fact, many of their paintings and images were assembled rather than created afresh each time.[67] This was, then, a veritable industry of image-making—mechanical reproduction without machines! This tradition has continued unbroken into our time: Dafen village, near Shenzhen, is today 'the world's largest production center for hand-painted art, China's model art industry, and the Western retailer's best source for oil reproductions of Western masterpieces'.[68]

Guangzhou's studios had artists with many different skill levels: the best of them were superb painters and sculptors, who created pioneering fusions of European and Chinese art. Some even found recognition in the West in their lifetimes. One artist, Tan Chet-qua, known to Europeans as Chitqua, travelled to London and exhibited his pictures in the Royal Academy to great acclaim as early as the 1760s.[69] He met many celebrities, including Josiah Wedgwood and James Boswell, and was received by King George III and Queen Charlotte at Buckingham Palace. He was even included in Johan Zoffany's famous painting *The Academicians of the Royal Academy*.[70]

Many other artists from Guangzhou also had their work shown in London and Boston in the early nineteenth century. Parsi traders like Jamsetji Tata, the founder of the Taj Mahal Hotel in Mumbai, brought back many paintings to India, some of which can still be seen in the hotel's old building, in the corridors overlooking the atrium. Sir Jamsetji Tata's sons, Sir Dorab and Sir Ratan Tata, also assembled large collections of Chinese art and artefacts, which are now in the collection of Mumbai's most prominent museum.[71]

The most notable of Guangzhou's artists from this period was Guan Qiaochang, known to Westerners as Lamqua (see insert image 17).[72] So exceptional was his work, and such was his mastery of Western techniques, that many foreigners believed he had studied with George Chinnery.[73]

In fact, Guan Qiaochang belonged to a prominent family of artists (as with the Patna School, many of Guangzhou's artists shared family ties), and he appears to have been a well-established painter even before Chinnery moved to Macao.[74] While Guan Qiaochang certainly knew Chinnery, and may even have been influenced by him, there is no evidence that he was his student—Chinnery himself vehemently denied that he was.[75] And unlike Chinnery, whose forte was landscapes and street scenes, Guan Qiaochang's was portraiture, a field in which he was arguably more accomplished than Chinnery.

It is interesting, in this regard, to compare a couple of paintings by Guan Qiaochang and George Chinnery on very similar subjects (see insert images 18 and 19). Chinnery's painting is a portrait of Dr Thomas Colledge, a famous English surgeon of Macao: he depicts the doctor in a heroic pose, with a sumptuous curtain sweeping down behind him.

Guan Qiaochang's picture is of Dr Peter Parker, an American surgeon who ran a charitable clinic in Guangzhou's Foreign Enclave: it depicts him seated in a chair, looking directly at the viewer while his Chinese assistant operates on a patient. As with the contrasting portrayals of the Patna Opium Factory by Sherwill and Shiva Lal, there is a striking difference here between the gaze of the European painter and that of the Asian artist: it is Guan Qiaochang's work that appears more realistic and 'natural'.

Some of Guan Qiaochang's most powerful paintings were, in fact, unflinchingly detailed portrayals of some of Dr Parker's patients, many of whom suffered from disfiguring diseases.[76]

Guan Qiaochang's work, like that of Sita Ram and Shiva Lal, is often described as 'Company Art'. But there were some major differences between the Company Art of India and that of China. The Indian schools never produced pictures on the industrial scale of the studios of Guangzhou; nor did the reputations of any Indian Company painters extend beyond the subcontinent. That Sita Ram was an exceptional artist may have been recognized by British officials in Calcutta, but his work was never shown at the Royal Academy like Tan Chet-qua's. Nor did any Indian 'Company artist' achieve a measure of renown in England. Why was this so?

I think I am not the first to ask this question: Sir Jamsetjee Jejeebhoy must have asked it too, for in the 1850s he did something quite remarkable—he donated Rs 1,00,000, an immense amount of money at that time, towards the founding of a school of art in Bombay.[77] This school, now known as the Sir J.J. School of Art, opened its doors in 1857: it has since exercised enormous influence, not only on Indian art and culture, but indeed on the entire visual landscape of the subcontinent. Many of the school's graduates went on to earn international acclaim, just as Sir Jamsetjee Jejeebhoy would have wanted.[78]

Most of the early teachers and principals of the Sir J.J. School of Art were from Britain. John Griffiths, who copied the Ajanta murals, was one of them, and Lockwood Kipling, father of the writer, was another. These two very English names might give the impression that the Sir J.J. School of Art was a chapter in the story of 'anglicization' or 'Westernization'—but, in fact, the genealogy of the school's founding points in a completely different direction. It was founded with money made in the China trade, by the most prominent of all Indian China traders—a man who had never ventured past the Cape of Good Hope but had travelled to Guangzhou four times and had sat for many artists, including George Chinnery. There is no doubt in my mind that it was Sir Jamsetjee Jejeebhoy's experience of Guangzhou— an experience that he shared with many in his community—that prompted the founding of this remarkable institution: the inspiration is evident even in the picture that graces the school's Wikipedia entry today—it is a painting of Sir Jamsetjee with his Chinese accountant, made in China, by George Chinnery.

Furniture was another specialty of Guangzhou's artisans. The city had many workshops that could create perfect imitations of Western-style furniture: many pieces that are passed off today as Chippendale, Hepplewhite or Shaker are actually reproductions that can be traced back to Guangzhou. But the finest items of furniture to come out of the city were often those where local artisans improvised freely, mixing many kinds of design elements: some of their pieces seem startlingly ahead of their time.[79]

Although capable of producing masterworks in many mediums, Guangzhou's artists and artisans were remarkable, most of all, for their adaptability and lack of pretension: if a buyer wanted something inexpensive, they would give it to them with as much readiness as they would something costly or sophisticated. While artisans in other parts of the world tended to cater to elites, Guangzhou's craftsmen seem always to have had an eye on the mass market. In this too they were ahead of their time. Anticipating Ikea by centuries, the city's carpenters even worked out a system whereby large pieces would leave their workshops in units that could be reassembled by the buyer.[80]

Perhaps the single most impressive collection of Chinese export objects, artwork and furniture is that of the Peabody Essex Museum in Salem, Massachusetts (which is not surprising since many of New England's Canton graduates were enthusiastic collectors of chinoiserie). Apart from several expensive rarities, the museum also has a large selection of everyday objects. Some of them, I was startled to realize when I visited, were distant ancestors of things that had long been a part of my own life but in different guises. In a superbly lacquered late-eighteenth-century powder cabinet, fitted with a hinged top and mirror, I saw the progenitor of the dressing tables that had been an indispensable part of my mother's life.[81] In an exquisite black-and-gilt lacquered sewing table I could see the ancestor of my mother's table-mounted Singer sewing machine (see insert image 22).[82] Only then did I understand why those old Singers had that shiny black patina—they were evidently trying to mimic the look of lacquer work.

Another set of objects that were prominently on display at the Peabody Essex were souvenirs, or curios (or 'tchotchkes', as they are known in Brooklyn): hand-painted fans, carved houseboats, lacquered boxes, moulded clay statuettes and figurines with heads that are balanced in such a way that they nod if touched or blown upon.

As was common among the middle class in Calcutta, my family always had a display case at one end of the living room, stuffed with tchotchkes: prominent among them were painted fans, decorative porcelain, lacquered boxes, carved houseboats and nodding figurines (see insert image 23). I remember, as a child, how disconcerting it was to watch the movement of those grinning, disarticulated heads: they would appear sometimes in my dreams, scaring me awake.

My first inklings of the unacknowledged presence of China in my life may have come to me in my two studies, in Calcutta and Brooklyn, but it was in Salem, Massachusetts, that I understood that my visual and tactile world had always been saturated, unbeknownst to me, by elements of design that could be traced back to the artisans of Guangzhou.

In India, Parsis were the counterparts of the elite New Englanders who introduced Chinese practices and products to America. This is a tiny community but it has had an influence that is completely disproportionate to its size: whether it be in politics or industry, science or philanthropy, many, if not most, of the institutions and practices that define modern India can be traced back to Parsi origins.[83] This is true even of the dominant popular culture of the subcontinent: the roots of the Bollywood film industry, for instance, go back to nineteenth-century Parsi theatre (travelling Parsi theatre troupes even created a new genre of performance in Malaysia and Indonesia—*wayang Parsi*.)[84] Similarly, the Parsis were instrumental in converting India to the religion of cricket.

It is my belief that the early Parsi experience of Canton put the community far ahead of their time also in another respect, one that has left a deep mark on contemporary India, and has also shaped certain facets of my own self. Let me put it like this: when I look at the middle-class culture of urban India, one aspect that strikes me very forcibly is the prevalence of what I shall call, for a lack of a better word, a certain style—a kind of social and linguistic adaptability, an ability to switch between languages, registers, cultures and even personalities. It is a style that makes a virtue of what Homi Bhabha—the most prominent Parsi intellectual of our time—calls 'hybridity'. It is an interactive mode that can confer a certain kind of cosmopolitanism on people who have never left home; it helps young professionals adapt to challenging work environments in foreign countries, and it has enabled many Indians to rise to the top of global corporations and institutions.

In my view, this style is a culture in its own right: it is what I was acculturated to through my education in English-speaking institutions in India. Now, if this is indeed a culture of sorts, then it is legitimate to ask: What are its antecedents? What is its genealogy? How did it evolve and where?

In the Indian subcontinent, Europeans and Indians did, of course, adapt to each other in many different ways, but after the 1760s it was almost always within a context of domination, of ruler and ruled. The military camps known as 'cantonments' are good examples of this: here, more than in any other institution, Indians and Britons co-existed in very close contact with each other. Yet, the cantonment was also a rigidly structured space, where Indian sepoys and British officers lived apart, with each group inhabiting buildings of different kinds, eating different sorts of food and being governed by different rules: instead of being a transactional space, the cantonment became a site of distancing, so that it was commonly said that 'out of uniform, the sepoys reverted to their "natural" character'.[85] The cantonment was, therefore, not a site of acculturation: if it had been, then the part of India to be 'Westernized' first would have been Purvanchal, which supplied the East India Company with its first sepoys. But this is conspicuously not the case.

In the major Presidency cities too there were very marked boundaries between groups and communities. 'Every Briton appears to pride himself on being outrageously a John Bull,' wrote Maria Graham in her 1812 memoir of India.[86] Another mid-nineteenth-century British observer was struck by 'the extreme contempt for the natives which characterizes the English in India, which is perhaps nowhere cherished more than in Calcutta, not only at government-house, but among the independent settlers, and which makes itself so felt of an evening on the esplanade'.[87]

This, precisely, is why pre-1840s Guangzhou is so unique and interesting: it was a place where the dominant power was Asian, not European; it was a place where Westerners, Indians and Chinese lived in close proximity, depending on each other commercially, politically and socially; the traders in Canton were, moreover, merchants rather than officials, and they were accustomed to transacting business with each other on equal terms because that was how they made their fortunes.

In the early colonial era very few Indians travelled to Europe but a significant number regularly made the journey to southern China.

This was a time when communities, Asian and European alike, placed great emphasis on adhering to their own customs—yet Guangzhou's Foreign Enclave was a place where exclusivity was impossible. The Parsis who lived there would inevitably have been forced to invent modes of social interaction that permitted them to live easily alongside foreigners of many different kinds—and were gloriously successful in doing so. That, perhaps, is why Mumbai is, and has always been, the city where the cultural styles of modern urban India have been practised with the greatest ease and facility.

Is it possible then that it was neither in India nor in Europe that the subcontinental styles of cultural adaptation were invented? Is it possible that they were actually invented in China? If so, then surely that process of acculturation that is called 'Westernization' should be termed, instead, 'Cantonization'?

It is not my intention to suggest that India became 'Sinicized' in the nineteenth century: the point, rather, is that Guangzhou played an essential role in the evolution of a kind of cosmopolitanism in which many different influences were merged.[88] The idea of Cantonization might seem outlandish at first—yet in the case of the Tanchoi saris, gardens, tea drinking, nodding dolls and much else, including the Sir J.J. School of Art, this characterization is self-evidently true.

FIFTEEN

The Sea-Calming Tower

For 900 years the central districts of Guangzhou were surrounded by an immense wall, over 7 metres high and 6 metres thick, with sixteen tower-crowned gates.[1] The wall, 10 kilometres in length, ran along the edge of the Pearl River and then circled around the city to meet at the top of Mt Yuexiu (Yuexiushan, North Hill), which overlooks the entire plain below (see insert image 14).[2] At the summit the walls were anchored by a stately, five-storeyed edifice with broad balconies and cascades of upturned eaves: this was the Zhenhai (literally, 'Sea-Calming') Tower.

Almost nothing remains of the old city walls today. They were torn down in the 1920s, during a modernization drive launched by Sun Yat-sen's son, who was then the city's mayor.[3] The only segment of the old fortifications that still exists is the Zhenhai Tower, which overlooks a large and skilfully landscaped public park. The Tower is now the city museum of Guangzhou, and its five floors house a large collection of eighteenth- and nineteenth-century objects, many of which are related to the Opium Wars.

On my trips to Guangzhou, I visited the Zhenhai Tower often, and it eventually came to play an important part in the Ibis Trilogy. In *River of Smoke*, the half-Indian artist Robin Chinnery experiences a moment of revelation in the Tower. On climbing up to the top floor, Robin discovers that he can see the whole city spread out below him. As the sights are pointed out to him, he is both surprised and delighted (as was I) to discover that India is deeply imprinted on the map of Guangzhou. Two of the city's oldest and most important Buddhist temples are associated with Indian monks—Dharmayasa, who was probably from Kashmir, is one; and the Bodhidharma, who was probably from southern India, is the second. The temples are thriving, with crowds of worshippers thronging their grounds every day. Close to the Zhenhai Tower, there also stands a temple dedicated to Guanyin, the city's guardian deity, who, according to some legends, was actually a Buddhist nun from India. Robin is stupefied to think (as was I) that Guangzhou's tutelary spirit was a woman who might once have worn a sari.

In *Flood of Fire*, the Zhenhai Tower figures in scenes of a completely different kind, set during the final stages of the First Opium War in May 1841. By this time, the British Expeditionary Force has been in China for a little less than eleven months. The force is small, consisting of around 4,000 fighting men, of whom about half are Indian sepoys.[4] But the expedition's naval wing is lethally powerful, primarily because it has a secret weapon, never before seen in these waters—a coal-powered, iron-hulled gunboat, aptly named *Nemesis*.[5] With the gunboat as its spearhead, the force has inflicted numerous defeats on the Qing forces, and has raided and ransacked many cities. But sporadic resistance continues, and China's rulers are reluctant to acknowledge defeat: they continue to baulk at Britain's conditions, which include a demand for 6 million silver dollars to be paid as 'reparations' for the losses sustained by foreign opium smugglers. In order to apply more pressure on the Qing state, the British high command decides to follow through on plans, which have long been in preparation, to attack the Zhenhai Tower and break into the walled city.[6]

Among the troops chosen for the strike is a company of 'Bengal Volunteers', consisting of 112 Bihari sepoys and four British officers. The most senior sepoy in the company is a sergeant, Havildar Kesri Singh, whose sister Deeti is the main character in *Sea of Poppies*. Kesri Singh is himself the central character in *Flood of Fire*.

On 24 May, Kesri Singh and his company of Bengal Volunteers are on a troop transport ship at Whampoa, 13 kilometres downriver from Guangzhou. They are part of a brigade that includes 215 sepoys from the 37th Madras Native Infantry and 273 British soldiers from the 49th Hertfordshire Regiment. This brigade is one of four that have been tasked with occupying four small fortresses that guard the slopes on the northern side of the Zhenhai Tower.

In the meantime, a massive storm is barrelling up the South China Sea, heading towards the Pearl River Delta; in anticipation of its arrival the weather in Guangzhou has turned muggy and oppressively hot. As he stews in the heat, Kesri Singh is impatient for the action to get under way. But it is Queen Victoria's birthday so a gun salute must be fired at noon, toasts must be drunk and an extra ration (batta) of porter and malt liquor must be distributed to the troops.[7]

The toasts, and the quaffing of the grog, take longer than expected and by the time the *Nemesis* begins towing the troop transport vessels upriver it is around 4 p.m. As planned, the convoy goes through Guangzhou, past the ransacked Foreign Enclave, to a designated landing ground north of the city. Night falls while hundreds of Indian support staff ('camp-followers') set up camp and start preparing the evening meal. But even after it grows dark they know they are being watched because every now and then rockets are launched from nearby villages, to light up the countryside. Late at night the corpse of an Indian camp-follower is found just outside the camp: the head is missing, which suggests that it has been carried off to claim a reward. The troops know now that there is a price on their heads.

The next morning the weather is, again, stiflingly sultry. There are signs of threatening preparations in the distance; Chinese soldiers are pouring out of the walled city, setting up artillery pieces to target the invaders.

Some 5-6 kilometres of flooded rice fields separate the invading forces from the Zhenhai Tower. The troops, and their army of camp-followers (four or five to every fighting man), must now slog through the mud, sweltering in their heavy uniforms, carrying enormous loads on their backs, and dragging their artillery and their baggage trains over the narrow paths that crisscross the brimming rice fields. As they struggle along, they come under continuous fire from the Chinese, and their rear guard is constantly harassed by groups of angry farmers.

Kesri's brigade's objective is to storm a small fortress that stands directly opposite the Zhenhai Tower (the location is now marked by a monument). By the time they reach their target, the troops are exhausted but they attack in echelon and succeed in scaling the walls; the small garrison inside is quickly overwhelmed. When Kesri climbs to the top of the battlements, he is presented with a wide view of the city beyond. Everything is in turmoil; thousands of people can be seen pouring out of the city gates, fleeing the imminent British assault.[8]

The attack on the Zhenhai Tower is meant to begin the next morning but before it can be launched the Chinese commanders hoist a white flag. Negotiations are opened, and the British now demand an 'indemnity' of 6 million silver dollars to spare the city.[9] The Chinese agree but ask for time to raise the money. The British forces remain where they are, in the forts, but as the days drag on, their provisions begin to run low. Foraging parties are sent to scour the countryside, and are met by hostile crowds wherever they go. The troops have been ordered not to pillage but the situation is such that they cannot collect provisions without using force.[10]

As tensions escalate, discipline begins to unravel.[11] British soldiers enter a temple and break open some coffins awaiting burial; the officer in charge later claims that he was only studying local mortuary rites. But in Chinese eyes, the stirring of the bones of the dead is an unforgiveable offence.[12] This is followed by accusations of sexual assault in a village called Sanyuanli: the British first deny the allegations and then put the blame, as usual, on the sepoys—but Chinese records show that the soldiers responsible for the assault were British.[13] Hundreds of people gather outside to confront the soldiers. Later, large numbers of local men and women come together in a temple and pledge to defend the village and drive away the foreigners.[14] They call themselves 'Soldiers of Righteousness' and paint the words on hundreds of banners.[15]

The days drag on until finally, five days after the initial attack, the 6-million-dollar indemnity is paid. The next morning, as the British forces begin to withdraw, they see the plain below swarming with thousands of men and women equipped with swords, spears, pikestaffs, scythes, cudgels and the like. Many are carrying banners that proclaim them to be Soldiers of Righteousness. The resistance of the militias is fiercer and more determined than anything the troops have encountered before in China. The invaders are constantly harassed as they retreat, and, as luck would have it, this is exactly when the storm breaks; rain comes pouring down in such thick sheets that visibility is greatly reduced and the rice fields become 'a sea of water'.[16] This is a disaster for the withdrawing troops, especially the Indian sepoys, because they are armed with old 'India pattern' Brown Bess flintlocks, which will not fire in damp or wet conditions (most British soldiers, on the other hand, have been issued percussion-fired, all-weather muskets).[17] With their flintlocks malfunctioning, the sepoys are now reduced to hand-to-hand combat with the militias: they flail about with their bayonets and swords while trying to keep their footing in the ankle-deep mud. The rain and wind are so intense that they cannot see where they are going; they lose their way and are cornered by the crowds near Sanyuanli.

The fighting is very fierce now, at close quarters, with the rain pouring down. Forming a defensive square, the sepoys struggle desperately for hours, and somehow manage to hold off their assailants until a detachment from the 26th Cameronian Regiment arrives, late in the evening, and beats back the militias with all-weather muskets.[18] It is largely a matter of luck that most of the sepoys get away with their lives.[19]

Thus ended the battle of Sanyuanli. Publicly the British high command was dismissive of it, declaring it to be a minor skirmish— although their internal communications, and the promotions that were handed out later, suggest that they took a different view in private.[20] As a result, vanishingly few Indians or Britons have heard of Sanyuanli. But in Chinese historical memory, the battle of Sanyuanli has acquired great symbolic importance, and is regarded as the event that marked the beginning of popular resistance to imperialism.[21] Mao Haijian, the leading Chinese historian of the First Opium War, has criticized some of the myths that have arisen around the battle of Sanyuanli, but he accepts that, '[t]he resistance against the British at Sanyuanli was the first link in a chain of transformations that led to modern Chinese nationalism'.[22] In China, every schoolchild knows the name of Sanyuanli.[23]

Today, the battle of Sanyuanli as well as many other events of the Opium Wars are commemorated in museums, some large and sophisticated, at many different sites in the Pearl River Delta. Some draw huge crowds.

It has been suggested that these museums, and the memorialization of the Opium Wars in general, are elements of a strategy to keep memories of China's 'century of humiliation' alive in order to stoke nationalism. But it is worth asking: would those memories have faded in the absence of such a strategy? In the Tuscan city of Arezzo, people still tell their children stories about the battle of Campaldino in 1289, when they were defeated and humbled by Florence. In Serbia, the 1389 battle of the 'Field of Blackbirds' is remembered and talked about to this day. In the United States, sites associated with the Civil War draw hundreds of thousands of visitors every year. As for World War II, hardly a day passes in the United States or Britain when it is not mentioned and cited in newspapers and on television.

Given the enormity of what happened in China in the nineteenth century, is it really conceivable that a people as historically minded as the Chinese would *not* remember the Opium Wars?

Today, Sanyuanli is just another busy, crowded neighbourhood engulfed by Guangzhou's suburban sprawl, with narrow lanes shaded under looping cobwebs of cables and electrical wiring. But tucked away inside the neighbourhood, in the very temple where the villagers had gathered to swear their pledge in 1841, is a museum that commemorates the battle of Sanyuanli. As with many other temple complexes in and around Guangzhou, the compound is startlingly tranquil, a throwback to a distant time.

The Sanyuanli Museum is small in comparison to some other Opium War museums, and its exhibits are modest. They include copies of Lin Zexu's proclamations, charts of opium consumption in China, displays of captured British uniforms and maps that mark the major engagements of the war. But pride of place is accorded to a collection of weapons said to have been used by the men and women of the militias during the battle: short swords, hammers, cudgels, spears, sickles, tridents and so on.

One exhibit that can be seen in many Opium War museums, including that of Sanyuanli, is a vitrine in which opium pipes and receptacles are arranged beside objects that look like black cannonballs: these are replicas of the painted clay containers in which opium was shipped abroad from the Ghazipur and Patna factories. [24]

There is something hypnotic about these bizarre objects: they are like black holes that suck you in and transport you across thousands of kilometres to the poppy fields of Bihar, where Kesri's brother and sisters are painstakingly scoring ripe poppy bulbs and gathering the raw gum, which they will later take to the Opium Factory in Ghazipur, where they will be paid a pittance for their labour.

Like many Bihari sepoys, Kesri is from a family of farmers who are obliged to cultivate poppies every winter under the aegis of the colonial Opium Department. This means, in China, Kesri is fighting on several fronts for different purposes. One is to force the Chinese to continue to import Indian opium. But this, in turn, means that he is also inadvertently ensuring that families like his own will have to go on cultivating poppies under the Opium Department's draconian regime. In this sense, Kesri is the colonial subject not just of the British but also of the opium poppy, since he is part of a campaign that is being fought to make sure that the plant will continue to expand its dominion. And as Kesri is a sepoy of the East India Company, it follows that the British, unbeknownst to themselves, are also sepoys of the opium poppy: they who believe themselves to be masters of all they survey are actually serving the purposes of a Being whose vitality and power they are incapable of acknowledging. In other words, in colonizing the poppy fields of Bihar, the colonizers have themselves been colonized—by a non-human entity whose intelligence, patience and longevity far exceed that of humans.

It is almost as if the elders of the plant kingdom, having concluded that *Homo sapiens* was too dangerous an animal to be allowed to survive, had given humankind a gift that they knew would be used by the most ruthless and powerful of the species to build economic systems that would slowly, inexorably, bring about the end of their civilizations.

One of the exhibits in the Sanyuanli Museum is a coloured illustration that depicts a scene from the battle, with a group of red- and blue-coated soldiers trapped between two militias. What is startling about the picture is that the artist who painted it does not seem to have been aware that the battle of Sanyuanli was basically a fight between Indian sepoys and Chinese villagers. All the visible faces, in the foreground, are white; only in the rear are there a few figures who might (or might not) be Indian sepoys. In other words, Indians have essentially been painted out of the picture: in this depiction they are as invisible as those other participants of this botanical war—the plants.[25]

At the time of the First Opium War, sepoys were by no means invisible to the Chinese. On the contrary, they occasioned great curiosity among Qing military leaders, who understood very well that 'black foreigners are the instruments of predation of the white foreigners, and should they be lost for a single day the white foreigners would find their forces diminished and lose courage'.[26]

The airbrushing of Indians from China's memorialization of the First Opium War happened only in retrospect. This can be interpreted in two ways: either as a wilful erasure, or as a gesture of historical generosity that recognizes that Indians were not the instigators of the war. In either case, Indians are relegated to the sidelines of the story.

As I wandered through Sanyuanli (where I met with nothing but politeness and amiability), I tried to imagine how those streets would have appeared to Kesri during the fighting. What was his state of mind on that day?

To imagine what a soldier feels during combat is one of the hardest tasks a writer can take on. This is partly because combat itself is the

most intense of psychoactives, a consciousness-altering experience
of an extreme kind. This is why, throughout history, soldiers have
been known to use psychoactive substances to help them enter the
necessary mental state.[27] For the colonial British army, the officially
designated substance was alcohol, which was distributed among the
troops with almost as much care as guns and bullets.[28]

The task of imagining the states of mind of British soldiers is made
easier by the fact that there are thousands of personal accounts written
by men who participated in combat. In the case of nineteenth-century
sepoys there is only one and that too is probably apocryphal.[29] This
silence is astounding in the length of its duration: millions of Indian
men served in British armies over several hundred years, going back
to the seventeenth century.[30] Many were upper caste, literate men,
yet it was not till 1902 that a soldier by the name of Thakur Gadadhar
Singh published a first-hand account of his wartime experiences:
written in Hindi, this book is about the British campaign against the
Boxer insurgents in China.[31]

Given the lack of documentary materials I had no choice but
to rely on later accounts authored by Indian sepoys and camp-
followers. I also drew on my father's World War II stories, and on my
own experiences of being under fire in Cambodia and at the Burma
border. But these are, at best, a poor guide to the inner life of a
nineteenth-century sepoy. A number of historical studies have shown
that for Indians, Hindus and Muslims alike, soldiering was not just a
profession but also a spiritual calling, tied to mystical experiences.[32]
Indeed, some of the fiercest warriors in India were Sufis and sadhus
of various different orders. The British recognized this and always
assigned a faqir or a sadhu to each battalion, along with run-of-the-
mill clerics like pundits and moulvis. The mendicants often insisted
on being naked when they marched with the battalions, which
caused great embarrassment to British officers and their wives. But
the mystics had to be tolerated because they were exceptionally good

collectors of information, and because the sepoys reposed greater faith in them than in traditional clerics.

Did those traditions help to sustain Kesri and his sepoy company on the night of the battle of Sanyuanli? It is impossible to know, so I had to accept this as an unavoidable limitation. It is impossible, equally, not to ask the question: would Kesri have regarded ordinary Chinese people as his enemies?

Thakur Gadadhar Singh's memoir suggests that this was not the case: he was actually, in many respects, sympathetic to the plight of the Chinese. Indeed, all the available material indicates that sepoys who served in foreign wars harboured very little rancour towards the people they were fighting: for them these conflicts were not, so to speak, personal. It was in their relations with their British officers and fellow soldiers that their feelings were really invested, in deeply conflicted ways.

Sepoys, more than any other Indians, had to deal with the constrictions of colonial hierarchies in their most systematized forms.[33] As a result, they were often teetering on the brink of rebellion, and sporadic mutinies were common, especially in units that were deployed for service in foreign wars. Mindful of this, the commander of the British Expeditionary Force in the First Opium War, Major General Sir Hugh Gough, specifically requested that the sepoys be regularly reminded of their extra pay for service abroad, and 'of every advantage they are to enjoy'.[34] Such blandishments were standard fare for sepoys serving overseas, but these were not always successful in preventing insubordination and disaffection: the year before the Opium War, for instance, the 8th Native Infantry at Malacca came close to rebelling.[35] And when sepoys did cross the rubicon of mutiny in large numbers, as in Bihar in 1857, Singapore in 1916 and Malaya in 1942, they fought the British with such a depth of passion that there can be no doubt that it was these conflicts that were, for them, truly, intensely personal.

Nothing is harder to capture on paper than this duality in the consciousness of a soldier like Kesri Singh, an inner conflict so powerful that it eventually impels him, sixteen years after that day in Sanyuanli, to join the sepoys of Bihar in their war against the colonizers.[36]

The historian Matthew Mosca has shown in a pioneering study that Qing officials conducted thorough interrogations of captured Indian lascars and camp-followers, and were well aware of the racial hierarchies in the British forces. They even made a few faltering efforts to exploit those tensions. One Chinese plan for fomenting rebellion noted:

> In every engagement they ['the black men'] have to bear the brunt of the battle, so that many of them are wounded or killed; and they complain frequently of this with tears, showing their unwillingness to engage in that which does not concern them in the least degree. Therefore, to effect a mutiny in the ranks of the enemy, we shall treat these men with leniency . . . with the secret understanding that they shall surrender to us their commanding officers.[37] [Long before the sepoys could even think about surrendering their commanding officers, the plan was discovered by the British.]

On occasion, Qing commanders also issued proclamations promising amnesty to sepoys who did not fire on Chinese soldiers. But it is very unlikely that the sepoys ever heard of these offers because the British, always alive to the possibility of disaffection in the ranks, were careful to limit the sepoys' contact with the Chinese.

The maladroitness of the Chinese attempts to court sepoys is surprising considering that Lin Zexu had a large retinue of translators and other informants who were fluent in Indian languages and were well-informed about the subcontinent.[38] Had he sought their advice, they would probably have told him that in order to switch sides the sepoys would need, above all, to be assured of safe passage back to their homes. This would not have been impossible for the Chinese to arrange, particularly through the overland route across Tibet. The sepoys would also have needed monetary incentives— they were mercenaries after all, and poorly paid ones at that. This approach may have proved expensive but it would certainly have cost the Qing far less than the untold millions they ended up paying the British in indemnities and reparations. But, instead of making such offers respectfully, through intermediaries who might have been able to make themselves understood to the sepoys, Chinese officials often treated captive Indians much more cruelly than they did white prisoners.[39]

There was another strategy that the Qing leadership could have used to mitigate, if not prevent, the disaster that was the Opium War. This was to attack the East India Company's territories in Bengal from the rear, in alliance with the Gurkha kingdom of Nepal, which was then in a tributary relationship with China.

Nepal and Tibet had long served as China's principal sources of information on the Indian subcontinent. For Nepal, this function became even more important after 1792, when the Qianlong Emperor sent an expedition against the Gurkha kingdom because of various disputes over the Qing territories in Tibet.[40] As the Manchu general Fuk'anggan advanced into Nepal, the Gurkhas reached out to the East India Company for troops and armaments. But their requests were rejected out of hand by the British, whose paramount consideration, at that time, was to maintain their access to Chinese tea. They could not risk antagonizing the Qing for fear of being ejected from Guangzhou, which would have deprived them of a vitally important source of revenue.[41]

So the Gurkhas came to terms with the Qing general, and thereafter made every effort to draw China into a military alliance against the East India Company.[42] They cautioned the Qing over and over that the British 'harbor ill-intentions and have occupied all the lands from the sea in the south to the mountains in the north; and the kings of each place have been subdued and incorporated'.[43] The Qing baulked, however, and refused to intervene when the Gurkhas fought a series of wars with the British between 1814 and 1816. But Beijing did send an Imperial Commissioner and a large military force to Tibet to keep an eye over the warring sides, and the envoy's diplomatic interventions ultimately played an important part in resolving the conflict, on terms that were relatively favourable to Nepal. It was because of the kingdom's tributary relationship with the Qing that the British allowed the Gurkha kingdom to remain mostly autonomous, and in possession of its core territories, at a time when the East India Company was on an expansionist spree, gobbling up state after state across the subcontinent.[44] Nepal continued to send five-yearly tribute missions to China till 1906.[45]

Over the next couple of decades, Nepalese emissaries in Beijing conveyed repeated warnings about British intentions, and urged the Qing to adopt the strategy of attacking the British from the rear, in alliance with the Gurkha kingdom.[46] This advice was reiterated even as the Chinese were suffering catastrophic defeats in the battles of the First Opium War.[47] In the aftermath of the First Opium War, the Gurkhas continued to urge the Chinese to adopt this strategy. In a letter addressed to the Qing Emperor in 1842, King Rajendra pleaded:

> [W]e request you to help us by sending your army to fight the British. The Chinese army can reach Calcutta within twenty

or twenty five days if it moved through the eastern way i.e. Sikkim and it takes about thirty five or forty days to reach Delhi if the Imperial army marched through the western side i.e. Taklakhar. Be it not possible to send army so far, give us some seventy or eighty million rupees so that we can expel the British Resident from our country and make an attack on India.[48]

Could this strategy have worked? That Gurkhas are great soldiers hardly needs to be said. As for the Chinese armed forces, although hopelessly outmatched at sea, they were not totally ineffective on land. Tactically too, the moment was favourable: it so happened that in 1841, even as the Opium War was raging, a British invasion force was annihilated in Afghanistan. Had the Qing provided the Gurkhas with a sufficiently large force and adequate material support, such an attack might certainly have caused enough of a diversion to delay the Opium War, giving the Qing enough time to make their own preparations. 'If only our ministers had known anything about geography or foreign politics, and allowed [the Gurkhas] to create a diversion,' the Chinese official Wei Yuan would lament later, 'then England's Indian troops would have had their hands full at home, and could not all have come to China.'[49] As for the Gurkha kingdom, in the best-case scenario it could possibly have expanded its territorial presence in northern India, perhaps even established itself in Delhi.

This is something we can only dream about, however, because the Qing rejected the Gurkhas' suggestions out of hand, because of a deep-seated reluctance to being drawn into conflicts by their tributaries.[50] Yet, the fact that Nepal remains, to this day, an independent country is a sign of the many ways in which the invisible hands of tea, opium and China have shaped not just the history but also the political geography of the Indian subcontinent.

SIXTEEN

Pillar of Empire

'You don't chase a market; you create it,' says a member of the Sackler family in the TV miniseries *Dopesick,* which tells the story of how their company, Purdue Pharma, made billions from the opioid-based painkiller OxyContin.[1]

In 1996, when Purdue Pharma introduced OxyContin, the sales of the drug amounted to 48 million dollars. Four years later its sales had grown to 1.1 billion dollars, an increase of 2,192 per cent.[2] The success of the East India Company's drug-pushing programme was not quite as spectacular but it was astounding nonetheless. In the 101 years between 1729 and 1830, the Company's opium exports to China rose from 200 to 30,000 chests, a 14,900 per cent increase.[3] The number kept rising steeply in the following years, reaching nearly 40,000 chests in 1840, just before the outbreak of the First Opium War.[4] In other words, in just ten years, from 1831 to 1840, China received as much opium from India as it had in the whole of the century before.[5] By 1837 opium accounted for 57 per cent of all of China's imports.[6] But this was just the beginning. After the two

Opium Wars, the British Empire's opium exports kept growing until they peaked at 105,507 chests in 1880.[7] The vast bulk of those exports ended up in China.

For the British colonial regime, this was nothing short of a financial bonanza. In the 1790s its annual earnings from opium were about 200,000 pounds sterling. This would rise to more than 10 million pounds sterling in the 1880s.[8] Writes Richards:

> By the 1880s, opium was one of the most valuable commodities moving in international trade. In an average year, export opium leaving Calcutta and Bombay averaged over 90,000 chests, containing more than 5,400 metric tons. This staggering amount would meet the annual needs of between 13 and 14 million opium consumers in China and Southeast Asia who smoked opium on a daily basis.[9]

Quite possibly, no single economic policy has ever been more successfully implemented than the British Empire's opium scheme. Within a few decades, exactly as intended, it solved the East India Company's balance of payments problem: the drain of silver from England to China ended, and huge quantities of bullion began to flow in the other direction.[10] In 1837 a Qing official estimated that the equivalent of 20 million pounds sterling was pouring out of China annually.[11]

For India's colonizers, opium was an economic mainstay, ostensibly the regime's third largest source of income, after the taxes on land and salt. But unlike the revenues from land and salt, which required a hugely expensive bureaucratic infrastructure, the earnings from opium were cheaply and easily collected: this was easy money, which could be used to finance the colonizers' unceasing wars of expansion. The entire imperial system on which Britain's trade was delicately balanced depended on the funds it could extract from other commodity trades through opium, either in tax or profit. And as the scale of the empire grew, so too did that dependence.'[12]

On paper, opium produced somewhere between 16 and 20 per cent of the British Raj's revenues through most of the nineteenth century. But these figures do not take into consideration all the ancillary industries that were supported by opium, the most notable of these being shipping and transportation. Not only did these industries generate large profits for businessmen, but the taxes on them also raised significant money for the Empire. If these other industries are taken into account, the net earnings from opium probably far exceeded those derived from the land and salt taxes. Indeed, the Sino-Indian historian Tan Chung estimated that in the 'China trade Britain had acquired such economic advantages as would amount to half the worth of her Indian colony'.[13] Other European empires in Asia were similarly dependent on opium: even though the Dutch East Indies and French Indochina did not produce any opium, the drug contributed 35 per cent of the revenues of the former, and was the single largest source of revenue in the latter.[14]

But it was in colonial India, the original source of Asia's opium, that the drug had its longest innings, continuing as a mainstay of Empire deep into the twentieth century. In the words of Richards (by no means a critic of Empire): 'From 1789–90 . . . to 1934–35, just before World War Two, opium and the Indian Empire marched together.'[15]

That opium played a crucial role in sustaining colonialism in Asia is largely forgotten today, because European empires have been astonishingly successful at whitewashing the historical record. But at the time, colonial grandees were much more candid. When Lord Aberdeen, the British Foreign Secretary, indicated in 1843 that he might authorize the prohibition of the opium trade in Hong Kong, he was told off in no uncertain terms by Lord Ellenborough, the then Governor General of India, who warned him against doing anything 'to place in peril our Opium Revenue. As for preventing the manufacture of opium, and the sale of it in China, that is far beyond your power.'[16]

Defenders of the British Empire's drug trade often drew parallels between alcohol and opium: like wine and spirits in Europe, went the argument, opium had been used in India for centuries, generally in moderation, so there was no reason why it should not be treated as a source of revenue, just as alcohol was.[17] This is how Charles Dickens, in an essay on opium, put it: '[I]f you were to check or prohibit this drug, a craving would arise for some other stimulus, like as in England, where an intemperate advocacy of temperance often leads to a secret indulgence in something fully as bad as ardent spirits.'[18] Similarly, in Java, Dutch colonizers believed that 'should Holland forbid the Javanese their opium, docile, placid, and harmless opium smokers would soon turn into rowdy, troublesome drunkards'.[19]

An Indian employee of the colonial regime was even more forthright in his testimony to the Royal Commission on Opium of 1893–95:

> Cannot we induce the people of England to eat opium instead of annually spending more than two hundred crores of rupees in the consumption of alcoholic liquors? Opium is amazingly cheap, duty included; it prolongs life after a certain age, and it can be asserted with all the force of truth and seriousness that its substitution in place of alcohol . . . will bring back happiness to thousands of families in Great Britain and Ireland where there is no happiness now . . . It will greatly benefit England if her people take to opium.[20]

In the same vein, the British medical journal *The Lancet* commented sarcastically on the reports of the 1895 Royal Commission on Opium:

> [S]uppose that the natives of India had sent a commission to this
> country to inquire into the drink question—into the sum spent
> per head by our population on alcohol, and the degradation,
> misery and crime which are too often the outcome of it all—
> can there be any reasonable doubt that the evils traceable to
> alcohol here would appear to such a commission, enormous,
> and those arising from the abuse of opium, there, in India,
> altogether insignificant in comparison with them.[21]

These arguments persuaded many people then, and are still cited sometimes by historians who defend the British Empire's opium policies. Critics, on the other hand, argued, as they do even now, that the chemical composition of opium was such as to make it far more addictive, and, therefore, more dangerous, than alcohol. In the words of one detractor: 'There is no slavery on earth, to be compared with the bondage into which opium casts its victim.'[22]

What both these arguments have in common is the assumption that the effects of substances like opium and alcohol will be similar everywhere, irrespective of time and place. However, with both alcohol and opium, the critical factor is not their chemical composition but their social history, that is to say the length, duration and historical circumstances of a population's exposure to the substance. When alcohol fell on 'virgin soil', as 'smoking opium' did in China and Southeast Asia, it too could have devastating consequences, as it did among Native Americans and indigenous Australians.[23] To this day, alcohol causes 8–10 per cent of Aboriginal deaths. In Western Australia, in 'the period 1981–1990 hospital admission rates for alcohol caused conditions were 8.6 times greater for Aboriginal men than for non-Aboriginal men, and 12.8 times greater for Aboriginal women than for non-Aboriginal women.'[24]

In Australia, the first British settlers in the late eighteenth century were quick to realize that the indigenous people had not had any prior exposure to alcohol, and they made extensive use of spirits in their dealings with them. 'It would not be too far-fetched to suggest,' writes the indigenous scholar Marcia Langton, 'that alcohol was from the very beginning of British settlement a crucially important strategy in dealing with Aboriginal people . . . [A]lcohol was, consciously or unconsciously used by the British as a device for seducing the Aboriginal people to engage economically, politically and socially with the colony.'[25]

The colonial officials who equated alcohol and opium would surely have known that whether alcohol was socially and administratively manageable or not depended on historical circumstances: for 'naïve' populations its effects could also be deadly, which was why it could sometimes serve as a biopolitical weapon. It is hard to believe that they did not know that opium was having similarly deadly effects in China and Southeast Asia.

Alcohol, however, could not have been weaponized in China and Southeast Asia in the same way that opium was because those regions had been exposed to it for a very long time. This is why alcohol, despite the analogies drawn by colonial officials, never produced revenue on the same scale as opium. Although both substances were managed in much the same way by European colonial regimes, especially in Southeast Asia, where the rights to distribute them were auctioned off annually to concessionaires (or 'farmers'), nowhere did alcohol generate the kind of revenues that opium did, nor did it come even remotely close to being a keystone of colonial economies. In Singapore, the annual rent paid to the colonial authorities for the opium farm was four times what was paid for alcohol; in Johor, it was eight times as much.[26] The colonial officials who equated opium and alcohol were being disingenuous; they knew perfectly well that the two substances had completely different properties even as sources of revenue.[27] In Indonesia, for example, the Dutch colonial regime

earned profits of 742 per cent from opium in some years; no other
commodity came even close to yielding such an astronomical gain
over costs.[28]

   While Southeast Asia and China had long been exposed to alcohol,
opium was a different matter. Not having had extensive exposure to
the drug, they had not developed protocols other than smoking for
the consumption of opium. Selling low-grade opium in India, where
it had long been consumed in a less addictive form, was, therefore,
a completely different matter from selling smoking-grade 'export'
opium in China and Southeast Asia, where a large part of the appeal of
the drug lay precisely in its novelty, in the idea that it was 'something
utterly new in the world, possessing an attraction that nothing else is
capable of encompassing.'[29]

   Curiously enough, the significance of the length of a society's exposure
to psychoactive substances was often implicitly acknowledged even
by those who equated opium with alcohol. 'You should remember,'
says an imagined anti-opium activist in Dickens's essay, 'that opium-
smoking is not an ancient habit in China; it is comparatively modern,
and therefore more easily eradicated.' Or, in the words of another
British writer: '[O]ne hundred years ago opium was used in China as
a medicine only. If any persons had learned to eat or smoke it, the
number must have been small indeed; for the quantity imported down
to that period had never exceeded two hundred chests per annum. The
quantity now imported is somewhere about sixty-five thousand.'[30]

   Equally striking are these sentences in an article by Richards:
'When first new drugs appear and spread in any society, there is a
period of adaptation that can often be devastating. This was true
of the Chinese who began smoking opium in pipes during the mid-
1700s'.[31] Yet, later in the same article Richards goes on to spell out,

with apparent sympathy, arguments that equated opium and alcohol in order to justify the export of drugs to China.

This suggests, I think, that Richards was torn between compassion for the Asian victims of colonial opium policies and admiration for the British Empire, a common attitude among Anglo-American historians of his generation. In an article published in 2002, for instance, Richards stated that there was 'a good deal of truth' to the view that the history of the colonial opium trade illustrated 'the cynicism and greed of the British regime in India and the harm imposed by imperial policies on the population of China'.[32] But in 2007 he wrote another article, where he forcefully criticized the historians who 'have deplored, in no uncertain terms India's role in the world opium trade'. He adds: 'In my view, this condemnation, heavily freighted with moral judgements, derives from the demonization of opiates by the rhetorical excesses of the world drug wars of today.'[33]

The change in Richards's position reflects, in my opinion, a broader cultural shift towards the rehabilitation of opiates that was partly the result of the devastating failure of the United States' decades-long 'war on drugs', which filled American prisons with people of colour and inflicted enormous violence on many countries and marginalized communities. But this shift also came about because of a more general change in attitudes in academic and medical circles. The hospice and palliative care movements of the 1960s were among the first to call for the use of opiates in the treatment of extreme pain, especially for patients who were near death.[34] Following this, several influential doctors began to actively campaign for the wider use of opioids in treating pain.[35]

It was against the background of this push for the rehabilitation of opioids that Richard Sackler, the head of Purdue Pharma, launched a massive drive to promote prescription opioids; recognizing that there was a stigma against strong opioids in the medical establishment, Purdue Pharma 'executed a brilliant strategy to remove that barrier and clear the way'. The Sacklers had long specialized in medical advertising, and the claim that opioids had been 'unfairly stigmatized' was a central plank of their strategy.[36] Richards's reference to the 'demonization of opiates' suggests that Purdue Pharma's propaganda might have had some influence on him, albeit subconscious.

Nor was Richards the only historian to offer alternative views of the colonial opium trade at this time when the calamitous failure of America's War on Drugs was becoming ever more evident; this was also when the movement for the legalization of marijuana was beginning to gain strength, which in turn lent credibility to the campaign to rehabilitate opioids.[37] Around that time, several other scholars also produced revisionist framings of the British Empire's colonial policies, arguing that the effects of opium were not as harmful as critics claimed; that only a small percentage of users were addicts; and that the reconsideration of 'drugs' in the present day requires also a reappraisal of the past, especially in relation to Chinese prohibition policies.[38] The implication is that the nineteenth-century opium trade now needs to be viewed through the prism of the more liberal attitudes that have replaced old prejudices against drugs.

Another revisionist framing rests on the term 'agency'.[39] To represent Asian drug addicts as helpless victims of colonial strategies, goes the argument, is to deny them agency and personal choice in the shaping of their habits and preferences.

It is no coincidence that this kind of revisionist thinking began to gain ground in academic circles at exactly the time when opioid advocates were waging a war on what they called 'opiophobia'.[40] Indeed, the fact that the forces behind the effort understood the talismanic power that neologisms like 'opiophobia' can wield among highly educated people like doctors and academics is a measure of the intelligence with which the campaign was waged. That such revisionist views on opium ran counter to socially prevalent opinions also probably helped them gain ground in the academy: there are few things experts and academics—especially economists and economic historians—relish more than contradicting commonly held beliefs.

Contemporary China's increasing repressiveness, and the rapid spread of anti-Chinese attitudes in the West, probably contributed in lending plausibility to revisionist views on opium: since China has been wrong about many things, then it might well be mistaken also in regarding the opium trade as a historical scourge. In addition, stories from Singapore and other Asian countries about young Westerners being harshly punished for the possession of small quantities of cannabis also helped create an impression that Asian attitudes towards drugs were excessively puritanical (and there is a good deal of truth to this, especially where it concerns grassroots psychoactives).[41]

But where the matter of agency is concerned, the obvious question is: what of the agency of the vast number of Asians who clamoured for the restriction of opiates? They surely outnumbered the users and addicts by a huge margin. And what, most of all, of the agency of the sovereigns of China, Thailand, Vietnam and innumerable smaller Asian states that tried to restrict opium, only to be forcibly prevented from doing so by European guns and gunboats? Those rulers and officials surely understood their compatriots far better than Western colonists did.

Conversely, we might ask, is the government of the United States suppressing the agency of Americans by banning the sale of prescription opioids? Or does the fact that prescription opioids disproportionately affect the white population completely change the complexion of the matter?

There is no reason why the United States' War on Drugs—a state-led enterprise undertaken by the world's most powerful government—should be regarded as the only possible strategy to deal with epidemics of addiction. The anti-opium campaigns of the nineteenth and early twentieth centuries were nothing like the War on Drugs. In fact, they were popular civil-society movements that aimed to apply pressure on the world's most powerful empire, which also happened to be the global sponsor of the drug trade. Politically speaking, the two campaigns were the exact inverse of each other. While the War on Drugs targeted consumers as well as producers, the anti-opium drive was aimed primarily at producers and dealers, not users or addicts.[42] Throughout Asia, doctors were at the forefront of the movement and, far from stigmatizing users, they showed keen concern for the treatment and rehabilitation of addicts, perhaps because of their experiences of treating addicted friends and relatives.[43] In many ways their approach was similar to the harm-reduction strategies of today.

Another significant problem with the revisionist arguments is that they share the most flawed premise of the War on Drugs, which lumps all psychoactives together under the same label. In reality, substances like cannabis, qat, coca, peyote, psilocybin mushrooms, kava, pituri etc. have different properties and, from a public health perspective, each should be assessed on their own merits. It does not, by any means, follow that if legalizing marijuana or peyote makes sense, then the same should also be true of prescription opioids or fentanyl.

In my view the legalization of marijuana is, without question, a necessary and sensible measure. Nor can it be doubted that the legalization of many other psychoactives, such as peyote and psilocybin mushrooms, would make equally good sense. Indeed, as I have noted before, 'grassroots psychoactives' are one of the few defences that could be effectively deployed against the continuing spread of opioids and cocainoids. The reality is that all other efforts at curbing the spread of opioids have failed: the opium poppy has always found a way of circumventing them.[44]

As a public policy legalization did not work in China.[45] Opium was legal there for almost a half-century, between 1860 and 1906, but not only did the number of users and addicts continue to grow at a phenomenal rate, so did criminality and corruption.[46] Even after the

Qing government imposed a tax and allowed opium to be sold freely, criminal networks continued to sell it illegally, at lower prices.

That opium and its derivatives are in a class by themselves has become starkly clear in the wake of the United States' OxyContin crisis, which, after devastating many parts of the country, led to a series of lawsuits against several pharmaceutical companies. It should be noted that these cases came before the courts at about the same time that marijuana was being legalized in a number of American states. But the courts, even as they were upholding the legalization of marijuana, decided to ban OxyContin and some other prescription opioids. They also imposed punitive liabilities on the companies that produced prescription opioids. These judgments, and the popular outrage that has forced many museums, galleries and universities to remove the Sackler name from their premises, are clear indications that while public attitudes to some psychoactive substances may have become more liberal, these have ceased to apply to opioids now that their dangers have been made evident, once again, by America's epidemic of addiction.

In effect, it has now come to be judicially recognized in the United States that opioids and their synthetic analogues pose greater dangers than other psychoactives, and must be dealt with in a different way. Opium itself has forced upon the world the recognition that it is an exceptional substance, and demands to be treated with precisely the kind of species-level humility that Robin Wall Kimmerer calls for.

> Opium's combination of danger and pleasure [write two Harvard economists] has led to repeated cycles of innovation, addiction, and correction, which begin when entrepreneurs produce an allegedly safer opioid. However, when purchasers begin consuming the new drug, they discover that this new innovation is as addictive and deadly as the old forms of opium. New consumers avoid the drug or are prohibited from

using it. Existing users pass away, and the fad dies down—until memories fade and the cycle begins again.[47]

In other words, opium creates its own temporalities: when opioid epidemics subside, they are followed by periods of amnesia, which, after a few decades, help to rehabilitate opioids all over again. These cycles are another sign of opium's potency as a historical actor in its own right.

I suspect that Richards, and other revisionist historians, came to the conclusion that the powers of opium had been unfairly demonized during one of those down cycles, when the memories of the harm that opioids can cause had temporarily faded.[48] Would Richards, for instance, have castigated the sanctions against Purdue Pharma for being 'heavily freighted with moral judgments' in light of what is now known about America's opioid crisis? I very much doubt that he, or anyone else, would write in that vein today if they knew that David Kessler, who headed the United States' Food and Drug Administration when OxyContin was approved, had later declared that the rehabilitation of opioid-based pharmaceuticals was one of the 'great mistakes of modern medicine'.[49]

That opioids form a class of their own is now recognized even by the most liberal advocates of psychoactives. Very few would argue today that OxyContin, heroin or fentanyl should be made freely available on the streets (although there are, of course, very good public health reasons for expanding the full gamut of harm-reduction strategies, including the distribution of clean needles to those who are already dependent on heroin). In the words of the two Harvard economists: 'Thousands of years of experience with the fruits of the poppy should have taught that opioids have never been safe and probably never will be.'[50]

Some might counter that the opium the British Empire was exporting to China was not as addictive as morphine or heroin. Strictly speaking, this is true, in the sense that the opium that was exported from India to

China had to undergo a further process of refinement to make chandu, the substance that was smoked, and this was usually done in the places where it was consumed. But the Opium Department's 'provision' or export opium was itself a more refined version of the drug than the akbari or excise opium sold by the colonial regime's outlets in India.[51] Not only was export opium produced expressly in order to make it suitable for processing into chandu, but the Opium Department's laboratories were also constantly experimenting to provide a grade of opium that was 'suited to the Chinese market'.[52] As James Rush points out, opium was known to be addictive 'even at the very modest levels consumed by most Javanese smokers'.[53] In the words of a Javanese addict: 'If I don't smoke for a day, I feel shivery and fatigued.'[54] In other words, much as they do today, opioids exerted their hold on nineteenth-century Asian addicts by creating an intense fear of being 'dopesick'.

Every era has its own threshold of tolerance with opioids: in the 1750s an unwary young Englishman in India happened merely to lick the head of a poppy bulb; he soon fell into a coma and died.[55] At that time, when opioids were not mixed into a wide range of medicines, most human bodies were 'naïve' and so just a taste of opium sap could kill a grown man, much like fentanyl can today.[56] Chandu or 'smoking opium', like later derivatives such as morphine, heroin and fentanyl, was the high-grade opioid of *its own time*.

In its impacts on society, chandu opium certainly stands comparison with OxyContin. Consider this passage, written by a high-born Javanese woman of the late nineteenth century: 'What are our daily murders, incendiary fires, robberies, but the direct result of the use of opium? . . . Hunger will make a man a thief, but the hunger for opium will make him a murderer. There is a saying here—"At first you eat opium, but in the end it will devour you."'[57]

These words sound hyperbolic until they are compared with descriptions of the effects of the opioid epidemic in America: '[OxyContin] took a hold of people's lives and turned them into thieves who stole from their families and neighbors to meet the cost of feeding an ever-demanding habit. It cost them their jobs, cars, houses, dignity and sometimes even their children.'[58]

Certain accounts of parts of rural China in the nineteenth century read eerily like descriptions of the small Appalachian communities that were worst hit by the prescription painkiller crisis. In China: 'The most dramatic pictures of opium devastation came in the form of what authors described as "opium villages", places that were extremely poor already but . . . were then "ravaged and desolated by opium". "All classes, all ages, both sexes" were victims.'[59] This is uncannily like Barry Meier's descriptions of the opioid epidemic in twenty-first-century Appalachia: 'Families saw their life's savings drained by a son or daughter's drug habit. Parents scoured pawnshops searching for family heirlooms hocked by an addicted child. The jail in Lee County swelled with young people arrested for drug-related crimes. Before long, the nephew of the local sheriff joined their ranks.'[60]

It is important to note that prescription opioids had these devastating impacts in America even though only a small percentage of those who took the drug became addicts—perhaps only 5 to 12 per cent.[61] In nineteenth-century China too, the number of actual addicts was only a fraction of all those who used the drug; most users were able to function normally, as is the case with most users of cocainoids and opioids in America today. However, the rate of addiction was probably higher in China.[62] After all, prescription opioids circulated in the United States for only a few decades, while in China the opium problem unfolded over more than a century and a half.

The overriding consideration that guided British and Dutch policies in their Asian colonies was always revenue, and this was frankly acknowledged by officials. 'Shall we sacrifice the whole or any portion of the opium duty?' asked Sir Cecil Beadon, a top-tier colonizer, in 1871. '[I]t seems to me that the present state of the Indian finances is such as to prevent us from giving any answer but one to that question—that we cannot give up any of the opium revenue; we cannot afford to do so.'[63]

To admit that public health played second fiddle to revenue was not easy for regimes that boasted about shouldering the white man's burden and bringing progress to natives. But many colonizers understood very well the damage that opium was causing in some parts of Asia, and were perfectly candid about it. The founder of Singapore, Sir Stamford Raffles, for example, wrote in his 1817 *The History of Java*:

> The use of opium, it must be confessed and lamented . . . [has] extended its malignant influence to the morals of the people, and is likely to perpetuate its power in degrading their character and enervating their energies, as long as the European government, overlooking every consideration of policy and humanity, shall allow a paltry addition to their finances to outweigh all regard to the ultimate happiness and prosperity of the country.'[64]

Yet, Singapore became the quintessential colonial opium-city, subsisting largely on opium revenues, which were by no means 'paltry'.[65]

John Cameron, owner and editor of Singapore's *The Straits Times*, was also candid in acknowledging that revenue was a far greater concern for British colonizers than public welfare. In 1865 he wrote in his own paper: 'With the East India Company revenue was a matter of considerably greater solicitude than the moral condition of the large populations under their rule; and there can be very little question that the opium farm had its origin in the necessities of the local exchequer.'[66]

In the late nineteenth century, when the global anti-opium movement began to gather strength, such views were stated with increasing vehemence. '[India] cannot afford,' declared *The Straits*

Times in 1881, 'to sacrifice an annual revenue of eight millions sterling at the bidding of sentimental fanatics and spurious philanthropy based on imaginary facts and false argumentation.'[67]

There is no better indicator of how important opium was to the colonial project than the ingenuity and persistence with which the British government defended its drug-running business well into the twentieth century in the face of overwhelming global criticism.[68] A considerable part of this criticism came from within Britain itself, which had long had a vocal anti-opium movement, with strong connections to anti-slavery campaigns.[69]

When international pressure, primarily from China and the United States, forced Britain to enter into drug-control negotiations, its government was characteristically ingenious in using diplomacy to delay any kind of effective action. Indeed, it could be said that opium provided the template that other dangerous industries would use later to forestall regulation; similar tactics are still being used by fossil fuel companies in relation to climate change. The difference is that in the case of opium, these tactics were employed not by a corporation but by a government that was then the world's most powerful state.

One of the British government's cleverest strategies in this regard was to field Indian spokesmen to justify its opium policies. These frontmen did their jobs with great skill and conviction. Nor is this surprising. By the late nineteenth century, opium had become so crucial to the colonial edifice that the industry was, in effect, deemed by many important people, both British and Indian, to be 'too big to fail'. 'Opium may be a great evil,' opined *The Hindu* newspaper in 1895, 'but national bankruptcy is a greater evil.'[70]

When defending the British opium racket in international forums, the industry's mouthpieces often cited the predicament of impoverished Indian peasants who would be ruined, or so they claimed, if poppy farming were to be banned (never mind that many farmers, by their own account, were producing opium at a loss to themselves, and desperately wanted to be freed of the burden).[71] These spokesmen were, in effect, using India's impoverished masses as an alibi to safeguard the interests of their own class.

Here again are striking parallels with modern-day corporate 'climate denial'. Energy corporations, and their defenders, frequently allude to the needs of the global poor as a reason why fossil fuel industries should continue to expand. The fact that it is the poor who will bear the brunt of the disastrous impacts of climate change is conveniently swept under the carpet, just as the protests of Bihari poppy farmers were in the nineteenth century.[72]

One argument that British and Dutch colonial officials relied on to defend their various opium regimes, ranging from the network of excise outlets in India to the 'farm' systems of British Singapore, French Indochina and the Dutch East Indies, was to present these as regulatory structures intended to control and reduce the consumption of opium. The fact that they also generated revenues that were essential for the sustenance of colonial states was obscured or relegated to the margins.

However, the objective of increasing revenues was never completely disavowed. In India, in 1878, the colonial regime passed a law that strengthened the harsh penalties that were already in place to curb the smuggling and possession of illicit opium.[73] The price of opium was also inflated repeatedly, ostensibly to deter abuse.

But raising revenues and limiting drug use were fundamentally incompatible objectives that implanted several contradictions at the heart of the policy. For instance, were the laws against smuggling and possession intended to curb the use of opium, or was the aim, rather, to boost the revenues the regime earned by selling its own, sanctioned variety of the drug? Also, so long as higher revenues remained a major objective, there was always an incentive for licensed opium outlets to drive up their sales. Contrary to its public declarations about reducing opium use, the internal documents of the Opium Department 'show that an increase in the sale of licit opium was always mentioned with pride by the opium officials'.[74] In reality, it was impossible to boost profits from the drug without also expanding opium use. No matter what the regime's professed intentions, statistics reveal that after the introduction of the restrictive new laws there was a gradual *rise* in opium consumption in India, and it was accompanied by a huge surge in revenue from 1885 to 1920.[75] (This occurred also in the Dutch East Indies where 'reforms' purportedly implemented in order to restrict opium consumption actually ended up boosting returns and making the drug legally available in more places than ever before.[76])

Nor did the draconian laws of 1878 help to prevent opium smuggling and drug-related crime. As long as the opium poppy remained a major crop and opium continued to be used widely in the country, quantities of the drug were bound to leach through from cultivators, licensed and illicit, to the consumers, no matter how strict the systems of surveillance and repression. Nor could the Opium Department crack down on those farmers who retained a part of their crop for their own use, or for the black market. Poppy growing required a great deal of skill and experience, so jailing farmers or taking away their licenses would have made it harder for the Opium Department to meet its production targets: 'the colonial state could not punish the opium growing *ryots* beyond a point for fear of killing the goose which laid the golden eggs'.[77]

That poppy growing was both economically and socially harmful for farmers was often acknowledged by British officials in their private correspondence. Here, for example, is an extract from a letter that I stumbled upon in my research, written by a senior British district official in Gujarat to a colleague in 1842:

I strongly urged them [farmers] to revert to the Cultivation of the Products they formerly had previous to the introduction of the Opium Culture . . . it is sincerely to be desired that with the disappearance of the poppy from the zilla they will themselves gradually forget its use and not feel the want of the stimulating and insinuating drug, a habit which has extended itself 100 fold since the first introduction of its growth in these parts.'[78]

The dangers of opium were certainly no secret to the British government. In 1843 twenty-five of Britain's most eminent doctors issued a statement saying: 'However valuable opium may be when employed as an article of medicine, it is impossible for anyone who is acquainted with the subject to doubt that the habitual use of it is productive of the most pernicious consequences'.[79]

The leadership of the British Empire was well aware that opium was indeed having 'the most pernicious consequences' in China in the nineteenth century. This was made clear to them by innumerable critics in Britain, by a burgeoning international anti-opium movement and by many British merchants in China.[80] Most of all, it was made clear to them, over centuries, by the government of China and by countless ordinary Chinese. Yet, the Empire persisted with its policies until it was finally forced to abandon them in the early twentieth century.

I can think of no principle of law, statecraft or morality that holds that a state does not have a right to stop the inflow of a commodity that endangers its people: if this is true of fentanyl today, then it was also true of opium in an earlier era. This principle was recognized even by Lord Palmerston, the British Foreign Secretary at the time of the First Opium War. 'The British Government acknowledges the right of every independent state,' he wrote at the start of the First Opium War, 'to regulate as it pleases the commercial intercourse of its subjects with foreigners; to permit or to forbid as it pleases, dealings in any commodity which is the produce of its own soil or industry, or which is brought from foreign ports'.[81] But Palmerston did not want to go down in history as the man who forced opium on China at gunpoint. His plan, marvellous in its deviousness, was to force the Chinese to legalize opium *of their own accord*, through behind-the-scenes pressure.[82] The Chinese, however, were unyielding on this score for a long time. 'It is true I cannot prevent the introduction of the flowing poison,' said the Emperor, 'gain-seeking and corrupt men will, for profit and sensuality, defeat my wishes; but nothing will induce me to derive a revenue from the vice and misery of my people.'[83] So it took another war—and the burning of Beijing's Summer Palace, one of the greatest acts of vandalism in history—before the British Empire and its allies were able to achieve their unstated object.[84]

At the time of the attack on China in 1839, and for decades afterwards, the British government, and historians sympathetic to it, argued that the war was not about opium; the main issues, rather, were China's treatment of foreigners as exemplified by the restrictions imposed on them in Canton, the Qing state's refusal to allow Western governments diplomatic access to Beijing, and much else, including the words used to refer to Westerners.[85] Put thus, a war was inevitable because of the Qing state's 'insolence'; opium was almost irrelevant to the conflict.[86] What was omitted from this picture, of course, was the fact that the Canton system, and the restrictions imposed on foreigners, had existed for over a century without resulting in military confrontation. It was only when the Qing state made a determined effort to put an end to opium smuggling that Britain went to war, following 'a strategy which corresponded very closely to the declared needs of the big opium smugglers'.[87] The connection could not be more obvious, and was plainly stated by the British Plenipotentiary, Charles Elliot, who wrote later: 'The real cause of the outbreak with China in 1839 was the prodigiously increased supply of opium from India.'[88]

In short, no amount of sophistry can disguise the fact that the British Empire's opium racket was a criminal enterprise, utterly indefensible by the standards of its own time as well as ours. That China is today an assertive and aggressive power, with many deplorable practices and policies, is beyond dispute. However, the fact that it is difficult to conceive of this behemoth as being wronged by history should not influence our assessment of the past; it should instead prompt us to reflect on the chain of causation that has made China what it is today. In doing so it is instructive to consider the words of warning that the Chinese statesman Ku Hung-ming addressed to the English writer W. Somerset Maugham in 1921:

Do you know that we tried an experiment that is unique in the history of the world? We sought to rule this great country not by force, but by wisdom. And for centuries we succeeded. Then why does the white man despise the yellow? Shall I tell you? Because he has invented the machine gun. That is your superiority. We are a defenseless horde and you can blow us into eternity. You have shattered the dream of our philosophers that the world could be governed by the power of law and order. And now you are teaching our young men your secret. You have thrust your hideous inventions upon us. Do you know that we have a genius for mechanics? Do you not know that there are in this country four hundred millions of the most practical and industrious people in the world? Do you think it will take us long to learn? And what will become of your superiority when the yellow man can make as good guns as the white and fire them as straight? You have appealed to the machine gun and by the machine gun shall you be judged.[89]

SEVENTEEN
Parallels

In the course of one century, after 1780, India's total opium exports to China increased hundred-fold, rising to a peak in the 1880s.[1] The numbers alone make it clear that there was something profoundly out of the ordinary about this surge. They become even more astounding when we consider that China had, in the meantime, developed a huge opium industry of its own. The industry emerged in the early nineteenth century, when farmers began to grow poppies in defiance of the prohibition imposed by the Qing.[2] Some of the regions that led the way in poppy cultivation were provinces of which it was proverbially said, 'Heaven is high, and the Emperor far away.'[3]

One such province was Yunnan, which was, and still is, a diverse region populated by many different ethnic groups, some of which had long been engaged in trading across the steep valleys and mountains that mark the frontiers of India, China and Burma. In the late nineteenth century, the opium trade brought great wealth to some of these communities, as will be evident to anyone who travels to the remote and marvellously picturesque villages and towns that dot the valleys around the Tiger Leaping Gorge. In the souvenir shops of these villages it is quite common to find finely crafted pipes and other opium paraphernalia being sold as antiques: I bought several when I travelled across the province with my son in 2012. Although poppies are no longer farmed there, the fact that this was once a major opium-producing region is amply evident.

The cultivation of opium poppies in Yunnan had probably started to increase around the 1830s, when the British colonial regime's opium exports to China were escalating steeply.[4] After the disastrous defeat of the First Opium War, which left the weakened Qing state even less able to combat opium trafficking, China's opium industry began to expand quickly, not just in Yunnan but also in several other provinces.[5] The growth was particularly rapid in the coastal region of Fujian: by 1845 the capital city, Fuzhou, had more than 100 opium dens and, according to one Qing official, 80 per cent of the residents were opium smokers.[6]

In the years between 1842 and 1858 China's opium industry was in a state that has been described by the historian Peter Thilly as one of 'negotiated illegality' because the Qing, despite their humiliating loss in the First Opium War, steadfastly refused to legalize the drug trade.[7] But after another catastrophic defeat, in the Second Opium War, the Qing state—also under attack from within, by the Taiping Rebellion, which had taken control of large parts of the country—was left with no option but to sign a new treaty with the British in 1860. China was effectively forced to legalize the opium trade, thus adopting the model that European empires had imposed on their Asian colonies, in which opium was a licit source of revenue. In the meantime, an enormous growth in opium smuggling along the coasts made it clear to the Qing state that its efforts to suppress the opium trade would never succeed so long as the British were holding a knife to its throat.[8] So the Qing then adopted a policy akin to that of British

India and the colonial regimes of Southeast Asia, whereby the opium industry came to be treated as a source of revenue. This led to a huge expansion in poppy cultivation, which meant that there was a sizeable increase also in opium use, because, as Spence notes, 'the growing of opium does indeed encourage the growers themselves to smoke'. It is estimated that Chinese poppy farmers consumed around a quarter of their opium themselves.[9]

In the later decades of the nineteenth century, opium became a major industry in China, and its revenue a cornerstone of the finances of the Qing state in much the same way that it already was in colonial India and Southeast Asia.[10] Even after the Qing were overthrown, opium continued to serve as 'the financial mainstay of virtually all of the warlord and republican regimes that dominated China in the period before 1950'.[11] Needless to add, opium also generated vast fortunes for many businessmen in China, Taiwan and, later, Japan.[12]

Foreign observers often cited China's flourishing domestic opium industry as evidence of the corruption of the Qing state, and the general insincerity of Chinese officialdom.[13] 'John C......n is the greatest hypocrite on the face of the earth,' says a character in *From London to Lucknow*, a mid-nineteenth-century memoir by a British chaplain. 'He grows annually fifty or sixty thousand chests of opium at home, yet affects to be scandalized when it is brought into the country from abroad.'[14]

This is a good example of how imperial rhetoric was used to shift blame away from the British Empire to its victims: having thwarted every Qing measure to suppress the opium trade, the colonizers then pointed fingers at China for allowing its domestic industry to thrive— instead of continuing to consume ever-increasing amounts of the product exported by the British Raj! The arrogance is breathtaking: it is as if a foreign drug cartel were to tell the United States that it should legalize cannabis but not produce it domestically.

The situation being what it was, the Qing decided on a course that any government would probably choose under similar circumstances: import substitution. If China was to be forced, at gunpoint, to continue to import opium, then it might as well grow the product domestically—that way at least it could cut back on paying for foreign imports. This line of thinking was supported by even the fiercest critics of the Qing state, such as Sun Yat-sen, who is known to have argued:

> [I]n the future, when opium cultivation has become widespread,
> it will surely preempt the profits from Indian opium . . . Once
> we have preempted the profits from Indian opium, the British
> will voluntarily stop importing it, and then we can stop planting
> it. If at that time we issue a decree prohibiting the consumption
> of opium, we can end this scourge of more than a century in
> a short time. So promoting the planting of poppies is actually
> the beginning of banning opium.[15]

The thinking behind the import-substitution policy might have made sense if opium had been a commodity like any other, subject to the same laws that governed, say, cotton and sugar cane. Instead, for three decades after the legalization of the drug, China's opium imports from India continued to grow steeply, peaking only in the late 1880s.[16] Though imports began to level off around this time, astoundingly, despite the phenomenal growth of the domestic industry, China went on importing large quantities of opium from Turkey and colonial India till the end of the nineteenth century.[17] By now China's domestic opium industry was far larger than India's; in the first decades of the twentieth century, it was the single largest producer of opium in the world, accounting for seven-eighths of global supply.[18] Although most of this opium was consumed domestically, China was now also the world's largest exporter of not just opium but also heroin, large quantities of which began to wash up on the shores of colonial Southeast Asia, and even Europe and the United States.[19]

Only in light of this is it possible to get a sense of the surge in opium use in China over a little more than a hundred years. Although the exact number of users and addicts in the country is hard to compute, it is conservatively estimated that by the early decades of the twentieth century, between 3 and 10 per cent of China's population—possibly as many as 50 million people—were using opium.[20] But other estimates suggest that the figure was at least double that and may even have been closer to 30 or 40 per cent of the population, possibly as many as 200 million people.[21]

How is this astonishing increase in opium production and consumption to be explained?

Approaches to this issue usually circle back, in one way or another, to the question of demand. Most nineteenth-century Western commentators tended to assume that the increase in imports was driven by the growth in demand. This was in keeping with free-market theories, which held that supply and demand were brought into equilibrium by the 'invisible hand' of the market. These ideas, which emerged in the late eighteenth century, when the British opium-pushing programme was in its infancy, would soon become completely hegemonic among the elites of the Anglosphere. They took it for granted that the laws of supply and demand functioned much like the laws of nature (or like the inscrutable will of the Protestant God).

The supposed primacy of demand provided one of the most important arguments in British justifications of the opium trade: it features constantly in nineteenth-century British writings on the drug trade. Here, for example, is what Charles Dickens had to say in one of his articles on opium: 'Nothing but the extraordinary corruption of the Chinese authorities can account for the recent vast increase of a trade prohibited by the laws; this increase is one among many proofs of the difficulty of putting in force, regulations at variance with popular habits and tastes.'[22]

A similar argument is phrased more playfully in *From London to Lucknow*.

> The fact is, [says a British merchant] the Chinese wanted opium, and would have it. But their great papa at Pekin, the brother of the sun and moon, said, 'No, my boys, you shan't have any.' The boys said, 'We are big enough to judge for ourselves, dear papa; and, although we love you very much, and are willing to obey you in reasonable things, we really must have our pipes.' Well, what did we do? We just quietly filled their pipes for them, and told them to hold their tongues, and then the old governor would be none the wiser. I can almost see a touch of benevolence and brotherly kindness in the transaction . . .'[23]

The import of these passages is that a large demand for opium existed in China, and would inevitably be met by an equivalent supply. If this supply were not provided by the colonial regime in India, it would come from somewhere else: this was inexorable, the result of a natural law, and any attempt to interfere with it was both foolish (for it was doomed to fail) and wrong (in the sense of being morally unjustifiable).

For those who subscribed to the view that demand was the essential factor behind the growth of the drug trade, the crux of the issue lay in explaining why the need for opium had increased at such a phenomenal pace in China. Of the suggested explanations, some of the most persistent were rooted in another set of ideas that was then becoming hegemonic among Western elites: conceptions of race and gender. It was often said that a propensity for drugs was characteristic of 'Asiatics' in general, and of the Chinese in particular, because they were 'effeminate' by nature and hence more inclined to indulge in opium, which induced passivity, rather than alcohol, which was connected with the 'active, impetuous disposition'.[24] '[I]n the dominant European rendition,' writes the historian Keith McMahon, 'opium was the perfect drug for the Chinese, who were seen to be sottish and addicted to pleasure by nature.'[25] In the words of a leading British politician, the issue was simply 'a matter of race': '[A]s the Aryan races prefer alcohol, so the Turanian consume opium.'[26] The increase in demand for opium was thus attributed to perceived flaws in Chinese bodies, Chinese ways of thought, Chinese culture and 'Chinese social depravity and deficient self-control'.[27]

Along with these, another aspect of the Chinese constitution that was often blamed was the Chinese body politic, which was said to be inherently riddled with corruption and venality. This is how Charles Dickens put it:

> It is known that, about eighteen years ago, the Emperor and his council discussed fully the opium-question; it was found that all attempts to check the contraband trade with the British, were rendered futile by the self-interested energy of the merchants, by the growing love of the Chinese for the drug, and by the venality of the Emperor's officers.

Or, more simply: 'The Chinese, impenetrable to every thing else, are never impenetrable to bribery. They are the most corrupt people on the face of the earth.'[28]

These views form an interesting contrast to earlier Western attitudes towards China, which tended to be generally respectful and even admiring.[29] The seventeenth-century German polymath Gottfried Leibniz, for instance, even inverted the order of venality: '[T]he state of our affairs, as corruptions spread among us without measure, seems to me such that it would appear almost necessary that Chinese missionaries should be sent to us to teach us the use and practice of natural religion . . .'[30] In that era the Chinese were regarded by many European thinkers as 'above all, masters in the great practical art of government'.[31]

In time European states did indeed borrow freely from Chinese models of governance. As the historian Stephen R. Platt has noted, the East India Company's adoption of a competitive examination system in 1806 was 'inspired largely by what its traders had learned of the Chinese system in Canton'. This in turn became 'the foundation of the British government's own civil service exams when they were established in the mid-nineteenth century'.[32] The genealogies of the civil service examinations that preoccupy millions of young Indians today thus lead directly back to China. Indeed, as Wengrow and Graeber have pointed out, the very idea of the contemporary nation-state as 'a population of largely uniform language and culture, run by a bureaucratic officialdom . . . whose members had succeeded in passing competitive exams' is 'almost exactly the system that had existed for centuries in China.'[33]

It was in the late eighteenth century, when Europeans, and especially the British, were becoming increasingly dominant globally, that Western attitudes towards China began to change.[34] It is no coincidence, I think, that Western perceptions became increasingly negative as China kept absorbing ever-growing quantities of opium. It is as though the very fact that the supposedly 'powerful' Qing Empire was unable to effectively curtail the drug trade was enough to make it worthy of contempt. It is of a piece with this that the people who were most derisive of the Chinese were often the very merchants who were most successful in bribing local officials and breaking the country's laws.

One such was Sir James Matheson, an opium trader who, over a career built on criminality in China, became the second-largest landowner in all of Britain, and bagged himself a baronetcy as well as a seat in Parliament.[35] In 1836, as a part of the (ultimately successful) lobbying effort to prod Britain into declaring war on China, Matheson wrote a book which begins thus: 'It has pleased Providence to assign to the Chinese—a people characterized by a marvellous degree of imbecility, avarice, conceit, and obstinacy—the possession of a vast portion of the most desirable parts of the earth, and a population estimated as amounting to nearly a third of the human race.'[36]

These attitudes echo those of contemporary drug lords, who are often contemptuous of the hapless governments whose laws they circumvent. They too often blame corrupt American and European officials for the constant rise in drug consumption in the West. Unlike today's drug lords, however, Matheson and his ilk came to be celebrated in their countries as paragons of imperial virtue.[37]

It is unarguable that the opium trade largely depended on the collusion of Chinese criminal networks, just as the drug trade in the West, and around the world, does today.[38] Nor can there be any doubt that there was a great deal of official corruption in China even before the large-scale importation of opium accelerated. Still, according to Jonathan Spence, one of the greatest historians of China, the country's 'standard of law and order was probably comparable to that prevalent in Europe or the US at the time'.[39] But money can corrupt the soundest institutions and Western drug runners had no shortage of funds. In one instance, in 1839, British smugglers paid two low-ranking Chinese officials 26,000 dollars in cash and kind, 'a truly monumental sum' in a region where 'one Spanish silver dollar was equivalent to several days wages for an ordinary boatman'.[40]

What is extraordinary about the views of merchants like Matheson, then, is that they blame China's corruption not only for the very existence of the opium trade but also for their own wrongdoings ('Look what you made me do!'). In retrospect it is clear that the pattern of causality was complicated, and that the drug-traders' exploitation of pre-existing vulnerabilities in the system contributed greatly to the steadily increasing corrosion of Chinese structures of governance in this period.

This too would establish a template for Western resource extraction around the world: mining and energy corporations that spend huge sums on bribing officials in poor countries frequently blame those very countries for their 'cultures of corruption'. (As I was writing this sentence, a headline appeared on my screen announcing that the giant commodities trading company Glencore had pleaded guilty to seven counts of bribery in relation to its oil operations in Africa, and would have to pay more than a billion dollars in fines.[41])

Much has been written in recent times about the possible causes for the phenomenal increase in opium use in nineteenth-century China. But this literature too usually circles back, one way or another, to the reasons for the growth in demand: the need for relaxation, for combating stress and isolation, for dealing with the strain of hard manual labour and so on.[42]

Some scholars have emphasized other reasons for the growth in demand, such as the downward percolation of opium use from China's upper classes and literati, who imparted a sense of sophistication to the practice, which, in turn, made it socially acceptable and led to its widespread adaptation throughout the country, especially among people with social aspirations. This was possible because the smoking of opium did not, by any means, automatically imply addiction. The great majority of those who smoked the drug were moderate users—just as the great majority of those who use prescription painkillers today do not become addicts. Then, as now, addiction was the exception, rather than the rule.[43] Nor can there be any doubt that opiates were then, as they still are, a great boon to those who are able to use them in moderation. They can provide stimulation for the weary, exhilaration for the jaded and relief for those racked by physical or psychological pain. These were precisely the properties that made it possible for purveyors of medicine in China to market opium as an effective remedy for all manner of ailments. In nineteenth-century Java too, 'many smokers first tried opium as a remedy of last resort for one of several conditions: headaches; fevers and chills (including malaria); stomach aches, diarrhea, dysentery, and asthma; tuberculosis ("bloody coughing"); fatigue and anxiety'.[44]

Indeed, the role of doctors and healers in creating surges of opioid addiction is one of the many threads of repetition that run through the history of opium. Iatrogenic, or doctor-caused, surges of opioid abuse have been especially characteristic of the history of opiates in America, going back to the widespread prescribing of morphine during the mid-nineteenth century and continuing into the epidemic of prescription painkillers.[45]

Opium addiction in nineteenth-century China has also been linked by many scholars to the various social, political and economic crises that convulsed the Qing Empire in this period. At the forefront of this multidimensional crisis, of course, was China's encounter with the West, which had repercussions that extended far beyond matters of trade, finance or even public health. The fact that the country's rulers were unable to end the influx of opium was not just a failure of trade policy; it also steadily eroded the machinery of the state and the legitimacy of the country's system of governance. All of this came to a head during the First Opium War, which put China's impotence in relation to the British Empire on spectacular display, further accelerating the country's many crises and leading directly to the Taiping Rebellion, which resulted in the death of some 20–30 million people.

What the Taiping Rebellion, with its messianic, missionary-inspired ideological underpinnings, also made clear was that China was facing a civilizational challenge in the deepest sense, one that called into question the culture's long-held views about its place in the world, and of its historical role as a model of governance. Within a few decades, every institution that had once commanded trust— the monarchy, the bureaucracy, the legal system—began to visibly crumble.[46] At the same time, the spread of opium dependency also destabilized the cornerstone of the Confucian order—the family— with parents abandoning their traditional duties and relatives stealing from each other to fund their habit.

This crisis of faith is vividly reflected in many literary works of the period. One of these is a short testament called *Opium Talk* by Zhang Changjia, a well-connected opium smoker of the late nineteenth century. As Keith McMahon has shown in his perceptive study of this text, Zhang believed that opium had revealed something to him that non-smokers were unable to adequately appreciate: that an era had passed and history had entered a new stage in which the teachings of the old Chinese seers and sages were irrelevant. 'Now that opium is present, nothing else is foreseeable.'

In Chinese, the words for 'opium' and 'smoke' are almost synonymous, so that the main expression for smoking opium, 'chi yan', means 'to eat smoke'. It was this, Zhang suggests, that made opium a means of coming to terms with a time of unprecedented change—because for him, this new era was quintessentially defined by smoke. Not the fumes of ordinary fires, but rather, those that pour out of the funnels of coal-powered steamers. Thus, in an uncannily perceptive leap of the imagination, Zhang came to identify fossil fuels as the defining characteristic of the new era.

When Western steamships are sufficiently fired up, they are keen and invincible and can sail a thousand miles in one journey. But when the fire is extinguished, the ship rests in complete silence, all night long, surrendering its ability to move. If you want it to go the next day, you must fire it up

again. The more fired, the more it can move. Upon reaching
full potential it is ready again for another journey of moving
without stopping.

It is the same with opium smokers. When their craving
comes on, their bodies feel shriveled and listless, their joints
all stiff. They must rely on opium to fire themselves up. At
the beginning of firing up, they wriggle like worms. A little
more fired up and they begin to flow like a great river. Fired
up for a good while, they brim and burst with energy, and
quickened in every limb they steam forth with indomitable
heat. By the middle of the night they have even more energy
to spare.[47]

Zhang's use of the words 'energy' and 'fire' has deeply unsettling
resonances in this age of intensifying climate change, when the
burning of fossilized forms of carbon has at once energized the
world into a stupendous dance of acceleration while simultaneously
entrapping it, like the body of an addict, in coils from which it may
never succeed in extricating itself. Today, the fact that the world's
relation with fossil fuels is indeed nothing other than a deadly and self-
destructive addiction is widely acknowledged. But Zhang Changjia
may have been the first to see the connection.

In the nineteenth century it was common for Westerners to blame
China's civilizational crisis on the country's inward-looking culture,
particularly the inflated sense of self that was implied in the idea
of the 'Middle Kingdom', and the pretensions to cultural (and even
racial) superiority that led many Chinese to refer to foreigners by
terms that Europeans generally chose to translate as 'barbarians' or
'devils'.[48]

This being a time when elite Westerners were beginning to sub-scribe, with increasing enthusiasm, to various cults of individualism, many also came to regard the collectivism of the Confucian order as one of the greatest of China's weaknesses, the root cause of its self-absorption and arrogance. Implicit in this was the belief that in individualistic, Western societies, where institutions were established through participatory processes, there could never be a similarly widespread breakdown of trust in institutions; nor, in such societies, would people ever be so deluded as to imagine that they were the cen-tre of the world and paramount among nations. China's crisis was, therefore, taken to be a special case, caused by conditions that were endogenous to the country and its culture.[49] Even today, China's ex-perience is generally thought to be irrelevant to the wider world, as is evident from the fact that the literature on the American opioid crisis very rarely mentions nineteenth-century China, and usually only in passing.

It is true, of course, that the Chinese predicament was unique in many ways, and it is also true that the past never reproduces itself in an exact fashion. But as Mark Twain famously observed, 'History never repeats itself but it does often rhyme.' It is a measure of opium's peculiar ability to insert itself into human affairs that it has created many echoes and rhymes between past and present.

Consider, for instance, the justifications that were used by the management of Purdue Pharma in their advocacy of OxyContin and other opioid-based painkillers: that they provided miraculous relief; that they were safe and addiction was extremely rare; that there was a large unmet demand; that opioid addicts and abusers were temperamentally inclined to addiction; that the problem really lay in lax law enforcement.[50] These arguments echo, to a degree that can only be described as uncanny, the voices of the merchants who built their fortunes by selling opium in China and Southeast Asia in the nineteenth century. Consider also that in the United States, as in China,

the demand for opioids increased at a staggering rate: OxyContin
came on the market in 1996 and just a couple of decades later, in 2019,
30 million people—about 3 per cent of the population—were believed
to be addicts. In Ohio alone, by 2016, 2.3 million people, around 20
per cent of the population, had received a prescription for opioids.[51]
During that time, opioid overdose became the leading cause of death
in America, surpassing gun-related fatalities and car accidents: in
2016 an average of 175 Americans were dying of overdoses every day,
adding up to an annual total of 64,000, equal to the entire population
of cities the size of Santa Fe, New Mexico. In 2017 there was a 10 per
cent rise, with 72,000 overdose deaths.[52] 'It was as if,' writes Barry
Meier, 'a plague had entered one of these towns and killed every
single inhabitant.'[53]

In nineteenth-century Asia, as well as in twenty-first-century
America, opiates provided relief to people engaged in hard physical
labour. Like the Chinese migrants who toiled in Southeast Asian
mines, mineworkers in Appalachia also took opioids because the drug
made it possible to go on working despite injuries and exhaustion. And
just as the retailers of opium in Southeast Asia specifically targeted
those miners, so did American pharmaceutical companies focus their
promotional efforts on areas like Appalachia, where there were larger
concentrations of people with work-related injuries.

'I have an opinion about Big Pharma and opioid medications,'
writes Ryan Hampton, a recovering user. 'To put it simply: They're
evil. I know that's not very nuanced, but I want to just come out and
say it.'[54] We can be sure that there were millions of people in China
who were saying the same thing about the merchants, Chinese and
foreign, who were selling opium to drug dealers.

It is now abundantly clear that the rapid rise in opioid addiction
in the United States is also closely related to a multidimensional crisis. The manner in which Purdue Pharma and other pharmaceutical
companies were able to obtain federal approvals for their opioid

painkillers; their enlisting of doctors and physicians in their distribution campaigns; their manipulation of the judicial system; their success in co-opting lawmakers at both the state and national levels; and
the fact that the company's top management was able to get away
with light sentences—all point to corruption on an astonishing scale.[55]
Today, American pharmaceutical companies outspend every other
industry in buying political influence.[56] As Patrick Radden Keefe
writes in *Empire of Pain*, 'The opioid crisis is, among other things, a
parable about the awesome capability of private industry to subvert
public institutions.'[57]

It is starkly evident that in the United States today, as in nineteenth-
century China, civil servants, doctors, prosecutors, police officers,
law enforcement agents and public figures from many walks of life
can be persuaded to look the other way with sufficient financial
inducements. And, as with China, the profits that opioids generate are
such that limitless amounts of money can be used for those purposes.
In the years between 2006 and 2015 alone, Purdue Pharma and
other drug companies spent roughly 700 million dollars on buying
political influence, eight times the amount spent by the gun lobby.[58]
To understand how opioids and their purveyors are able to seek out
and exploit pre-existing weaknesses in the system we have only to
look at the example of Qing China.

Again, in the United States, as in nineteenth-century China, the
expansion in the use of opioids has also been accompanied by a steady
erosion of trust in figures and institutions that had long commanded
authority and respect. How was it that 400,000 American lives, more
than all American military deaths in World War II, were lost in an
epidemic without anybody taking notice? Chris McGreal writes:

> As grief gave way to anger, the families of the dead and
> the survivors wanted to know why opioids were so easily
> prescribed, and why doctors told them these pills were safe.

They asked how it was that those who Americans expect to
protect them—the medical profession, the government, the
federal regulators—seemed to stand idly by, or worse, as the
bodies piled up year after year.[59]

The involvement of small-town pharmacists and doctors (like the
principal character in Dopesick) is particularly shocking in this regard
because they are traditionally the most trusted people in their
communities. This is how Ryan Hampton, whose life was upended
by pills prescribed by a doctor, puts it: 'I was given the prescription in
a doctor's office, a place we are all taught to trust. My "dealer" was a
source we are taught to believe has our best interests at heart.'[60]

The actions of the rural doctors and pharmacists who vouched for
opioids and doled out prescriptions affected many beyond those who
fell victim to addiction. The damage seeped deep into communities,
often in exactly those parts of the country where, like in China, the
family was regarded as the sacrosanct cornerstone of social life. For
these Americans, the ease with which opioids were prescribed and
obtained represented a betrayal not just on the part of individual
doctors and pharmacists but also of the sciences that lent them their
authority.[61] By giving their imprimatur to opioids these widely trusted
figures helped to make opioids socially acceptable. The same could be
said of the Food and Drug Administration (FDA), which had long
been one of the most trusted institutions in the country: it conducted
only cursory, two-week trials on OxyContin before approving it. Two
of the examiners involved in the FDA's approval process later went
on to work for Purdue Pharma. In 2002, when the FDA convened
a group of experts to 'examine the harms from OxyContin, eight
of the ten had ties to pharmaceutical firms'. The link between the
regulatory body and the corporations it oversaw was a prime example
of 'regulatory capture'.[62] All of this resulted in an erosion of trust that
would have bitter consequences during the COVID-19 pandemic.

The opioid epidemic, it is worth recalling, unfolded against the backdrop of other massive institutional failures, like the financial crisis of 2008. Opioid use surged in the wake of the crash not only because it thrust large numbers of people into poverty, but also because of the revelation that banks, once the most dependable of institutions and the bedrock of many small communities, had become predators that sought to profit from the systematic duping of their clients. Rising inequalities and disappearing jobs in sectors like mining and manufacturing, which had provided secure employment for generations of Americans, compounded the crisis further.

As the journalist Sam Quinones, among others, has shown, many of the communities that have been worst affected by prescription opioids are in regions that were severely impacted by post-industrial blight, with factories closing, tax bases shrinking and cities sinking into abandonment and neglect. The changing economy and extreme rates of unemployment have left rural populations in the heartlands of America devastated.[63] In 2012 15 per cent of rural residents had more than one opioid prescription.[64] Nor is it a coincidence that some of these regions send disproportionate numbers of young people into the military, to fight overseas wars from which they return traumatized in mind and body. Not for nothing have overdose fatalities been described as 'deaths of despair'.[65]

In many parts of the United States, the opioid crisis has overlapped with a more general loss of faith in political institutions, including the electoral process, which is the very foundation of democratic systems of governance. Since 2000, when the presidential election was decided by 'hanging chads', trust in the electoral system has declined steadily, hitting new lows after the elections of 2016 and 2020. This has contributed, in no small measure, to the deepening of political rifts—to an extent where it has become commonplace for political pundits to lay odds on the likelihood of a new civil war. In all of this there are echoes of nineteenth-century China.

There is another, very important, way in which the contemporary American experience rhymes with the situation in nineteenth-century China: the loss of people's sense of their place in the world, and the dissipation of long-held beliefs in the centrality and primacy of their country, not just as the world's paramount economic, political and military power but also as a model of good governance. Why this feeling should be widespread in the United States is not easy to fathom, since the US still is, unquestionably, the world's foremost economic and geopolitical power. Yet, the fact that many Americans believe their country is in decline was made evident by the slogan that carried Donald Trump to power: 'Make America Great Again'.

It is no coincidence that the need to believe in the continuing superiority of the United States is felt most strongly in precisely the regions that are the epicentres of the opioid problem, where the idea of decline is perceived as a threat to national, and even racial, identity. Evidently, despite America's vaunted traditions of individualism, the necessity for a collective sense of primacy is powerful for many Americans, much as it once was for countless Chinese. Indeed, what the United States is experiencing today is, in many ways, a reversal of the civilizational shock that traumatized China in the nineteenth century.

There are many other parallels. In nineteenth-century China, as in the United States today, there was an outpouring of noir literature related to the opioid crisis; there too drugs came to be associated with nightlife and partying. In both countries drug addiction did not spare the families of the highest in the land, mandarins and emperors, senators and presidents. In nineteenth-century China, as in the United States today, the inflow of opioids was often described as a security threat and a national emergency. But the strangest aspect of the crises, in Qing China as in contemporary America, was that on the surface everything seemed normal, so that it was possible for visitors and even large sections of the population to be completely unaware of the very existence of a problem.

That these parallels have gone totally unnoticed in the United States is itself another way in which contemporary America rhymes with nineteenth-century China.

There can be no doubt whatsoever that rates of addiction in a society are closely connected to economic, political and cultural problems, so it is not surprising that scholars should choose to focus on those issues, especially since they allow for many kinds of imaginative speculations.[66] But it is important to note that framing the matter thus is to automatically place the emphasis on demand, when the fact, which has long been glaringly evident to countless people— from Col. Watson of the East India Company to Qing Emperors and their mandarins, from the Americans who campaigned to shut down Purdue Pharma to the judges who decided those cases, or indeed to the Sackler scion who said, 'You don't chase a market; you create it'— is that with opioids the factor that is most responsible for increasing use is not demand but supply. Where plentiful supplies of opioids exist, they will create their own demand; that is precisely why opium is, in its own right, a force in history.[67]

This fact, which has long been apparent to many, has recently been corroborated in a study of America's opioid epidemic conducted by two Harvard economists. Their study looked 'at available measures of physical and mental pain, despair, and the opportunity cost of time, which is associated with joblessness and social isolation', and found 'that changes in demand-side factors alone, such as physical pain, depression, despair, and social isolation can only explain a small fraction of the increase in opioid use and deaths from 1996 to 2012.'[68] The conclusion they came to was that: 'the direct effect of economic change on opioid deaths is modest. Changes in supply seems to be far more likely causes of the opioid epidemic than changes in demand-side factors including pain and despair.'[69] These findings are completely consistent with the story told by many journalists and scholars: 'Over and over again the epidemiologic data affirm a simple truth: those groups who, for whatever reason, have had the greatest exposure to opiates have had the highest rates of opiate addiction.'[70] Or, as the writer William S. Burroughs put it: 'Addiction is an illness of exposure. By and large those who have access to junk become addicts.'[71]

In effect, Purdue Pharma invented an opioid-based painkiller and then, through clever marketing, created a demand for it.[72] As Keefe notes: 'Prior to the introduction of OxyContin, America did not have an opioid crisis. After the introduction of OxyContin, it did.'[73]

Similarly, another group of economists has shown that when OxyContin was released in 1996, five American states happened to have additional regulations in place to restrict doctors' ability to write prescriptions for narcotics. Those states experienced 'uniquely low' growth in overdose deaths even as the opioid epidemic devastated other parts of the country.[74] The five states—California, Idaho, New York, Texas and Illinois—have very little in common geographically, so clearly it was the limitation in supply that provided a layer of protection.[75]

At Purdue Pharma it was often said that OxyContin would sell itself—and it did. In the words of one sales rep, 'There was growth instantly, from the beginning. Phenomenal growth.'[76] These words might well have been uttered by British colonial officials in Calcutta: the East India Company shipped opium to China in ever-increasing quantities and the market essentially created itself.

It could be argued that by the 1830s, when poppy farming was surging in Malwa, it would have been impossible for the colonial regime to stop the outflow of opium from India. After all, native merchants and trading networks had successfully circumvented

British efforts to control the trade in Malwa, and they would surely have found some way to smuggle opium out of India. But, while Indian criminal networks might well have tried to send drugs into China, there is no way they could, on their own, have forced the Chinese to abandon their efforts to ban opium if the British had not defeated the Qing by force of arms.

But of course, the British Empire had no interest in stopping Indian opium exports in the 1830s or even afterwards; quite the contrary. The argument that defenders of the colonial opium policy often put forward, that China was 'perfectly free to stop the import of opium if she desires', was completely disingenuous. 'We did stop it once,' a Chinese official once retorted, 'and it caused a war.'[77] Not only were the Qing forcibly prevented from stopping the inflow of opium, but they were also forced to pay 21 million silver dollars, amounting to more than 5 million pounds sterling, in reparations to drug smugglers.[78]

It might be said that one major difference between the Chinese and the American opioid epidemics is that in the United States the state machinery worked—after all, Purdue Pharma was ultimately forced into bankruptcy. However, it is apparent from almost everything that has been written about the prescription opioid epidemic that the American system did *not* work. The Sackler family was able to use its money to not only interfere in legal proceedings at every level but also protect a significant portion of its assets: Purdue Pharma's bankruptcy was actually a strategy for protecting those assets. The story, as told by Keefe, Quinones, McGreal and others who have studied America's opioid crisis, is a shocking narrative of corruption and institutional breakdown at every level. Nor is the crisis over by any means: even though the supply of prescription painkillers has been drastically reduced, the number of opioid-related deaths has not declined. In fact, the shutting down of Purdue Pharma led to a spike in the use of heroin, and the numbers have continued to rise since then, hitting new peaks during the COVID-19 pandemic.[79] Evidently the wave of demand for opioids that was so ingeniously created by Purdue Pharma is now being met by increasingly resourceful criminal networks.

Remarkably, it was in China that the system did work—or would have if the British assault had not derailed it. The Qing administrative machinery did actually succeed in shutting off the inflow of opium between January 1839, when Lin Zexu took up his duties as governor of Guangdong, and 1840, when the British Expeditionary Force overwhelmed China's defences.

In thinking about the opium poppy's role in history it is hard to ignore the feeling of an intelligence at work. The single most important indication of this is the poppy's ability to create cycles of repetition, which manifest themselves in similar phenomena over time. What the opium poppy does is clearly not random; it builds symmetries that rhyme with each other.

It is important to recognize that these cycles will go on repeating, because the opium poppy is not going away anytime soon. In Mexico, for instance, despite intensive eradication efforts the acreage under poppy cultivation has continued to increase.[80] Indeed, there is more opium being produced in the world today than at any time in the past.

Only by recognizing the power and intelligence of the opium poppy can we even begin to make peace with it. To do so, however, would mean parting company with many ideas that have long been dominant, such as the notion that the earth is inert and humans are the only agents of history. Clearly, there are many other entities and beings that have not only shaped history but have also used humans for their own ends. The opium poppy is, undoubtedly, one of the most powerful of these because of its unmatched ability to propagate itself by bonding with humanity's darkest propensities.

Today, in a world where climate disruptions are intensifying, and many formerly stable institutions are crumbling, it is more and more evident that much of what we have been taught about the past is untrue. Indeed, what was truly new about the great 'take-off' of the nineteenth century was that it created a system in which indifference to human suffering was not just accepted by ruling elites but was justified and promoted by a plethora of false teleologies and deceptive theories. What this led to was, for the most part, a kind of 'slow violence', inflicted not by weaponry but rather by inaction, and refusals to intervene. Such violence gives the appearance of being—and indeed, often is—unintentional, because it is enabled principally by institutional indifference. It is this that made it possible for European empires to push opium on China and Southeast Asia, and it is what makes it possible today for the wealthy and powerful to be suicidally indifferent to the prospect of a global catastrophe.

In such a world, does it serve any purpose to recount this bleak and unedifying story?

This question has haunted me since I first started working on this book, many years ago. It was the reason why, at a certain point, I felt I could not go on, even though I had already accumulated an enormous amount of material. It seemed to me then that Tagore had got it exactly right when he wrote: 'in the Indo-China opium traffic, human nature itself sinks down to such a depth of despicable meanness, that it is hateful even to follow the story to its conclusion.'

So persuaded was I of this that I decided to abandon the project: I cancelled the contracts I had signed, and returned the advances I had been paid by my publishers.

304 SMOKE AND ASHES

Looking back now I realize that it was not only because of the 'despicable meanness' of the story that I gave up on the project. There is also an inherent conceptual difficulty in telling a story of this kind: the problem lies in the inescapable presence of a non-human protagonist, a plant. This is, I think, one of the principal reasons why many histories of India, China, the British Empire and the United States skirt around this subject: it is very difficult to narrate a story in which a botanical entity is both instrument and protagonist.

It was not because of a conceptual breakthrough that I decided to take up the challenge once again. Rather it was the increasingly evident vitality of the Earth—or rather, Gaia—that gave me the impetus to carry on. The climate-intensified events of recent years have made it abundantly clear that there are many kinds of forces— biological, geological and atmospheric—that possess vital, agentive properties of their own. These forces may give the impression of being temporarily under human control, but beyond a certain point they are fully capable of asserting their independence and ascendancy. There is no better example of this than the story of the opium poppy; it is at once a cautionary tale about human hubris, and a lesson about humanity's limits and frailties.

At a time when elite hucksters and all-powerful billionaires are trying to peddle the idea of solar geoengineering there is nothing more important than to remember that every one of the interconnected crises that humanity now confronts is the unintended consequence of interventions conceived of by men who believed that their superior education and privilege entitled them to over-ride all customary, common-sense constraints.

Now, if ever, is the time for humility, in relation to other species and to the Earth itself.

EIGHTEEN
Portents

There are many differences between the ways in which opioids circulated in the nineteenth century and today. Back then the supply chains that distributed opium and cocaine were under the control of colonial regimes, so when the earliest internationally accepted drug control measures were enacted, between 1907 and 1920, it was possible for those regimes to scale back the supply. This certainly made a huge impact on China's problem, even though it did not solve it: opium continued to circulate within the country for decades afterwards, until the Communist Party instituted draconian anti-opium measures in the 1950s.[1]

Today, however, the international situation is completely different. The influence that any government can now exert on drug supplies is much more limited than it was then because the traffic is controlled by criminal networks that operate outside state control. New technologies have also given poppy farming many new fields in which to flourish, like Tasmania, which has been described as the 'breadbasket of the opioid boom', because it grows a genetically engineered 'super poppy' that produces 'a higher proportion of thebaine, an alkaloid that is the key chemical precursor for Oxycodone'.[2] It is only a matter of time before this variety spreads into other parts of the world, like Afghanistan, where opium production is increasing. As wars and failed states multiply around the world, it is quite likely that poppy farming, especially of genetically engineered varieties, will also spread to conflict-ridden areas in Syria, Iraq and Libya. The rekindled civil unrest in Burma may also initiate a new surge of poppy farming in borderlands where it was only recently suppressed. In a world that is increasingly destabilized by war, internecine conflict and climate change, it will be very hard to curtail the global flows of opium and its derivatives.

Most of the supply chains that distribute opioids and other drugs are now controlled by criminal networks which have shown themselves to be fully able to hold their own against the heavily funded, massively armed and increasingly militarized law enforcement system of the United States. While the American stance may well be counterproductive, it is by no means clear that the less oppressive methods of some European countries have been effective either. Vast quantities of illegal substances continue to flow across the Mediterranean, into southern Europe.

Another untoward portent is the steep rise, in recent years, in the use of other prescription drugs, such as Adderall and Ritalin, which are generally prescribed for attention deficit disorders. These drugs, which may have 'helped lay a foundation for the rise of opioids in universities', are now routinely prescribed for some 10 per cent of Americans under the age of seventeen: it is impossible to know what the long-term effects will be.[3]

Advances in communications technologies have further compounded the problem. Today China is the world's leading producer of fentanyl and the precursor chemicals needed to make heroin. These substances are often marketed through the internet and delivered through the US Postal Service: being odourless they are difficult to detect.[4] In a world where algorithms send merchandise spinning around the planet without interruption, it will be ever more difficult to trace contraband. 'Indeed, the ability to access an Asian supplier of fentanyl over the internet may be far more revolutionary than the ability to buy consumer goods on Amazon.'[5] With Artificial Intelligence and disinformation thrown in, the mix is bound to become even more volatile.

For countries with weaker law enforcement systems, such as those of the Indian subcontinent and Africa, it will be close to impossible to regulate the flow of opiates. Pakistan already has a major heroin problem because of the steady inflow from Afghanistan. The same is true of the Indian state of Punjab. Matters are likely to become much worse in the near future, especially if the many insurgencies of the region resort to poppy farming or drug running to fund their causes.

In short, every trend suggests that opioids and cocaine will become an even more powerful force than they already are in undermining nation-states as well as global systems of governance. It is very unlikely that any country will be able to reduce drug use in the ways that India, China and other Asian countries did in the 1950s. Those successes were the product of deeply rooted anti-colonial movements. It seems improbable that any country will ever again be able to recreate that kind of fervour, especially in the teeth of intensifying climate change.

It would appear, then, that the poppy, having been a major force in the making of modernity, will also be instrumental in its unmaking, a role that it will share with fossil fuels. In both cases, the dangers inherent in the use of these substances have been long known, but either denied or systematically suppressed.

Those who find it difficult to believe that giant energy corporations would be depraved enough to conceal the dangers that fossil fuels pose

to future generations—dangers revealed by their own scientists—
should remember that this kind of depravity has been built into the
system and can only be overcome by concerted collective action.

These sinister portents notwithstanding, the history of opium also
offers an important augury of hope for global environmental movements: they could look to the example of the transnational, multiethnic,
multiracial coalition of civil society groups that was eventually able to
drastically curtail the opium trade despite the determined and skilful
resistance of the British Empire, which was, at the time, even more
powerful than today's giant energy corporations.

Ironically, the credit for the successes of the anti-opium movement
was largely appropriated by colonial powers, which have always been
proficient in shaping historical narratives. This was the case also with
abolition: just as the role of black resistance to slavery was, until
recently, written out of the dominant narrative, so too has the story
of drug regulation generally been presented as one in which Christian
missionaries and Western statesmen were the chief protagonists.[6] But
as the historian Steffen Rimner has shown in his excellent 2018 study,
Opium's Long Shadow: From Asian Revolt to Global Drug Control, it was the
dogged determination of Chinese civil society groups, as well as the
adroit diplomacy of a few figures in the Qing hierarchy, that provided
the main impetus for the emergence of 'a worldwide covenant on
drug control'.[7] This happened, furthermore, at a time when the prime
movers of the opium trade—that is to say Western colonial powers—
were in complete control of the entire world: decolonization and
the emergence of a plethora of independent nation-states were such
distant prospects that they were hardly even dreamed of. Yet, against
all odds, a coalition of grassroots movements successfully joined
forces and, through the mobilization of international public opinion,

was able to turn a trade which had long been conducted under the aegis of the world's most powerful states into an activity that involved serious reputational damage.

One of the key figures in this long struggle was a Qing statesman, Prince Gong (also known, in English, as Prince Kung and Yixin). A half-brother of the Xianfeng Emperor, Prince Gong, while still in his twenties, played an important part in negotiating the unequal treaties that led to the legalization of opium after China's devastating defeat in the Second Opium War. But for the Prince, as for many other Qing statesmen, this was never anything other than a profoundly repugnant move, a step taken under duress. They shared, with most of their compatriots, the view that 'the opium trade was still what it had been before 1860: malevolent in conception, harmful and frequently fatal to the individual, corrosive in its social effects'.[8]

Soon after the conclusion of the Second Opium War, Prince Gong founded the Qing state's first bureau of foreign affairs, which made him, in effect, China's foreign minister. In that capacity, at a meeting with the British diplomat Rutherford Alcock in 1869, the Prince made an impassioned protest that was later submitted also as a written memorial:

> '[A]ll say that England trades in opium because she desires to work China's ruin . . . the Chinese merchant supplies your country with his goodly tea and silk, conferring thereby a benefit upon her, but the English merchant empoisons China with pestilent opium. Such conduct is unrighteous. Who can justify it? What wonder if officials and people say that England is willfully working out China's ruin . . . ?'[9]

These words—especially the refrain, 'All say that England trades in opium because she desires to work China's ruin'—resonated around the world, being carried far afield by newspapers and journals. The presence of the international press within China was a relatively new development that had followed after the First Opium War: the same processes of imperial aggression that had ripped open China's economy had also ensured that the country was no longer shut off from the world's gaze. Prince Gong evidently understood that the international press could amplify his message; in the years to come his bureau of foreign affairs would actively form alliances with activists in other parts of the world and play an important part in disseminating information about opium internationally. As a result, the Prince's protest had 'momentous, sustained and long-term consequences . . . [its] sustained and comprehensive reception by audiences from Asia to western Europe and North America made it the first stimulus behind a mobilization of anti-opium sentiment on a global scale.'[10]

The Prince's words fell on fertile soil in Britain and the United States, where anti-opium sentiment, and even organized activist groups, had long been in existence. Soon anti-opium groups began to spring up also in China and other parts of Asia, with many of them developing close ties of cooperation with each other. A growing number of books, pamphlets and articles on the issue also began to be published around the world. So (not unlike the global climate movement) a broad-based transnational effort began to take shape, one that colonial powers could not ignore because by this time public opinion had come to be recognized as an increasingly important factor in global geopolitics.

In India, as in China, opposition to the opium trade gathered momentum in the 1880s.[11] There, as in the United States and elsewhere, women played a major role in the drive (yet another prefiguration of the climate movement). A very important figure in the Indian campaign was Pandita Ramabai, the founder of Sharada Sadan, an institution that provided education and shelter for Hindu girls and widows.[12] Pandita Ramabai made Sharada Sadan into a major centre for the global struggle against the colonial opium trade, forming many partnerships with women's groups in other countries. Particularly important in this regard was an American group, the Women's Christian Temperance Union (WCTU), which sponsored a lobbying tour of the United States for Ramabai in 1887. As one of the earliest and most important women's organizations, the WCTU's influence was unrivalled at the time: 'No male anti-opium group had ever launched a comparable fight for its voice.'[13]

Another very important figure in the Indian anti-opium movement was Ramabai's mentor, the prominent social reformer Soonderbai H. Powar. In 1892 she authored an influential pamphlet titled *An Indian Woman's Impeachment of the Opium Crime of the British Government*. On speaking tours her audiences were so moved by her speeches that at one meeting a woman said: 'Tell the English government that if they will stop the Opium curse, I and other women in India will willingly take off the skin of our bodies to make shoes for the English Government and its people.'[14]

Yet another major voice in India's anti-opium movement was Rabindranath Tagore, who returned to this subject again and again over the course of his life. In 1933, twenty years after he was awarded the Nobel Prize for Literature, he wrote: 'It has gradually become clear that outside of Europe the torch of European civilization was not intended to light the way, but to start fires. That is why, one day, cannonballs and pellets of opium rained down together on the heart of China. Never in history has such an atrocity occurred before.'[15]

In Burma, Sri Lanka and Indonesia too there was growing public outrage against the colonial regime's opium policies.[16] Inspired by anti-opium activists and social reformers in mainland China, Java's Peranakan-dominated Chinese Chambers of Commerce took the lead in disseminating anti-opium propaganda and sponsoring pro-grammes to discourage opium use. Among the Javanese as well, the opposition to opium became far more vocal. In 1899 a Javanese no-blewoman called Kartini wrote in a letter to a Dutch correspondent in Holland:

Opium is the pest of Java. Yes, opium is far worse than the pest . . . It spreads more and more, and will never leave us, never grow less—for to speak plainly—it is protected by the Government! The more general the use of opium in Java, the fuller the treasury. The opium tax is one of the richest sources of income of the Government—what matter if it go well or ill with the people?—the Government prospers. This curse of the people fills the treasury of the Dutch Indian Government with thousands—nay, with millions . . . It is terrible to see so much evil and to be powerless to fight against it.[17]

Such protests found a ready audience because anti-opium sentiment had been gathering strength in Holland as well, partly inspired by novels that depicted the atrocities of the opium trade in vivid detail.[18] In 1887 the editor of the most important Dutch paper in the East Indies wrote a detailed critique of colonial opium policies and appealed to politicians in Holland to 'bring an end to the "moral, physical and financial" ruin of the Javanese perpetrated in the interests of state income'.[19] In 1899 a prominent Dutch lawyer called on Holland to pay a 'Debt of Honor' in reparation for its neglect of its colonies, a sentiment echoed by the country's monarch, Queen Wilhelmina, who, in marked contrast to her counterpart in Britain, publicly 'lamented "the diminished welfare of the population of Java"'.[20]

The United States was another country where concerns about opium became widespread in the late nineteenth century, not least because it was then dealing with its own addiction problem brought on by the invention of the hypodermic syringe and the extensive use of opiates during the Civil War.[21] Morphine dependence came to be known as 'morphinism' or 'soldier's disease', and the German pharmaceutical company Bayer Laboratories soon came up with a 'cure' that was touted as non-addictive, even though it was also an opioid. This was none other than heroin, the name of which was 'derived from the German for "heroic"'.[22] Packaged in bottles with colourful labels, heroin, writes Beth Macy, was 'sold widely from drugstore counters, no prescription necessary, not only for veterans but also for women with menstrual cramps and babies with hiccups'.[23] At the start of the twentieth century some 300,000 Americans were addicted to opioids. President Theodore Roosevelt, in 1908, appointed a special commissioner, Dr Hamilton Wright, to deal with the problem.[24]

As the campaign against opium intensified, it became steadily more militant, and the colonial regimes in India and Indonesia—in yet another foreshadowing of the present predicament of the climate movement—responded with outright repression, exiling and prosecuting activists and critics.[25] But these measures only helped to further energize the anti-opium movement.

So, led by early feminists, writers, public figures, Christian missionaries and religious reformers of many nationalities, the Indian anti-opium campaign implanted its ideas deep within the public sphere. A particularly important figure, in this regard, was Dadabhai Naoroji, who had been one of the earliest to make opium a central plank in his critique of the British Empire. As a founding member of the Indian National Congress, Naoroji, and other like-minded figures, ensured that opposition to the colonial drug trade was incorporated early into the programme of India's most important political organization.

By the 1890s anti-opium sentiment had coalesced into a global movement, with a substantial representation in legislatures across Europe and America. At the same time opioids were also becoming a matter of concern for European colonial authorities now that China itself had emerged as the world's largest producer of opium and heroin: criminal networks, of the kind that had previously carried drugs into China, were now smuggling them into Southeast Asia, India and, increasingly, Europe.

These concerns, along with the election to Parliament of some 240 supporters of the anti-opium cause, ultimately led to the setting up of the Royal Commission on Opium in 1893 by Prime

Minister William Gladstone.[26] Although Gladstone had been a
fierce critic of the First Opium War in his youth, denouncing it as
'morally indefensible', after many decades in politics he had learnt
to be far more accommodating of Britain's imperial realities. The
Commission was set up in such a fashion as to ensure, through
its membership and methods, that the final outcome would be
favourable for the British Raj.[27] And it ably fulfilled this mission: after
interviewing hundreds of witnesses, the Commission produced a
set of voluminous reports that fully endorsed the British Empire's
opium policies.

One of the men in the Commission who belonged to the 'anti-
opium party' was a member of Parliament by the name of Henry J.
Wilson; he wrote a striking note of dissent in which he pointed
out that among the 722 witnesses who had appeared before the
Commission, the defenders of the system outnumbered the critics by
more than two to one.

> I do not think that the whole of the facts were presented to
> us with the impartiality and completeness due to such an
> inquiry. The Report adopted by my colleagues appears to me
> to partake more of the character of an elaborate defence of
> the opium trade of the East India Company, and of the present
> Government of India, than of a judicial pronouncement on
> the immediate questions submitted by us.[28]

The Royal Commission was intended, from the start, to silence the
anti-opium movement in Britain, and in this it certainly succeeded:
the movement was essentially defunct there for several years
afterwards.[29] But elsewhere the campaign continued to gain strength,
so that in the end the Commission, and its report, came to be 'the
last and ultimately futile governmental attempt to mute anti-opium
energies in Asia and around the world'.[30]

The year in which the Commission began to publish its reports, 1894, was when China suffered another major defeat, this time in the First Sino-Japanese War. In the aftermath, the Qing state was forced to cede Taiwan and some other territories to the victor. This had crucial repercussions for the politics of drugs: since opium was completely banned in Japan, Taiwan was where Japanese administrators had their first encounter with large-scale opium addiction. The policy they adopted stopped short of an outright ban on opium; instead, the drug was tightly regulated, and provision was made for the treatment of addicts and for anti-opium education. Most significantly perhaps, the Japanese broke with European colonial policies in Asia by refusing to treat opium as a source of revenue (though this would change when they expanded into China).

Shortly after this, in 1898, the United States took control of the Philippines, where it encountered widespread opium use, especially among the migrant Chinese population. In trying to formulate an appropriate opium policy for its new colony, the American administration decided to set up its own commission to conduct a comparative inquiry into opium governance across East and Southeast Asia.[31] The Philippines Commission concluded that the 'opium farm' system that the British, French and Dutch had established in their colonies, far from being a regulatory mechanism, as claimed by colonial authorities, actually led to increases in opium use. Rejecting outright the European colonial model of using opium as a source of revenue, the Commission recommended instead the Japanese model.[32] The Philippines Commission's report thus became a standing rebuke to European colonial policies, and a refutation of the findings of the Royal Commission on Opium. As a result, 'Britain edged closer than ever to becoming the opium villain of Asia'.[33]

The Philippines Commission's report was published in 1905. By then the anti-opium movement had become so internationalized, with information flowing continually in all directions, that the report even

affected China. In 1906, in a momentous move, the Qing Emperor
Guangxu reversed the legalization that had been in effect for almost
half a century.[34] The imperial edict noted that far from solving the
drug problem, legalization had exacerbated it:

> Since the restrictions against the use of opium were removed,
> the poison of the drug has practically permeated the whole of
> China. The opium smoker wastes times and neglects work,
> ruins his health, and impoverishes his family, and the poverty
> and weakness which for the past few decades have been daily
> increasing amongst us are undoubtedly attributable to this
> cause.[35]

The Qing state's new ban envisaged a gradual phasing out of
opium production and consumption over ten years, and ordered the
setting up of anti-opium societies across the country. The renewed
criminalization of the opium trade was enacted under the world's
gaze and it left the British Empire, which had long cited China's
legalization as justification for its own drug-trafficking activities, with
little room for manoeuvre. In the meantime, as the historian Diana
Kim has shown, many colonial bureaucrats had also undergone a
change of heart.[36]

In 1907 Britain signed an agreement with China, undertaking
to phase out all opium exports from India, over a ten-year period,
provided that China's suppression of its domestic drug industry met
similar annual targets.[37] Many British colonial officials assumed, no
doubt, that China would fail to meet its targets, thereby giving them
an excuse to resume exports from India.[38] But, in the event, China
disappointed them by actually exceeding its targets.[39] In some regions,
like Sichuan, conscientious officials succeeded in almost eliminating
opium in just four years.[40] 'China's crusade to free her people from
the opium curse,' wrote a contemporary American observer, 'may be

justly reckoned one of the greatest moral achievements in history—
a challenge to our Western world.'[41]

The Sino-British accord of 1907 was a turning point in the
evolution of an international regulatory framework for opium, which
proceeded apace over the next few years. In 1911 the Patna Opium
Factory was shut down, and the acreage under poppy cultivation
in India was greatly reduced.[42] Within a few years the Sino-Indian
opium relationship had effectively ended.[43] Although the process
was disrupted by World War I the anti-opium movement was strong
enough by then to ensure that the cause would be taken up again—
and the League of Nations did indeed treat it as a major priority.
By the mid-1920s this regulatory framework was securely in place,
with severe restrictions on the export of opium from India. In 1930
legislation was introduced to strictly control the circulation of opium
within the Indian subcontinent (although in a contradictory move, the
colonial regime also opened the Neemach Opium Factory in 1935).[44]

Needless to add, the establishment of the global regulatory
framework for opium did not succeed in putting the genie back
in the bottle: far from it. In the 1920s and 1930s, as Japan seized
more and more Chinese territory, it abandoned the policies
it had followed in Taiwan and became deeply involved in drug
trafficking itself, continuing through World War II.[45] Immediately
after the War, opium played an important part in financing the
anti-colonial struggle in Vietnam. In Indonesia, similarly, the
infant independent republic was forced to sell leftover stocks of
the colonial regime's opium in order to fund its fight against the
Dutch, from 1945 to 1949.[46]

In the post-War period, India and China appeared as the two
leaders of 'the offensive against opium'.[47] Two years after India gained
independence in 1947, a national opium conference was held in New
Delhi, where it was decided that 'the use of opium for other than
scientific and medical purposes should be totally prohibited'.[48] Every

state was asked to reduce its purchases of opium from the Ghazipur factory by 10 per cent annually. The following years saw a steep decline in the consumption of opium across the country. The total amount of opium consumed in India went from 2,22,700 kilograms in 1936 to 1,56,784 kilograms in 1951.[49] After 1950,

> the quantity of opium released for oral consumption declined steadily from 150 tonnes to 2.5 tonnes in 1966. Simultaneously the number of registered addicts dropped from 200,000 in 1956 to 124,904 at the end of 1963. The number of opium smokers went down from 2,504 in 1953 to 1,822 in 1966. Some of these figures may not be exact but they certainly reflect the state resolve in independent India to overcome the ill-effects of British opium policy in the shortest possible time.[50]

The Indian's state's resolve was certainly strong enough to reduce the total area under poppy cultivation to a tenth of what it was in 1947; the colonial infrastructure for the distribution of opium within India was also dismantled.[51] Contrary to the confident predictions of colonial apologists, India's rural economy did not collapse, Bihari peasants did not rise up in defence of poppy cultivation, and there was no sudden rise in fatal illnesses in remote villages.

Meanwhile, elsewhere in Asia, opium once again came to be implicated in strategic manoeuvring. As Alfred McCoy has shown, between 1955 and 1975 the French and American secret services made extensive use of opium during the wars in Vietnam, and in other conflicts. When returning soldiers planted the problem of addiction in the heart of Middle America, the United States' violent and blundering response, in the form of the War on Drugs, created disastrous consequences for large parts of Latin America, and for minorities at home, while also accelerating the growth of the carceral state.

In India too the early successes in curtailing the circulation of opium were reversed within a couple of decades. This came about primarily because India, unlike China, did not entirely renounce the colonial practice of treating opium as a source of revenue: the government's two state-run factories continued to produce opium for the international market.[52] Through international agreements it remained the world's single largest source of licit opium during the 1960s and 1970s. Soon enough history repeated itself, and a great deal of 'licit' opium began to find its way into the hands of criminal networks, which used it to manufacture heroin. Eventually, opiates started leaving India once again through the ports that had once been used by the old Malwa smuggling networks.[53] By 1988, according to the United States House Committee on Foreign Affairs, 'the diversion of licit stocks in India was creating "a billion dollars' worth of street heroin"'.[54]

Since then there has been a steep rise in heroin production across the Indian subcontinent, not to mention the huge surge that occurred in Afghanistan after the American invasion of 2001, which sent fresh waves of opioids sweeping across the region. Today, many parts of India, Pakistan, Nepal and Bangladesh are experiencing new epidemics of addiction, and drugs have again become a major factor in the politics of the region.[55] A historian has noted, ominously, that 'international observers have listed opium production and traffic as one of the greatest threats to India's social structure, security and status as a regional superpower . . . In Pakistan drugs are an immediate threat to the survival of the state.'[56]

In short, the anti-opium movement certainly did not succeed ultimately in containing the global flow of opium. However, it is also true that in the early decades of the twentieth century it was able to prevail against an industry that had generated fabulous profits for some of the world's most powerful states.

The success of the anti-opium movement in building a transnational coalition of civil society organizations and religious groups, many of which did not see eye to eye on any other matter, suggests that such a strategy might also work in relation to energy corporations today. But to achieve that enough people would have to come together, in an organized fashion, to ensure that the reputational damage of selling fossil fuels would outweigh the profits. This is, of course, precisely the strategy that activist organizations have followed in their campaign to get universities, churches, pension funds, and even governments to disinvest from energy corporations. With enough momentum it is possible that the reputational damage of trafficking in fossil fuels will lead to a significant reduction in their use.

On an increasingly dark horizon, this is a rare, but bright, ray of hope.

Notes

1: Here Be Dragons

1. The word is 'likely a Portuguese corruption of *Guangdong*, of which Guangzhou was the administrative center, where Portuguese travelers were conducted in the late 16 century . . .' (Graham E. Johnson and Glen D. Peterson, *Historical Dictionary of Guangzhou (Canton) and Guangdong* (Lanham, MD, and London: The Scarecrow Press, 1999), p. xi.

2. For the geopolitical significance of the southern slope of the Himalayas see John W. Garver, *Protracted Contest: Sino-Indian Rivalry in the Twentieth Century* (Seattle, WA: University of Washington Press, 2001). For a Chinese view see Lin Xuecheng, *The Sino-Indian Border Dispute and Sino-Indian Relations* (New York, NY: University Press of America, 1994).

3. Avtar Singh Bhasin, *Nehru, Tibet and China* (Gurgaon: Penguin Random House India, 2021), p. 319.

4. In the words of former Indian Foreign Secretary Shyam Saran: 'India found itself in an unexpected clash of arms mainly as a result of its unfamiliarity with Chinese culture and ways of thinking. Indian leaders failed to pick up cues and oblique hints which if understood accurately may have led to a different outcome than humiliating defeat.' (quoted in Bhasin, *Nehru, Tibet and China*, 318).

5. Much has been written about these issues by specialists in international relations and strategic studies. See for example Kanti Bajpai, *India Versus*

China: Why They Are Not Friends (New Delhi: Juggernaut Books, 2021); Zorawar Daulet Singh, *Powershift: India–China Relations in a Multipolar World* (New Delhi: Pan Macmillan Publishing India, 2020); and Shyam Saran, *How China Sees India and the World* (New Delhi: Juggernaut Books 2022). These issues, important as they are, have only a tangential bearing on this book.

6. See Zhang Xing and Tansen Sen, 'The Chinese in South Asia', in *Routledge Handbook of the Chinese Diaspora*, ed. Chee-Beng Tan (London: Routledge, 2012), p. 206; Tansen Sen, *India, China and the World: A Connected History* (London: Rowman & Littlefield Publishers, 2017), p. 271; Ramakrishna Chatterjee, 'The Chinese Community of Calcutta: Their Early Settlement and Migration', in *India and China in the Colonial World*, ed. Madhavi Thampi (New Delhi: Social Science Press, 2005), pp. 55–65; and Jayani Jeanne Bonnerjee, 'Neighbourhood, City, Diaspora: Identity and belonging for Calcutta's Anglo-Indian and Chinese communities' (Thesis submitted in partial fulfilment of the requirements for the degree of PhD in Geography at the Department of Geography, Queen Mary, University of London, 2010), p. 10.

7. Sen, *India, China and the World*, 271.

8. See, for example, *Painted Encounters: Parsi Traders and the Community*, eds Pheroza J. Godrej and Firoza Punthakey Mistree (New Delhi: National Gallery of Modern Art, 2016), p. 10.

9. Sanjay Subrahmanyam, 'Hearing Voices: Vignettes of Early Modernity in South Asia, 1400-1750', *Daedalus*, Vol. 127, no. 3 (1998): 100.

10. See Christiaan J.A. Jörg, 'Porcelain: China in the Netherlands', in *Sailing to the Pearl River: Dutch Enterprise in South China 1600–2000*, ed. Cai Hongsheng, Leonard Blussé et al. (Guangzhou: Guangzhou Publishing House, 2004), pp. 17–19.

11. Sucheta Mazumdar, *Sugar and Society in China: Peasants, Technology and the World Market* (Cambridge: Harvard University Press, 1998), p. 109; and Tan Chung, 'The British-China-India Trade Triangle, 1771-1840', *Proceedings of the Indian History Congress* 34 (1973): 429.

12. Robin Wall Kimmerer, *Braiding Sweetgrass: Indigenous Wisdom, Scientific Knowledge, and the Teachings of Plants* (Minneapolis, MN: Milkweed Editions, 2013), p. 346.

2: Seeds

1. Erika Rappaport, *A Thirst for Empire: How Tea Shaped the Modern World* (Princeton, NJ: Princeton University Press, 2017), p. 27.

2. Andrew B. Liu, *Tea War: A History of Capitalism in China and India* (New Haven, CT: Yale University Press, 2020), p. 31; and Rappaport, *A Thirst for Empire*, 35. The first recorded instance of an Englishman drinking tea dates back to 1637, when a merchant by the name of Peter Mundy tasted a beverage called 'Chaa' on the Pearl River (Stephen R. Platt, *Imperial Twilight: The Opium War and the End of China's Last Golden Age* [New York, NY: Knopf, 2018], p. 12).

3. From the mid-eighteenth to the mid-nineteenth century, the British customs duty on tea varied between 75 per cent, 127 per cent and 100 per cent (although at times it also dipped to 12.5 per cent). From 1835 to 1858, this duty accounted for 20.95 per cent of Britain's entire customs revenue and constituted 8.68 per cent of total gross revenues. These figures are from J.Y. Wong's *Deadly Dreams: Opium, Imperialism and the Arrow War (1856–1860) in China* (Cambridge: Cambridge University Press, 1998), pp. 346–60.

4. Rappaport, *A Thirst for Empire*, 42.

5. Michael Greenberg, *British Trade and the Opening of China* (Cambridge: Cambridge University Press, 1951), p. 3; and Platt, *Imperial Twilight*, 12.

6. Liu, *Tea War*, 32.

7. Wong, *Deadly Dreams*, 343.

8. Ibid., 342–43.

9. Tan Chung, 'The British-China-India Trade Triangle, 1771–1840', *The Indian Economic and Social History Review*, Vol. 11, no. 4 (1974): 416; and Greenberg, *British Trade*, 3.

10. Wong, *Deadly Dreams*, 350–55.

11. Ibid., 357.

12. Harry G. Gelber, 'China as "Victim"? The Opium War That Wasn't' (Working Paper Series 136, Center for European Studies, Harvard University, 2019), p. 5.

13. Jonathan Spence, *The Search for Modern China* (New York, NY: W.W. Norton, 1990), p. 122; and Platt, *Imperial Twilight*, 43. In the words of a British director of Chinese customs: '[The] Chinese have the best food in the world, rice; the best drink, tea; the best clothing, silk, and fur. Possessing these staples and their innumerable native adjuncts, they do not need to buy a penny's worth elsewhere . . .' (Greenberg, *British Trade*, 5). Rajat Kanta Ray, attributes Chinese self-sufficiency to the great variety of climates in China ('Asian Capital in the Age of European Domination: The Rise of the Bazaar, 1800–1914', *Modern Asian Studies*, Vol. 29, no. 3 [1995]: 474).

14. 'The Chinese appeared self-sufficient and impervious to foreign science and products. In other words they had all the earmarks of another master

race.' (Keith MacMahon, *The Fall of the God of Money: Opium Smoking in Nineteenth-Century China* [Lanham, MD: Rowman & Littlefield Publishers, 2002], p.11.)

15. See Matthew Wormer, 'Opium, Economic Thought, and the Making of Britain's Free Trade Empire, 1773–1839' (Ph.D. diss., Stanford University, Stanford, CA, 2022), p. 206, fn. 2. I am grateful to Dr Priya Satia for bringing this thesis to my attention.

16. David Edward Owen, *British Opium Policy in China and India* (New Haven, CT: Yale University Press, 1934), p. 61.

17. Jayeeta Sharma, 'Making Garden, Erasing Jungle: The Tea Enterprise in Colonial Assam' in *The British Empire and the Natural World: Environmental Encounters in South Asia*, ed. Deepak Kumar, Vinita Damodaran and Rohan D'Souza (New Delhi: Oxford University Press, 2011), pp. 119–41.

18. See Philip Lutgendorf, 'Making Tea in India: Chai, Capitalism, Culture', *Thesis Eleven*, Vol. 113, no. 1 (2012): 13–21; and Gautam Bhadra, *From an Imperial Product to a National Drink: Culture of Tea Consumption in Modern India* (Kolkata: Tea Board, Department of Commerce, 2005): https://archive.org/details/fromanimperialproducttoanationaldrinkcultureofteaconsumptioninmodern indiagautambhadra_17_I.

19. Rappaport, *A Thirst for Empire*, 33.

20. Sharma 'Making Gard-en Erasing Jungle', 122.

21. Ibid., 121.

22. Today, two varieties of the plant are recognized: *Camellia sinensis (var. sinensis)* and *Camellia sinensis (var. assamica)*, Liu, *Tea War*, p. 27.

23. See Rappaport, *A Thirst for Empire*, 92–103.

24. Sharma, 'Making Garden, Erasing Jungle', 123.

25. William S. Ruschenberger, *Narrative of a Voyage Around the World, During the Years 1835, 36, and 37* (London: Richard Bentley, 1838), p. 252. See also: Stan Neal, 'Opium and Migration: Jardine Matheson's Imperial Connections and the Recruitment of Chinese Labour for Assam, 1834–39', *Modern Asian Studies*, Vol. 51, no. 5 (2017): 1–30.

26. Liu, *Tea War*, 82.

27. Ibid.

28. The English translation was published in 2018 by Pan Macmillan, New Delhi.

29. Rappaport, *A Thirst for Empire*, 28. See also Ruschenberger, *Narrative of a Voyage*, 244.

30. Rappaport, *A Thirst for Empire*, 103–104.

31. Liu, *Tea War*, 117. See also Sharma, 'Making Garden, Erasing Jungle', 127.

32. Tea, as Erika Rappaport observes, 'especially thrived in colonial conditions . . . because colonial states fertilized this industry with cheap land, labor, and other requirements.' (118).

33. Liu, *Tea War*, 132–35.

34. See for example, this list published by Greenpeace media: https://media. greenpeace.org/archive/Owner-of-Makaibari-Tea-Estate-in-Darjeeling-27MZIF3DABH5.html.

35. Rappaport, *A Thirst for Empire*, 8.

36. Liu, *Tea War*, 1.

37. Ibid., 9

38. Ibid., 5.

39. For more on this, see my book *The Nutmeg's Curse: Parables for a Planet in Crisis* (Gurugram: Penguin Random House, 2021).

40. David Graeber and David Wengrow, *The Dawn of Everything: A New History of Humanity* (New York, NY: Farrar, Strauss and Giroux, 2021), pp. 17–20, 30–37. For the unacknowledged influence of Chinese ideas on Immanuel Kant, see Yu Liu, *Seeds of a Different Eden: Chinese Gardening Ideas and a New English Aesthetic Ideal* (Columbia, SC: University of South Carolina Press, 2008), p. 159.

3: 'An Actor in Its Own Right'

1. See David T. Courtwright, *Forces of Habit: Drugs and the Making of the Modern World* (Cambridge, MA: Harvard University Press, 2001), p. 31.

2. Martin Booth, *Opium: A History* (New York, NY: St. Martin's Press, 1999), p. 4.

3. Carl A. Trocki, *Opium, Empire and the Global Political Economy: A Study of the Asian Opium Trade, 1750–1950* (New York, NY: Routledge, 1999), p. 16.

4. Booth, *Opium*, 15-16.

5. Rudi Matthee, *The Pursuit of Pleasure: Drugs and Stimulants in Iranian History, 1500–1900* (Princeton, NJ: Princeton University Press, 2009), p. 97.

6. Nathan Allen, *The Opium Trade; Including a Sketch of Its History, Extent, Effects Etc. as Carried on in India and China* (Lowell, MA: James P. Walker, 1853), p. 6.

7. David M. Cutler and Edward L. Glaeser, 'When Innovation Goes Wrong: Technological Regress and the Opioid Epidemic', *The Journal of Economic Perspectives*, Vol. 35, no. 4 (2021): 174.

8. See, for instance, Gunnel Cederlöf, 'Poor Man's Crop: Evading Opium Monopoly', *Modern Asian Studies*, Vol. 53, no. 2 (2019): 645.

9. Quoted in Barry Meier, *Pain Killer: An Empire of Deceit and the Origin of America's Opioid Epidemic* (New York, NY: Penguin Random House, 2018), p. 64. Ironically, Purdue Pharma would make extensive use of this quote in its marketing campaigns for its prescription painkiller Oxycontin. See also David T. Courtwright, *Dark Paradise: A History of Opiate Addiction in America* (Cambridge, MA: Harvard University Press, 2001), p. 43.

10. Meena Bhargava, 'Narcotics and Drugs: Pleasure, Intoxication or Simply Therapeutic – North India, Sixteenth- Seventeenth Centuries', *The Medieval History Journal*, Vol. 15, no. 1 (2012): 104. Pituri is a narcotic used by Indigenous Australians (see Mike Letnic and Luke Keogh, 'Pituri Country', in *Desert Channels: The Impulse to Conserve,* eds Libby Robin, Chris Dickman and Mandy Martin [Clayton: CSIRO Publishing, 2010], pp. 61–79.

11. Courtwright, *Forces of Habit*, 91. Courtwright attributes this observation to Andrew Weil.

12. Ibid., 139.

13. Unlike these other psychoactives, the use of qat also began relatively recently. See Hans Derks, *History of the Opium Problem: The Assault on the East, ca. 1600–1950* (Leiden: Brill, 2012), p. 29.

14. See Derks, *History of the Opium Problem*, 343. See also Steffen Rimner, *Opium's Long Shadow: From Asian Revolt to Global Drug Control* (Cambridge, MA: Harvard University Press, 2018), p. 232.

15. In *The Po: An Elegy for Italy's Longest River* (London: Head of Zeus, 2022), Tobias Jones notes that in 1870 'about 15 percent of all arable land in the provinces of Bologna and Ferrara was dedicated to hemp . . .' (p. 111). However, 'there's no record of *Cannabis sativa* being used as a psychoactive substance in Piemonte prior to the twentieth century . . .' (p. 222).

16. Courtwright, *Forces of Habit*, 39.

17. Trocki, *Opium, Empire*, 91.

18. For a detailed account of the use of opium in the courts of Safavid Persia, see Matthee, *The Pursuit of Pleasure*, 97–116. For the adoption of opium by Southeast Asian elites, see Trocki, *Opium, Empire*, 52. For China, see Zheng Yangwen, *The Social Life of Opium in China* (Cambridge: Cambridge University Press, 2005), pp. 48–55; Jonathan Spence, 'Opium Smoking in Ch'ing China', in *Conflict and Control in Late Imperial China*, eds Frederic Wakeman Jr and Carolyn Grant (Berkeley, CA: University of California Press, 1975), pp. 229–31; and Peter Lee, *Opium Culture: The Art and Ritual of the Chinese Tradition* (Rochester, VT: Park Street Press, 2005), pp. 11–17.

19. Patrick Radden Keefe, *Empire of Pain: The Secret History of the Sackler Dynasty* (New York, NY: Doubleday, 2021), p. 37.

20. For the history of mahua, see David Hardiman, *The Coming of the Devi: Adivasi Assertion in Western India* (New Delhi: Oxford University Press, 1987); and Ajay Skaria, *Hybrid Histories: Forest, Frontiers and Wilderness in Western India* (New Delhi: Oxford University Press, 1999), pp. 46–48.

21. For more on the aestheticization of opiates, see Lucy Inglis, *Milk of Paradise: A History of Opium* (New York, NY: Pegasus Books, 2019), p. 330.

22. Beth Macy, *Dopesick: Dealers, Doctors, and the Drug Company that Addicted America* (Boston, MA: Little, Brown and Co., 2018), pp. 58–59.

23. Alfred W. McCoy, *The Politics of Heroin: CIA Complicity in the Global Drug Trade, Afghanistan, Southeast Asia, Central America, Colombia* (Chicago, IL: Lawrence Hill Books, 2003), p. 3.

24. For an example from eastern Kentucky, see Tarence Ray, 'United in Rage: Half-truths and Myths Propelled Kentucky's War on Opioids', *The Baffler*, no. 58 (2021).

25. William B. McAllister, '"Wolf by the Ears": The Dilemmas of Imperial Opium Policymaking in the Twentieth Century', in *Drugs and Empires: Essays in Modern Imperialism and Intoxication, c.1500–c.1930*, eds James H. Mills and Patricia Barton (New York, NY: Palgrave Macmillan, 2007), p. 216.

26. Matthee, *The Pursuit of Pleasure*, 97. See also Bhargava, 'Narcotics and Drugs', 105.

27. S.P. Sangar, 'Intoxicants in Mughal India', *Indian Journal of History of Science*, Vol. 16, no. 2 (1981): 202.

28. N.P. Singh, *The East India Company's Monopoly Industries in Bihar with Particular Reference to Opium and Saltpetre, 1773–1833* (Muzaffarpur: Sarvodaya Vangmaya, 1980), p. 11.

29. As David Courtwright observes, 'Diseases and drug exchanges have many close parallels'. (*Forces of Habit*, 3.)

30. Matthee, *The Pursuit of Pleasure,* 110.

31. Ibid., 12. 'French observers of Safavid society likened [opium's] use to that of wine in their home country, arguing that Iranians knew how to deal with it and generally did not succumb to its addictive qualities.'

32. The historian N.P. Singh writes: 'We know from *Bahadur Shahnamah* of 1709 that during the Mughal period no attempt was made to encourage or restrict the cultivation of opium.' (*The East India Company's Monopoly Industries*, 12.)

33. 'Indian society regarded medicinal opium-taking by mouth as normal and valuable,' writes the historian Richard Newman, 'but saw the recreational

smoking of opiates as a perversion.' (Richard Newman, 'Early British Encounters with the Indian Opium Eater', in *Drugs and Empires: Essays in Modern Imperialism and Intoxication, c.1500–c.1930*, eds James H. Mills and Patricia Barton [New York, NY: Palgrave Macmillan, 2007], p. 69.)

34. See Keith McMahon, *The Fall of the God of Money: Opium Smoking in Nineteenth-Century China* (Lanham, MD: Rowman & Littlefield Publishers, 2002), p. 4; Derks, *History of the Opium Problem*, 194; and Gregory Blue, 'Opium for China: The British Connection', in *Opium Regimes: China, Britain, and Japan, 1839–1952*, eds Timothy Brook and Bob Tadashi Wakabayashi (Berkeley, CA: University of California Press, 2000), p. 37. For patterns of opium consumption in nineteenth-century America, see Courtwright, *Dark Paradise*.

35. See James H. Mills, 'Drugs, Consumption, and Supply in Asia: The Case of Cocaine in Colonial India, c. 1900–c.1930', *The Journal of Asian Studies*, Vol. 66, no. 2 (2007): 345–62.

36. Mathee, *The Pursuit of Pleasure*, 110. Another popular compound was *madak*, see Rolf Bauer, *The Peasant Production of Opium in Nineteenth-Century India* (Leiden: Brill, 2019), p. 46; and Courtwright, *Forces of Habit*, 33.

37. W.M. Thackston Jr., trans., *The Baburnama: Memoirs of Babur, Prince and Emperor* (New York, NY: Penguin Random House, 2002), p. 443. See also, Matthee, *The Pursuit of Pleasure*, 42.

38. Humayun's sister, in her account of his reign, records an incident when he excused himself for having failed to turn up for a party thrown by his female relatives by claiming that he was an opium addict (Gulbaden Begum, *Humayunnama* [Delhi: Idarah-i Adabiyar-i Delhi, 1972] Persian text, p. 131). I am grateful to Dr Lisa Balabanlilar for this reference.

39. Newman, 'Early British Encounters', 58.

40. The earliest estimate of opium production in Bihar is from 1688, when Dutch factors estimated that 4,350 chests were produced there (Om Prakash, 'Opium monopoly in India and Indonesia in the eighteenth century', *The Indian Economic and Social History Review*, Vol. 24, no. 1 [1987]: 71). But another Dutch source provides a much lower estimate of around 2,96,235 kgs (8,700 maunds, with 1 maund being equal to 34.05 kg). (Om Prakash, *The Dutch East India Company and the Economy of Bengal, 1630-1720* (New Jersey, NJ: Princeton University Press, 1985), p. 57. This is equal to about 3,936.31 'chests' of opium, calculated at 75.257 kg (160 lbs) per chest, as estimated for 'Bengal' opium by Amar Farooqui ('Opium Enterprise and Colonial Intervention in Malwa and Western India, 1800-1824', *The Indian*

Economic and Social History Review, Vol. 32, no. 4 [1995]: 451, fn.). This is a plausible figure, because the total Bihar production hovered around 4,000 chests through much of the eighteenth century. But it should be noted that by 1688 increased Dutch demand had already driven up the production of opium in Bihar, so it would have been lower earlier in the century. I am grateful to Rolf Bauer for his help with these calculations. He is in no way responsible for the inferences that I have drawn from them, or from his book in general.

41. Derks, *History of the Opium Problem*, 187. For population estimates see Irfan Habib, 'Population', in *The Cambridge Economic History of India, c. 1200–c.1750*, eds Tapan Raychaudhuri and Irfan Habib (Cambridge: Cambridge University Press, 1982), Chapter VI; and Shireen Moosvi and Roland Lardinois, 'Une estimation de la population de l'Inde en 1601', *Population* (French Edition), Vol. 39 (1984): 9–25.
42. Derks, *History of the Opium Problem*, 188.
43. John F. Richards, 'The Opium Industry in British India', *The Indian Economic and Social History Review*, Vol. 39, nos. 2-3 (2002): 159–61.

4: Frenemies

1. It has been estimated that for a farmer to produce the equivalent of one 'ball' of raw opium (about 1.6 kg), required 387 man-hours of labour. Carl A. Trocki, *Opium, Empire and the Global Political Economy: A Study of the Asian Opium Trade, 1750–1950* (New York, NY: Routledge, 1999), p. 68. N.P. Singh notes: 'Poppy cultivation was not liked at all since it was far more laborious and troublesome,' in *The East India Company's Monopoly Industries in Bihar with Particular Reference to Opium and Saltpetre, 1773–1833* (Muzaffarpur: Sarvodaya Vangmaya, 1980), p. 23.
2. Hans Derks, *History of the Opium Problem: The Assault on the East, ca. 1600–1950* (Leiden: Brill, 2012), p. 430.
3. Singh, *The East India Company's Monopoly Industries*, 23–24.
4. Derks, *History of the Opium Problem*, 177.
5. Om Prakash, *The Dutch East India Company and the Economy of Bengal, 1630–1720* (Princeton, NJ: Princeton University Press, 1985), p. 47. See also Derks, *History of the Opium Problem*, 150, 159 and 229.
6. Derks, *History of the Opium Problem*, 208.
7. '[T]he Dutch created opium as a commercial mass product in the Malabar coastal region after 1663.' (Ibid., 236.)
8. Prakash, *The Dutch East India Company*, 145.

9. J.F. Scheltema, 'The Opium Trade in the Dutch East Indies', *American Journal of Sociology*, Vol. 13, no. 1 (1907): 80.

10. Ibid., 80-81.

11. Prakash, *The Dutch East India Company*, 145.

12. Derks, *History of the Opium Problem*, 231.

13. Ibid., 208–13.

14. Ibid., 200.

15. Om Prakash, 'Opium monopoly in India and Indonesia in the eighteenth century', *The Indian Economic and Social History Review*, Vol. 24, no. 1 (1987): 64.

16. See Wormer, 'Opium, Economic Thought, and the Making of Britain's Free Trade Empire, 1773–1839' (Ph.D. diss., Stanford University, Stanford, CA, 2022), p. 32.

17. Jonathan Spence, 'Opium Smoking in Ch'ing China', in *Conflict and Control in Late Imperial China*, eds Frederic Wakeman Jr and Carolyn Grant (Berkeley, CA: University of California Press, 1975), pp. 213–14; Prakash, *The Dutch East India Company*, 145; Introduction to *Opium Regimes: China Britain, and Japan, 1839-1952*, eds Timothy Brook and Bob Tadashi Wakabayashi (Berkeley, CA: University of California Press, 2000), p. 6; and Tansen Sen, *India, China and the World: A Connected History* (London: Rowman & Littlefield Publishers, 2017), pp. 232–33.

18. Hsin-Pao Chang, *Commissioner Lin and the Opium War* (Cambridge, MA: Harvard University Press, 1964), p. 16. See also Sen, *India, China and the World*, 233.

19. Peter Lee, *Opium Culture: The Art and Ritual of the Chinese Tradition* (Rochester, VT: Park Street Press, 2005), pp. 8–9.

20. Zheng Yangwen, *The Social Life of Opium in China* (Cambridge: Cambridge University Press, 2005), pp. 81–86. See also Betty Peh-T'i Wei, *Ruan Yuan, 1764–1849: The Life and Work of a Major Scholar-Official in Nineteenth-Century China before the Opium War* (Hong Kong: Hong Kong University Press, 2006), pp. 155–58.

21. Hosea Ballou Morse, *The International Relations of the Chinese Empire; Vol. I, The Period of Conflict 1834–1860* (London: Longmans, 1910), p. 173. See also Frederic Wakeman Jr, *Strangers at the Gate: Social Disorders in South China 1839–1861* (Berkeley, CA: University of California Press, 1966), p. 32: 'The imperial government had banned opium smoking in 1729, but the prohibition had been so ignored that further edicts were issued in 1796 and 1800, finally forbidding any importation of the drug at all.' See also Hsin-Pao Chang, *Commissioner Lin*, 19; and Stephen R. Platt, *Imperial Twilight*:

The Opium War and the End of China's Last Golden Age (New York, NY: Knopf, 2018), p. 224.

22. Keith McMahon, *The Fall of the God of Money: Opium Smoking in Nineteenth-Century China* (Lanham, MD: Rowman & Littlefield Publishers, 2002), p. 36.

23. David T. Courtwright, *Dark Paradise: A History of Opiate Addiction in America* (Cambridge, MA: Harvard University Press, 2001), pp. 35–36.

24. Spence, 'Opium Smoking in Ch'ing China', 233.

25. Ong Tae-hae, *The Chinaman abroad, or, A desultory account of the Malayan Archipelago, particularly of Java* (Shanghai: Mission Press, 1849), pp. 18-19. In a similar vein, a senior Qing official observed in a memorial to the Emperor: 'In the history of Formosa, written by Yu Wáneě [it is] mentioned that the inhabitants of Java were originally nimble, light-bodied, expert in war: but when the [European] . . . came among them, these prepared opium and seduced them into the use of it; whereupon they were subdued, brought into subjection and their land taken possession of.' ('Memorial from Hwang Tseŏtse, soliciting increased severity in the punishments of the consumers of opium; and the imperial reply', in *The Chinese Repository*, Vol. VII [Elibron Classics Reprints, 2005], p. 277).

26. See James R. Rush, *Opium to Java: Revenue Farming and Chinese Enterprise in Colonial Indonesia, 1860-1910* (Indonesia: Equinox Publishing, 2007) pp. 237–41.

27. See, for instance, Derks, *History of the Opium Problem*, 276.

28. Ibid., 213.

29. Ibid., 247.

30. Ibid., 226–27.

31. Ibid., 331–33.

32. Ibid., 286.

33. Ibid., 245.

34. Prakash, 'Opium monopoly in India and Indonesia', 75.

35. Derks, *History of the Opium Problem*, 239–54.

36. Ibid., 307–13.

37. Ibid., 317.

38. See Zach Boren, Alexander C. Kaufman and Lawrence Carter, 'Revealed: BP and Shell Back Anti-Climate Lobby Groups Despite Pledges', *Huffington Post*, 28/09/2020: https://www.huffingtonpost.co.uk/entry/bp-shell-climate_n_5f6e3120c5b64deddeed6762; Benjamin Franta, 'Shell and Exxon's secret 1980s climate change warnings', *The Guardian*, 19/9/2018: https://www.theguardian.com/environment/climate-consensus-97-per-cent/2018/sep/19/shell-and-exxons-secret-1980s-climate-change-warnings; and Scott Waldman, 'Shell Grappled with Climate Change 20 Years Ago, Documents

Show', *Scientific American*, 5 April 2018: https://www.scientificamerican.com/article/shell-grappled-with-climate-change-20-years-ago-documents-show/.

39. Ibid., 310.

40. Ibid., 295–305.

41. Ibid., 236.

42. See Alison Games, *Inventing the English Massacre: Amboyna in History and Memory* (New York, NY: Oxford University Press, 2020); and Adam Clulow, *Amboyna 1623: Fear and Conspiracy on the Edge of Empire* (New York, NY: Columbia University Press, 2019).

43. The British called Easterners 'poorbeahs'. See T.A. Heathcote, *The Military in British India: The Development of British Land Forces in South Asia 1600–1947* (Manchester, and New York, NY: Manchester University Press, 1995), p. 29.

44. Tapan Raychaudhuri, 'The State and Economy', in *The Cambridge Economic History of India: c. 1200–c.1750*, eds Tapan Raychaudhuri and Irfan Habib (Cambridge: Cambridge University Press, 1982), Chapter VII, p. 179. See also D.H.A. Kolff, *Naukar, Rajput, and Sepoy: The Ethnohistory of the Military Labour Market of Hindustan, 1450–1850* (Cambridge: Cambridge University Press, 2002), pp. 3–5. Heathcote notes: 'Centuries of warfare in northern India had encouraged the development of a society in which everyone of the slightest consequence carried weapons.' (*The Military in British India*, 29). Similarly Bishop Heber noted, of his travels in Punjab in 1824, 'every traveller whom we met, even the common people going to market, had either swords and shields, spears, or match-lock guns'. (D.H.A. Kolff, *Grass in Their Mouths: The Upper Doab of India under the Company's Magna Charta, 1793–1830* [Leiden: Brill, 2010], p. 439.)

45. Kolff, *Naukar, Rajput, and Sepoy*, 185–87.

46. Heathcote, *The Military in British India*, 76; H. Dodwell, *Sepoy Recruitment in the Old Madras Army* (Calcutta: Indian Historical Records Commission, 1922), p. 14 and Rajesh Rai, 'Sepoys, Convicts and the "Bazaar" Contingent: The Emergence and Exclusion of "Hindustani" Pioneers at the Singapore Frontier', *Journal of Southeast Asian Studies*, Vol. 35, no. 1 (2004): 9.

47. The historian Emdad-ul Haq argues that the Battle of Plassey (1757) and the Battle of Buxar (1764) were fought largely in order to establish control over the opium trade (Haq, *Drugs in South Asia: From the Opium Trade to the Present Day* [New York, NY: St. Martin's Press, 2000], p. 16).

48. Ibid., 20.

49. J.F. Richards, 'The Indian Empire and Peasant Production of Opium in the Nineteenth Century', *Modern Asian Studies*, Vol. 15, no. 1 (1981): 63.

50. Singh, *The East India Company's Monopoly Industries*, 26.

51. Sen, *India, China and the World*, 253.
52. See Derks, *History of the Opium Problem*, 245.
53. Some Company officials doubted that the Chinese market could be expanded. For a detailed account of debates among British officials and merchants, see Wormer, 'Opium, Economic Thought', 79–82, 179.
54. Samuel Warren, *The Opium Question* (London: James Ridgway, 1840), p. 51. Warren cites an earlier article that mentions Col. Watson in this role, so it was evidently widely believed in British mercantile circles that he was the first to propose this idea.
55. Nathan Allen, *The Opium Trade; Including a Sketch of Its History, Extent, Effects Etc. as Carried on in India and China* (Lowell, MA: James P. Walker, 1853), p. 12. See also *The Chinese Repository*, Vol. VII (Elibron Classics Reprints, 2005), p. 609.
56. Dilip K. Basu, 'Asian Merchants and Western Trade: A Comparative Study of Calcutta and Canton 1800–1840 (Ph.D. diss., University of California, Berkeley, CA, 1975), p. 116.
57. Ibid., 118.
58. In 1839, more than seventy years later, an article in *The Chinese Repository* credited Colonel Watson with having been the first to suggest that more opium be exported from Bengal to China (Vol. VII, p. 609).
59. Wormer writes: 'So convinced were Company leaders that opium's profitability depended on monopoly control that they embarked on an intensive, if fruitless, search for historical evidence for the existence of a similar institution "from time immemorial" under the old Mughal administration. ('Opium, Economic Thought', 67.)
60. See Rolf Bauer, *The Peasant Production of Opium in Nineteenth-Century India* (Leiden: Brill, 2019), p. 12 and Singh, *The East India Company's Monopoly Industries*, 28.
61. Derks, *History of the Opium Problem*, 56.
62. Emdad-ul Haq discusses the purported Mughal monopoly at some length, and concludes that it was a fabrication (*Drugs in South Asia*, 17–19).
63. For a fuller discussion of this, see my book, *The Nutmeg's Curse: Parables for a Planet in Crisis* (Gurgaon: Penguin Random House India, 2021), Chapter 4.
64. See Priya Satia, *Time's Monster: How History Makes History* (Cambridge, MA: Harvard University Press, 2020), pp. 3–8.
65. See Priya Satia, *Empire of Guns: The Violent Making of the Industrial Revolution* (Stanford, CA: Stanford University Press, 2019), p. 154.

5: The Opium Department

1. Rolf Bauer writes: 'When I tell someone about my research one of the first things that I do is to ask them if they are familiar with Amitav Ghosh's Ibis Trilogy . . . these novels are so profoundly researched and well-written that I consider them among the best material available on the subject.' (*The Peasant Production of Opium in Nineteenth-Century India* [Leiden: Brill, 2019], p. 1.)

    Matthew Wormer writes: 'In the words of the historical novelist Amitav Ghosh, the most prominent recent chronicler of the trade, opium is "the guilty secret of the birth of capitalism.". . . This dissertation takes that claim as its starting point.' ('Opium, Economic Thought, and the Making of Britain's Free Trade Empire, 1773–1839' [Ph.D. diss., Stanford University, Stanford, CA, 2022], p. 2.)

    Needless to add neither of them is any way responsible for the inferences I have drawn from their work.

    See also 'Roundtable: History Meets Fiction in the Indian Ocean: On Amitav Ghosh's Ibis Trilogy', *The American Historical Review*, Vol. 121, no. 5 (2016): 1521–22.

2. My own research was largely focused on the military history of the First Opium War, but I often stumbled upon documents related to the production of opium. The following are just two instances of such folders: British Library; India Office Records, Board's Collections 8675 to 8750, 1812–13, Vol. 359 (F/4/359) and Board's Collections 19297 to 19375, 1823–24, (F/4/710).

3. See Wormer, 'Opium, Economic Thought', 49–51. For a detailed discussion of the Company's internal debates on the management of opium, see Wormer, 65–69.

4. Ibid., 31.

5. John F. Richards, 'The Indian Empire and Peasant Production of Opium in the Nineteenth Century'. *Modern Asian Studies*, Vol. 15, no. 1 (1981): 64.

6. Bauer, *The Peasant Production of Opium*, 133.

7. N.P. Singh, *The East India Company's Monopoly Industries in Bihar with Particular Reference to Opium and Saltpetre, 1773–1833* (Muzaffarpur: Sarvodaya Vangmaya, 1980), p. 138.

8. Wormer, 'Opium, Economic Thought', 220.

9. Ibid.

10. John Henry Rivett-Carnac, *Many memories of life in India, at home, and abroad* (Edinburgh: William Blackwood, 1910), p. 327.

11. Ibid., 329.

12. Ibid., 330.

13. Bauer, *The Peasant Production of Opium*, 72.

14. Rivett-Carnac, *Memories*, 306.

15. Ibid., 307.

16. Also sometimes spelled *kooties* (Singh, *The East India Company's Monopoly Industries*, 49).

17. Rivett-Carnac, *Memories*, 308.

18. Darcy Moore, *The Diaries of Henry Osborne (Part I)*, 2018: http://www.darcymoore.net/2018/04/23/diaries-henry-osborne-part/.

19. Darcy Moore, *The Diaries of Henry Osborne (Part II)*, 2018: http://www.darcymoore.net/2018/05/12/diaries-henry-osborne-part-2/.

20. See Orwell's essay 'Such, Such Were the Joys', published in the *Partisan Review*, Sept–Oct 1952, but probably written earlier.

21. See Darcy Moore, 'Orwell and the Appeal of Opium', in *George Orwell Studies*, Vol. 3, no. 1, ed. Richard Lance Keeble (Suffolk: Abramis Academic, 2018).

22. Some of these terms occur often in The Ibis Trilogy, and are listed in the 'Chrestomathy': http://amitavghosh.com/chrestomathy.html.

23. Bauer, *The Peasant Production of Opium*, 72–76.

24. Wormer, 'Opium, Economic Thought', 84, 218.

25. Ibid., 210–11.

26. *The Chinese Repository*, Vol. VIII (Elibron Classics Reprints, 2005), p. 519.

27. Wormer, 'Opium, Economic Thought', 121.

28. Ibid., 123.

29. Carl A. Trocki, *Opium, Empire and the Global Political Economy: A Study of the Asian Opium Trade, 1750–1950* (New York, NY: Routledge, 1999), pp. 66–68.

30. Bauer, *The Peasant Production of Opium*, 160.

31. See Wormer, 'Opium, Economic Thought', 125; and Bauer, *The Peasant Production of Opium*, 160. Bauer devotes an entire chapter to calculating the costs of opium cultivation (pp. 132–62).

32. Bauer, *The Peasant Production of Opium*, 162.

33. Singh, *The East India Company's Monopoly Industries*, 52.

34. Bauer, *The Peasant Production of Opium*, 177.

35. See Emdad-ul Haq, *Drugs in South Asia: From the Opium Trade to the Present Day* (New York, NY: St. Martin's Press, 2000), p. 24; and Singh, *The East India Company's Monopoly Industries*, 52 and 81–84.

36. A.S. Thelwall, *The Iniquities of the Opium Trade with China; Being a Development of the Main Causes which Exclude the Merchants of Great Britain*

from the Advantages of an Unrestricted Commercial Intercourse with that Vast Empire (London: W.H. Allen & Co., 1839), 25–29.

37. In 1777, a few years after Bengal had been devastated by a terrible famine, an official letter notes 'a considerable tract of land in the neighborhood of Ghya (Gaya) was covered with green corn and which would have been fit to cut in a month or six weeks: this corn was suddenly cut down in order that the land might be prepared for the immediate cultivation of the poppy.' (Quoted in Singh, *The East India Company's Monopoly Industries*, 81.)

38. Bauer, *The Peasant Production of Opium*, 90.

39. Wormer, 'Opium, Economic Thought', 216.

40. Singh, *The East India Company's Monopoly Industries*, 170–72.

41. Anirudh Deshpande, 'An Historical Overview of Opium Cultivation and Changing State Attitudes Towards the Crop in India, 1878–2000 A.D.', *Studies in History*, Vol. 25, no. 1 (2009): 109–43.

42. L.C. Reid, the Collector of Kaira to the Revenue Commissioner: Board's Collections, 83888 to 84180, 1841-42, Vol. 1938 (India Office: F/4/1938).

43. Deshpande, 'An Historical Overview', 118.

44. Quoted by Bauer, *The Peasant Production of Opium*, 89.

45. Quoted in Deshpande, 'An Historical Overview', 117.

46. Wormer, 'Opium, Economic Thought', 223.

47. Ibid., 238.

48. See Bauer's charts for Bengal Opium chests sold, and concurrent increase in cultivated area. (*The Peasant Production of Opium*, 24.)

49. Hsin-Pao Chang, *Commissioner Lin and the Opium War* (Cambridge, MA: Harvard University Press, 1964), p. 19. See also, *The Chinese Repository*, Vol. VII (Elibron Classics Reprints, 2005), p. 609.

50. Jonathan Spence, *The Search for Modern China* (New York, NY: W.W. Norton, 1990), p. 129.

51. See Trocki, *Opium, Empire*, 59.

52. Celina B. Realuyo, 'The New Opium War: A National Emergency', *Prism: The Journal of Complex Operations*, 8:1 (2019): 133. https://cco.ndu.edu/News/Article/1767465/the-new-opium-war-a-national-emergency/.

53. See Ruth Wilson Gilmore, foreword to *Cedric J. Robinson: On Racial Capitalism, Black Internationalism, and Cultures of Resistance*, ed. H.L.T. Quan (London: Pluto Press, 2019), pp xi–xiv.

6: Big Brother

1. Rudyard Kipling, 'In an Opium Factory', 1899, http://www.telelib.com/authors/K/KiplingRudyard/prose/FromSeaToSea/opiumfactory.html.

2. J.W.S. MacArthur, *Notes on an Opium Factory* (Calcutta: Thacker, Spink & Company's Press, 1865) p. 1.

3. Another factory, now known as The Opium Factory and Alkaloid Works at Neemuch (or Nimach), in present-day Madhya Pradesh, was built by the colonial regime in the 1930s. This is today the biggest opium processing plant in Asia. According to Wikipedia it contains the world's largest opium receptacle, which resembles a 'backyard swimming pool' and holds '450 tons of opium worth 36 US billion in 1992.'; https://en.wikipedia.org/wiki/Opium_and_Alkaloid_Works#See_also.

4. The various steps of the production process are described in detail in MacArthur, *Notes*. As Caitlin Rosenthal has shown in *Accounting for Slavery: Masters and Management* (Cambridge, MA: Harvard University Press, 2018), Frederick W. Taylor's 'scientific management' had its origins in plantation slavery. The labour processes of the East India Company's opium factories also anticipated Taylorite scientific management.

5. MacArthur, *Notes*, 2.

6. According to Professor Gautam Choubey, an eminent scholar of Bhojpuri, and translator of Pandey Kapil's acclaimed Bhojpuri novel *Phoolsunghi*, 'no one has written on the subject' of the opium factories of Ghazipur and Patna in Bhojpuri or Hindi: 'not even a short story. While there is plenty on the indigo trade, possibly because it is reminiscent of Gandhi and represents a much-romanticised episode in the local history, the opium factories remain unexplored.' [Personal communication.]

7. Matthew Wormer, 'Opium, Economic Thought, and the Making of Britain's Free Trade Empire, 1773–1839' (Ph.D. diss., Stanford University, Stanford, CA, 2022), p. 210.

8. See Emily Eden, *Up the Country: Letters to Her Sister from the Upper Provinces of India* (London: Richard Bentley, 1867), p. 14.

9. 'Government literature shows that discussions around skilled labor or positions of authority in the opium factory hinged on a broader belief in the untrustworthiness of Indian workers.' Hope Marie Childers, 'Spectacles of Labor: Artists and Workers in the Patna Opium Factory in the 1850s', *Nineteenth-Century Contexts*, Vol. 39, no. 3 (2017): 184.

10. Ibid., 178.

11. W.S. Caine, 'Mr Caine's letter on India', *Times of India*, 19 March 1889, p. 7.

12. See 'Gajipur mein Gurudeb', gajipur.blogspot.com, 9 May 2011: https://gajipur.blogspot.com/2011/05/blog-post.html?m=1. I am grateful to Dr Gautam Choubey for bringing this article to my notice.

13. Swarnakumari Devi: *Gazipur Patra*. I am grateful to Dr Sukanta Chaudhuri for bringing this piece to my attention.

14. The title of the article was 'Chine Maraner Byabsa'. See Steffen Rimner, *Opium's Long Shadow: From Asian Revolt to Global Drug Control* (Cambridge, MA: Harvard University Press, 2018), p. 107.

15. The article was translated into English under the title 'The Death Traffic' and was published in the *Modern Review*, Vol. 37, May 1925.

16. See Childers, 'Spectacles of Labor', 173.

17. W.S. Sherwill, *Illustrations of the Mode of Preparing Indian Opium Intended for the Chinese Market* (London, 1851).

18. The originals that I viewed are in the collection of the Yale Center for British Art, New Haven, CT. My thanks to the Center and its staff for their generosity with their time and expertise.

19. See Daniel J. Rycroft, *Representing Rebellion: Visual Aspects of Counter-Insurgency in Colonial India* (New Delhi: Oxford University Press, 2006), pp. 17–43.

20. Childers, 'Spectacles of Labor', 177.

21. Ibid., 183.

22. Art historian Hope Marie Childers writes of the prints that they 'echo early, celebratory portrayals of the British Industrial Revolution, with not only the rectilinear order of the structures, but also the uniformity and repetitiveness that generate a cool, mechanical feel.' (Ibid., 173.)

23. Annette S. Beveridge, quoted in Childers's 'Spectacles of Labor', p. 178.

24. Carl A. Trocki, *Opium, Empire and the Global Political Economy: A Study of the Asian Opium Trade, 1750–1950* (New York, NY: Routledge, 1999), pp. 89–90.

25. Rimner, *Opium's Long Shadow*, 20.

26. Diana S. Kim, *Empires of Vice: The Rise of Opium Prohibition across Southeast Asia* (Princeton; NJ: Princeton University Press, 2020), p. 32.

27. A strict ban on opium was also passed in 1839. *The Chinese Repository*, Vol. VIII (Elibron Classics Reprints, 2005), p. 125.

28. Rimner, *Opium's Long Shadow*, 20; and Kim, *Empires of Vice*, 32.

29. Alfred W. McCoy, *The Politics of Heroin: CIA Complicity in the Global Drug Trade, Afghanistan, Southeast Asia, Central America, Colombia* (Chicago, IL: Lawrence Hill Books, 2003), pp. 110–11.

30. Rimner, *Opium's Long Shadow*, 179.

31. Gregory Blue, 'Opium for China: The British Connection', in *Opium Regimes: China, Britain, and Japan, 1839–1952*, eds Timothy Brook and Bob Tadashi Wakabayashi (Berkeley, CA: University of California Press, 2000), pp. 32–33. British officials were well aware of the ban (see for example John Barrow, *Travels in China from Pekin to Canton* [London, 1806], p. 344).

32. Tan Chung, 'The British-China-India Trade Triangle, 1771-1840', *Proceedings of the Indian History Congress*, Vol. 34 (1973): 422; Hsin-Pao Chang,

Commissioner Lin and the Opium War (Cambridge, MA: Harvard University Press, 1964), pp. 18–19.

33. Hosea Ballou Morse, *The International Relations of the Chinese Empire; Vol I, The Period of Conflict 1834–1860* (London: Longmans, 1910), pp. 178-79. See also Dael A. Norwood, *Trading Freedom: How Trade with China Defined Early America* (Chicago: University of Chicago Press, 2022), p. 66.

34. Peter Ward Fay, *The Opium War: 1840-42* (Chapel Hill, NC: University of North Carolina Press, 1975), pp. 45–46.

35. Charles C. Stelle, 'American Trade in Opium to China, 1821–39', *Pacific Historical Review* Vol. 10, no. 1 (1941): 62. In Cantonese slang they were also known as 'glued-on wings' (Jonathan Spence, 'Opium Smoking in Ch'ing China', in *Conflict and Control in Late Imperial China*, eds Frederic Wakeman Jr and Carolyn Grant [Berkeley, CA: University of California Press, 1975], p. 246).

36. For detailed accounts of the 'Lintin System', see Morse, *The International Relations*, 178–80; Norwood, *Trading Freedom*, 66; and Jacques M. Downs, *The Golden Ghetto: The American Commercial Community at Canton and the Shaping of American China Policy, 1784–1844* (Bethlehem: Lehigh University Press, 1997), pp. 170–72. For a contemporary account, see Charles Toogood Downing, *The Fan-Qui in China, in 1836-7, Vol. III* (London: H. Colburn, 1838), pp. 167–68.

37. Jacques M. Downs, 'American Merchants and the China Opium Trade, 1800-1840', *The Business History Review*, Vol. 42, no. 4 (1968): 433. See also Trocki, *Opium, Empire*, 52.

38. Bills were basically a system of using credit to leverage opium sales. For a full account see John R. Haddad, *America's First Adventure in China: Trade, Treaties, Opium, and Salvation* (Philadelphia: Temple University Press, 2013), Kindle edn, locs. 1188–1214.

39. See Norwood, *Trading Freedom*, 65.

40. The documents are reproduced in full in J. Lewis Shuck, *Portfolio Chinensis; Or, a Collection of Authentic Chinese State Papers Illustrative of the History of the Present Position of Affairs in China* (Macao, 1840), pp. 1–127. See also *The Chinese Repository*, Vol. VII (Elibron Classics Reprints, 2005), pp. 639–41. For a vivid description of Lin Zexu's actions at this time, see A. Haussmann, 'A French Account of the War in China', *United Service Magazine*, Vol. 1, no. 71 (1853): 54.

41. The American merchant William Hunter wrote a detailed account of the merchants' confinement: E.W. Ellsworth, W.C. Hunter, J.L. Cranmer-Byng and Lindsay T. Ride, 'Journal of Occurrances at Canton: During the Cessation of Trade at Canton 1839', *Journal of the Hong Kong Branch of the Royal Asiatic Society*, Vol. 4 (1964). See also Stephen R. Platt, *Imperial*

Twilight: The Opium War and the End of China's Last Golden Age (New York, NY: Knopf, 2018), pp. 370–72.

42. See Arthur Waley, The Opium War through Chinese Eyes (London: George Allen & Unwin Ltd., 1958), pp. 23–38; Julia Lovell, The Opium War: Drugs, Dreams and the Making of China (New York, NY: Overlook Press, 2014), pp. 55–72; and Jack Beeching, The Chinese Opium Wars (New York, NY: Harcourt Brace, 1976), pp. 74–81.

43. Samuel Warren, The Opium Question (London: James Ridgway, 1840), p. 5.

44. Christopher Munn, 'The Hong Kong Opium Revenue 1845–1885', in Opium Regimes: China, Britain, and Japan, 1839–1952, eds Timothy Brook and Bob Tadashi Wakabayashi (Berkeley, CA: University of California Press, 2000), p. 107. See also Beeching, The Chinese Opium Wars, 159.

45. Rolf Bauer, The Peasant Production of Opium in Nineteenth-Century India (Leiden: Brill, 2019), p. 24.

7: Visions

1. See J.P. Losty, 'The rediscovery of an unknown Indian artist: Sita Ram's work for the Marquess of Hastings', British Library 'Asian and African Studies' blog, 4 Jan 2016: https://blogs.bl.uk/asian-and-african/2016/01/the-rediscovery-of-an-unknown-indian-artist-sita-rams-work-for-the-marquess-of-hastings.html.

2. J.P. Losty, Sita Ram: Picturesque Views of India – Lord Hastings's Journey from Calcutta to the Punjab, 1814-15 (New Delhi: Roli Books, 2015). See also Sita Ram's Painted Views of India (London: Thames & Hudson, 2015).

3. See: http://www.sackler.org/piranesi/.

4. See Patrick Conner, Chinese Views – Western Perspectives 1770-1870: The Sze Yuan Tang of China Coast Paintings & The Wallen Collection of China Coast Ship Portrait (Asia House, 1997), p. 13.

5. See Mildred Archer, Natural History Drawings in the India Office Library (London: Her Majesty's Stationery Office, 1962), p. 72.

6. See P.C. Manuk, 'The Patna School of Painting', Journal of the Bihar Research Society, XXIX: 143–69.

7. See Mildred Archer, Patna Painting (London: David Marlowe Ltd, 1948).

8. Neel Rekha, 'The Patna School of Painting: A Brief History (1760–1880)', Proceedings of the Indian History Congress, Vol. 72, Part-I (2000): 1000.

9. Emdad-ul Haq notes: 'In his work Reminiscences of the Great Mutiny 1857–59, William Forbes-Mitchell, a sergeant who took part in the suppression of

the uprising in UP, argued that the introduction of forced poppy cultivation sparked mass rebellion in the region.' (*Drugs in South Asia: From the Opium Trade to the Present Day* [New York, NY: St. Martin's Press, 2000], p. 25).

10. Heather Streets, *Martial Races: The Military, Race and Masculinity in British Imperial Culture, 1857–1914* (Manchester: Manchester University Press, 2004), pp. 38–45.

11. Matthew Wormer, 'Opium, Economic Thought, and the Making of Britain's Free Trade Empire, 1773–1839' (Ph.D. diss., Stanford University, Stanford, CA, 2022), p. 239.

12. An 1888 photograph of the Ghazipur factory can be found here: https://www.nationalgalleries.org/art-and-artists/10557/ghazipur-opium-factory.

13. Jonathan Lehne, 'An opium curse? The long-run economic consequences of narcotics cultivation in British India', publication of the Paris School of Economics, 10 June 2018. http://barrett.dyson.cornell.edu/NEUDC/paper_364.pdf. Accessed 7/26/2021.

14. N.P. Singh, *The East India Company's Monopoly Industries in Bihar with Particular Reference to Opium and Saltpetre, 1773–1833* (Muzaffarpur: Sarvodaya Vangmaya, 1980), pp. 170–72.

15. Lehne, 'An opium curse?', 27.

16. D.H.A. Kolff, *Naukar, Rajput, and Sepoy: The Ethnohistory of the Military Labour Market of Hindustan, 1450–1850* (Cambridge: Cambridge University Press, 2002), pp. 176–80; and Channa Wickremesekera, *'Best Black Troops in the World': British Perceptions and the Making of the Sepoy, 1746–1805* (New Delhi: Manohar, 2002), pp. 96–105.

17. Kaushik Roy, 'Recruitment Doctrines of the Colonial Indian Army: 1859–1913', *The Indian Economic and Social History Review*, Vol. 34, no. 3 (1997): 345.

18. The doctrine behind the recruitment of Punjabis and some other groups was the theory of 'martial races'. (For a full treatment of this subject, see Heather Streets, *Martial Races*.)

19. See Streets, *Martial Races*, 65–67.

20. Abhijit Banerjee and Lakshmi Iyer, 'History, Institutions, and Economic Performance: The Legacy of Colonial Land Tenure Systems in India', *American Economic Review*, Vol. 95, no. 4 (2005): 1210.

8: Family Story

1. Although Bhojpuri is now regarded as a dialect of Hindi, in the opinion of many linguists it is very much a language in its own right, with its own distinctive literature, folklore and culture.

2. See Latika Chaudhary, 'Taxation and educational development: Evidence from British India', *Explorations in Economic History*, Vol. 47, no. 3 (2010): 279–93. Using district-level data Chaudhary shows that there has been a huge and persistent lag in literacy in Bihar.

3. The certificates are divided into ten columns: No; Name; Father's Name; Caste; Age; Height (in feet and inches) Village; Pegunnah; Zillah; Remarks. Below these is a printed line: 'I hereby certify that the Man above described, has appeared before me, and I have explained to him all matter concerning him as an Emigrant proceeding to the Mauritius according to Clause 3 of Schedule attached to her Majesty's Order in Council of 15th January 1842.' Each certificate is dated and signed and counter signed by three officers: Medical; Treasurer & Asst. Emigration Agent.

4. Certificate number 28989 was issued to a man whose name is recorded as Curooah. He is described as a twenty-year-old, 5'5" Bhooya from Gaya district: 'Good teeth a mole on the left back'. But the note on the verso suggests his name was 'Kehua'. Similarly, certificate number 28986 was issued to a man whose name is recorded as Cabul but the notation on the verso records his name as Keban.

5. I have told this story in my book *In an Antique Land*.

6. For instance, certificate number 28956 [18/9/43], issued to Ramkurna M. of Googarpore, Arrah district, notes that he had 'Uneven teeth, a small mark on the forehead; a mark on the left leg'. On the verso, in Bengali, there is the name of the *dafaadaar* who recruited him: 'Thakari'.

7. Kapil Pandey, *Phoolsunghi*, trans. Gautam Choubey (Gurugram: Penguin Random House India, 2020).

8. Quoted in Matthew Wormer, 'Opium, Economic Thought, and the Making of Britain's Free Trade Empire, 1773–1839' (Ph.D. diss., Stanford University, Stanford, CA, 2022), p. 221.

9. Pandey, *Phoolsunghi*, p. 4.

10. Wormer, 'Opium, Economic Thought', 227.

11. As Marc Gilbert points out, even for defenders of the regime 'it was hard to argue that any increase in opium consumption was unrelated to British dominion over India, since opium production and trade contributed so greatly to the rise and expansion of their Raj . . .'(Marc Jason Gilbert, 'Empire and Excise: Drugs and Drink Revenue and the Fate of States in South Asia', in *Drugs and Empires: Essays in Modern Imperialism and Intoxication, c. 1500–1930*, 116–41, eds James Mills and Patricia Barton [Basingstoke: Palgrave Macmillan, 2007], p. 117.)

9: Malwa

1. This section is based almost entirely on Chapter Three of Amar Farooqui, *Smuggling as Subversion: Colonialism, Indian Merchants and the Politics of Opium* (Lanham, MD: Rowman & Littlefield Publishers, 2005). See also Farooqui, 'Opium Enterprise and Colonial Intervention in Malwa and Western India, 1800-1824', *The Indian Economic and Social History Review* 32:4 (1995): 456.
2. Matthew Wormer, 'Opium, Economic Thought, and the Making of Britain's Free Trade Empire, 1773–1839' (Ph.D. diss., Stanford University, Stanford, CA, 2022), p. 159.
3. The poppies cultivated in nineteenth-century China were also multicoloured 'pink, lilac and white'. In the words of a British traveller: '[T]he appearance of the beds of poppies on the terraces of the hill-sides among the other crops is very beautiful.' (Thomas W. Blakiston, *Five Months on the Yang-Tsze* [London: Murray, 1862], p. 148.)
4. Nathan Allen, *The Opium Trade; Including a Sketch of Its History, Extent, Effects Etc. as Carried on in India and China* (Lowell, MA: James P. Walker, 1853), p. 11. See also N.P. Singh, *The East India Company's Monopoly Industries in Bihar with Particular Reference to Opium and Saltpetre, 1773–1833* (Muzaffarpur: Sarvodaya Vangmaya, 1980), p. 153.
5. Wormer, 'Opium, Economic Thought', 160.
6. See Joya Chatterjee, *Shadows at Noon: The South Asian Twentieth Century* (London: The Bodley Head, 2023), p. 209.
7. See Randolf G.S. Cooper, 'Wellington and the Marathas in 1803', *The International History Review*, Vol. 11, no. 1 (1989): 31–38.
8. Ibid., 34.
9. Lakshmi Subramaniam, *Three Merchants of Bombay: Business Pioneers of the Nineteenth Century* (Gurgaon: Penguin Random House, 2011), p. 97.
10. See Wormer, 'Opium, Economic Thought', 167–68.
11. Farooqui, 'Opium Enterprise', 468–70.
12. Ibid., 451.
13. Alexander Klimburg, 'Some research notes on Carl A. Trocki's publication *Opium, Empire and the Global Political Economy*', *Bulletin of the School of Oriental and African Studies*, Vol. 64, no. 2 (2001): 264.
14. Wormer, 'Opium, Economic Thought', 52.
15. Farooqui, 'Opium Enterprise', 450.
16. Cooper, 'Wellington and the Marathas', 37.

17. Randolf G.S. Cooper, *The Anglo-Maratha Campaigns and the Contest for India: The Struggle for Control of the South Asian Military Economy* (Cambridge: Cambridge University Press, 2003), p. 293.

18. In Amar Farooqui's words: 'What has to be appreciated is that historically the balance of forces in western and central India was not the same as that which obtained in eastern and northern India. Consequently, rather than merely extending the Bengal monopoly to western and central India, colonial administrators had to continuously modify their strategies vis-à-vis Malwa opium . . .' ('Opium Enterprise', 455.)

19. Ibid., 451.

20. In colonial terminology, these networks were usually characterized as 'smugglers', but as Kate Boehme notes, 'this was, in many instances, simply a re-labelling of established pre-colonial networks and trade practices'. (Kate Boehme, 'Smuggling India: Deconstructing Western India's Illicit Export Trade, 1818–1870', *Journal of the Royal Asiatic Society*, Vol. 25, no. 4 [2015]: 701.)

21. See *The Nutmeg's Curse: Parables for a Planet in Crisis* (Gurgaon: Penguin Random House India, 2021), pp. 74–75.

22. Margaret Makepeace, 'Gerald Wellesley's Secret Family', British Library 'Untold Lives' blog, 20 April 2017: https://blogs.bl.uk/untoldlives/2017/04/gerald-wellesleys-secret-family.html.

23. Singh, *The East India Company's Monopoly Industries*, 159.

24. C.U. Aitchison, *A Collection of Treaties, Engagements and Sanads Relating to India and Neighbouring Countries*, Vol. III (Calcutta: Government of Indian Central Publication Branch, 1876), p. 349.

25. See John Phipps, *A Practical Treatise on the China and Eastern Trade* (Calcutta: W. Thacker and Co. 1836), p. 225.

26. Farooqui, *Smuggling as Subversion*, 61.

27. Ibid., 10.

28. See Claude Markovits, 'The Political Economy of Opium Smuggling in Early Nineteenth Century India: Leakage or Resistance?', *Modern Asian Studies*, Vol. 43, no. 1 (2009): 103.

29. As Alfred McCoy notes: 'Washington's massive military juggernaut has been stopped in its steel tracks by a small pink flower—the opium poppy.' ('How the Heroin Trade Explains the US-UK Failure in Afghanistan', *The Guardian*, 9 Jan 2018: https://www.theguardian.com/news/2018/jan/09/how-the-heroin-trade-explains-the-us-uk-failure-in-afghanistan?s=03).

30. David Mansfield, *A State Built on Sand: How Opium Undermined Afghanistan* (London: C. Hurst & Co., 2016), pp. 104–105 and 109.

31. As Melissa Macauley notes, in regard to both Qing China and contemporary Afghanistan 'drug-smuggling networks historically have subverted the efforts of statebuilders to extend central governmental authority into the local arena.' ('Small Time Crooks: Opium, Migrants, and the War on Drugs in China, 1819–1860', *Late Imperial China*, Vol. 30, no. 1 [2009]: 2).
32. See Wormer, 'Opium, Economic Thought', 202.
33. Rolf Bauer, *The Peasant Production of Opium in Nineteenth-Century India* (Leiden: Brill, 2019), p. 22.
34. Boehme, *Smuggling India*, 701.
35. Markovits, 'The Political Economy of Opium Smuggling', 92.
36. For a detailed discussion of the role of opium in the British conquest of Sind, see J.Y. Wong, *Deadly Dreams: Opium, Imperialism and the Arrow War (1856–1860) in China* (Cambridge: Cambridge University Press, 1998), pp. 417–25. See also Markovits, 'The Political Economy of Opium Smuggling', 90.
37. Bauer, *The Peasant Production of Opium*, 33; and Wong, *Deadly Dreams*, 420.
38. Wong, *Deadly Dreams*, 420.
39. Singh, *The East India Company's Monopoly Industries*, 139.
40. Wormer, 'Opium, Economic Thought', 204. The last quotation is from John F. Richards, 'The Opium Industry in British India', *The Indian Economic and Social History Review*, Vol. 39, nos. 2–3 (2002): 166.
41. Bauer, *The Peasant Production of Opium*, 37.
42. This problem eventually became so acute that the major Malwa opium trader had to pay a Chinese expert by the name of Samsing to move to Bombay to certify their product (See Thomas N. Layton, *The Voyage of the Frolic: New England Merchants and the Opium Trade*, [Stanford, CA: Stanford University Press, 1997], p. 99.)
43. Bauer, *The Peasant Production of Opium*, 38–39. See also Singh, *The East India Company's Monopoly Industries*, 139.
44. Anirudh Deshpande, 'An Historical Overview of Opium Cultivation and Changing State Attitudes Towards the Crop in India, 1878–2000 A.D.', *Studies in History*, Vol. 25, no. 1 (2009): 120–21.
45. *The Chinese Repository*, Vol. VIII (Elibron Classics Reprints, 2005), p. 513.
46. See also Madhavi Thampi, *Indians in China, 1800–1949* (New Delhi: Manohar, 2005), p. 51.
47. Amar Farooqui, *Opium City: The Making of Early Victorian Bombay* (Gurgaon: Three Essays Collective, 2016), p. 7.
48. Ibid., 8–9.

49. As the business historian Lakshmi Subramaniam notes: 'It was really opium that made Bombay's fortunes and those of its notable commercial men.' (Subramaniam, *Three Merchants*, 103).

50. Farooqui, *Smuggling as Subversion*, 10.

51. Farooqui, *Opium City*, 17–18.

52. Lord Palmerston, for instance, explained why Britain had to go to war against China with these words: 'The rivalship of European manufactures is fast excluding our productions from the markets of Europe, and we must unremittingly endeavour to find in other parts of the world new vents for our industry . . . if we succeed in our China expedition, Abyssinia, Arabia, the countries of the Indus and the new markets of China will at no distant period give us a most important extension to the range of our foreign commerce.' (Jack Beeching, *The Chinese Opium Wars* [New York, NY: Harcourt Brace, 1976], p. 95.)

10: East and West

1. John F. Richards, 'The Opium Industry in British India', *The Indian Economic and Social History Review*, Vol. 39, nos. 2-3 (2002): 173-74.

2. N.P. Singh, *The East India Company's Monopoly Industries in Bihar with Particular Reference to Opium and Saltpetre, 1773–1833* (Muzaffarpur: Sarvodaya Vangmaya, 1980), p. 155; and Claude Markovits, 'The Political Economy of Opium Smuggling in Early Nineteenth Century India: Leakage or Resistance?', *Modern Asian Studies*, Vol. 43, no. 1 (2009): 92.

3. Richards, 'The Opium Industry', 173–74.

4. See, for example, Manu S. Pillai's *False Allies: India's Maharajahs in the Age of Ravi Varma* (New Delhi: Juggernaut Books, 2021).

5. Lakshmi Iyer, 'Direct versus Indirect Colonial Rule in India: Long-Term Consequences', *The Review of Economics and Statistics*, Vol. 92, no. 4 (2010): 707.

6. Amar Farooqui, *Smuggling as Subversion: Colonialism, Indian Merchants and the Politics of Opium* (Lanham, MD: Rowman & Littlefield Publishers, 2005), p. 221. Richards notes, similarly, 'I speculate that much, if not most, of the capital accumulated by Indian investors, traders and industrialists manifest in nineteenth-century Bombay was the result of the Malwa or western opium trade.' ('The Opium Industry', 180.)

7. Thomas N. Layton, *The Voyage of the Frolic: New England Merchants and the Opium Trade* (Stanford, CA: Stanford University Press, 1997), pp. 73–76.

8. Dilip Kumar Basu, 'Asian Merchants and Western Trade: A Comparative Study of Calcutta and Canton 1800–1840 (Ph.D. diss., University of

California, Berkeley, CA, 1975), p. 129. Tansen Sen cites his name as 'Bahadur Mullshet' (*India, China and the World: A Connected History* [London: Rowman & Littlefield Publishers, 2017], pp. 254–55).

9. Amar Farooqui, 'Opium Enterprise and Colonial Intervention in Malwa and Western India, 1800-1824', *The Indian Economic and Social History Review*, Vol. 32, no. 4 (1995): 471; and Markovits, 'The Political Economy of Opium Smuggling', 107–109.

10. Jenny Rose, *Between Boston and Bombay: Cultural and Commercial Encounters of Yankees and Parsis, 1771–1865* (Cham: Palgrave Macmillan, 2019), p. 153.

11. Rajat Kanta Ray, 'Asian Capital in the Age of European Domination: The Rise of the Bazaar, 1800–1914', *Modern Asian Studies*, Vol. 29, no. 3 (1995): 484.

12. Farooqui, *Smuggling as Subversion*, 198.

13. See Markovits, 'The Political Economy of Opium Smuggling', 107–109.

14. Quoted in Madhavi Thampi and Shalini Saksena, *China and the Making of Bombay* (Mumbai: K.R. Cama Oriental Institute, 2009), pp. 70–71.

15. Asiya Siddiqi, 'Pathways of the Poppy: India's Opium Trade in the Nineteenth Century', in *India and China in the Colonial World*, ed. Madhavi Thampi (New Delhi: Social Science Press, 2010), p. 21.

16. See Farooqui, 'Opium Enterprise'.

17. See James W. Furrell, *The Tagore Family: A Memoir* (New Delhi: Rupa & Co., 2004), pp. 14–19.

18. Basu, 'Asian Merchants and Western Trade', 233–36.

19. Matthew Wormer, 'Opium, Economic Thought, and the Making of Britain's Free Trade Empire, 1773–1839' (Ph.D. diss., Stanford University, Stanford, CA, 2022), p. 169.

20. Govind Narayan, *Govind Narayan's Mumbai: An Urban Biography from 1863*, ed. and trans. Murali Ranganathan (New York, NY: Anthem Press, 2009), pp. 122–23.

21. Nariman Karkaria, *The First World War Adventures of Nariman Karkaria: A Memoir*, trans. Murali Ranganathan (Gurugram: HarperCollins India, 2021), pp. 6–7.

22. See Pernilla Ståhl, *The Triumphal Arch of Mogadishu: Colonial Architecture and Urban Planning*, trans. Benjamin Hein and Katarina Trodden (2022), p. 33.

23. E.H. Nolan, *The Illustrated History of the British Empire in India and the East: from the earliest times to the suppression of the Sepoy Mutiny in 1859* (London: Virtue & Co.).

24. C.T. Buckland, 'The Opium-Poppy Cultivation of Bengal', in *The Living Age*, Vol. 168, eds Eliakim Littell and Robert S. Littell (1886), p. 31.

25. Richards, 'The Opium Industry', 150. Richards also suggests that 'tazi' was 'teji' (strong, vigorous), which would provide a completely different etymology for the term.

26. *Flood of Fire* (Gurugram: Penguin Random House, 2015), p. 272.

27. Nolan, *The Illustrated History*.

28. Thomas A. Timberg, 'Hiatus and Incubator: Indigenous Trade and Traders, 1837–1857', in *Trade and Finance in Colonial India, 1750–1860*, ed. Asiya Siddiqi (New Delhi: Oxford University Press, 1995) pp. 258-59. In the same vein John Richards notes: 'Merchants from Marwar, such as the Aggarwals, began to move into North Indian markets along the Ganges River route in the early 19th century. By the 1830s they had reached Calcutta and were active as agents, brokers, and, as they acquired capital, exporters of auctioned opium to China.' (Richards, 'The Opium Industry', pp. 178-79.)

29. Carl Trocki also suggests that 'the company monopoly stifled native Indian capitalism in Calcutta . . .' (*Opium, Empire and the Global Political Economy: A Study of the Asian Opium Trade, 1750–1950* [New York, NY: Routledge, 1999], pp. 84–85.)

30. Maya Palit, 'Chhath puja celebrations in Mumbai: MNS' attack on performers stems from a class hatred', Firstpost, 11 November 2016. https://www .firstpost.com/india/chhath-puja-celebrations-in-mumbai-mns-attack-on -performers-stems-from-a-class-hatred-3101128.html.

31. Amar Farooqui, *Opium City: The Making of Early Victorian Bombay* (Gurgaon: Three Essays Collective, 2016), p. 18.

32. Claude Markovits, *Merchants, Traders, Entrepreneurs: Indian Business in the Colonial Era* (Basingstoke: Palgrave Macmillan, 2008), pp. 128–51.

33. Ibid.

34. Ibid.

35. Quoted in Thampi and Saksena, *China and the Making of Bombay*, 81.

36. Fakrul Alam and Radha Chakravarty, eds, *The Essential Tagore* (London: Harvard University Press, 2011), p. 753.

37. See Dinyar Patel, *Naoroji: Pioneer of Indian Nationalism* (Cambridge, MA: Harvard University Press, 2020), pp. 13–21.

38. Dadabhai Naoroji, *Poverty and Un-British Rule in India* (London: Swan Sonnenschein & Co., 1901), p. 215.

39. Steffen Rimner, *Opium's Long Shadow: From Asian Revolt to Global Drug Control* (Cambridge, MA: Harvard University Press, 2018), pp. 84–86.

40. Emdad-ul Haq, *Drugs in South Asia: From the Opium Trade to the Present Day* (New York, NY: St. Martin's Press, 2000), p. 52.

11: Diasporas

1. Sebouh Aslanian, 'Trade Diaspora versus Colonial State: Armenian Merchants, the English East India Company, and the High Court of Admiralty in London, 1748-1752', *Diaspora: A Journal of Transnational Studies*, Vol. 13, no. 1 (Spring, 2004): 41. See also Dhrubajyoti Banerjea, *European Calcutta: Images and Recollections of a Bygone Era* (New Delhi: UBSPD, 2005), pp. 91–92.
2. Aslanian, 'Trade Diaspora', 41.
3. See R.W. Ferrier, 'The Armenians and the East India Company in Persia in the Seventeenth and Early Eighteenth Centuries', *The Economic History Review*, Vol. 26, no. 1 (1973): 38–62.
4. An Armenian merchant magnate called Khwaja Waheed was the 'most honored and respected businessman throughout early eighteenth-century Bengal'. (Kumkum Chatterjee, *Merchants, Politics and Society in Early Modern India Bihar 1733–1820* [Leiden: Brill, 1996], p. 71.)
5. See M.J. Seth, *The Armenians in India, from the Earliest Times to the Present Day* (Calcutta: P.C. Ray and Sri Gouranga Press, 1937; repr. New Delhi: Oxford University Press and IBH, 1983). See also Sushil Chaudhury, *From Prosperity to Decline: Eighteenth Century Bengal* (New Delhi: Manohar, 1995), p. 31.
6. James R. Rush, *Opium to Java: Revenue Farming and Chinese Enterprise in Colonial Indonesia, 1860–1910* (Indonesia: Equinox Publishing, 2007), p. 68.
7. See for instance British Library; India Office Records, Madras Despatches 4 Jan to 28 Aug 1839 [Br. Lib. IOR/E/4/952], letter of 4 Jan 1839 referring to the seizure of the Armenian-owned ship *Angelica*.
8. Madhavi Thampi and Shalini Saksena, *China and the Making of Bombay* (Mumbai: K.R. Cama Oriental Institute, 2009), p. 15; and Madhavi Thampi, *Indians in China, 1800–1949* (New Delhi: Manohar, 2005), p. 52. The surname 'Readymoney' derived from this merchant's plentiful supplies of cash.
9. Lakshmi Subramaniam, *Three Merchants of Bombay: Business Pioneers of the Nineteenth Century* (Gurgaon: Penguin Random House, 2011), p. 99.
10. Thampi and Saksena, *China and the Making of Bombay*, 29.
11. Ibid., 24.
12. Ibid., 55.
13. The eighteenth-century Chinese traveller, Ong Tae-hae, noted of Java: 'It is now several hundred years since the Dutch ... by artifice obtained possession of the soil of Batavia; for by rich presents and sweet words they induced the natives of the country to give them as much ground as could

be included within a cow's hide, where they might carry on their trade; and now they have strengthened their citadel, and rigidly enforced their severe enactments; until the natives of every island, far and near, not presuming to resist, have paid them tribute; thus they have possessed themselves of a wealthy and powerful kingdom.' (Ong Tae-hae, *The Chinaman abroad, or, A desultory account of the Malayan Archipelago, particularly of Java* [Shanghai: Mission Press, 1849], p. 18.). Eighteenth-century Bengal is also a good example of how this pattern worked.

14. Valery M. Garrett, *Heaven Is High, the Emperor Far Away: Merchants and Mandarins in Old Canton* (China: Oxford University Press, 2002), p. 52.

15. Tan Chung, *China and the Brave New World: A Study of the Origins of the Opium War 1840–42* (New Delhi: Allied Publishers, 1978), p. 42.

16. Stephen R. Platt, *Imperial Twilight: The Opium War and the End of China's Last Golden Age* (New York, NY: Knopf, 2018), pp. 10–11.

17. See Dael A. Norwood, *Trading Freedom: How Trade with China Defined Early America* (Chicago, IL: University of Chicago Press, 2022), pp. 5–6. See also Goran Aijmer and Virgil K.Y. Ho, *Cantonese Society in a Time of Change* (Hong Kong: The Chinese University Press, 2000), p. 19; and Hsin-Pao Chang, *Commissioner Lin and the Opium War* (Cambridge, MA: Harvard University Press, 1964), pp. 3–9. Paul Λ. Van Dyke argues that 'there is much justification for calling the entire period from about 1700 to 1842 the Canton System' (*The Canton Trade: Life and Enterprise on the China Coast, 1700-1845* [Hong Kong: Hong Kong University Press, 2007], p. 10).

18. See Weng Eang Cheong, *The Hong Merchants of Canton: Chinese Merchants in Sino-Western Trade 1684–1798* (London: Routledge, 1997). See also Frederic Wakeman Jr, *Strangers at the Gate: Social Disorders in South China 1839–1861* [Berkeley, CA: University of California Press, 1966], p. 45); and Tan Chung, *China and the Brave New World*, 55–59.

19. For a complete list of regulations see William C. Hunter, *The Fan-Kwae at Canton Before Treaty Days, 1825–1844* (London: Kegan Paul, Trench & Co., 1882), pp. 28–30.

20. See Peter Ward Fay, *The Opium War: 1840–42* (Chapel Hill, NC: University of North Carolina Press, 1975), pp. 19–25.

21. For the regulation that prohibited compradors from providing 'boys or courtesans', see Wakeman, *Strangers*, 55.

22. See John R. Haddad, *America's First Adventure in China: Trade, Treaties, Opium and Salvation* (Philadelphia, PA: Temple University Press, 2013), Kindle edn., loc. 661. As Haddad notes, the conditions in the Foreign Enclave were designed to be so restrictive that foreigners would not be

tempted to stay too long. Yet, many spent decades there and found it hard to leave (loc. 809).

23. An American writer described one factory as 'nothing more nor less than a range of houses built one back of the other, and entered by arches, with a passage under the houses to get to each.' (Harriet Low, quoted in Michael Wise and Mun Him Wise, eds, *Travellers' Tales of Old Hong Kong and the South China Coast* (Brighton: In Print, 1996), p. 29.

24. Shen Fu, *Six Records of a Floating Life* (New York, NY: Penguin Random House, 1983), p. 122.

25. For detailed descriptions of the Foreign Enclave, see Garrett, *Heaven Is High*, chap. 7; and Patrick Conner, *The Hongs of Canton: Western Merchants in South China 1700-1900, as Seen in Chinese Export Paintings* (London: Martyn Gregory, 2009), chap. 5. For a detailed contemporary description see Hunter, *The Fan Kwae at Canton*, 20–25.

26. Platt, *Imperial Twilight*, 74, 202.

27. Jacques M. Downs, *The Golden Ghetto: The American Commercial Community at Canton and the Shaping of American China Policy, 1784–1844* (Bethlehem, PA: Lehigh University Press, 1997).

28. The writer is William Henry Low of Brooklyn, New York. See, James Duncan Phillips, ed., *The Canton Letters 1839-1841 of William Henry Low* (The Essex Institute Historical Collections LXXXIV, 1948, p. 27). I have retained his spellings and usages.

29. Downs, *The Golden Ghetto*, 43.

30. Platt, *Imperial Twilight*, xx–xxii.

31. Samuel Shaw, *The Journals of Major Samuel Shaw, the First American Consul at Canton, with a Life of the Author by Josiah Quincy* (Boston, MA: Wm Crosby and H.P. Nichols, 1847), p. 179.

32. Downs, *The Golden Ghetto*, 57.

33. For residential disputes between Parsis and other foreign merchants see Thampi, *Indians in China*, 82.

34. See Guo Deyan, 'The Dutch and the Parsees in Canton during the Qing Dynasty', in *Sailing to the Pearl River: Dutch Enterprise in South China, 1600–2000*, eds Cai Hongseng, Leonard Blussé et al. (Guangzhou: Guangzhou Publishing House, 2004), pp. 77–79.

35. Hunter, *The Fan-Kwae at Canton*, 63.

36. The influence of Parsi merchants over the Malwa market is described in detail in Weng Eang Cheong's *Mandarins and Merchants: Jardine Matheson & Co., A China Agency of the Early Nineteenth Century* (London: Curzon Press, 1979). See, for example, pp. 123–24.

37. Subramaniam, *Three Merchants*, 115; Richard J. Grace, *Opium and Empire: The Lives and Careers of William Jardine and James Matheson* (Montreal: McGill-Queen's University Press, 2016), p. 206; Tansen Sen, *India, China and the World: A Connected History* (London: Rowman & Littlefield Publishers, 2017), p. 256; and Cheong, *Mandarins and Merchants*, 122–24.

38. Pallavi Aiyar, 'Sea slugs and Jain diets: The real reason for the mutual incomprehension that plagues India-China relations', The Global Jigsaw, 2 July 2021. https://pallaviaiyar.substack.com/p/sea-slugs-and-jain-diets.

39. Garrett, *Heaven Is High*, 79.

40. A contemporary estimated Howqua's fortune to be 26,000,000 silver dollars in 1834 (Hunter, *The Fan-Kwae at Canton*, 48). John Haddad estimates that he was worth 'roughly $52 million in the 1830s . . . perhaps the wealthiest commoner on earth'. (*America's First Adventure*, loc. 733.) See also Sen, *India, China and the World*, 257.

41. See Hsin-Pao Chang, *Commissioner Lin and the Opium War*, pp. 191–92.

42. Grace, *Opium and Empire*, 224.

43. Phyllis Forbes Kerr, ed., *Letters from China: The Canton-Boston Correspondence of Robert Bennet Forbes, 1838–1840* (Carlisle, MA: Applewood Books, 1996), p. 88.

44. Gideon Nye, *The Morning of My Life in China: Comprising an Outline of the History of Foreign Intercourse from the Last Year of the Regime of Honorable East India Company, 1833, to the Imprisonment of the Foreign Community in 1839* (Whitefish, MT: Kessinger Publishing, 2008), p. 57.

45. Kerr, *Letters from China*, 89.

46. The custom of excarnation, or exposing corpses in dakhmas, or Towers of Silence, was not followed by Parsis living outside certain specific locations in Iran and India. See Shernaz Italia, 'Letter in More on Zoroastrian Rites', blog, amitavghosh.com, 27 March 2012: https://amitavghosh.com/blog/?p=2992.

47. Ibid.

48. See Amitav Ghosh, 'Zoroastrian Hong Kong', blog, amitavghosh.com, 19 March 2012: http://amitavghosh.com/blog/?p=2902.

49. HK_Heritage, 'The Parsees: Hong Kong's Disappearing Community', 28 June 2019. https://hongkongrefuge.wordpress.com/2019/06/28/hong-kongs-disappearing-communities/.

50. For general background on the role of Parsi seths in the Indian economy, see Amalendu Guha, 'Parsi Seths as Entrepreneurs: 1750–1850', *Economic and Political Weekly*, Vol. 5, no. 35 (1970): M-107–15; and Amalendu Guha, 'Comprador Role of Parsi Seths: 1750–1850', *Economic and Political Weekly*, Vol. 5, no. 48 (1970), 1933–36.

51. Thampi and Saksena, *China and the Making of Bombay*, 70–71.

52. Ibid., 72–76.

53. Downs, *The Golden Ghetto*, 157. See also Norwood, *Trading Freedom*, 64.

54. See Shalva Weil, ed., *The Baghdadi Jews in India: Maintaining Communities, Negotiating Identites and Creating Super-Diversity* (London: Routledge, 2019), pp. 3–4.

55. Carl A. Trocki, *Opium, Empire and the Global Political Economy: A Study of the Asian Opium Trade, 1750–1950* (New York, NY: Routledge, 1999), p. 114.

56. See, for example, Joseph Sassoon, *The Sassoons: The Great Global Merchants and the Making of an Empire* (New York, NY: Penguin Random House, 2022).

57. Thampi, *Indians in China*, 94–95.

58. Ibid., 103.

59. Thampi and Saksena, *China and the Making of Bombay*, 70–71.

60. Carl A. Trocki, *Opium and Empire: Chinese Society in Colonial Singapore, 1800-1910* (Ithaca, NY: Cornell University Press, 1990), pp. 50, 224.

61. Ibid., 56–57.

62. Rush, *Opium to Java*, 1. See also Rajat Kanta Ray, 'Asian Capital in the Age of European Domination: The Rise of the Bazaar, 1800–1914', *Modern Asian Studies*, Vol. 29, no. 3 (1995): 468.

63. Rush, *Opium to Java*, 66–67.

64. Diana S. Kim, *Empires of Vice: The Rise of Opium Prohibition across Southeast Asia* (Princeton, NJ: Princeton University Press, 2020), p. 33.

65. Rush, *Opium to Java*, 29–30.

66. Ibid., 20.

67. Trocki, *Opium and Empire*, 31–33.

68. Ibid., 67.

69. See Lee Poh Ping, *Chinese Society in Nineteenth Century Singapore* (Kuala Lumpur: Oxford University Press, 1978), pp. 27–30.

70. Trocki, *Opium and Empire*, 15–23. See also Lee, *Chinese Society*, 45–49.

71. Trocki, *Opium and Empire*, 197. See also Ray, 'Asian Capital', 521.

72. Rush, *Opium to Java*, 231.

73. Ibid., 208.

74. Warren Hastings cited this a reason for creating the EIC's opium monopoly in 1817 (Trocki, *Opium, Empire*, 75). See also Rush, *Opium to Java*, 148. See also Siddharth Chandra, 'The Role of Government Policy in Increasing Drug Use: Java, 1875–1914', *The Journal of Economic History*, Vol. 62, no. 4 (2002): 1116–21.

75. Siddharth Chandra, 'What the Numbers Really tell us about the Decline of the Opium Regie', *Indonesia*, No. 70 (2000): 101–23.

76. Ibid. See also Trocki, *Opium and Empire*, 204. In Java the sales of opium surged after the official monopoly was declared; in 1910 the Dutch Opium Regie yielded 137 per cent more than the opium farms had done. See Rush, *Opium to Java*, 237–40; and Siddharth Chandra, 'Economic Histories of the Opium Trade', EH.Net Encyclopedia, 10 February 2008. http://eh.net/encyclopedia/economic-histories-of-the-opium-trade/.

77. Hans Derks, *History of the Opium Problem: The Assault on the East, ca. 1600–1950* (Leiden: Brill, 2012), p. 336.

78. Trocki, *Opium and Empire*, 147.

12: Boston Brahmins

1. Jacques M. Downs, *The Golden Ghetto: The American Commercial Community at Canton and the Shaping of American China Policy, 1784–1844* (Bethlehem, PA: Lehigh University Press, 1997), p. 19.

2. See Frederick D. Grant, introduction to *The Golden Ghetto*, by Jacques M. Downs, p. 14 fn.

3. Letter dated 10 March 1839. Phyllis Forbes Kerr, ed., *Letters from China: The Canton-Boston Correspondence of Robert Bennet Forbes, 1838–1840* (Carlisle, MA: Applewood Books, 1996), p. 105.

4. Downs, *The Golden Ghetto*, 157.

5. Dael A. Norwood, *Trading Freedom: How Trade with China Defined Early America* (Chicago, IL: University of Chicago Press, 2022), p. 7.

6. Jenny Rose, *Between Boston and Bombay: Cultural and Commercial Encounters of Yankees and Parsis, 1771–1865* (Cham: Palgrave Macmillan, 2019), p. 40.

7. Francis Ross Carpenter, *The Old China Trade: Americans in Canton, 1784–1843* (New York, NY: Coward, McCann & Geoghegan, 1976), p. 11.

8. Norwood, *Trading Freedom*, 14–16; Jonathan Goldstein, *Philadelphia and the China Trade 1682–1846: Commercial, Cultural and Attitudinal Effects* (University Park and London: The Pennsylvania State University Press, 1978), p. 25.

9. Norwood, *Trading Freedom*, 15.

10. Goldstein, *Philadelphia and the China Trade*, 27.

11. For a full account of Samuel Shaw's voyage on the *Empress of China*, see John R. Haddad, *America's First Adventure in China: Trade, Treaties, Opium, and Salvation* (Philadelphia, PA: Temple University Press, 2013), Kindle edn., chapter 1.

12. Ibid., loc. 259.

13. Goldstein, *Philadelphia and the China Trade*, 41.

14. Charles C. Stelle, 'American Trade in Opium to China, Prior to 1820', *Pacific Historical Review*, Vol. 9, no. 4 (1940): 429.

15. Ibid., 425.

16. Rose, *Between Boston and Bombay*, 41.

17. Haddad notes that 'Of all the China dreams imagined by Americans, few matched Astor's in grandiosity' (*America's First Adventure*, loc. 1057).

18. See Carpenter, *The Old China Trade*, 80–88; and Alfred Tamarin and Shirley Glubok, *Voyaging to Cathay: Americans in the China Trade* (New York, NY: Viking Press, 1976), pp. 122, 156–58. See also Stelle, 'American Trade', 425. Haddad notes that the 'drive of traders to locate goods for the China market yielded' many ecological horror stories (*America's First Adventure*, loc. 970).

19. Stelle writes: 'Samuel Shaw had early noted that a "handsome profit" could be made on opium and that a "good market" existed for it in China, where it could be "smuggled with the utmost security".' 'American Trade', 427.

20. Carl A. Trocki, *Opium, Empire and the Global Political Economy: A Study of the Asian Opium Trade, 1750–1950* (New York, NY: Routledge, 1999), p. 76.

21. Jacques M. Downs, 'American Merchants and the China Opium Trade, 1800–1840', *The Business History Review*, Vol. 42, no. 4 (1968): 420.

22. Ibid., 421.

23. Goldstein, *Philadelphia and the China Trade*, 53.

24. Alfred W. McCoy, *The Politics of Heroin: CIA Complicity in the Global Drug Trade, Afghanistan, Southeast Asia, Central America, Colombia* (Chicago, IL: Lawrence Hill Books, 2003), p. 82.

25. Goldstein, *Philadelphia and the China Trade*, 54.

26. Thomas N. Layton, *The Voyage of the Frolic: New England Merchants and the Opium Trade* (Stanford, CA: Stanford University Press, 1997), p. 28.

27. Quoted in Stelle, 'American Trade', 429.

28. Stelle, 'American Trade', 434–36.

29. Downs, 'American Merchants', 424.

30. Stelle, 'American Trade', 440–41.

31. Ibid., 440.

32. Ibid., 442.

33. Charles C. Stelle, 'American Trade in Opium to China, 1821–39', *Pacific Historical Review*, Vol. 10, no. 1 (1941): 69.

34. Rose, *Between Boston and Bombay*, 46.

35. Ibid., 60, 67.

36. Ibid., 151.

37. Ibid., 145.

38. Ibid., 152.

39. Downs, 'American Merchants', 429.

40. Rose, *Between Boston and Bombay*, 158.

41. Downs, *The Golden Ghetto*, 177.

42. Ibid., 321. Among the Americans who prospered in Guangzhou there was only one who was not from the Northeast: William Hunter, who was a Midwesterner.

43. For Brown University's ties to slavery, see the University's report: 'Slavery, the Slave Trade and Brown University': https://slaveryandjusticereport .brown.edu/sections/slavery-the-slave-trade-and-brown/. For the founding family's connections with opium and the China trade see Downs, *The Golden Ghetto*, 202, 223.

44. Daniel Irving Larkin, ed., *Dear Will: Letters from the China Trade, 1833–1836* (New York, NY: D.I. Larkin, 1986), p. 168.

45. Ibid., 262.

46. Elma Loines, ed., *The China Trade Post-Bag of the Seth Low Family of Salem and New York, 1829-1873* (Falmouth, MA: Falmouth Publishing House, 1953), p. 61.

47. William C. Hunter, *The Fan-Kwae at Canton before Treaty Days, 1825–1844* (London: Kegan Paul, Trench & Co., 1882), p. 110.

48. Larkin, *Dear Will*, 207.

49. Ibid., 169.

50. Ibid., 203.

51. Ibid., 184.

52. Ibid., 185.

53. Ellen M. Oldham, 'Lord Byron and Mr Coolidge of Boston', *The Book Collector*, Vol. 13, no. 2 (1964): 211–13.

54. Robert Bennet Forbes, for example, wrote after one of Coolidge's departures, 'I trust Coolidge will not come out [to Canton] he has pocketed over One hundred thousand dollars out of the [firm] he ought to retire and stay at home.' Kerr, *Letters from China*, 83.

55. Haddad describes the Boston merchants' reliance on their relatives as 'meritocratic nepotism' because they were careful to choose only the most promising amongst them (*America's First Adventure*, loc. 570). Needless to add, this was the case also with Scottish, Indian and Chinese merchants: none of them would have recruited incompetent relatives. William Jardine, for example, 'showed a peculiar addiction to helping his own and James Matheson's several impecunious nephews'. But in a letter to one of them, he warned: 'I can never consent to assist idle and dissipated characters

however nearly connected with me, but am prepared to go to any reasonable extent in supporting such of my relatives as conduct themselves prudently and industriously.' (Weng Eang Cheong's *Mandarins and Merchants: Jardine Matheson & Co., A China Agency of the Early Nineteenth Century* [London: Curzon Press, 1979], pp. 207-8).

56. Downs, *The Golden Ghetto*, 315.

57. This was true also of many British merchants. Michael Greenberg notes: 'It is a remarkable characteristic of the expansion of Britain's Eastern trade that it was largely developed by family and clan groups.' (Michael Greenberg, *British Trade and the Opening of China* [Cambridge: Cambridge University Press, 1951], p. 37).

58. See Basil Lubbock, *The Opium Clippers* (Glasgow: Brown, Son & Ferguson, 1953), p. 19.

59. John Haddad, 'New England's Opium Overlords', *Tablet*, 23 November 2022: https://www.tabletmag.com/sections/history/articles/new-england-opium-overlords.

60. Norwood, *Trading Freedom*, 1-2; and Tamarin and Glubok, 107.

61. Haddad, *America's First Adventure*, loc. 607.

62. Cohong was the *anglice* of *gonghang*. For a detailed account, see Frederic Delano Grant Jr, *The Chinese Cornerstone of Modern Banking: The Canton Guaranty System and the Origins of Bank Deposit Insurance 1780–1933* (Leiden: Brill, 2014), pp. 57–60.

63. Strictly speaking he was Howqua II. 'In their trading names, the hong merchants came to generally adopt the suffix "qua" (*guan* as in *guan shang*), indicating official merchant status.' Ibid., 49. See also J.M. Braga, 'A Seller of "Sing-Songs": A Chapter in the Foreign Trade of China and Macao', *Journal of Oriental Studies*, Vol. 6 (1961–64): 105.

64. Carpenter, *The Old China Trade*, 36. See also Haddad, *America's First Adventure*, loc. 725.

65. Haddad, *America's First Adventure*, loc. 1698.

66. See Letter dated 28 January 1839, fn. 111. Kerr, *Letters from China*, 91; and Sarah Forbes Hughes, ed., *Letters and Recollections of John Murray Forbes, Vol. I* (Boston, MA: Houghton, Mifflin and Co. 1899), p. 53.

67. Hughes, *Letters and Recollections*, 62-63. See also Stephen R. Platt, *Imperial Twilight: The Opium War and the End of China's Last Golden Age* (New York, NY: Knopf, 2018), pp. 449–52.

68. Ibid., 101.

69. Layton, *The Voyage of the Frolic*: 31.

70. Ibid.

71. Downs, *The Golden Ghetto*, 317.

72. See Christine Dobbin, *Asian Entrepreneurial Minorities: Conjoint Communities in the Making of the World Economy* (London: Routledge, 1996), p. 7.

73. Max Weber, *The Protestant Ethic and the Spirit of Capitalism* (London: Routledge, 2001), p. 27.

13: American Stories

1. John Cushing played an important part in devising the Lintin system of 'floating warehouses' (see John R. Haddad, *America's First Adventure in China: Trade, Treaties, Opium, and Salvation* [Philadelphia, PA: Temple University Press, 2013], Kindle edn., loc. 767).

2. Octavius T. Howe and Frederick G. Matthews, *American Clipper Ships 1833–1858*, Vol. 1 (New York, NY: Dover Publications, 1986), pp. v–vi.

3. Charles G. Davis, *American Sailing Ships: Their Plans and History* (New York, NY: Dover Publications, 1984), p. 37.

4. Basil Lubbock, *The Opium Clippers* (Glasgow: Brown, Son & Ferguson, 1953), p. 188. See also Basil Greenhill and Ann Giffard, *The Merchant Sailing Ship: A Photographic History* (New York, NY: Praeger Publishers, 1970), p. 90.

5. Thomas N. Layton, *The Voyage of the Frolic: New England Merchants and the Opium Trade* (Stanford, CA: Stanford University Press, 1997), p. 42.

6. Frederick Douglass, *My Bondage and My Freedom* (New York, NY: Penguin Classics, 2003), pp. 227–30.

7. Mark Ravinder Frost, 'Asia's Maritime Networks and the Colonial Public Sphere, 1840-1920', *New Zealand Journal of Asian Studies*, Vol. 6, no. 2 (2004): 69.

8. Jenny Rose, *Between Boston and Bombay: Cultural and Commercial Encounters of Yankees and Parsis, 1771–1865* (Cham: Palgrave Macmillan, 2019), p. 203.

9. See Alfred H. Tamarin and Shirley Glubok, *Voyaging to Cathay: Americans in the China Trade* (New York, NY: Viking, 1976), p. 143.

10. See Clare Anderson, 'Convicts and Coolies: Rethinking Indentured Labour in the Nineteenth Century', Slavery and Abolition, Vol. 30, no. 1 (2009): 93–109; and Clare Anderson, *Indian Convict Ship Mutinies in the mid-nineteenth century*, 2011. See also Madhavi Thampi, *Indians in China, 1800–1949* (New Delhi: Manohar, 2005), p. 55.

11. See Janet J. Ewald, 'Crossers of the Sea: Slaves, Freedmen and Other Migrants in the Northwestern Indian Ocean, c. 1750–1914', *American Historical Review*, Vol. 105, no. 1 (2000): 76.

12. Anne Bulley, *The Bombay Country Ships, 1790–1833* (Richmond, Surrey: Curzon Press, 1999), pp. 12–15. See also Ruttonjee Ardeshir Wadia, *The Bombay Dockyard and the Wadia Master-Builders* (Bombay: R.A. Wadia, 1955).

13. Rose, *Between Boston and Bombay*, 130.

14. Eleanor Roosevelt Seagraves, ed., *Delano's Voyages of Commerce and Discovery: Amasa Delano in China, the Pacific Islands, Australia and South America, 1789–1807* (Stockbridge, MA: Berkshire House Publishers, 1994).

15. Phyllis Forbes Kerr, ed., *Letters from China: The Canton-Boston Correspondence of Robert Bennet Forbes, 1838–1840* (Carlisle, MA: Applewood Books, 1996), p. 90.

16. Arthur Waley, *The Opium War through Chinese Eyes* (London: George Allen & Unwin Ltd., 1958), p. 92; Gideon Chen, *Lin Tse-hsu: Pioneer Promoter of the Adoption of Western Means of Maritime Defense in China* (Peiping: Dept of Economics, Yengching University, 1934), p. 14.

17. Haddad, *America's First Adventure*, loc. 1988. See also Jonathan Spence, *The Search for Modern China* (New York, NY: W.W. Norton, 1990), p. 155.

18. Joseph Archer, quoted by Jacques M. Downs, *The Golden Ghetto: The American Commercial Community at Canton and the Shaping of American China Policy, 1784–1844* (Bethlehem, PA: Lehigh University Press, 1997), p. 296.

19. Dael A. Norwood, *Trading Freedom: How Trade with China Defined Early America* (Chicago, IL: University of Chicago Press, 2022), pp. 93, 139.

20. Stephen R. Platt, *Imperial Twilight: The Opium War and the End of China's Last Golden Age* (New York, NY: Knopf, 2018), p. 204.

21. Norwood, *Trading Freedom*, 39.

22. Francis Ross Carpenter, *The Old China Trade: Americans in Canton, 1784–1843* (New York, NY: Coward, McCann & Geoghegan, 1976), p. 123.

23. Ibid., 124.

24. Ibid., 130.

25. Ibid., 132.

26. Frederic Delano Grant Jr., *The Chinese Cornerstone of Modern Banking: The Canton Guaranty System and the Origins of Bank Deposit Insurance 1780–1933* (Leiden: Brill, 2014), p. 2.

27. Ibid.

28. Sarah Forbes Hughes, ed., *Letters and Recollections of John Murray Forbes, Vol. I* (Boston, MA: Houghton, Mifflin and Co. 1899), pp. 98–99. See also Platt, *Imperial Twilight*, pp. 339–40.

29. Hughes, *Letters and Recollections*, 81.

30. Downs, *The Golden Ghetto*, 209.

31. Carpenter, *The Old China Trade*, 139-40; and Downs, *The Golden Ghetto*, 329–30.
32. Downs, *The Golden Ghetto*, 330.
33. Platt, *Imperial Twilight*, 450.
34. Downs, *The Golden Ghetto*, 331.
35. Martha Bebinger, 'How Profits from Opium Shaped 19th-Century Boston', WBUR: https://www.wbur.org/news/2017/07/31/opium-boston-history.
36. Downs, *The Golden Ghetto*, 349.
37. See William K. Selden, 'John Cleve Green and the Beginnings of Science and Engineering at Princeton', *The Princeton University Library Chronicle*, Vol. 50, no. 3 (1989): 262–75.
38. Patrick Radden Keefe, *Empire of Pain: The Secret History of the Sackler Dynasty* (New York, NY: Doubleday, 2021), p. 3.
39. Barry Meier, *Pain Killer: An Empire of Deceit and the Origin of America's Opioid Epidemic* (New York, NY: Penguin Random House, 2018), p. 45.
40. Downs, *The Golden Ghetto*, 344.
41. Gerpha Gerlin, 'Architecture and Opium at Russell House', The Wesleyan Argus, 1 November 2012. http://wesleyanargus.com/2012/11/01/then-and-now-a-look-at-russell-house-past-and-present/.
42. Haddad, *America's First Adventure*, loc. 834.
43. Downs, *The Golden Ghetto*, 336–43.
44. Platt, *Imperial Twilight*, 449.
45. Downs, *The Golden Ghetto*, 347.
46. Haddad, *America's First Adventure*, loc. 834.
47. Jonathan Goldstein, *Philadelphia and the China Trade 1682–1846: Commercial, Cultural and Attitudinal Effects* (University Park and London: The Pennsylvania State University Press, 1978), p. 2.
48. Ibid.
49. Quoted in Downs, *The Golden Ghetto*, 339.
50. Ibid., 346.
51. Ibid., 335. As Haddad notes, John Cushing's true home was Canton. "'I feel better satisfied here,' he wrote of Canton, 'than I ever expect to anywhere else.'" (*America's First Adventure*, loc. 809).
52. Capt. Charles P. Low, *Some Recollections by Captain Charles P. Low, Commanding the Clipper Ships 'Houqua,' 'Jacob Bell,' 'Samuel Russell,' and 'N.B. Palmer,' in the China Trade, 1847–1873* (Boston, MA: Geo. H. Ellis Company, 1906), p. 2.
53. The two boys were born the same year, 1816, and died within months of each other in 1841 (Patrick Conner, *Chinese Views – Western Perspectives 1770–1870: The Sze Yuan Tang of China Coast Paintings & The Wallen Collection of*

China Coast Ship Portrait [Asia House, 1997], p. 16). See also Robin Hutcheon, *Chinnery: The Man and the Legend* (Hong Kong: South China Morning Post, 1975), p. 18.

54. See Peter Moss, *Chinnery in China* (Hong Kong: FormAsia, 2007), pp. 59–69.
55. Harriet Low described this visit at length in a letter to her mother. (Michael Wise and Mun Him Wise, eds, *Travellers' Tales of Old Hong Kong and the South China Coast* [Brighton: In Print, 1996], pp. 27–30.)
56. William C. Hunter, *The Fan-Kwae at Canton before Treaty Days, 1825–1844* (London: Kegan Paul, Trench & Co., 1882), pp. 121–22.
57. Nan Powell Hodges and A.W. Hummell, eds, *Lights and Shadows of a Macao Life: The Journal of Harriet Low, Travelling Spinster* (Creative Options, 2002), 7–9.
58. Ibid., 7.
59. E.J. Wagner, 'A Murder in Salem', *Smithsonian Magazine*, November 2010: https://www.smithsonianmag.com/history/a-murder-in-salem-64885035/.
60. Hodges and Hummell, *Lights and Shadows*, 14-15. See also Haddad, *America's First Adventure*, loc. 1804.
61. Elma Loines, ed., *The China Trade Post-Bag of the Seth Low Family of Salem and New York, 1829–1873* (Falmouth, MA: Falmouth Publishing House, 1953), p. 66.
62. Ibid., 72.
63. Platt, *Imperial Twilight*, 78. See also Haddad, *America's First Adventure*, locs. 1796–1807.
64. Ibid., 67. 'Quite a good sized fortune' was his brother Charles's comment (Low, *Some Recollections*, 13).
65. Loines, *The China Trade Post-Bag*, 82.
66. Ibid., 59; and Low, *Some Recollections*, 13.
67. Loines, *The China Trade Post-Bag*, 59.
68. Annie Doge, 'Matt Damon Checks Out Brooklyn's Most Expensive House, a Brooklyn Heights Mansion with a Mayoral Past', 29 September 2016. https://www.6sqft.com/matt-damon-checks-out-brooklyns-most-expensive-house-a-brooklyn-heights-mansion-with-a-mayoral-past/.
69. Keefe, *Empire of Pain*, 67–72.
70. Ibid., 147.
71. Ibid., 226.
72. *Adirondack Journal*, A.A. Low's Empire, https://www.theadkx.org/a-a-lows-empire/.
73. Donald Matheson, a young member of the great Scottish clan of drug dealers, resigned from the family firm in 1849, saying: 'It was intolerable

to me to continue in such a business . . .' (Carl A. Trocki, *Opium, Empire and the Global Political Economy: A Study of the Asian Opium Trade, 1750–1950* [New York, NY: Routledge, 1999], p. 163).

74. Bebinger, 'How Profits from Opium Shaped 19th-Century Boston'.
75. Keefe, *Empire of Pain*, 282.
76. Ibid., 431.
77. Ibid., 251.
78. Downs, *The Golden Ghetto*, 318.
79. Ibid., 331.
80. Ibid., 329.
81. Letter dated 4 February 1839. Kerr, *Letters from China*, 93.
82. This pact is known as 'The Treaty of Wanghia (Wangxia)'. Mao Haijian, *The Qing Empire and the Opium War: The Collapse of the Heavenly Dynasty*, ed. Joseph Lawson (Cambridge: Cambridge University Press, 2016), pp. 455, 467. See also, Spence, *The Search for Modern China*, 161.
83. For the influence of American missionaries on this treaty, see Michael C. Lazich, 'American Missionaries and the Opium Trade in Nineteenth-Century China', *Journal of World History*, Vol. 17, no. 2 (2006): 210–14.
84. See Haddad, *America's First Adventure*, loc. 1820–28.
85. Hodges and Hummell, *Lights and Shadows*, 351 and 348.
86. Charles W. King, *Opium Crisis: A Letter Addressed to Charles Elliot, Esq., Chief Superintendent of the British Trade with China* (London: Hatchard & Son, 1839), p. 8.
87. Peter Ward Fay, *The Opium War: 1840–42* (Chapel Hill, NC: University of North Carolina Press, 1975), p. 126.
88. King, *Opium Crisis*, 49.
89. Haddad, *America's First Adventure*, loc. 1764.
90. Downs, *The Golden Ghetto*, 452.
91. Bebinger, 'How Profits from Opium Shaped 19th-Century Boston'.
92. Downs, *The Golden Ghetto*, 448.
93. Ibid., 332.
94. Ibid., 456.
95. The opium trade has been described as a species of 'collaborative competition' between Britons and Americans (Norwood, *Trading Freedom*, 63).
96. Letter dated 10 March 1839. Kerr, *Letters from China*, 101.
97. Haddad, *America's First Adventure*, loc. 1728.
98. Ellen Newbold La Motte, *The Opium Monopoly* (New York, NY: Macmillan, 1920), p. 5.
99. Norwood, *Trading Freedom*, p. 89.

100. The US government actually recognized the distinction between the two and taxed smoking opium at a much higher rate than crude opium (David T. Courtwright, *Dark Paradise: A History of Opiate Addiction in America* [Cambridge, MA: Harvard University Press, 2001], p. 17).

101. The Royal Commission on Opium of 1894-95 questioned many 'Europeans' who had long been resident in Asia, whether 'people of European race contract the opium habit in any numbers? If not, why not? And what makes Asiatics more liable to contract the habit?' The answers to these questions reveal a great deal about contemporary British attitudes: many of the respondents stated that 'people of European race' were constitutionally averse to smoking opium. A fairly typical response was: 'Natives of a colder climate and of a more vigorous temperament Europeans prefer alcohol to the soothing drug which harmonises better with the impassive nature of the C......n. The former, as a rule, is fond of outdoor life, sports and athletic exercises, with the enjoyment of which the opium habit would greatly interfere . . .' (Royal Commission on Opium, *Proceedings*, Vol. V, 1894, p. 217).

102. Courtwright, *Dark Paradise*, 62.

103. Ibid., 71.

104. Ibid., 78–79.

105. Virginia Berridge and Griffith Edwards, *Opium and the People: Opiate Use in Nineteenth-Century England* (New York, NY: St. Martin's Press, 1981), pp. 113–22.

106. In the words of a British anti-opium activist: 'And what should we do, if the case were reversed, and China was to attempt upon our coasts, the violent, the avaricious, and the unfeeling contraband trade in poison which we practice against her?' (Horatio Montagu, *A Voice for China: . . . demonstrating that the War with China arises out of our British National Opium Smuggling* [London: Nisbet & Co., 1840], p. 17.)

107. *The Chinese Repository*, Vol. VIII (Elibron Classics Reprints, 2005), p. 500.

108. See Norwood, *Trading Freedom*, 67.

109. King, *Opium Crisis*, 11.

110. Downs quoting John Fairbanks's *Trade and Diplomacy on the China Coast: The Opening of the Treaty Ports, 1842–1854* (Stanford, CA: Stanford University Press, 1969) in *The Golden Ghetto*, 454.

111. See Alfred W. McCoy, *The Politics of Heroin: CIA Complicity in the Global Drug Trade, Afghanistan, Southeast Asia, Central America, Colombia* (Chicago, IL: Lawrence Hill Books, 2003).

112. King, *Opium Crisis*, 58.

113. Chris McGreal, *American Overdose: The Opioid Tragedy in Three Acts* (New York, NY: Hachette Book Group, 2018), p. 287.

114. Ibid., 292.

115. As Keefe points out, the opioid epidemic was one instance in which structural racism actually protected minorities in America because they were less likely to be issued prescription opioids. However, they suffered disproportionately in the law enforcement campaigns that were launched when prescription opioids led to a heroin epidemic. (*Empire of Pain*, 320.)

116. Karl E. Meyer, 'The Opium War's Secret History', *New York Times*, 28 June 1987. https://www.nytimes.com/1997/06/28/opinion/the-opium-war-s-secret-history.html.

117. *The Chinese Repository*, Vol. VIII, 499.

118. Naomi Oreskes and Erik M. Conway, *The Big Myth: How American Business Taught Us to Loathe Government and Love the Free Market* (New York, NY: Bloomsbury, 2023).

14: Guangzhou

1. Valery M. Garrett, *Heaven Is High, the Emperor Far Away: Merchants and Mandarins in Old Canton* (China: Oxford University Press, 2002), p. 126.

2. See Johnathan Farris, 'Thirteen Factories of Canton: An Architecture of Sino-Western Collaboration and Confrontation', *Buildings & Landscapes: Journal of the Vernacular Architecture Forum*, Vol. 14 (2007): 66–83.

3. Garrett, *Heaven Is High*, 133.

4. Graham E. Johnson and Glen D. Peterson, *Historical Dictionary of Guangzhou (Canton) and Guangdong* (Lanham, MD, and London: The Scarecrow Press, 1999), p. 73.

5. Quoted in Jessica Hanser, *Mr. Smith Goes to China: Three Scots and the Making of Britain's Global Empire* (New Haven, CT: Yale University Press, 2019), p. 63.

6. William S. Ruschenberger, *Narrative of a Voyage Around the World, During the Years 1835, 36, and 37* (London: Richard Bentley, 1838), p. 216.

7. Shen Fu, *Six Records of a Floating Life* (New York, NY: Penguin Random House, 1983), p. 124.

8. James Johnson, *The Oriental Voyager: Or, Descriptive Sketches and Cursory Remarks, on a Voyage to India and China, in His Majesty's Ship Caroline, Performed in the Years 1803–4–5–6* (London: J. Asperne, 1807), pp. 173–74.

9. David Abeel, *Journal of a Residence in China and the Neighboring Countries from 1829 to 1833* (New York, NY: Leavitt, Lord & Co., 1834), p. 60.

10. Patrick Conner, *The Hongs of Canton: Western Merchants in South China 1700–1900, as Seen in Chinese Export Paintings* (London: Martyn Gregory, 2009), p. 76. See also John Glasgow Kerr, *A Guide to the City and Suburbs of Canton* (Canton: Chinese Materials Center, 1974), p. 10.

11. Ruschenberger, *Narrative of a Voyage*, 232.

12. Quoted in Aldous Colin Ricardo Bertram, 'Chinese Influence on English Garden Design and Architecture Between 1700 and 1860', Ph.D. diss., University of Cambridge, Cambridge, 2012), p. 186.

13. Ibid., 187.

14. Peter Valder, *The Garden Plants of China* (London: Weidenfeld and Nicholson, 1999), p. 12.

15. Shen Fu, *Six Records*, 122.

16. Kerr, *A Guide to the City and Suburbs of Canton*, 43.

17. Garrett, *Heaven Is High*, 113.

18. Shen Fu, *Six Records*, 122.

19. Fan Fa-ti, 'British naturalists in China, 1760–1910' (Ph.D. diss., University of Wisconsin–Madison, Madison, WI, 1999), p. 37.

20. Valder, *The Garden Plants of China*, 66–67.

21. Hazel Le Rougetel, 'The Fa Tee Nurseries of South China', *Garden History*, Vol. 10, no. 1 (1982): 70–73.

22. Fan Fa-ti, 'British naturalists in China', 14.

23. Desmond Ray, *Kew: The History of the Royal Botanic Gardens* (London: Harvill Press with the Royal Botanic Gardens, Kew, 1995), pp. 89–104.

24. Fan Fa-ti, 'British naturalists in China', 44; and Le Rougetel, 'The Fa Tee Nurseries', 71.

25. Fan Fa-ti, 'British naturalists in China', 25; and F. Nigel Hepper, *Plant Hunting for Kew* (London: HMSO, 1989), p. 6.

26. Ray, *Kew*, 102.

27. Alice M. Coats has the Chinese gardener's name as 'Ah Hey' (*The Plant Hunters: Being a History of the Horticultural Pioneers, Their Quests, and Their Discoveries from the Renaissance to the Twentieth Century* [New York, NY: McGraw Hill, 1970], p. 99).

28. During the First Opium War, the Expeditionary Force was explicitly instructed to collect specimens: 'There will no doubt be in the fleet many Officers of Science and of acquirement in various branches of natural history, who will be ready to avail themselves of every opportunity for making Observations, the report of which may be interesting or of forming Collections, the possession of which in Europe or in India would be considered to be of much value.' [British Library, India Office Records,

Board's Collections 83888 to 84180, 1841-42, Vol.1938; F/4/1938; no. 235; *Extract from the Proceedings of the Right Hon'ble the Governor General of India in Council in the Secret and Confidential Dept under date the 11 May 1840.*]

29. Jane Kilpatrick, *Gifts from the Gardens of China* (London: Frances Lincoln, 2007), p. 9.

30. James Wong, "What 'English style" owes to Asia's gardens', *The Guardian*, 10 November 2019.

31. Quoted in Bertram, 'Chinese Influence on English Garden Design', 5.

32. Quoted in Bertram, 'Chinese Influence on English Garden Design', 6.

33. Bertram, 'Chinese Influence on English Garden Design', 6.

34. Quoted in Yu Liu, 'The Inspiration for a different Eden: Chinese Gardening Ideas in England in the Early Modern Period', *Comparative Civilizations Review*, Vol. 53, no. 53 (2005): 89.

35. Yu Liu, *Seeds of a Different Eden: Chinese Gardening Ideas and a New English Aesthetic Ideal* (Columbia, SC: University of South Carolina Press, 2008), p. 23.

36. Ibid., 16; and Peter Valder, *Gardens in China* (Portland, OR: Haseltine Press, 2002), p. 21.

37. Yu Liu, *Seeds*, 10. It is possible that Chambers was also familiar with a Chinese monograph by Ji Cheng called *Yuanye* ('The Craft of Gardening'). Published in 1631, this is thought to be 'the world's first practical treatise on gardening' (Bertram, 'Chinese Influence on English Garden Design', 30).

38. Bertram, 'Chinese Influence on English Garden Design', 182–83.

39. Kilpatrick, *Gifts*, 31.

40. Anthony Huxley, *An Illustrated History of Gardening* (Essex, CT: Lyons Press, 1998), p. 70.

41. Bertram, 'Chinese Influence on English Garden Design', 32.

42. My translation of George-Louis Le Rouge's words: '*Les Jardins Anglais ne sont qu'une imitation de ceux de la Chine.*' Quoted in Bertram, 'Chinese Influence on English Garden Design', 6. See also Yu Liu, 'The Inspiration for a different Eden', 86.

43. Bertram, 'Chinese Influence on English Garden Design', 36.

44. See Le Rougetel, 'The Fa Tee Nurseries', 72.

45. This was perhaps an extension of the prevalent colonial view that Chinese workers were generally more skilful than Indians and other Asians. For instance, John Crawfurd, resident of Singapore from 1823 to 1827 wrote: 'I entertain so high an opinion of the industry, skill and capacity of consumption of the Chinese, that I consider one C......n equal in value to the state to *two* natives of the Coromandel Coast and to four Malays at least.' (Quoted in Carl A. Trocki's, *Opium and Empire: Chinese Society in*

Colonial Singapore, 1800–1910 [Ithaca, NY: Cornell University Press, 1990], p. 224 fn.)

46. Huxley, *An Illustrated History*, 66. There is a picture of a contemporary nursery in Guangdong that conveys an idea of what the Fa Tee nurseries might have looked like (Valder, *The Garden Plants*, 66).

47. Some scholars continue to believe this even today. Eugenia W. Herbert, for example, writes that gardens 'were one of the most *visible* manifestations on British presence and British civilization' and that their influence was amplified by 'subject peoples [who] aped the ways of the British, not least of all their gardens'. (*Flora's Empire: British Gardens in India* [Philadelphia, PA: University of Pennsylvania Press, 2011], p. 306.)

48. See Herbert, *Flora's Empire*, 306.

49. 'A very large number of beautiful Asiatic primulas [primroses] was introduced at the end of the nineteenth and the first quarter of the present century; and many of them have proved more hardy and accommodating in the garden than the difficult Alpine species of Europe' (Alice M. Coats, *Flowers and their Histories* [New York, NY: McGraw Hill, 1956], p. 217).

50. See Patrick Conner, '"Mysteries of Deeper Consequences": Westerners in Chinese Reverse-Glass Painting of the 18th Century', *Arts of Asia*, Vol. 46, no. 5 (2016): 124–36.

51. Paul L.F. van Dongen, '"Sensitive Plates": Nineteen Chinese Paintings on Glass' (Sassenheim: Sikkens Paint Museum, Leiden: National Museum of Ethnology, 1997), p. 30.

52. Jérôme Samuel, 'Naissances et Renaissance de la peinture sous verre à Java', *Archipel*, Vol. 69 (2005): 91. I am grateful to Michael Feener for bringing this article to my notice.

53. Ibid., 92.

54. Madhavi Thampi and Shalini Saksena, *China and the Making of Bombay* (Mumbai: K.R. Cama Oriental Institute, 2009), p. 98.

55. Kalpana Desai, 'The Tanchoi and the Garo: Parsi Textiles and Embroidery', in *A Zoroastrian Tapestry: Art, Religion and Culture*, ed. Sudha Seshadri (Ahmedabad: Mapin Publishing, 2002), p. 591.

56. Ibid., 98–99: 'Jamsetjee Jeejeebhoy is said to be the man responsible for sending Indian weavers to China to learn the art of producing the fine satin brocade. Three (*tan*) Joshi brothers from Surat went to Shanghai to learn the art from a master weaver whose name has come down to us as "Choi". The material they produced after they returned to India came to be known as *tan-choi*. As in the case of the *gara*, the motifs are recognizably Chinese

in inspiration, although some Indian innovations, such as the mango motif, have also been introduced.'

57. Ibid., 577: 'The training of these brothers was sponsored by the First Baronet Sir Jamsetjee Jejeebhoy who, intrigued by this particular technique of weaving, had his baronet's emblem woven as a motif in *tanchoi* material.'

58. Ibid., 586.

59. The blouse-like Parsi garment was known as a jabla. There are some fine pictures of the garment in *Painted Encounters: Parsi Traders and the Community*, eds Pheroza J. Godrej and Firoza Punthakey Mistree (New Delhi: National Gallery of Modern Art, 2016), p. 127. Dr Kalpana Desai also includes several pictures of early Parsi 'blouses' in her article (most of them from the collection of the Prince of Wales Museum in Mumbai). The Chinese influence on these garments is quite apparent.

60. This happened to be a period in which there was a great efflorescence in vernacular painting in China. See James Cahill *Pictures for Use and Pleasure: Vernacular Painting in High Qing China* (Berkeley, CA: University of California Press, 2010), pp. 3–12.

61. Carl L. Crossman's *The Decorative Arts of the China Trade: Paintings, Furnishings and Exotic Curiosities* (Woodbridge, Suffolk: Antique Collectors Club Ltd, 1991) includes many fine portraits. Several excellent portraits of Parsis, painted in Guangzhou, are included in Godrej and Mistree, *Painted Encounters*.

62. Robin Hutcheon, *Chinnery: The Man and the Legend* (Hong Kong: South China Morning Post, 1975), p. 77. See also Johnson, *The Oriental Voyager*, 176.

63. John C. Dann, ed., *The Nagle Journal: A Diary of the Life of Jacob Nagle, Sailor, from the Year 1775 to 1841* (New York, NY: Weidenfeld & Nicholson, 1988), p. 273.

64. Fan Fa-ti, 'British naturalists in China', pp. 58–72.

65. Peter Valder provides a useful overview of the history of Chinese botanical paintings in *The Garden Plants*, 53–56. Osvald Sirén's *Gardens of China* (New York, NY: Ronald Press, 1949) has a longer treatment of the subject.

66. Wilfrid Blunt, *The Art of Botanical Illustration: An Illustrated History* (New York, NY: Dover, 1994), notes the influence of eighteenth-century Chinese botanical painters on their European counterparts such as Jospeh Pierre Buc'hoz (1731–1807): 'In some of [his] works, considerable use is made for the first time of drawings of Chinese plants executed by native artists, and much of Buc'hoz's other work also has a distinctly oriental flavour . . . The Far East has not only provided us with many of the loveliest shrubs and flowers in our gardens; it offers us a salutary object lesson in humility towards Nature.' (p. 160)

67. See Charles Toogood Downing, *The Fan-Qui in China, in 1836–7*, Vol. II (London: H. Colburn, 1838), pp. 95–108.

68. Winnie Won Yin Wong, *Van Gogh on Demand: China and the Readymade* (Chicago, IL: University of Chicago Press, 2013), p. 5.

69. Tan Chet-qua is a conjecture because: 'The full Chinese name of Chitqua has not come down to us with certainty . . .' (David Clarke, *Chinese Art and Its Encounter with the World* [Hong Kong: Hong Kong University Press, 2011], p. 22.)

70. For a detailed account of Chitqua's visit to London, see Clarke, *Chinese Art*, 21–84.

71. See Terese Tse Bartholomew and He Li, *The Tate Collection of Chinese Antiquities in the Chhatrapati Shivaji Maharaj Vastu Sangrahalaya* (Mumbai: Chhatrapati Shivaji Maharaj Vastu Sangrahalaya, 2002).

72. See Downing, *The Fan-Qui in China*, Vol. II, 90–93.

73. See Hutcheon, *Chinnery*, 73.

74. See Patrick Conner, *George Chinnery: 1774–1852: Artist of India and the China Coast* (Woodbridge, Suffolk: Antique Collectors Club Ltd, 1983), pp. 263–67.

75. See Capt. Arthur Cunynghame, *The Opium War: Being Recollections of Service in China* (Philadelphia, PA: G.B. Zieber & Co., 1845), p. 217. For a detailed discussion of this issue see Larissa N. Heinrich, *The Afterlife of Images: Translating the Pathological Body between China and the West* (Durham, NC: Duke University Press, 2008), pp. 48–49.

76. These paintings, which were made without charge, are now in the collection of the Cushing-Whitney Medical Library at Yale. See Heinrich, *The Afterlife of Images*, 49–65.

77. Thampi and Saksena, *China and the Making of Bombay*, 88.

78. To look at the list of the school's alumni is to recognize that this institution has had an enormous impact on the world of Indian art: the list includes Dadasaheb Phalke, Uday Shankar, Homai Vyarawalla, M.F.Husain, Tyeb Mehta, Francis Newton Souza, and such contemporary luminaries as Jitish Kallat and Atul Dodiya.

79. See, in particular, the lacquered and gilded rosewood bookcase on p. 241 in Crossman, *The Decorative Arts*. Crossman describes it as 'a *tour de force* of Chinese and western elements cleverly used together to form a unique furniture form. The door with its "cracked ice" pattern and three shaped panels is clearly the most imaginative to be seen on any piece of export furniture'.

80. Ibid., 264.

81. Ibid., 272.

82. Ibid., 269.

83. Lakshmi Subramaniam, *Three Merchants of Bombay: Business Pioneers of the Nineteenth Century* (Gurgaon: Penguin Random House, 2011), p. 129.

84. Jan van der Puten, 'Wayang Parsi, Bangsawan, and Printing', in *Islamic Connections: Muslim Societies in South and Southeast Asia*, eds R. Michael Feener and Terenjit Sever (Singapore: Institute of Southeast Asian Studies, 2009), pp. 91–92.

85. See, for example: Douglas M. Peers, 'Imperial Vice: Sex, drink and the health of British troops in North Indian cantonments, 1800–1858', in *Guardians of Empire: The Armed Forces of the Colonial Powers c. 1700–1964* (Manchester: Manchester University Press, 2017), p. 33; and Douglas M. Peers, 'Privates Off Parade: Regimenting Sexuality in the Nineteenth-Century Indian Empire', *The International History Review*, Vol. 20, no. 4 (1998): 836–37.

86. Maria Graham, 'Journal of a Residence in India', in *The Monthly Magazine*, Vol. 34 (1812): 645.

87. E.H. Nolan, *The Illustrated History of the British Empire in India and the East: from the earliest times to the suppression of the Sepoy Mutiny in 1859* (London: Virtue & Co.). The historian Anthony Webster notes: 'During the first three decades of the nineteenth century, a note of contempt in European commentaries on Indians became louder.' (*The Richest East India Merchant: The Life and Business of John Palmer of Calcutta, 1767–1836* [Martlesham, Suffolk: Boydell & Brewer, 2007], p. 79). Similarly D.H.A. Kolff notes: 'The British, in other words, chose to remain outsiders: tourists in India who refused to communicate with the Indian people.' (*Grass in Their Mouths: The Upper Doab of India under the Company's Magna Charta, 1793–1830* [Leiden: Brill, 2010], p. 435).

88. My argument here owes a great deal to Sanjay Subrahmanyam's idea of 'connected history', and his long-held position that 'modernity is historically a global and *conjunctural* phenomenon, not a virus that spreads from one place to another.' ('Hearing Voices: Vignettes of Early Modernity in South Asia, 1400-1750', *Daedalus*, Vol. 127, no. 3 (1998): 99–100). See also Kenneth Pomeranz, 'Teleology, Discontinuity and World History: Periodization and Some Creation Myths of Modernity', *Asian Review of World History*, Vol. 1, no. 2 (2013): 191.

15: The Sea-Calming Tower

1. Frederic Wakeman Jr, *Strangers at the Gate: Social Disorders in South China 1839–1861* (Berkeley, CA: University of California Press, 1966), p. 14.

2. Peter Valder, *Gardens in China* (Portland, OR: Haseltine Press, 2002), p. 226.

3. Graham E. Johnson and Glen D. Peterson, *Historical Dictionary of Guangzhou (Canton) and Guangdong* (Lanham, MD, and London: The Scarecrow Press, 1999), p. 11.

4. Mao Haijian, *The Qing Empire and the Opium War: The Collapse of the Heavenly Dynasty*, trans. Joseph Lawson, Craig Smith and Peter Lavelle, ed. Joseph Lawson (Cambridge: Cambridge University Press, 2016), p. 127.

5. See W.D. Bernard and W.H. Hall: *The Nemesis in China: comprising a history of the late war in that country; with a complete account of the colony of Hong-Kong* (London: Henry Colburn, 1846), pp. 2–4.

6. The attack on the Zhenhai Tower had been in the planning since March 1841 (British Library, India Office Records, Despatch no. 15 of 1841, to Lord Palmerston from C. Elliot, 28 March 1841; China Records Miscellanious [sic] Vol. 4 R/10/72; 1841). It is clear from this collection of dispatches that the British high command had also made plans (later aborted) to occupy large parts of China.

7. For the troops liquor rations see, the British Library's India Office Records, Madras Despatches 13 July to 31 Dec 1841; p. 96, Record Department; IOR/E/4/956; 201–208.

8. Lt. John Ouchterlony, *The Chinese War: An Account of All the Operations of the British Forces from the Commencement to the Treaty of Nanking* (London: Saunders and Otley, 1844), p. 145.

9. The file 'China Foreign Office Instructions and Correspondence, 1842–43 [L/PS/9/195]', in the British Library's India Office Records, contains many letters from leading British politicians and diplomats that bear witness both to the extreme bellicosity of many high-ranking British officials in London, and to their determination to humiliate the Chinese and extract crippling reparations. The Plenipotentiary Charles Elliot was moderate by comparison.

10. 'There was no question that the British looted. In fact, the very word "loot" (of Indian derivation) was first used by the English during the Opium War.' (Wakeman, *Strangers at the Gate*, 16). See also Mao Haijian, *The Qing Empire*, 251, on foraging: 'This sort of "foraging" is very unlikely not to have involved "plundering".'

11. Gerald Graham, *The China Station: War and Diplomacy, 1830–1860* (Oxford: Clarendon Press, 1978), p. 167.

12. Mao Haijian, *The Qing Empire*, 251; and Julia Lovell, *The Opium War: Drugs, Dreams and the Making of China* (New York, NY: Overlook Press, 2014), p. 159.

13. For the Chinese sources, see Mao Haijian, *The Qing Empire*, 252. The violations are also described in John Elliot Bingham, *Narrative of the*

Expedition to China: From the Commencement of the War to Its Termination in 1842; with Sketches of the Manners and Customs of the Singular and Hitherto Almost Unknown Country, Vol. I (London: Henry Colburn, 1843), pp. 149–150; and there is an oblique reference to rapes in Ouchterlony, *The Chinese War*, 151; and by other British officers (David McLean, for example, quotes an officer who wrote: 'I am sorry to say that many most barbarous things occurred disgraceful to our men' ('Surgeons of The Opium War: The Navy on the China Coast, 1840–42', *The English Historical Review*, Vol. 121, no. 491 [2006]: 492). Similarly *The Chinese Repository*, Vol. X (Elibron Classics Reprints, 2005), p. 530, refers to 'doings of which it is a shame even to speak'. Unfortunately, Frederic Wakeman Jr accepted uncritically the British story that 'sepoy troops had indeed violated native women around San-yuan-li.' (*Strangers at the Gate*, 16-17.)

14. According to a Chinese account, the oath-taking was led by a market gardener by the name of Wei Shao-kuang (*The Opium War* [Beijing: Foreign Languages Press, 1976], p. 54).

15. Bingham, *Narrative of the Expedition*, 160.

16. Duncan Mcpherson, M.D., *The War in China: Narrative of the Chinese Expedition, from Its Formation in April, 1840, to the Treaty of Peace in August, 1842* (London: Saunders and Otley, 1843), p. 155.

17. 'It had been intended to arm the Bengal Volunteer Battalion, proceeding on Service to China with percussion Muskets, but with reference to the small number of Percussion caps which the Board reported would remain in store after the transmission of the above mentioned quantity to Delhi, we have considered it advisable for the Regiment to be provided, in the first instance, with flint Arms, to be exchanged for Percussion in the event of a sufficient supply of Copper caps being received, either from Madras or Europe, previous to the embarkation of the Corps.' The copper caps never arrived. [British Library, India Office Records, Bengal Military Letters Received, 1842; L/MIL/3 48; No 26 of 1842.]

18. '[T]he value of the new percussion musket . . . was at once seen.' Henry Meredith Vibart, *Military History of the Madras Engineers and Pioneers, from 1743 Up to the Present Time, Vol. 2* (London: W.H. Allen & Co., 1881), p. 150. See also, British Library, India Office Records, Madras Despatches 12 Jan to 29 June 1842 [E/4/957]; Draft Military, 2 March No. 8, 1842: 'Looking to the great superiority of the Percussion Arms . . .'

19. My account of the battle of Sanyuanli is based on the following sources: Maj. Mark S. Bell, *China: Being a Military Report on the North-Eastern Portions of the Provinces of Chih-Li and Shan-Tung; Nanking and its Approaches; prepared*

in the Intelligence Branch of the Quarter Master General's Department in India, 1882, Vol. I Confidential, Vol. II Secret (Simla: Government Central Branch Press, 1882, British Library; India Office Records) British Library, India Office Records, L/P&S/20/D28/2; Bingham, *Narrative of the Expedition*; 'Official Accounts of the Late Naval and Military Operations in China', *The Nautical Magazine and Naval Chronicle* (London: Simpkin, Marshall & Co., London, 1841), pp. 56–63, 262–68, 331–36, 408–16, 473–84, 765–76 and 849–62; 'Despatches; China', *The Annual Register or a View of the History and Politics of the Year 1841* (London, 1842) pp. 468–527); Capt. Sir Edward Belcher, *Narrative of A Voyage Round the World Performed in Her Majesty's Ship Sulphur During the Years 1836–42 Including Details of the Naval Operations in China* (London: Henry Colburn, 1843); Rick Bowers, 'Notes from the Opium War: Selections from Lieutenant Charles Cameron's Diary during the period of the Chinese War, 1840–41', *Journal of the Society for Army Historical Research* 86 (2008): 190–203; Lt. John Ouchterlony, *The Chinese War*; Dallas and Hall, *The Nemesis in China*; 'Frontier and Overseas Expeditions from India,' Anon., Compiled in the Intelligence Branch, Army HQ, India, Vol. VI (Expeditions Overseas), 1911, pp. 379–80; Vibart, *Military History*; McPherson, *The War in China*; *Diary of events kept by Capt. H. Giffard, HMS Volage & Cruiser, 1833–40* (British Library); Lt W.S. Birdwood, 'Plan of Attack on the Heights and Forts near the City of Canton Under the Command of Major General Sir Hugh Gough, 25 May 1841' (British Library, India Office Records). Among the military dispatches in the collection of the India Office Records of the British Library, the most useful were the following: Board's Collections 83888 to 84180, 1841–42, Vol. 1938; Madras Despatches 13 July to 31 Dec 1841 [E/4/769]; Madras Despatches 4 Jan to 28 Aug 1839 [E/4/952]; Madras Despatches 4 Jan to 28 Aug 1839 [IOR/E/4/952]; Madras Despatches 12 Jan to 29 June 1842 [E/4/957]; Madras Despatches 13 July to 31 Dec 1841; 96 Record Department, [IOR/E/4/956]; Bengal Military Letters Received 1840 [L/MIL/3/46]; Bengal Military Letters Received 1841 [L/MIL/3/47]; Bengal Military Letters Received, 1842 [L/MIL/3/48]; Bengal Military Letters Received, 1842 [L/MIL/3/48]; Board's collections 1841–42 [IOR/F/4/1954/85080]; India and Bengal Despatches 12 Jan to 30 March 1842 [E/4/769]; and India and Bengal Despatches 13 July to 1 Sept 1841 [E/4/769]; China Foreign Office Instructions and Correspondence 1841, Secret Department, [L/PS/9/194]; China Foreign Office Instructions and Correspondence, 1839–40 [L/PS/9/193]; China Foreign Office Instructions and Correspondence, 1842-43 [L/PS/9/195]; China Records Miscellanious [sic] Vol. 4 [R/10/71]

1840–41; and China Records Miscellanious [sic] Vol. 4 [R/10/72; 1841]. Among secondary sources the most useful were: Wakeman, *Strangers at the Gate*; Hsin-Pao Chang, *Commissioner Lin and the Opium War* (Cambridge, MA: Harvard University Press, 1964); Arthur Waley, *The Opium War Through Chinese Eyes* (Stanford, CA: Stanford University Press, 1958); *The Chinese Repository*, Vols VIII, IX and X; *The Canton Register*, Vols. 13, 14 and 15; and Lovell, *The Opium War*.

20. Two of the British officers involved in the battle received promotions, and the 37 Madras Native Infantry was upgraded to a Grenadier Regiment, in order 'to mark our sense of the gallantry and steadiness displayed under most trying circumstances . . .' [British Library, India Office Records, Madras Despatches 13 July to 31 Dec 1841; 96 Record Department; IOR/E/4/956 (letter dated 27th October/No 77/ 1841).] In 1842 it was again brought to the notice of the EIC's Court of Directors that 'no boon whatever has been conferred on a company of the 37th Regiment Madras Native Infantry whose steady and gallant conduct during the operations before Canton was favorably brought to the notice of Government by Sir Hugh Gough, Commander in Chief of the China Expedition.' (British Library, India Office Records, Board's Collections 1841–42 [IOR/F/4/1954/85080]; collection No. 14, Ft St George Military Dept., Letter dated Jan 21, 1842, no. 3.). In response the Court directed that 'the name of each European and Native Commissioned Officer, Non Commissioned Officer and Sepoy who composed the Company of that Regiment detached under Lt Hadfield and who by their steady courage and discipline successfully defeated the repeated attacks of a large body of the enemy and thus nobly sustained the credit of the Native Army be entered in the Regimental Order Book of that Corps with a record of the transactions to which it refers. We also desire that the Native Officers Non Commissioned Officers and Sepoys of that Company be granted an addition to their pay and pensions on retirement either by admitting them to the advantages of the "Order of Merit" or in any other manner which you may consider desirable.' [British Library, India Office Records, Board's Collections 1841–42. [IOR/F/4/1954/85080]; Military Letter to Fort St. George, dated 27 October 1841.] Some of the sepoys who received promotions were Havildar Goorapah; Jemadar Naique Narrapah; Lance Naique Dawood Khan, and Private Lutchman (British Library, India Office Records, Board's Collections 1841–42 [IOR/F/4/1954/85080]; Regimental Orders by Captain Bedingfield; Hong Kong, 3 July 1841).

21. See James M. Polachek, *The Inner Opium War* (Cambridge, MA: Harvard University Asia Center, 1992), p. 165; and Lovell, *The Opium War*, 156–64.

22. Mao Haijian, *The Qing Empire*, 267.

23. Lovell, *The Opium War*, 159.

24. These containers were only for export or 'provision' opium. The opium that was marketed in India was known as 'excise' or *akbari* opium and was packaged differently.

25. It's interesting that Mao Haijian, whose revisionist history of the Opium War, has been influential around the world, makes no mention of the presence of Indians at Sanyuanli in his detailed account of the battle. He also seems hardly to notice the critical role that opium played in this conflict.

26. Matthew W. Mosca, *From Frontier Policy to Foreign Policy: The Question of India and the Transformation of Geopolitics in Qing China* (Stanford, CA: Stanford University Press, 2013), p. 252.

27. David T. Courtwright, *Forces of Habit: Drugs and the Making of the Modern World* (Cambridge, MA: Harvard University Press, 2001), p. 140.

28. British military dispatches on the subject of alcohol are astonishing in their attention to detail. See, for instance, British Library, India Office Records, Madras Despatches 12 Jan to 29 June 1842 [E/4/957]; Draft Military, 2 March No. 8, 1842; and Bengal Military Letters Received 1840 [L/MIL/3/46]; No. 46 of 1840. Erica Wald notes that British commanders saw drinking as 'an integral part of the soldier's composition.' ('Health, Discipline and Appropriate Behaviour: The Body of the Soldier and Space of the Cantonment', *Modern Asian Studies*, Vol. 46, no. 4 [2012]: 834).

29. The only extant nineteenth-century memoir by a sepoy is *From Sepoy to Subedar: Being the Life and Adventures of Subedar Sita Ram, a Native Officer of the Bengal Army, Written and Related by Himself*, trans. James Thomas Norgate, ed. James D. Lunt (London, 1873; also Calcutta: Baptist Mission Press, 1911). First published in 1873, it is said to have been dictated to an English officer and is widely believed to be apocryphal. The original text, if there was one, has never been found, so only the English version exists. While parts of the memoir may have been made up by Norgate, some of the narrative is certainly authentic. The writer Madhukar Upadhyaya has published a beautiful reimagining of the text in Awadhi (*Kissa Pande Sitaram Subedar* [Delhi, Saaransh Prakashan, 1999]).

30. For a detailed account see T.A. Heathcote, *The Military in British India: The Development of British Land Forces in South Asia 1600–1947* (Manchester, and New York, NY: Manchester University Press, 1995), pp. 21–37.

31. Anand A. Yang, Kamal Sheel, Ranjana Sheel, Prasenjit Duara and Tansen Sen, *Thirteen Months in China: A Subaltern Indian and the Colonial World—An Annotated Translation of Thakur Gadadhar Singh's* Chīn Me Terah Mās (New

Delhi: Oxford University Press, 2017). See also: Anand A. Yang, 'An Indian Subaltern's Passage to China in 1900', *Education About Asia* Vol. 11, no. 3 (2006).

32. As William Pinch notes: 'The popular religious world that the English East India Company encountered in the seventeenth century was defined less by Hinduism and Islam than by asceticism.' (William R. Pinch, *Warrior Ascetics and Indian Empires* [Cambridge: Cambridge University Press, 2006], p. 82). Pinch's book is a detailed study of the religious lives of warrior ascetics. For a study of spirituality among Muslim soldiers see: Nile Green, *Islam and the Army in Colonial India: Sepoy Religion in the Service of Empire* [Cambridge: Cambridge University Press, 2009]). Nile Green notes: 'Stories of soldiers falling into states of ecstasy and distraction were by no means uncommon' ('Jack Sepoy and the Dervishes: Islam and the Indian Soldier in Princely India', *Journal of the Royal Asiatic Society* Vol. 18, no. 1 [2008]: 39). See also D.H.A. Kolff, 'Sanyasi Trader-Soldiers', *The Indian Economic and Social History Review*, Vol. 8 (1971); and D.N. Lorenzen, 'Warrior Ascetics in Indian History', *Journal of the American Oriental Society*, Vol. 98, no. 1 (1978): 61–75.

33. It was not uncommon for British officers to abuse and beat their orderlies, sometimes to death. In one such case in which a British lieutenant called Charles Mann killed his orderly, the punishment he received was just two years imprisonment and dismissal from service (British Library, India Office Records, Madras Despatches 1 Jan to 2 July 1841 [Br. Lib. E/4/955] Draft Military 19 May, no. 37, 1841, Madras).

34. British Library, India Office Records, Madras Despatches 1 Jan to 2 July 1841 [Br. Lib. E/4/955] Military 28 April No. 28 1841. See also Madras Despatches 12 Jan to 29 June 1842 [E/4/957] No. 26 (2 July 1841) where Sir Hugh Gough writes: 'We fully approve of the measures taken for ensuring to the Native Troops of your Establishment the several advantages to which they were entitled by the rules of your Presidency whilst serving beyond the sea.'

35. British Library, India Office Records, Madras Despatches 1 Jan to 2 July 1841 [Br. Lib. E/4/955]; Military 28 April No. 28 1841. See also Heathcote, *The Military in British India*, 77–81.

36. I hope to be able someday to write an account of Kesri's role in the war of 1857.

37. Mosca, *From Frontier Policy*, 253.

38. Ibid., 242. See also: Lawrence Wang-chi Wong, 'Translators and Interpreters During the Opium War between Britain and China (1839–1842)', in

Translating and Interpreting Conflict, ed. Myriam Salama-Carr, Editions Rodopi B.V. (New York and Amsterdam, 2007), pp. 41–60.

39. For instance, in 1842, when a large number of shipwrecked crewmen were taken captive in Taiwan, the lascars were treated much worse than the white prisoners. See John Lee Scott, *Narrative of a Recent Imprisonment in China After the Wreck of the Kite* (London: W.H. Dalton, 1842).

40. Amish Raj Mulmi, *All Roads Lead North: Nepal's Turn to China* (Chennai: Context, 2021), pp. 63–66. See also Mahesh C. Regmi, *Kings and Political Leaders of the Gorkhali Empire 1768–1814* (Hyderabad: Orient Blackswan, 1995), p. 66; and Tansen Sen, *India, China and the World: A Connected History* (London: Rowman & Littlefield Publishers, 2017), pp. 252–53.

41. This was not an unreasonable apprehension since cancelling trade privileges (what today would be called 'sanctions') was one of the strategies that the Qing used to 'bring foreigners to heel' (Mao Haijian, *The Qing Empire*, 94).

42. See Vijay Kumar Manandhar, ed., *A Documentary History of Nepalese Quinquennial Missions to China 1792–1906* (Delhi; Adroit Publishers, 2001).

43. Mosca, *From Frontier Policy*, 179.

44. Ibid., 180–83.

45. Manandhar, *Documentary History*, 'Background'.

46. See E.H. Parker, *Chinese Account of the Opium War* (Shanghai: Kelly & Walsh, 1888), p. 72.

47. Mosca, *From Frontier Policy*, 260–62.

48. Manandhar, *Documentary History*, 87.

49. Parker, *Chinese Account*, 72.

50. Mosca, *From Frontier Policy*, 190–94. Wei Yuan notes that the Qing response to the Gurkhas as 'the Heavenly Dynasty never concerns itself with the mutual tiltings of savages' (Parker, *Chinese Account*, 73).

16: Pillar of Empire

1. *Dopesick* is a Hulu miniseries.

2. Art Van Zee, 'The Promotion and Marketing of OxyContin: Commercial Triumph, Public Health Tragedy', *American Journal of Public Health*, Vol. 99, no. 2 (2009): 221–27.

3. The figure for 1729 is from Jonathan Spence, *The Search for Modern China* (New York, NY: W.W. Norton, 1990), p. 129; and the figure for 1830 is from Peter Thilly, *The Opium Business: A History of Crime and Capitalism in Maritime China* (Stanford, CA: Stanford University Press, 2022), p. 7. Each

chest contained between 140 and 160 pounds of opium depending on its point of origin,

4. Thilly, *The Opium Business*, 7.
5. Tan Chung, *China and the Brave New World: A Study of the Origins of the Opium War 1840–42* (New Delhi: Allied Publishers, 1978), p. 86.
6. Thomas N. Layton, *The Voyage of the Frolic: New England Merchants and the Opium Trade* (Stanford, CA: Stanford University Press, 1997), p. 29.
7. John F. Richards, 'The Opium Industry in British India', *The Indian Economic and Social History Review*, Vol. 39, nos. 2–3 (2002): 159–161.
8. Ibid., 156.
9. John F. Richards, 'Opium and the British Indian Empire: The Royal Commission of 1895', *Modern Asian Studies*, Vol. 36, no. 2 (2002): 377.
10. Michael Greenberg, *British Trade and the Opening of China* (Cambridge: Cambridge University Press, 1951), p. 10.
11. Dilip K. Basu, 'Asian Merchants and Western Trade: A Comparative Study of Calcutta and Canton 1800–1840 (Ph.D. diss., University of California, Berkeley, CA, 1975), p. 58.
12. Introduction to *Opium Regimes: China, Britain, and Japan, 1839–1952*, eds Timothy Brook and Bob Tadashi Wakabayashi (Berkeley: University of California Press, 2000), p. 7.
13. Tan Chung, *China and the Brave New World*, 94.
14. Carl A. Trocki, *Opium, Empire and the Global Political Economy: A Study of the Asian Opium Trade, 1750–1950* (New York, NY: Routledge, 1999), p. 138. See also Hans Derks, *History of the Opium Problem: The Assault on the East, ca. 1600–1950* (Leiden: Brill, 2012), pp. 401–11; and Diana S. Kim, *Empires of Vice: The Rise of Opium Prohibition across Southeast Asia* (Princeton, NJ: Princeton University Press, 2020), p. 3.
15. Richards, 'The Opium Industry', 154–55.
16. Jack Beeching, *The Chinese Opium Wars* (New York, NY: Harcourt Brace, 1976), p. 159.
17. '[O]pium apologists pointed to the financial interests of India and equated consumption of opium in the Orient to that of alcohol in the West.' Richards, 'Opium and the British Indian Empire', 383. See also John R. Haddad, *America's First Adventure in China: Trade, Treaties, Opium, and Salvation* (Philadelphia, PA: Temple University Press, 2013), Kindle edn., loc. 1741.
18. Charles Dickens, 'Opium', *Household Words*, 22 August 1857, p. 185.
19. James R. Rush, *Opium to Java: Revenue Farming and Chinese Enterprise in Colonial Indonesia, 1860–1910* (Indonesia: Equinox Publishing, 2007) p. 140.

20. Richards, 'Opium and the British Indian Empire', 420.

21. Ibid., 408.

22. Nathan Allen, *The Opium Trade; Including a Sketch of Its History, Extent, Effects Etc. as Carried on in India and China* (Lowell, MA: James P. Walker, 1853), p. 32.

23. See David T. Courtwright, *Forces of Habit: Drugs and the Making of the Modern World* (Cambridge, MA: Harvard University Press, 2001), p. 147.

24. Sherry Saggers and Dennis Gray, 'Supplying and Promoting "Grog": The Political Economy of Alcohol in Aboriginal Australia', *Australian Journal of Social Issues*, Vol. 32, no. 3 (1997): 215.

25. Marcia Langton, 'Rum, Seduction and Death: "Aboriginality" and Alcohol', *Oceania*, Vol. 63, no. 3 (1993): 201. See also Simone Pettigrew and Ronald Groves, 'Australia, Alcohol and the Aborigine: Alcohol Consumption Differences between Non-Indigenous and Indigenous Australians', *ACR Asia-Pacific Advances*, Vol. 5 (2002). https://www.acrwebsite.org/volumes/11787/volumes/ap05/AP-0.

26. Carl A. Trocki, *Opium and Empire: Chinese Society in Colonial Singapore, 1800–1910* (Ithaca, NY: Cornell University Press, 1990), p. 201.

27. In the words of the historian Siddharth Chandra: 'What differentiates opium from other tradable commodities, such as rubber and sugar, for example, is its highly addictive nature. Because of the physical and psychological dependence that it is capable of creating in significant numbers of its users, as a commodity, opium possesses a potential for economic gain (especially for producers) and loss (especially for consumers) that surpasses the potential of most commodities.' Siddharth Chandra, 'Economic Histories of the Opium Trade', EH.Net Encyclopedia, 10 February 2008. http://eh.net/encyclopedia/economic-histories-of-the-opium-trade/.

28. Derks, *History of the Opium Problem*, 364.

29. Keith McMahon, *The Fall of the God of Money: Opium Smoking in Nineteenth-Century China* (Lanham, MD: Rowman & Littlefield Publishers, 2002), p 105.

30. James MacKay, *From London to Lucknow, with memoranda of mutinies, marches, flights, fights, and conversations. To which is added, an opium-smuggler's explanation of the Peiho massacre* (London: James Nisbet, 1860), p. 525.

31. Richards, 'Opium and the British Indian Empire', p. 375.

32. Richards, 'The Opium Industry', 163.

33. John F. Richards, '"Cannot We Induce the People of England to Eat Opium?" The Moral Economy of Opium in Colonial India', in *Drugs and Empires: Essays in Modern Imperialism and Intoxication, c. 1500–c.1930*, eds James H. Mills and Patricia Barton (New York, NY: Palgrave Macmillan, 2007), p. 73.

34. Chris McGreal, *American Overdose: The Opioid Tragedy in Three Acts* (New York, NY: Hachette Book Group, 2018), p. 20.

35. For the opioid advocacy movement see Barry Meier, *Pain Killer: An Empire of Deceit and the Origin of America's Opioid Epidemic* (New York, NY: Penguin Random House, 2018), pp. 34–40.

36. Patrick Radden Keefe, *Empire of Pain: The Secret History of the Sackler Dynasty* (New York, NY: Doubleday, 2021), p. 366.

37. McGreal, *American Overdose*, 165.

38. See, for instance, Frank Dikotter, Lars Laamann and Xun Zhou, 'China, British Imperialism and the Myth of the "Opium Plague"', in *Drugs and Empires: Essays in Modern Imperialism and Intoxication, c. 1500–c.1930*, eds James H. Mills and Patricia Barton (New York, NY: Palgrave Macmillan, 2007), p. 19–38.

39. James H. Mills, 'Drugs, Consumption, and Supply in Asia: The Case of Cocaine in Colonial India, c. 1900–c.1930', *The Journal of Asian Studies*, Vol. 66, no. 2 (2007): 361.

40. McGreal, *American Overdose*, 40.

41. See Kim, *Empires of Vice*, 204.

42. Steffen Rimner, *Opium's Long Shadow: From Asian Revolt to Global Drug Control* (Cambridge, MA: Harvard University Press, 2018), p. 10.

43. See Trocki, *Opium and Empire*, 210.

44. In the words of the historian of narcotics David Courtwright, 'no narcotic policy, either premaintenance or antimaintenance, has come close to eradicating addiction'. David T. Courtwright, *Dark Paradise: A History of Opiate Addiction in America* (Cambridge, MA: Harvard University Press, 2001), Kindle edn, loc. 122.

45. Stephen R. Platt, *Imperial Twilight: The Opium War and the End of China's Last Golden Age* (New York, NY: Knopf, 2018), p. 446.

46. See Thilly, *The Opium Business*, 85–86.

47. David M. Cutler and Edward L. Glaeser, 'When Innovation Goes Wrong: Technological Regress and the Opioid Epidemic', *The Journal of Economic Perspectives*, Vol. 35, no. 4 (2021): 174.

48. By the same token, I should note that I am writing in an 'up' cycle.

49. Keefe, *Empire of Pain*, 344.

50. Cutler and Glaeser, 'When Innovation Goes Wrong' 192.

51. Excise opium had a lower morphine content (see United Nations Office on Drugs and Crime, *Quasi-Medical Use of Opium*, 1953; https://www.unodc.org/unodc/en/data-and-analysis/bulletin/bulletin_1953-01-01_3_page008.html). It was also produced and packaged in a manner quite

different from 'provision' opium (J.W.S. MacArthur, *Notes on an Opium Factory* [Calcutta: Thacker, Spink & Company's Press, 1865] p. 28).

52. Tan Chung, *China and the Brave New World*, 87. In the words of the nineteenth-century writer Nathan Allen, 'The great object of those in India who prepare opium for the China market is, to inspissate the crude juice as to leave a very hot-drawn, watery extract, which will, being dried, possess the greatest amount of purity and strength of flavor when smoked through a pipe.' Allen, *The Opium Trade*, 8.

53. Rush, *Opium to Java*, 38.

54. Ibid.

55. Richard Newman, 'Early British Encounters with the Indian Opium Eater', in *Drugs and Empires: Essays in Modern Imperialism and Intoxication, c. 1500–c.1930*, eds James H. Mills and Patricia Barton (New York, NY: Palgrave Macmillan, 2007), p. 57.

56. A seventeenth-century European herbalist noted that a 'dose of as little as a single grain [of opium] may prove fatal to a European . . .'. Trocki, *Opium, Empire*, 25. See also S.P. Sangar, 'Intoxicants in Mughal India', *Indian Journal of History of Science*, Vol. 16, no. 2 (1981): 203.

57. Raden Adjeng Kartini, *Letters of A Javanese Princess*, 25 May 1899 (trans. 1921).

58. McGreal, *American Overdose*, 50.

59. McMahon, *The Fall of the God of Money*, 98.

60. Meier, *Pain Killer*, 64.

61. McGreal, *American Overdose*, 61.

62. See Zheng Yangwen, *The Social Life of Opium in China* (Cambridge: Cambridge University Press, 2005), p. 98.

63. Trocki, *Opium and Empire*, 237.

64. Quoted by Derks, *History of the Opium Problem*, 289.

65. See Derks, 450.

66. Quoted, Trocki, *Opium and Empire*, 77.

67. Ibid.

68. For a full account of British narco-diplomacy between 1909 and 1925, see Emdad-ul Haq, *Drugs in South Asia: From the Opium Trade to the Present Day* (New York, NY: St. Martin's Press, 2000), pp. 69–95.

69. Platt, *Imperial Twilight*, 392.

70. Richards, 'Opium and the British Indian Empire', 381.

71. For an account of such arguments see J. Spencer Hill, *The Indo-Chinese Opium Trade: Considered in Relation to Its History, Morality, and Expediency, and Its Influence on Christian Missions* (London: Henry Frowde, 1884), p. 68.

72. See Rob Hopkins, 'Review: "The Moral Case for Fossil Fuels" — Really?', *Our World*, 5 February 2015: https://ourworld.unu.edu/en/review-the-moral-case-for-fossil-fuels-really.

73. Anirudh Deshpande, 'An Historical Overview of Opium Cultivation and Changing State Attitudes Towards the Crop in India, 1878–2000 A.D.', *Studies in History*, Vol. 25, no. 1 (2009): 115.

74. Ibid., 119.

75. Between 1885 and 1920, the British Raj's revenues from opium rose from Rs 16,75,363 to Rs 44,12,308 (Deshpande, *An Historical Overview*, 122).

76. Rush, *Opium to Java*, 237.

77. Deshpande, 'An Historical Overview', 119.

78. The Collector's name was L.C. Reid. British Library, India Office Records, Board's Collections 83888 to 84180, 1841-42, Vol. 1938 (India Office: F/4/1938).

79. Virginia Berridge and Griffith Edwards, *Opium and the People: Opiate Use in Nineteenth-Century England* (New York, NY: St. Martin's Press, 1981), p. 175.

80. In 1841 a number of British merchants wrote a letter to Lord Palmerston in which they appealed for a ban on the opium industry. The first three paragraphs of the letter are as follows:

    1. That the traffic in Opium carried on by subjects of Gt Br has been for many years a source of irritation and of interruption to lawful trade; and that as the Chinese Govt is fully alive to its baneful effects, so long as that trade is carried on as it has been during the last forty five years, no solid and lasting peace between the two Empires can be established. 2. That the traffick in Opium operates injuriously to large classes of the The Queens Subjects; to the Merchants and Mariners whom it accustoms to clandestine and dishonourable transactions; to the natives of India, by whom it is cultivated under oppressive restrictions; and to our home manufacturers who are deprived of the custom of the Chinese as purchasers of the Woollens and Cottons, the importation of which into China has declined as that of Opium as increased. 3. That the traffick in Opium is dishonourable to the British Character and impedes the progress of Christianity among the Eastern Nations; the people who are engaged in it, and the religion which they profess, being disgraced in the apprehension of all considerate men, whether Chinese or Hindoo, who observe the effects of the Drug upon the morals and health of its infatuated consumers. 4.

That it is in the power of the British Government to put a stop to the growth of opium in the Provinces of Behar and Benares where alone in British India it is produced—the monopoly which the East India Company retains extending all over British India, the cultivation of the Poppy could be prevented in the Distts in which it is at present encouraged, just as easily as it is now prevented in all other Provinces of the Company's Dominions.

British Library, India Office Records, China Foreign Office Instructions and Correspondence 1841, Secret Department, [L/PS/9/194]. Needless to add, this made no impression on the Lord.

81. Viscount Palmerston to Captain Elliot, 4 November 1839 (Ian Nish, ed., *British Documents on Foreign Affairs: Reports and Papers from the Foreign Office Confidential Print, Part 1, Series E. Asia, Vol. 16, Chinese War and its Aftermath, 1839–49* [Frederick, MD: University Publications of America, 1994.] p. 2). Palmerston stated this again two years later in his instructions to the British representatives who were negotiating the Treaty of Nanjing: 'The Chinese government is fully entitled to prohibit the importation of opium, if it pleases; and British subjects who engage in a contraband trade must take the consequences of doing so.' (Quoted in Rimner, *Opium's Long Shadow*, 31).

82. Mao Haijian, *The Qing Empire and the Opium War: The Collapse of the Heavenly Dynasty*, ed. Joseph Lawson (Cambridge: Cambridge University Press, 2016), p. 187.

83. Allen, *The Opium Trade*, 57.

84. Erik Ringmar, 'Malice in Wonderland: Dreams of the Orient and the Destruction of the Palace of the Emperor of China', *Journal of World History*, Vol. 22, no. 2 (2011): 291–94.

85. The dispute centered on the word 'yi' which some translators inaccurately glossed as 'barbarian' (its connotations were more like the word 'alien' in modern American usage). The man mostly responsible for the mischief was a missionary, Robert Morrison, who claimed in 1827 that the British would not use that word to refer to themselves. This was untrue, because British merchants did use it in their correspondence with the authorities in Guangzhou. And, as Prof. Tan Chung points out, the word was used by the Qianlong Emperor in his letter to King George III in 1793, 'but the British government never complained about any Chinese discourtesy in that letter.' (Tan Chung, *China and the Brave New World*, 20). For a full treatment of this subject see Lydia H. Liu, *The Clash of Empires: The Invention of China in Modern World Making* (Cambridge, MA: Harvard University Press, 2006), pp. 92–95; and Dilip K. Basu, 'Chinese Xenology

and the Opium War: Reflections', *The Journal of Asian Studies*, Vol. 73, no. 4 (2014): 927–40.

86. See Dilip K. Basu, 'The Opium War and the Opening of China: A Historiographical Note', *Ch'ing-shih wen-t'i*, Vol. 3, no. 11 (1977): 2–16; Tan Chung, *China and the Brave New World*, 2–20.

87. Beeching, *The Chinese Opium Wars*, 106.

88. Platt, *Imperial Twilight*, 431.

89. Quoted in Liu, *The Clash of Empires*, 170.

17: Parallels

1. *The Chinese Repository*, Vol. VII (Elibron Classics Reprints, 2005), p. 609.

2. Zheng Yangwen, *The Social Life of Opium in China* (Cambridge, MA: Cambridge University Press, 2005), p. 102.

3. Stephen R. Platt, *Imperial Twilight: The Opium War and the End of China's Last Golden Age* (New York, NY: Knopf, 2018), p. 71. According to a source quoted by Keith McMahon, by 1906 'Sichuan, Yunnan, Shaanxi, Shanxi, Guizhou and Gansu provinces produced over 80 percent of China's opium.' (*The Fall of the God of Money: Opium Smoking in Nineteenth-Century China* [Lanham, MD: Rowman & Littlefield Publishers, 2002], p. 98).

4. David Bello, 'The Venomous Course of Southwestern Opium: Qing Prohibition in Yunnan, Sichuan, and Guizhou in the Early Nineteenth Century', *Journal of Asian Studies*, Vol. 62, no. 4 (2003): 1114.

5. Stephen R. Halsey, *Quest for Power: European Imperialism and the Making of Chinese Statecraft* (Cambridge, MA: Harvard University Press, 2016), pp. 59–61.

6. Peter Thilly, *The Opium Business: A History of Crime and Capitalism in Maritime China* (Stanford, CA: Stanford University Press, 2022), p. 58.

7. Thilly, *The Opium Business*, 9.

8. Zheng Yangwen, *The Social Life of Opium*, 105–10.

9. Jonathan Spence, 'Opium Smoking in Ch'ing China', in *Conflict and Control in Late Imperial China*, eds Frederic Wakeman Jr and Carolyn Grant (Berkeley, CA: University of California Press, 1975), p. 237.

10. Thilly, *The Opium Business*, 2–4.

11. Carl A. Trocki, *Opium, Empire and the Global Political Economy: A Study of the Asian Opium Trade, 1750–1950* (New York, NY: Routledge, 1999), p. xiii.

12. Thilly, *The Opium Business*, Ch. 6.

13. A commonly repeated accusation in the British Parliament was: 'The Chinese were not in earnest in the wish to prohibit opium. Why had they

not put down the cultivation of the poppy in China?' (*The Chinese Repository*, Vol. IX [Krauz Reprint Ltd], 251).

14. James MacKay, *From London to Lucknow, with memoranda of mutinies, marches, flights, fights, and conversations. To which is added, an opium-smuggler's explanation of the Peiho massacre* (London: James Nisbet, 1860), p. 518.

15. Quoted in Steffen Rimner, *Opium's Long Shadow: From Asian Revolt to Global Drug Control* (Cambridge, MA: Harvard University Press, 2018), p. 201.

16. Trocki, *Opium, Empire*, 126.

17. Thilly, *The Opium Business*, 88.

18. Edward R. Slack, *Opium, State and Society: China's Narco-Economy and the Guomindang* (Honolulu, HI: University of Hawaii Press, 2001), p. 3.

19. Thilly, *The Opium Business*, 14.

20. See Rimner, *Opium's Long Shadow*, 6. It has been argued that 3 to 16 per cent, with 10 per cent being 'the most referenced figure' tends to be the typical rate of substance abuse in a population (Barry Meier, *Pain Killer: An Empire of Deceit and the Origin of America's Opioid Epidemic* [New York, NY: Penguin Random House, 2018], p. 39).

21. Slack, *Opium, State and Society*, 4. See also McMahon, *The Fall of the God of Money*, 156; and David M. Cutler and Edward L. Glaeser, 'When Innovation Goes Wrong: Technological Regress and the Opioid Epidemic', *The Journal of Economic Perspectives*, Vol. 35, no. 4 (2021): 174.

22. Charles Dickens, 'Opium; Chapter the Second, China', *Household Words* (22 August 1857), pp. 181–86.

23. MacKay, *From London to Lucknow*, 527.

24. The words are those of one Rev. Graves, quoted by McMahon, *The Fall of the God of Money*, 76.

25. McMahon, *The Fall of the God of Money*, 4.

26. Gregory Blue, 'Opium for China: The British Connection', in *Opium Regimes: China, Britain, and Japan, 1839–1952*, eds Timothy Brook and Bob Tadashi Wakabayashi (Berkeley, CA: University of California Press, 2000), p. 37.

27. Rimner, *Opium's Long Shadow*, 34.

28. James Matheson, quoting a British merchant. (*Present Position and Prospects of the British Trade with China: Together with an Outline of Some Leading Occurrences in Its Past History* [London: Smith, Elder and Co., 1836], p. 62.)

29. Jonathan Spence, *The Search for Modern China* (New York, NY: W.W. Norton, 1990), pp. 132–34.

30. Arthur Lovejoy, 'The Chinese Origin of a Romanticism', in *Essays in the History of Ideas* (New York, NY: George Braziller, 1955), p. 106.

31. Ibid., 103.
32. Platt, *Imperial Twilight*, 53–54.
33. David Graeber and David Wengrow, *The Dawn of Everything: A New History of Humanity* (New York, NY: Farrar, Strauss and Giroux, 2021), p. 30.
34. See Platt's *Imperial Twilight* for an account of the changes in Western attitudes (pp. 162–65). See also Yu Liu, *Seeds of a Different Eden: Chinese Gardening Ideas and a New English Aesthetic Ideal* (Columbia, SC: University of South Carolina Press, 2008), p. 8.
35. Platt, *Imperial Twilight*, 432.
36. Matheson, *Present Position and Prospects*, 1.
37. Platt, *Imperial Twilight*, 431.
38. For a detailed study of criminal networks in 1840s China see Melissa Macauley, 'Small Time Crooks: Opium, Migrants, and the War on Drugs in China, 1819–1860', *Late Imperial China* Vol. 30, no. 1 (2009): 1–47.
39. Spence, *The Search for Modern China*, 126.
40. Thilly, *The Opium Business*, 21.
41. Jasper Jolly, 'Glencore to pay $1bn settlement amid US bribery and market abuse allegations', *Guardian*, 24 May 2022: https://www.theguardian.com/business/2022/may/24/glencore-to-pay-1bn-settlement-amid-us-bribery-and-market-abuse-allegations?s=03.
42. See Spence, *The Search for Modern China*, 131.
43. David T. Courtwright, *Forces of Habit: Drugs and the Making of the Modern World* (Cambridge, MA: Harvard University Press, 2001), p. 95.
44. James R. Rush, *Opium to Java: Revenue Farming and Chinese Enterprise in Colonial Indonesia, 1860–1910* (Indonesia: Equinox Publishing, 2007) p. 34.
45. David T. Courtwright, *Dark Paradise: A History of Opiate Addiction in America* (Cambridge, MA: Harvard University Press, 2001), pp. 42–54.
46. For the psychological impact of the shock, see Mark Elvin, 'How did the cracks open?: The origins of the subversion of China's late-traditional culture by the West', *Thesis Eleven*, Vol. 57, no. 1 (1999): 2–5.
47. McMahon, *The Fall of the God of Money*, 205–206.
48. See chapter 16, note 84.
49. The historian Howard Slack wrote: 'The most interesting and perplexing relationship that ever evolved between a narcotic drug and a culture is the one involving opium and the Chinese people.' (*Opium, State and Society*, 1.)
50. Patrick Radden Keefe, *Empire of Pain: The Secret History of the Sackler Dynasty* (New York, NY: Doubleday, 2021), pp. 229–236. See also Meier, *Pain Killer*, 73.
51. Keefe, *Empire of Pain*, 370.

52. Celina B. Realuyo, 'The New Opium War: A National Emergency', *Prism: The Journal of Complex Operations*, 8:1 (2019): 133. https://cco.ndu.edu/News/Article/1767465/the-new-opium-war-a-national-emergency/.

53. Meier, *Pain Killer*, ix.

54. Ryan Hampton, *American Fix: Inside the Opioid Addiction Crisis—and How to End It* (New York, NY: St. Martin's Publishing Group, 2018), p. 114.

55. Ibid., 115.

56. Chris McGreal, *American Overdose: The Opioid Tragedy in Three Acts* (New York, NY: Hachette Book Group, 2018), p. 165.

57. Keefe, *Empire of Pain*, 363.

58. Ibid., 345.

59. McGreal, *American Overdose*, xii.

60. Hampton, *American Fix*, 10.

61. See Keefe, *Empire of Pain*, 244–49.

62. Cutler and Glaeser, 'When Innovation Goes Wrong', 186.

63. Ibid., 179.

64. Ibid., 177.

65. This phrase is open to criticism, however, because it places 'implicit judgement' on affected communities and diminishes the 'unique impact' of opioids (McGreal, *American Overdose*, 112).

66. Writing in the *American Journal of Public Health*, a team of researchers notes: 'Intensifying substance use may be a normal societal response to mass traumatic events, especially when experienced by people in lower socioeconomic strata.' (Nabarun Dasgupta, Leo Beletsky and Daniel Ciccarone, 'Opioid Crisis: No Easy Fix to Its Social and Economic Determinants,' Vol. 108, no. 2 (2018): 182–86).

67. 'Oversupply in a narcotic has a rather different effect on its market than does a glut in most commodities. Excess supply, if maintained year after year, will tend to produce the dynamic needed to take it off the market.' (Jacques M. Downs, *The Golden Ghetto: The American Commercial Community at Canton and the Shaping of American China Policy, 1784–1844* [Bethlehem, PA: Lehigh University Press, 1997], p. 165.) Or, as one conscientious American merchant pointed out to the British emissary to China, the demand for opium had increased with the supply 'growing by what it feedeth on'. (Charles W. King, *Opium Crisis: A Letter Addressed to Charles Elliot, Esq., Chief Superintendent of the British Trade with China* [London: Hatchard & Son, 1839], p. 5.)

68. Cutler and Glaeser, 'When Innovation Goes Wrong', 173.

69. Ibid., 184.

70. Courtwright, *Dark Paradise*, 6.

71. Quoted in ibid.
72. Cutler and Glaeser, 'When Innovation Goes Wrong', 172.
73. Keefe, *Empire of Pain*, 4.
74. Ibid., 407.
75. Ibid. See also Meier, *Pain Killer*, 35.
76. Keefe, *Empire of Pain*, 213.
77. Rimner, *Opium's Long Shadow*, 147.
78. Trocki, *Opium, Empire*, 163.
79. McGreal, *American Overdose*, 260.
80. Realuyo, 'The New Opium War'.

18: Portents

1. For a detailed account see Zhou Yongming, 'Nationalism, Identity, and State-Building: The Antidrug Crusade in the People's Republic, 1949–1952', in *Opium Regimes: China, Britain, and Japan, 1839–1952*, eds Timothy Brook and Bob Tadashi Wakabayashi (Berkeley, CA: University of California Press, 2000).
2. Patrick Radden Keefe, *Empire of Pain: The Secret History of the Sackler Dynasty* (New York, NY: Doubleday, 2021), p. 363.
3. Chris McGreal, *American Overdose: The Opioid Tragedy in Three Acts* (New York, NY: Hachette Book Group, 2018), p. 147.
4. Celina B. Realuyo, 'The New Opium War: A National Emergency', *Prism: The Journal of Complex Operations*, 8:1 (2019): 137. https://cco.ndu.edu/News/Article/1767465/the-new-opium-war-a-national-emergency/.
5. David M. Cutler and Edward L. Glaeser, 'When Innovation Goes Wrong: Technological Regress and the Opioid Epidemic', *The Journal of Economic Perspectives*, Vol. 35, no. 4 (2021): 188.
6. On the role of missionaries, see Michael C. Lazich, 'American Missionaries and the Opium Trade in Nineteenth-Century China', *Journal of World History*, Vol. 17, no. 2 (2006); and Diana S. Kim, *Empires of Vice: The Rise of Opium Prohibition across Southeast Asia* (Princeton, NJ: Princeton University Press, 2020), p. 67.
7. Steffen Rimner, *Opium's Long Shadow: From Asian Revolt to Global Drug Control* (Cambridge, MA: Harvard University Press, 2018), p. 6.
8. Ibid., 60.
9. J. Spencer Hill, *The Indo-Chinese Opium Trade: Considered in Relation to Its History, Morality, and Expediency, and Its Influence on Christian Missions* (London: Henry Frowde, 1884), p. 25.

10. Rimner, *Opium's Long Shadow*, 57.
11. Emdad-ul Haq, *Drugs in South Asia: From the Opium Trade to the Present Day* (New York, NY: St. Martin's Press, 2000), pp. 49–54.
12. Rimner, *Opium's Long Shadow*, 84.
13. Ibid., 122.
14. Ibid., 92.
15. *Rabindra-Rachanabali*, Visva-Bharati edition, vol. 24 (Kolkata, 1354/1947 rpt. 1365/1958), p. 250. My translation.
16. Haq, *Drugs in South Asia*, 54–57.
17. Raden Adjeng Kartini, *Letters of A Javanese Princess*, May 1899 (trans. 1921).
18. James R. Rush, *Opium to Java: Revenue Farming and Chinese Enterprise in Colonial Indonesia, 1860–1910* (Indonesia: Equinox Publishing, 2007) pp. 202–203.
19. Ibid., 205.
20. Ibid., 218.
21. David T. Courtwright, *Dark Paradise: A History of Opiate Addiction in America* (Cambridge, MA: Harvard University Press, 2001), pp. 54–56; and Haq, *Drugs in South Asia*, 39.
22. Courtwright, *Dark Paradise*, 54–56.
23. Ibid.
24. Barry Meier, *Pain Killer: An Empire of Deceit and the Origin of America's Opioid Epidemic* (New York, NY: Penguin Random House, 2018), p. 25.
25. Rimner, *Opium's Long Shadow*, 142; and Haq, *Drugs in South Asia*, 69.
26. Virginia Berridge and Griffith Edwards, *Opium and the People: Opiate Use in Nineteenth-Century England* (New York, NY: St. Martin's Press, 1981), p. 185.
27. See Kathleen L. Lodwick, *Crusaders Against Opium: Protestant Missionaries in China, 1874–1917* (Lexington, KY: University Press of Kentucky, 2009), pp. 97–109. See also Gregory Blue, 'Opium for China: The British Connection', in *Opium Regimes: China, Britain, and Japan, 1839–1952*, eds Timothy Brook and Bob Tadashi Wakabayashi (Berkeley, CA: University of California Press, 2000), p. 39.
28. Royal Commission on Opium, *Proceedings*, Vol. V, appendices, 1894, p. 151.
29. Berridge and Edwards, *Opium and the People*, 186–94. See also Marc Jason Gilbert, 'Empire and Excise: Drugs and Drink Revenue and the Fate of States in South Asia', in *Drugs and Empires: Essays in Modern Imperialism and Intoxication, c. 1500–1930*, eds James Mills and Patricia Barton (New York, NY: Palgrave Macmillan, 2007), p. 133.
30. Rimner, *Opium's Long Shadow*, 152.
31. Lodwick, *Crusaders Against Opium*, 109–14.

32. Courtwright, *Dark Paradise*, 81.
33. Rimner, *Opium's Long Shadow*, 189. The conclusions of the Philippines Commission's report were endorsed also by the Ceylon Commission, set up by the British in 1907 (Haq, *Drugs in South Asia*, 49).
34. For the full text of the edict see Alan Baumler, ed., *Modern China and Opium: A Reader* (Ann Arbor, MI: University of Michigan Press, 2001), pp. 66–71.
35. Quoted in Rimner, *Opium's Long Shadow*, 198.
36. Kim, *Empires of Vice*, 217.
37. See R. Bin Wong, 'Opium and Modern Chinese State-Making' in *Opium Regimes: China, Britain, and Japan, 1839–1952*, eds Timothy Brook and Bob Tadashi Wakabayashi (Berkeley, CA: University of California Press, 2000), pp. 190–99; and Kim, *Empires of Vice*, 64.
38. See Joyce A. Madancy, *The Troublesome Legacy of Commissioner Lin: The Opium Trade and Opium Suppression in Fujian Province, 1820s to 1920s* (Cambridge, MA: Harvard University Asia Center, 2003), p. 202.
39. Blue, 'Opium for China', 41; Rimner, *Opium's Long Shadow*, 212.
40. Carl A. Trocki, *Opium, Empire and the Global Political Economy: A Study of the Asian Opium Trade, 1750–1950* (New York, NY: Routledge, 1999), p 130.
41. Quoted in Rimner, *Opium's Long Shadow*, 8.
42. Haq, *Drugs in South Asia*, 76.
43. Madancy, *The Troublesome Legacy*, 342. The achievements of the anti-opium movement were reversed in the following decades as civil war engulfed China. Madancy's book provides an excellent account of the movement's ups and downs in Fujian.
44. Haq, *Drugs in South Asia*, 100.
45. Zheng Yangwen, *The Social Life of Opium in China* (Cambridge, MA: Cambridge University Press, 2005), pp. 194–202; Rimner, *Opium's Long Shadow*, 247–52; and introduction to *Opium Regimes: China, Britain, and Japan, 1839–1952*, eds Timothy Brook and Bob Tadashi Wakabayashi (Berkeley, CA: University of California Press, 2000), pp. 15–19.
46. See Robert Cribb, 'Opium and the Indonesian Revolution', *Modern Asian Studies* Vol. 22, no. 4 (1988): 701–22; and Kim, *Empires of Vice*, 192.
47. Anirudh Deshpande, 'An Historical Overview of Opium Cultivation and Changing State Attitudes Towards the Crop in India, 1878–2000 A.D.', *Studies in History*, Vol. 25, no. 1 (2009): 112.
48. Ibid., 124–25.
49. Ibid., 126.
50. Ibid., 126.
51. Haq, *Drugs in South Asia*, 116.

52. Ibid., 114.
53. Ibid., 130–43.
54. Ibid., 142.
55. For a full account of the rise in heroin production in South Asia, see ibid., 106–256.
56. Gilbert, 'Empire and Excise', 136.

Acknowledgements

This book brings to a close a cycle of work that began with the Ibis Trilogy. In the course of writing those novels I came to be indebted to many people and institutions, all of whom are listed in the acknowledgements to each volume. I would not have been able to write the novels, or this book, if not for the enormous body of research produced by scholars and historians: I owe them all an enormous debt of gratitude.

But in writing this book I also incurred some new debts. I would especially like to express my gratitude to Sukanta Chaudhuri, Manan Ahmed, Amish Mulmi, Ajay Skaria, Partha Shrungarpure, Rahul Srivastava, and the staff of the Jefferson-Madison Regional Library, Central Branch, Charlottesville, Virginia, for their help with tracking down sources. Raj Patel provided many useful suggestions and comments; Karina Corrigan of the Peabody Essex Museum in Salem, Massachusetts, was enormously helpful in providing images; and my editor at HarperCollins India, Udayan Mitra, and his colleague Shatarupa Ghoshal did a great deal of invaluable work on the text: I am deeply grateful to all of them.

I owe an especial debt of gratitude to Chris Clark, who has been a close friend since long before he rose to his present eminence as Sir Christopher Clark, Regius Professor of History at the University of Cambridge. Through all these years he has been the most patient and meticulous reader of my manuscripts, and with none more so than this one. Inasmuch as there is a voice in my head calling insistently for restraint, it is his. My debt to him is inexpressible.

My greatest debt is to Deborah Baker, who, apart from being one of the finest writers of our time, also happens to be my wife. Without her I would not have started this book, far less finished it.

Illustration Credits

1. Poster by Annada Munshi
Gautam Bhadra, *From an Imperial Product to a National Drink: The Culture of Tea Consumption in Modern India*, p. 19: (https://archive.org/details/froman imperialproducttoanationaldrinkcultureofteaconsumptioninmodernindia gautambhadra_17_I/page/19/mode/2up).

2 and 3. The Stacking Room, opium factory at Patna, India and The Mixing Room, opium factory at Patna, India
Illustrations of the mode of preparing the Indian opium intended for the Chinese market from drawings made by Captain Walter S. Sherwill. Lithographs, hand coloured. (London: James Madden, 1851). Courtesy of the Yale Center for British Art, Paul Mellon Collection.

4. Bird's-eye view from above the opium godown at Patna
Sita Ram (fl.c.1814–23)
British Library, London, UK © British Library Board. All Rights Reserved/ Bridgeman Images. BL7393108.

5. *The Round Tower* (c. 1749) by Giovanni Battista Piranesi
(Italian, 1720 –78)
The Muriel and Philip Berman Gift, acquired from the John S. Phillips bequest of 1876 to the Pennsylvania Academy of the Fine Arts, with funds contributed by Muriel and Philip Berman, gifts (by exchange) of Lisa Norris Elkins, Bryant W. Langston, Samuel S. White 3rd and Vera White, with additional funds contributed by John Howard McFadden, Jr., Thomas Skelton Harrison, and the Philip H. and A.S.W. Rosenbach Foundation, 1985. Accession Number: 1985-52-1301.

6. The inside of the opium godown at Patna
Sita Ram (fl.c.1814–23)
British Library, London, UK © British Library Board. All Rights Reserved/ Bridgeman Images. BL7393109.

7. The opium being tested for purity
Shiva Lal. Patna, India, mid-nineteenth century © Victoria and Albert Museum, London. 2006AY5524.

8. Opium being moulded into balls and put into brass cups
Shiva Lal. Patna, India, mid-nineteenth century © Victoria and Albert Museum, London. 2006BB8373.

9. Jamsetjee Jejeebhoy by Unidentified Chinese Artist
Parsi-Times.com: https://parsi-times.com/2018/04/sir-jamsetjee-jejeebhoy -visionary-of-education/.

10. A View of the European Factories at Canton
William Daniell, 1769–1837, British,
The European Factories at Canton, China, 1806
Oil on canvas, 34 x 50 inches (86.4 x 127 cm)
B1981.25.210. Courtesy of the Yale Center for British Art, Paul Mellon Collection.

11. The Thirteen Factories
Artists in Guangzhou, China
A View of the Foreign Factory Site, Guangzhou, 1830s
Oil on canvas
Gift of Madeline A. Kidder, 1981.
M20558. Courtesy of the Peabody Essex Museum.

12. Portrait of Howqua
Artists in Guangzhou, China
Wu Bingjian, Known as Houqua, about 1835
Oil on canvas
Gift of Rebecca B. Chase, Ann B. Mathias, Robert H. Bradford, and Charles E. Bradford in memory of their mother and father, Rebecca Brown Bradford and Robert Fiske Bradford, 1990.
M23228. Courtesy of the Peabody Essex Museum.

13. Portrait of Harriet Low
George Chinnery, 1774–1852
Portrait of Harriet Low, 1833
Oil on canvas, 9¾ x 8⁹⁄₁₆ inches (24.765 x 21.749 cm)
Museum purchase, made possible by the Lee and Juliet Folger Fund, Joan Vaughan Ingraham, and an anonymous donor, 2001.
M18709. Courtesy of the Peabody Essex Museum.

14. Bird's-eye view of Guangzhou
Yee Cheong, Active 1880s
Bird's-eye view of Guangzhou (Canton) with Shamian Island, about 1880
Oil on panel, 25¼ x 41½ inches (64.135 x 105.41 cm)
Museum purchase, made possible by the Fellows and Friends Fund, 1961
M10867. Courtesy of the Peabody Essex Museum.

15. Chinese Merchant's House
The House of Consequa, a Chinese merchant, in the suburbs of Canton (Guangzhou), China, circa 1845. Engraved by S. Bradshaw from a drawing by T. Allom. (Photograph by Hulton Archive/Getty Images)

17. Self-portrait of Guan Qiaochang (Lamqua), before 1851.
Lamqua
Self-portrait, before 1851
Oil on canvas, 10⅝ × 8¹⁵⁄₁₆ inches (27 × 22.7 cm)
Gift of Robert S. Sturgis, 1983.
M20158. Courtesy of the Peabody Essex Museum.

18. Dr Thomas Colledge
George Chinnery, 1774–1852
Dr. Thomas Richardson Colledge and His Assistant Afun in Their Ophthalmic Hospital, Macau, 1833
Oil on canvas, 33⅛ x 33¼ inches (84.138 x 84.455 cm)
Gift of Cecilia Colledge, in memory of her father, Lionel Colledge, FRCS, 2003.
M23017. Courtesy of the Peabody Essex Museum.

19. Dr Peter Parker
Wikipedia: https://en.wikipedia.org/wiki/File:Dr._Peter_Parker.jpg.

21. Portrait of an American Merchant
Spoilum, Active 1765–1810
Portrait of Captain Richard Wheatland, about 1803
Oil on canvas, Frame 27¼ x 21⅝ x 2 inches (69.215 x 54.928 x 5.08 cm)
Gift of Richard Wheatland II, Alice Wellman, Mary Schley and Sarah Richards, 1991.
M22878. Courtesy of the Peabody Essex Museum.

22. Sewing Table
Artists in Guangzhou, China
Sewing table, about 1837
Lacquered wood, ivory, and gold, with reproduction silk bag
Gift of Francis B. Lothrop, 1970.
E82997. Courtesy of the Peabody Essex Museum.

23. Pair of Nodding-head Figures
Artists in Guangzhou, China
Pair of nodding-head figures, about 1803
Unfired clay and human hair, 26¼ x 12⅝ x 9½ inches (66.675 x 32.068 x 24.13 cm)
Gift of Captain Richard Wheatland, 1803.
E7098 and E7097. Courtesy of the Peabody Essex Museum.